101

The Critical Response
to Gertrude Stein

The Critical Response to Gertrude Stein

Edited by
Kirk Curnutt

Critical Responses in Arts and Letters, Number 36
Cameron Northouse, Series Adviser

GREENWOOD PRESS
Westport, Connecticut • London

Library of Congress Cataloging-in-Publication Data

The critical response to Gertrude Stein / edited by Kirk Curnutt.
  p.   cm.—(Critical responses in arts and letters, ISSN 1057–0993 ; no. 36)
  Includes bibliographical references and index.
  ISBN 0–313–30475–0 (alk. paper)
  1. Stein, Gertrude, 1874–1946—Criticism and interpretation. 2. Women and
literature—United States—History—20th century. I. Curnutt, Kirk, 1964– II. Series.
PS3537.T323Z5855   2000
823′.912—dc21   00–020765

British Library Cataloguing in Publication Data is available.

Library of Congress Catalog Card Number: 00–020765
ISBN: 0–313–30475–0
ISSN: 1057–0993

First published in 2000

Greenwood Press, 88 Post Road West, Westport, CT 06881
An imprint of Greenwood Publishing Group, Inc.
www.greenwood.com

Printed in the United States of America

The paper used in this book complies with the
Permanent Paper Standard issued by the National
Information Standards Organization (Z39.48–1984).

10 9 8 7 6 5 4 3 2

Copyright Acknowledgments

The editor and publisher gratefully acknowledge permission for use of the following material:

"A Cubist Treatise," H. L. Mencken, *Baltimore Sun*. Reprinted by permission of the Enoch Pratt Free Library in accordance with the terms of the will of H. L. Mencken.

"Medals for Miss Stein," Carl Van Vechten, *The New York Herald Tribune*. Reprinted by permission of the Estate of Carl Van Vechten.

"Everybody is a Real One," Katherine Anne Porter, *The New York Herald Tribune*. Reprinted by permission of Barbara Thompson Davis, Literary Trustee for the Estate of Katherine Anne Porter.

"We Ask for Bread," Conrad Aiken, *The New Republic*. Reprinted by permission.

"Hogarth Essays," Anonymous, Copyright © 1926 *Times Literary Supplement*. Reprinted by permission.

"From a Litterateur's Notebook," Elliot H. Paul, © Copyrighted Chicago Tribune Company. All rights reserved. Used with permission.

"Nonsense," Edmund Wilson, *The New Republic*. Reprinted by permission.

"Words and Waste," Sylva Norman, *The Nation and Athenæum*. Copyright © *New Statesman*. Reprinted by permission.

"Stein on Picasso," Nathalie Swan, *The New Republic*. Reprinted by permission.

"History Tramps Down the Champs-Elysées," Janet Flanner, *The New York Herald-Tribune Books*. Reprinted by permission of William Murray, literary executor of the Estate of Janet Flanner.

"Briefly Noted: *Paris France* by Gertrude Stein," *The New Yorker*. Reprinted by permission; copyright © July 13, 1940 The New Yorker Magazine, Inc. All rights reserved.

"Miss Stein and France," Justin O'Brien, *The Nation*. Reprinted with permission from the July 27, 1940 issue of *The Nation*.

"Her France, Her Paris," Dorothy Chamberlain, *The New Republic*. Reprinted by permission.

"War," Katharine Brégy, *Commonweal* 23 August 1940: 373. Reprinted by permission.

"In Brief: *What Are Masterpieces*," *The Nation*. Reprinted by permission from the November 23, 1940 issue of *The Nation*.

"And Paris," Jerome Mellquist, *Commonweal,* 29 November 1940: 148. Reprinted by permission.

"All About Ida," W. H. Auden. Copyright © by the Estate of W. H. Auden.

"Matron's Primer," Djuna Barnes, *Contemporary Jewish Record*. Copyright © The Authors League Fund, as literary executor of the Estate of Djuna Barnes.

"Gertrude Stein's Wars," Delmore Schwartz, *The Nation*. Reprinted with permission from the March 24, 1945 issue of *The Nation*.

"Gerty and the G. I.s," Robert S. Warshow, *The Nation*. Reprinted with permission from the October 5, 1946 issue of *The Nation*.

Contents

2. Contemporary Commentary: Style, Influence, and the Debate over Stein's Purpose

Series Foreword

Critical Responses in Arts and Letters is designed to present a documentary history of highlights in the critical reception to the body of work of writers and artists and to individual works that are generally considered to be of major importance. The focus of each volume in this series is basically historical. The introductions to each volume are themselves brief histories of the critical response an author, artist, or individual work has received. This response is then further illustrated by reprinting a strong representation of the major critical reviews and articles that have collectively produced the author's, artist's, or work's critical reputation.

The scope of *Critical Responses in Arts and Letters* knows no chronological or geographical boundaries. Volumes under preparation include studies of individuals from around the world and in both contemporary and historical periods.

Each volume is the work of an individual editor, who surveys the entire body of criticism on a single author, artist, or work. The editor then selects the best material to depict the critical response received by an author or artist over his/her entire career. Documents produced by the author or artist may also be included when the editor finds that they are necessary to a full understanding of the materials at hand. In circumstances where previous isolated volumes of criticism on a particular individual or work exist, the editor carefully selects material that better reflects the nature and directions of the critical response over time.

In addition to the introduction and the documentary section, the editor of each volume is free to solicit new essays on areas that may not have been adequately dealt with in previous criticism. Also, for volumes on living writers and artists, new interviews may be included, again at the discretion of the volume's editor. The volumes also provide a supplementary bibliography and are fully indexed.

While each volume in *Critical Responses in Arts and Letters* is unique, it is also hoped that in combination they form a useful, documentary history of the critical response to the arts, and one that can be easily and profitably employed by students and scholars.

Cameron Northouse

Acknowledgments

This book could not have been written without the support of colleagues and friends. First and foremost, I appreciate the assistance of Troy State University Montgomery. Both Glenda Curry and Livingston Alexander, president and vice president of academic affairs when this book was compiled, were unfailingly encouraging during their tenure. Members of TSUM's Professional Development Committee voted to fund research and permissions fees through a scholarly activity grant; I thus owe Drs. Don McDonald, Lan Lipscomb, John Patrick, Tom Mathew, Patrice Williams, James Macey, and Mr. Walter Hollon my gratitude for their collegiality. Additionally, the TSUM library staff diligently worked to track down ephemeral reviews and notices of Stein; for his patience and stamina in processing dozens of interlibrary loans alone, reference librarian Tim Bailey deserves special mention. Finally, for their administrative and technical support, special thanks are due to Kay Dobbs and Berniece Thomas, both of whom set aside their own deskful of duties to assist at critical moments. I am also grateful to Patricia Willis and her staff at the Beinecke Rare Book and Manuscript Library at Yale University for their guidance in locating the obscure newspaper commentaries on Stein housed in the American Literature Collection in New Haven. It is doubtful that my interest in Stein would have blossomed had J. Gerald Kennedy not introduced me to her work years ago;

similarly, Linda Wagner-Martin's kind words about the project's viability during a 1997 luncheon conversation motivated its completion. I was also lucky that my good friend James Meredith introduced me to Edward Burns at an American Literature Association conference; Professor Burns's willingness to critique an early prospectus helped clarify my thinking about the book's scope. Bruce Kellner, whose own Greenwood Press compilation of Stein commentary is indispensable, kindly pointed me to some unheralded Carl Van Vechten material on Stein. Thanks as well to the various permissions officers of the publications from which the material here is drawn; several of them fielded multiple requests and renegotiations as the table of contents changed from draft to draft. Finally, I must thank my very loyal and forgiving family, whose flowers of friendship never faded even when the book demanded my time and attention: to Beverly, Kip, and Kelley, this one's for you.

Checklist of Works
by Gertrude Stein

Alphabets and Birthdays. Introduction by Donald Gallup. New Haven: Yale UP, 1957.

As Fine as Melanctha, 1914-1930. Foreword by Natalie Clifford Barney. New Haven: Yale UP, 1954.

The Autobiography of Alice B. Toklas. New York: Harcourt, Brace, 1933.

Bee Time Vine and Other Pieces, 1913-1927. Preface and notes by Virgil Thomson. New Haven: Yale UP, 1953.

Before the Flowers of Friendship Faded Friendship Faded. Paris: Plain Edition, 1931.

Blood on the Dining-Room Floor. Pawlet, Vt.:Banyan, 1948.

A Book Concluding with As a Wife Has a Cow a Love Story. Paris: Daniel-Henry Kahnweiler, 1926.

Brewsie and Willie. New York: Random House, 1946.

Composition as Explanation. London: Hogarth, 1926.

Everybody's Autobiography. New York: Random House, 1937.

Fernhurst, Q.E.D., and Other Early Writings. Ed. Leon Katz. New York: Liveright, 1971.

Four in America. Introduction by Thornton Wilder. New Haven: Yale UP, 1947.

Four Saints in Three Acts. New York: Random House, 1934.

G. M. P. or *Matisse Picasso and Gertrude Stein with Two Shorter Stories*. 1933. Reprint, New York: Something Else, 1972.

The Geographical History of America; or, the Relation of Human Nature to the Human Mind. Introduction by Thornton Wilder. New York: Random House, 1936.

Geography and Plays. Foreword by Sherwood Anderson. 1922. Reprint, Madison: U of Wisconsin P, 1993.

Gertrude Stein, A Stein Reader. Ed. Ulla E. Dydo. Evanston: Northwestern UP, 1993.

Gertrude Stein on Picasso. Ed. Edward Burns. New York: Liveright, 1970.

How to Write. Paris: Plain Edition, 1931.

How Writing Is Written. Ed. Robert Bartlett Haas. Los Angeles: Black Sparrow, 1974.

Ida. New York: Random House, 1941.

Last Operas and Plays. Introduction by Carl Van Vechten. 1949. Reprint, Baltimore: Johns Hopkins UP, 1995.

Lectures in America. New York: Random House, 1935.

The Letters of Gertrude Stein and Carl Van Vechten, 1913-1946. Ed. Edward Burns. 2 vols. New York: Columbia UP, 1986.

Lucy Church Amiably. Paris: Plain Edition, 1930.

The Making of Americans. 1925. Reprint, Dalkey: Dalkey Archive, 1995.

Mrs. Reynolds and Five Earlier Novelettes, 1931-1942. Foreword by Lloyd Frankenberg. New Haven: Yale UP, 1952.

Narration: Four Lectures by Gertrude Stein. Introduction by Thornton Wilder. Chicago: U of Chicago P, 1935.

A Novel of Thank You. Introduction by Carl Van Vechten. New Haven: Yale UP, 1958.

Operas and Plays. Paris: Plain Edition, 1932.

Painted Lace and Other Pieces, 1914-1937. Introduction by Daniel-Henry Kahnweiler. New Haven: Yale UP, 1955.

Paris France. London: Batsford, 1940.

Picasso. London: Batsford, 1938.

Portraits and Prayers. New York: Random House, 1934.

A Primer for the Gradual Understanding of Gertrude Stein. Ed. Robert Bartlett Haas. Los Angeles: Black Sparrow, 1971.

Reflection on the Atomic Bomb. Ed. Robert Bartlett Haas. Los Angeles: Black Sparrow, 1973.

Selected Writings of Gertrude Stein. Ed. Carl Van Vechten. New York: Random House, 1946.

Stanzas in Meditation and Other Poems, 1929-1933. Preface by Donald
    Sutherland. New Haven: Yale UP, 1956.
Tender Buttons. New York: Claire Marie, 1914.
Three Lives. New York: Grafton, 1909.
*Two: Gertrude Stein and Her Brother and Other Early Portraits, 1908-
    1912*. Foreword by Janet Flanner. New Haven: Yale UP, 1951.
Useful Knowledge. New York: Payson and Clarke, 1929.
What Are Masterpieces and Why Are There So Few of Them? Foreword by
    Robert Bartlett Haas. Los Angeles: Conference, 1940.
The World Is Round. New York: Scottbooks, 1939.

Gertrude Stein Chronology

1874 Born 3 February in Allegheny, Pa., the fifth and final surviving child of German-Jewish immigrants Daniel and Milly Stein

1878 Moves to Passy, France with family

1880 Moves to Oakland, California, where father works in the cable-car industry

1888 Milly Stein dies

1891 Daniel Stein dies; oldest Stein son Michael assumes responsibility for family fortune, providing monthly allowance to Stein and second-youngest sibling Leo

1893 After living in Baltimore, Maryland, enrolls at Harvard Annex (subsequently Radcliffe College), where she begins writing

1894 Studies under William James and Hugo Münsterberg at Radcliffe

1897 Despite failing to earn undergraduate degree, enters Johns Hopkins School of Medicine

1898 Belatedly receives B. A. in medicine from Radcliffe

1900 Enters first significant relationship with fellow student May Bookstaver

1902 Abandoning studies, travels Europe with Leo

1903 Writes *Q.E.D.*, a novel about affair with Bookstaver; joins Leo at 27, rue de Fleurus, which she will occupy until 1938

1904 Visits America for the last time until 1934

1905   Begins writing *Three Lives*, which will not be published until 1909; with Leo, buys first Matisse and Picasso paintings; Saturday salons with Parisian artists begin at 27, rue de Fleurus

1906   Begins writing *The Making of Americans;* Picasso paints her portrait

1907   meets Alice B. Toklas in Paris; despite their secret "marriage" the following year, Toklas does not begin living at 27, rue de Fleurus until 1910

1913   Friend Mabel Dodge publishes "Speculations, or Post-Impressionism in Prose," the first critical essay on Stein's work; Leo abandons Paris for Italy, beginning lifelong alienation from Gertrude; through Dodge, meets Carl Van Vechten

1914   *Tender Buttons* published

1917   Works for the American Fund for French Wounded during WWI

1921   meets Sherwood Anderson

1922   meets Ernest Hemingway

1925   *The Making of Americans* published

1926   Lectures at Oxford and Cambridge at the invitation of Edith Sitwell; meets Bernard Faÿ and Virgil Thomson

1930   With Toklas, establishes Plain Edition to privately publish work

1932   Writes autobiography in six weeks in Bilignin in Southern France

1933   *The Autobiography of Alice B. Toklas* becomes a bestseller

1934-5 Collaboration with Thomson, *Four Saints in Three Acts,* produced in New York; returns to America for lecture engagements; meets Thornton Wilder

1937   *Everybody's Autobiography*, a memoir of American travels, is published

1938   Lease on 27, rue de Fleurus not renewed; moves to 5, rue Christine

1939   Forced to leave Paris as WWII looms

1940   As Paris is occupied, resides with Toklas first in Bilignin and later nearby Culoz; begins *Wars I Have Seen*

1944-5 After being "liberated" by American forces, becomes friends with G. I.s; tours American military installations in occupied Germany; begins *Brewsie and Willie*, an affectionate account of soldiers

1946   After suffering intestinal attack, is diagnosed with colon cancer; dies 27 July in surgery; later buried in Pére Lachaise Cemetery in Paris

Introduction

The critical response to Gertrude Stein offers one of the most intriguing chapters of American literary history. Between 1909 and 1933, Stein published some ten full-length volumes of her *sui generis* poetry, prose, and closet drama. This influential body of work, including the modernist landmarks *Three Lives* (1909) and *The Making of Americans* (1925), appeared under the aegis of either small, fly-by-night firms or through what is uncharitably called the vanity press—meaning that Stein had to pay for the privilege of seeing her name on a title page. While contemporaries like Ezra Pound and James Joyce embraced such outlets in avant-garde protest against the conservatism of mainstream publishing, Stein longed for the credibility (and remuneration) that a major imprimatur would bring. Because she had to wait nearly thirty years for these rewards, it is not surprising that in *The Autobiography of Alice B. Toklas* (published by Harcourt, Brace in 1933), she was tempted to bite the hand that finally agreed to feed her. Comparing American publishers unfavorably to the Paris art entrepreneurs who risked solvency to elevate Picasso and Matisse to their proper fame, Stein condemned the major houses for not supporting experimental authors. "There are many Paris picture dealers who like adventure in their business," she wrote. "There are no publishers in America who like adventure in theirs." While dealers "make their money as they can and they keep on buying something for which there is no present sale and they do so persistently until they create its public," publishers, instead of "gradually creating a public for Gertrude Stein's work," had for decades "procrastinated and then said no." At this point in her career, Stein feigned indifference at her constant rejection: "I suppose this was inevitable. However that was the matter as it was and as it continued to be" (241-42).

Beneath the blasé attitude, however, Stein remained frustrated, and understandably so, for the smaller firms that did agree to publish her lacked the resources to "create a public." Press runs for Stein's early books were invariably small, usually 500 to 1,000 copies. Distribution was so poor that retailers and libraries were rarely afforded the opportunity to stock them. Stein claimed she never saw a book of hers in a store until 1931, when she and Alice B. Toklas founded Plain Edition to print works like *Lucy Church Amiably* themselves (*Autobiography* 243). More frustrating, some of these small presses were one-man operations whose temperamental owners didn't always exhibit sound business sense. For years after *Tender Buttons* was published by the short-lived Claire Marie Press, Stein badgered founder Donald Evans for a royalty statement. Because Evans disliked letter writing, he never bothered to respond. In 1925, when *The Making of Americans* finally saw the light of day after circulating for nearly a quarter century in manuscript, the notoriously unstable expatriate publisher Robert McAlmon threatened to pulp the entire press run when Stein inquired once too often about her promised complimentary copies. After such dispiriting incidents, Stein had reason to believe her discouragement was over when her autobiography became a surprise bestseller. But she soon learned that the backing of a commercial publisher did not guarantee an audience. Between 1934 and 1946, Random House published eight Stein titles, including two more memoirs, *Everybody's Autobiography* (1937) and *Wars I Have Seen* (1945), but none sold enough to dispel the notion in publishing circles that *Alice B. Toklas* was a fluke. In 1942, Random House editor Bennett Cerf insisted in *The Saturday Review* that he had never lost money on Stein, but he also acknowledged that he hedged his bets by ordering modest press runs of 2,000 copies (20). Additionally, because Random House would only publish one Stein work per year, other fruits of her productivity, including *Narration* (1935) and *The World Is Round* (1939), were farmed out to the same small presses whose unreliability she thought she had escaped.

Yet Stein's frustration with publishers does not mean that she toiled in obscurity. Far from it. As early as 1913, with only *Three Lives* and the privately printed "Mabel Dodge at the Villa Curonia" to her credit, she became a long-running topic of consternation and concern in the American media. Initially, her notoriety was the product of a campaign to publicize her writing. As the Armory Show, the first exhibition of modernist art in America, prepared to open in New York in February 1913, Stein's socialite friend Mabel Dodge approached the show's publicity director, F. J. Gregg, hoping to spark moribund sales of *Three Lives* by exploiting the Stein family's support of Cubist painters to promote Gertrude's own efforts. "Oh! I'm all up in the air about this post-impressionistic literature—now this Gertrude Stein!" Gregg purportedly exclaimed (Dodge 159). Nevertheless, he invited Dodge to explicate Stein's methods, and the resulting essay, "Speculations, or Post-Impressionism in Prose," was duly published in *Arts and Decoration*. "Thousands will read it," Dodge promised Stein. "It *will* make your name known by & large" (159).

The boast was prophetic, but not perhaps in the way Dodge intended. While Stein's self-proclaimed "faithful & incomprehending Boswell" (160) interested a *New York Times* reporter, Carl Van Vechten, in writing on Stein, opposition from newspaper columnists and editorial writers was already taking shape. Even before Dodge and Van Vechten's essays hit the news stands, Stein had already provided an unflattering end rhyme for a bit of *Chicago Tribune* doggerel ridiculing Matisse's *Blue Nude*: "I called the canvas *Cow with Cud* / And hung it on the line / Altho' to me 'twas vague as mud, / 'Twas clear to Gertrude Stein" (qtd. in Brown 138). The jibe not only inaugurated a long tradition in which Stein's name served as a convenient punch line for spoofs of modern art, but it also marked the American press's fascination with her personality and its absolute lack of interest in her writing.

The concurrence of the Dodge and Van Vechten pieces with the *Chicago Tribune* parody ignited a heated debate between supporters and detractors not over Stein's merits as a writer but over her intent. Did she mean for her abstruse flights into repetition to be taken seriously, or was she pulling a Dadaist hoax by mocking the high seriousness of the literary establishment? The pro-Stein camp, which included lifelong members like Van Vechten and Sherwood Anderson, as well as passing admirers such as Edmund Wilson, Ernest Hemingway, Katherine Anne Porter, and Thornton Wilder, labored to validate her experiments as revolutionizing the verbal representation of perception and consciousness. Anti-Stein factions, meanwhile, fixated on her corpulence, her burgeoning reputation as an egotistical preceptor, her mannish appearance, and her stylistic propensity for what was derisively dubbed "baby talk." While the former celebrated Stein as the expatriate mater of modernism, the latter dismissed her as a "self-advertiser of pseudo-intellectual antics" (Burton 5). As her motives were alternately derided and defended, the actual content of her writing was relegated to the background, becoming a tangential issue until it was seen largely as an adjunct of her overpowering persona. An offhand comment from Edmund Wilson's *Axel's Castle* (1929) epitomizes the sentiments of many engaged in arguments over her art: "However unintelligible we may find [her writing]," Wilson wrote, "we are aware of a literary personality of unmistakable originality and distinction" (202).

While many scholars have lamented the overemphasis placed upon Stein the Personality during her lifetime, Gertrude's curious position of "being more talked about by more people who have never read a line of hers than any other author" (R.M.C. 69) is hardly an aberration. The early 20th century marked the first great age of modern celebrity in which audiences eagerly greeted news of the exploits of individuals whose genius seemed wholly tied to their talent for generating good copy. Alongside Stein's name in newspaper columns of the 1920s and 1930s, one finds less mention of Joyce, Hemingway, or Eliot than such now-forgotten figures as the hapless lothario "Peaches" Browning and the conniving adulteress-murderer Ruth Snyder. Because the extremeness of her art raised questions about just who she was (or who she thought she was), Stein was often lumped in with these pseudo-celebrities who fed the media maw for no other reason than they were curious, intriguing, and unique. These pop-culture luminaries were among the first to demonstrate that the art of notoriety had become an achievement unto itself. As Walter Lippmann warned in 1927, they were well-known only because they managed to manipulate a burgeoning "publicity machine" that, like "the beam of a powerful lantern," played "somewhat capriciously upon the course of events, throwing now this and now that into brilliant relief, leaving the rest in comparative darkness" (121). As Lippmann and other commentators cautioned readers that fame was no longer a gauge of achievement, Stein's reputation was sullied by association. She became someone whose perceived thirst for adoration, as Rose Macaulay put it, seemed "a trifle blatant" and "undignified": "To go down to history, to become a byword with posterity—is not this a little obvious and crude?" (549).

As a result of such reactionary ridicule, Stein's work—were it even to overcome her publisher problems to land in the hands of the common reader—had little chance of winning serious consideration; her public image *a priori* tainted perceptions of her writing. Even a loyal supporter like Anderson was prone to believing that she was "putting something across ... that by a strange freakish performance, [she] managed to attract attention to herself, get herself discussed in the newspapers, become for a time a figure in our hurried, harried lives" (15). The presumption that Stein's talents had less to do with writing than with getting noticed appears as early as 1914, when *New York Sun* humorist Don Marquis answered a self-proclaimed "puzzled reader" who demanded to know what exactly Gertrude Stein had done to merit public interest. "All we know of Gertrude really is that she is Gertrude Stein," Marquis responded in doggerel. "Let us search not, seek not, ask not, why the blessing has been sent / Little Groups, we have our Gertrude: worship her and be content!" (10).

Such was the tenuous state of Stein's critical reputation that when she died in August 1946 many observers of the literary scene assumed that her artistic legacy lay in the influence she bore on more conventional modernist literature, whether Hemingway's *The Sun Also Rises* or Wilder's *Our Town*. Malcolm Cowley's comments are typical: "I think of her often not as a writer primarily but as a scientist in his laboratory working at some problem that apparently has no connection with man or society," he wrote a few months after Stein's passing. "Her style is like a chemical useless in its pure state but powerful when added to other mixtures" (1). The best that could be said for her "often incomprehensible" efforts was that they were a catalyst—self-contained, of minor importance in and of themselves, yet essential for precipitating the modernist revolution. Accordingly, Stein the Personality persevered for nearly three decades in biographies like John Malcolm Brinnan's *The Third Rose* (1959) and James Mellow's *Charmed Circle* (1973), while the art itself was doomed to relative obscurity.

To be sure, a handful of critics and scholars devoted themselves to legitimating the actual texts. William Gass's 1958 essay "Gertrude Stein: Her Escape from Protective Language" eloquently testified to the value of her stylistic experiments, while Richard Bridgman's *Gertrude Stein in Pieces* (1970) set out to prove that her work was amenable to the same formalist scrutiny that established the canon-worthiness of *The Waste Land* and *Ulysses*. While critics like Leon Katz, Marianne DeKoven, and Wendy Steiner clarified the unity of aesthetic and philosophical thought beneath the deceptive surface confusion of *Buttons* and *Americans*, other scholars, including Donald Gallup, Ulla Dydo and Edward Burns, began editing the letters, manuscripts, and archival material necessary for a large-scale academic renaissance of interest. Yet the "Gertrude industry"did not truly establish itself until the 1980s and 1990s, when a plethora of interpretive methodologies shifted the focus of critical inquiry from content to context. As feminism, poststructuralism, and cultural studies interrogated the orthodoxies and ideologies that substantiated traditional literary values, the qualities that once made Stein easy to dismiss now made her essential. Whereas editorialists once ridiculed her as meaningless, Shari Benstock could now boast that Stein "did what no other author has quite had the courage to do … to relinquish the right to make language submit to the writer's will" (159). And if her harshest critics snidely alluded to her lesbianism to explain away her peculiarity, aficionados like Catharine R. Stimpson explored how these slurs revealed anxious efforts "to fix the monstrous qualities of the female body" and "stabilize" idealized images of femininity (183). In 1996, DeKoven summarized the transformation her reputation enjoyed as a result of interest in gender and other contextual issues: "Sometime in the past decade or two, she has been upgraded from noteworthy eccentric to figure of enduring gravitas …. We can [now] take for granted the diverse meaningfulness of all of Stein's writing, and the dazzlying, varyingly significant originality of her forms: the battles waged around questions of her quality or even viability have largely been won" (469, 473).

A further consequence of this victory is that we no longer need to ignore the long history of ridicule and hostility she suffered from the press. Previous compilations of Stein criticism, published at a time when one *did* have to argue her significance, drew largely from Stein admirers like Dodge, Van Vechten, and Wilder. Collections like G. K. Hall's *Critical Essays on Gertrude Stein* (1986) or Chelsea House's *Gertrude Stein* (1987) nominally chart the develop of her reception history by anthologizing both her contemporary supporters and the scholarly advocates responsible for her posthumous status. Yet because these resources generally draw from efforts aimed at ameliorating Stein's reputation, they perforce do an injustice by ignoring the bewilderment, protestation, and outright venom she inspired. The present volume is thus designed to give a more comprehensive overview of the range of response she inspired between 1909 and 1946.

The first and largest chapter, "Contemporary Reviews: The Making of a Reputation," gathers reviews of works published in Stein's lifetime, including *Selected Writings of Gertrude Stein*, for which she wrote an introductory note shortly before succumbing to cancer. (Because Stein and Toklas's Plain Edition venture suffered such poor distribution, at least three of her books from 1930-32—*Before the Flowers of Friendship Faded Friendship Faded, How to Write,* and *Operas and Plays*—were barely reviewed at all; Lindley Williams Hubbell's enthusiastic 1933 *Contempo* essay, included here, is one of the few pieces of the period to take notice of them. A later work, 1940's *What Are Masterpieces*, suffered only a slightly more enviable fate). The second section, "Contemporary Commentary: Style, Influence, and the Debate over Stein's Purpose," focuses on essays addressing the motives behind her hermeticism and its potential effect on standards of taste and appreciation. Chapter Three, "Veneration and Vituperation: The Making of a Celebrity," compiles parodies, doggerel, and selected pro-Stein pieces that illuminate her public imagine as "the Mother Goose of Montparnasse." Included here is Hemingway's satirical piece "The True Story of My Break with Gertrude Stein," reprinted for the first time since its initial appearance in *The New Yorker* in 1927.

The final section, "Remembrances, Memorials, and the Posthumous Reputation," begins with elegies that Stein's passing inspired over the late summer and fall of 1946. Among these tributes are the previously unpublished comments of Carl Van Vechten at a May 1947 Stein memorial in New York that featured performances of her major theatrical pieces *Four Saints in Three Acts* and *The Mother of Us All*. The book then concludes with five scholarly essays that provide an overview of the vagaries of Stein's posthumous reception. B. L. Reid's *Art By Subtraction* (1958), a self-described "essay in decapitation" (vii), may be the single-most negative academic book that Stein's work has inspired. Nevertheless, its central chapter, included here, is important inasmuch as Reid's objections to her style and the question of its content have been reiterated by subsequent critics. Catharine R. Stimpson's 1992 essay on *The Autobiography of Alice B. Toklas* challenges assumptions about Stein's lesbianism that became commonplace among academicians in the 1980s and 90s, while Maria Damon's complex 1996 study of Stein's Jewishness draws parallels between her attitude toward her ethnicity and the similar ambivalence of several 20th-century Jewish social scientists. Contributions by two of Stein's most recent biographers, Linda Wagner-Martin and Brenda Wineapple, are doubly interesting. Their insights into Stein's relationship with her mother and her attitudes toward feminism (1993 and 1997, respectively) are original and provocative. Equally important, they explore problems in writing *and* selling women's biography in the popular marketplace. Obviously, five essays fall far short of being exhaustive, yet by addressing Stein's aesthetics, lesbianism, ethnicity, her family relations and gender attitudes, this quintet of selections provides readers an introduction to the focal issues of contemporary Stein criticism.

In his 1947 remarks, Van Vechten describes visiting an exhibition of Stein memorabilia sponsored by Yale University Library, the repository for her papers. "As I examined the photographs made of her from childhood on," he writes, "it seemed to me that Gertrude Stein is more alive than she has ever been before." The motley assortment of pieces that make up *The Critical Response to Gertrude Stein* offers comparable snapshots of the artist and her era, demonstrating that for fans and foes alike she was indeed alive with the bustling energy of the early 20th century.

Works Cited

Anderson, Sherwood. "The Work of Gertrude Stein." *Sherwood Anderson./ Gertrude Stein: Correspondence and Personal Essays.* Ed. Ray Lewis White. Chapel Hill: U of North Carolina P, 1972. 14-17.

Benstock, Shari. *Women of the Left Bank: Paris, 1900-1940.* Austin: U of Texas P, 1986.

Bridgman, Richard. *Gertrude Stein in Pieces.* New York: Oxford U P, 1970.

Brinnan, John Malcolm. *The Third Rose: Gertrude Stein and Her World.* Boston: Little, Brown, 1959.

Brown, Milton. *The Armory Show.* 1963. New York: Abbeville, 1988.

Burton, Richard. "Posing." *Minneapolis Bellman* 17 October 1914: 5.

C., R. M. "Books, Books, Books." *The New Yorker* 20 February 1932: 69.

Cerf, Bennett. "Trade Winds." *The Saturday Review* 5 September 1942: 20.

Cowley, Malcolm. "Gertrude Stein, Writer or Word Scientist?" *The New York Herald-Tribune Weekly Book Review* 24 November 1946: 1.

DeKoven, Marianne. "Introduction: Transformations of Gertrude Stein." *Modern Fiction Studies* 42 (Fall 1996): 469-83.

Dodge, Mabel. *A History of Having a Great Many Times not Continued to be Friends: The Correspondence Between Mabel Dodge and Gertrude Stein.* Ed. Patricia R. Everett. Albuquerque: U of New Mexico P, 1994.

Lippmann, Walter. "Blazing Publicity: Why We Know So Much about 'Peaches' Browning, Valentino, Lindbergh, and Queen Marie." *Vanity Fair: A Cavalcade of the 1920s and 1930s.* Ed. Cleveland Amory and Frederic Bradlee. New York: Viking, 1960.

Macaulay, Rose. "Celebrities." *Forum* 80 (October 1928): 545-50.

Marquis, Don. "Gertrude Is Stein, Stein Gertrude." *The New York Sun* 15 October 1914: 10.

Mellow, James C. *Charmed Circle: Gertrude Stein & Co.* Boston: Houghton, 1973.

Stein, Gertrude. *The Autobiography of Alice B. Toklas.* 1933. New York: Vintage, 1990.

Stimpson, Catharine R. "The Somagrams of Gertrude Stein." *Critical Essays on Gertrude Stein.* Ed. Michael J. Hoffman. Boston: Hall, 1986. 171-83.

Wilson, Edmund. *Axel's Castle: A Study in the Imaginative Literature of 1870-1930.* 1931. London: Fontana, 1984.

1

Contemporary Reviews: The Making of a Reputation

Reviews of *Three Lives* (1909)

"Three Lives."

Anonymous

Three Lives by Gertrude Stein is a rather peculiar exposition of the art of character delineation, in which is shown the constant repetition of ideas in minds of low caliber and meager cultivation, the three lives depicted being those of three servant women, one of whom is a mulatto. The thing is novel in that it departs of traditional lines, the method of the great masters in this respect being one of summing up, or statement of ultimate and fixed condition, rather than a detailed showing of the repeated thoughts in the brain by which such conditions are arrived at. Of course, it must be admitted that such repetition does occur, even in cultivated and brilliant minds, but it is a question if the mind-working of such persons as Miss Stein has chosen could be made interesting by any process whatsoever. If she should attempt the same things with minds of a higher caliber, the result might be more entertaining.

Washington (D. C.) Herald, December 12, 1909.

"Fiction, But Not Novels."

Anonymous

Three Lives by Gertrude Stein is fiction which no one who reads it can ever forget, but a book for a strictly limited audience. The three lives are "The Good Anna," "The Gentle Lena," and "Melanctha." The good Anna was Miss Mathilda's housekeeper. The gentle Lena, when she had been in this country long enough to know the English, married the good son of German parents. Melanctha is a colored girl, her lover the very best type evolved in the race, a young physician. In this remarkable book one watches humanity groping in the mists of existence. As character study one can speak of it only in superlatives. The originality of its narrative form is as notable. As these humble human lives are groping in bewilderment so does the story telling itself. Not written in the vernacular, it yet gives that impression. At first one fancies the author using repetition as a refrain is used in poetry. But it is something more subtle still; something involved, something turning back, for a new beginning, for a lost strand in the spinning. It makes of the book a very masterpiece of realism, for the reader never escapes from the atmosphere of those lives, so subtly is the incantation wrought into these seeming simple pages. Here is a literary artist of such originality that is not easy to conjecture what special influences have gone into the making of her. But the indwelling spirit of it all is a sweet enlightened sympathy, an unsleeping sense of humor, and an exquisite carefulness in detail. But it is tautology to praise Miss Stein's work for this quality or that. Enough has surely been said to call the attention of those who will value her work to this new and original artist to come into the field of fiction.

Kansas City Star, December 18, 1909.

"Notable Piece of Realism."

Anonymous

Three Lives is in some respects a remarkable piece of realism. The author, Gertrude Stein, has given expression to her own temperament, to her own way of seeing the world. The style is somewhat unusual; at times it is a little difficult to follow, and sometimes it becomes prosy. It is only when one has read the book slowly—not as a story, but as a serious picture of life—that one grasps the author's conception of her humble characters, their thought and their tragedies.

Boston Evening Globe, December 18, 1909.

"Three Lives. **By Gertrude Stein."**

Anonymous

These stories of the Good Anna, Melanctha, and the Gentle Lena have a quite extraordinary vitality conveyed in a most eccentric and difficult form. The half-articulated phrases follow unrelentingly the blind mental and temperamental gropings of three humble souls wittingly or unwittingly at odds with life. Whoever can adjust himself to the repetitions, false starts, and general circularity of the manner will find himself very near real people. Too near, possibly. The present writer had an uncomfortable sense of being immured with a girl wife, a spinster, and a woman who is neither, between imprisoning walls which echoed exactly all thoughts and feelings. These stories utterly lack construction and focus but give that sense of urgent life which one gets more commonly in Russian literature than elsewhere. How the Good Anna spent herself barely for everybody in reach, the Gentle Lena for the notion of motherhood, while the mulattress Melanctha perished partly of her own excess of temperament, but more from contact with a life-diminishing prig and emotionally inert surroundings, readers who are willing to pay a stiff entrance fee in patient attention may learn for themselves. From Miss Stein, if she can consent to clarify her method, much may be expected. As it is, she writes quite as a Browning escaped from the bonds of verse might wallow in fiction, only without his antiseptic whimsicality.

The Nation, January 20, 1910.

"Curious Fiction Study."

Anonymous

It is probable that for every reader who accepts Gertrude Stein's first published book, *Three Lives*, there will be many who reject it. The broken rhythm of the prose, the commonness of the wording will probably be so repellant that the reader will not linger long enough to permit these qualities to produce their rightful effect and swing him into the imaginative understanding of the simple, mystic, humble lives of the women of whom the author writes.

It is hard to discuss the book without quoting the style, and it is impossible to quote unless whole pages be quoted. But it can be said that the slow, broken rhythm of the prose corresponds to the rhythm of the "lives" and to the reader's rhythmic comprehension; and that by this very token it is artistically justified, crudely inartistic as it may at first seem.

The subjects of the three tales Miss Stein tells are Anna and Lena, both servants, one good, the other gentle, one always managing the people about her, the other molded passively and almost uncomprehendingly by the people around her, and finally Melanctha, a colored girl, wandering and experiencing and learning, but never well utilizing what she has learned.

Nothing could be concretely more unlike the work of Henry James than is this work of Miss Stein's, and yet there is one most interesting relationship. James is the great master of conversation because his conversations are not patched up like mosaics out of separate people's remarks, but are themselves living, moving "situations" which must be understood as wholes if the words are to have real meaning. And James presents us the world he knows largely through these conversations.

Now, Miss Stein has no such tense, active, intellectual world to show us as James. She presents obscure, humble, vague, flowing, undefined life; but she presents us by an analogous method. She gives us no mosaics of life bits, but the living mass as it flows. Her murmuring people are as truly shown as are James' people who not only talk but live while they talk.

The place of such work as this is always obscure when first examined. It is certainly worth considering as a curiosity; doubtless also as an artist's story; possibly as much more than this.

Chicago Record Herald, January 22, 1910.

"A Futurist Novel."

Anonymous

Style is a matter of little importance when a certain effect is sought. Gertrude Stein knows this well when she merely sketches her *Three Lives*. There is a spirit in the method with which she tells us of the lives of three simple souls, and by this spirit, which comes from an instinctive feeling toward her subjects, Miss Stein accomplishes more than she could by any rhetorical or academic "style." Take, for example, this passage:

"It was very hard for Jeff Campbell to make all this way of doing, right, inside him. If Jeff Campbell could not be straight out, and real honest, he never could be very strong inside him. Now, Melanctha, with her making him feel, always, how good she was and how very much she suffered in him, made him always go so fast then, he could not be strong then, to feel things out straight then inside him."

If we try to analyze this from the point of view of "good English" construction it would seem incomprehensible. But analyze it from the view point of effectiveness, character picture and feeling, and there can be no doubt of the end accomplished. There is a picture of an emotional situation before us which arouses a deeper understanding and interest than could be done by the very best of conventional English.

To the willing reader of *Three Lives* each sketch means the acquaintance of an intimate life, its passions, emotions, feelings and happenings. We go through all the intimacies of "Good Anna's" soul. Physically and spiritually she stands before us unmasked. We see all her struggles with other humans. Her simple life passes on undramatically, with no events of worldwide importance to give us "thrills." We pass with her through the changes which life brings, and finally sit with her in the hospital in her last illness. And we weep when that simple soul is no more. We have known "Good Anna" in all her human weakness, and we have loved her as Miss Stein loved her.

For "Melanctha" and the "Gentle Lena," Miss Stein's other sketches, we can say as much. We are never burdened with a mass of detail, but when these lives are over—as all lives must be over some day—we have learned to understand passion, feelings and thought which we seldom recognize in ourselves, much less in others.

We cannot read these lives without thinking and sensitive minds. We must study the lines, the colors, the directions and, above all else, the spirit of the author. The mind must be keen and alert. For the blur which this futurist in writing at first creates cannot be cleared until we are willing to bring the thought and intelligence to its interpretation which we needed when examining *The Nude Descending the Stairs*. Let us welcome the new art, if it brings such wealth of simplicity and effectiveness as Miss Stein has shown in these sketches.

Philadelphia Public Ledger, April 10, 1915.

Reviews of *Tender Buttons* (1914)

"Officer, She's Writing Again."

Anonymous

Miss Gertrude Stein, who is at the head of the Cubists and Futurists in Paris, has produced *Tender Buttons* recently. The volume, according to one description, is "a sort of trilogy" on "Objects," "Foods" and "Rooms." After reading excerpts from it a person feels like going out and pulling the Fime Bank building over onto himself.

Detroit News, June 6, 1914.

"A Cubist Treatise."

H. L. Mencken

The small xanthous volume entitled *Tender Buttons*, by Gertrude Stein, late of Baltimore but now of Paris and the Cubist movement, is not a work for boneheads. Its emanations are too delicate to penetrate even the thinnest scum of cranial ivory. There must be a soft envelope to let them in—and within there must be a velvety substance for them to fall upon. As witness these transcendental strophes under the heading of "Way Lay Vegetables":
    "Leavens in grass and mow potatoes, have a skip, hurry you up flutter.
    Suppose it is as a cake suppose it is new mercy and leave charlotte and nervous bed rows. Suppose it is a meal. Suppose it is sam."
    "What Sam?" demand the vulgar. "Sam who? Certainly not the *geiger spieler*? And Charlotte? Who the deuce is Charlotte?" Thus the brutes and the osseocaputs. One hears the same idiotic questions about Cubist paintings. But to the illuminati the picture is vivid, succinct, comprehensible. A single reading, and the whole scene is there: the quiet, pastoral landscape, with Charlotte sitting on the fence nervously eating cake, and Sam mowing potatoes with a hop, skip and jump. Nothing photographic, nothing crudely representative, but how clear the image, how poignant the emotion! .... As the publishers frankly admit, the emotions aroused by a first reading of Miss Stein are "something like terror," but as one proceeds the beauty of these super-sentences begins to caress the refined mind, and in the end the effect is almost electrical. Not, however, upon the bonehead. The common

earthworm will gag at such filaments of fancy. They will demand a special education. They presuppose a Cubist and resilient cerebrum.

Baltimore Sun, June 6, 1914.

"Gertrude Stein."

Anonymous

From Claire Marie, publisher of books for people of "exotic tastes," comes at last a Gertrude Stein volume, a slim little book bound in bright canary covers called *Tender Buttons: Objects, Food, Rooms*. Those who are in the know about Gertrude Stein tell us that *Tender Buttons* is in the new Stein manner. The old Stein manner, it appears, was too easy. Too many people "got it." Some of those who read the famous "Portrait of Mabel Dodge," for example, are even said to have recognized Mabel Dodge when they met her at her "salon" on lower Fifth Avenue.

The new Stein manner, so it has been explained to us, is founded on what the Germans call "Wort-salad," a style particularly cultivated by crazy people. Miss Stein, it is known, has gone deeply into psychological matters. Although now living in Paris, she is an American, and has pursued her studies at both Radcliffe and Johns Hopkins.

The way to make a word-salad is to sit in a dark room, preferably between the silent and mystic hours of midnight and dawn, and let the moving fingers write whatever comes. The idea is not to think. Thinking would be ruinous. So this is how Miss Stein works, and we have some results in *Tender Buttons*.

E. S. Martin and his fellow-workers on that once humorous publication called *Life*, who are so solicitous for "home and mother," should be pleased at the warm domesticity revealed on every page of *Tender Buttons*. Here is no sex talk and unladylike feminism, but for the most part such homely topics are described as onions and turnips and roast beef and dress. One of the longest pieces in the book is on roast beef, which would make Charles Lamb, if he were alive—and recognized the beef—jealous for the fame of roast pig.

The titles are on the whole admirably simple and matter-of-fact: shoes, handkerchiefs, eyeglasses, cutlet, celery, eggs, etc. Miss Stein is known to be a patroness of the new art, and to have prospered by dealing in the pictures of Matisse, knowing when to buy, and also—it is supposed—when to sell.

But the Brancusi bust of Mlle. Pogany, popularly known as *The Lady or the Egg*, is plain as the nose, which isn't on the face, compared with Miss Stein's portrait of "Eggs" in this volume. But as to the titles, they, too, once in a while call for a little patience, as "A Piece of Coffee," or "A Little Called Pauline," or "Peeled Pencil, Choke," and "It was Black, Black Took."

The most "unique" volume ever written, the publisher says of *Tender Buttons*, but we go further and say "Most Uniquest." Do you remember the game (if your memory goes that far back) when everybody sat around in a circle, and each one wrote down a word, and when all the words were read in a sequence, the results were often screamingly funny? That was when you were young.

Also, did you ever amuse yourself with the "plachette," the "Ouija" board, as it is sometimes called, and do you recall how with a little coaxing and petting the things could sometimes be made to spell out something approximating the intelligible?

And what was that university that Gulliver visited on his travels? Were the professors there not busy with a wheel that turned and stopped at certain letters, which were then handed out in the name of profound learning?

Have you ever had the charade habit? And have you wrestled with Baconian ciphers and cryptograms?

If you have ever done any or all of these things you will enjoy *Tender Buttons*. Miss Stein, as she has been seen in Paris, is described as a mountainous lady, wearing a voluminous (necessarily voluminous) monkish robe of brown, roped—where the waist should be—with a cord. On her feet she wears carpet slippers, which may have suggested the bit on "Shoes," which we have quoted. At least this is how she appeared to my informant who saw her in Paris.

New York City Call, June 7, 1914.

"Gertrude Stein, Plagiary."

Anonymous

Not even the unkindest of Miss Gertrude Stein's critics accuses her of plagiary. There may be differences of opinion on the value of her discoveries in prose composition, but apparently no one questions them on the score of novelty and originality. The worst that has been said of her latest book, *Tender Buttons*, is that it is a farrago of nonsense, a meaningless medley of ill-assorted words. This judgment might possibly be attributed to prejudice, to a too-academic conception of language, and the defense offered by her admirers is in fact that she has found an entirely new use for words, arranging them, indeed, without too nice a regard for sense, but with clear and telling emotional intent. To this argument her critics have no answer, except that her prose means nothing to them. They are obliged, however, to admit that it is at least new.

Let us consider this new prose, picking a few passages at random from the *Tender Buttons*: "Aider, why aider why whow, whow stop touch, aider whow, aider stop the muncher, muncher munchers."

Similar passages might be quoted by the score, but these will do. It must be understood that they are not all by Miss Stein. Half of them are drawn from other authors, our purpose being to show that Miss Stein was not really the first to hit on this form of prose. We have taken care to draw on books published before Miss Stein discovered her literary gift in order that there may be no dispute on the question of priority. It is much to be regretted that the names of the earlier authors are not recorded, but the examples are all drawn from trustworthy editors, and most of them are to be found in classic textbooks. They are supposed to illustrate the way in which linguistic conceptions smother the content of thought in certain forms of insanity or how mere sound association sometimes overcomes the orderly association of ideas.

It is the belief of an ingenious lady, whose lectures have lately been published in the *Athenæum*, that some of those whom we call insane are in a state of spiritual or intellectual transition, preparing, as it were, to emerge "into a higher form of being." It may be then, that hitherto we have misunderstood what is commonly called confusion of speech in catatonic excitement, and that dementia praecox really represents a step towards perfection. That is a question which may be left to others. Our only object has been to show, with authentic examples from the writings and speeches of various men and women who came before her that Miss Gertrude Stein has had much more than her due share of homage at the hands of the critics.

New York Evening Sun, June 13, 1914.

"New Outbreaks of Futurism: 'Tender Buttons,' Curious Experiment of Gertrude Stein in Literary Anarchy."

Robert Emons Rogers

There is in New York a new publishing company called simply the "Claire Marie," which issues occasionally slender books bound in pale blues and greens, oranges and light lemons. The titles are, for instance, *Sonnets from the Patagonian, Saloon Sonnets and Sunday Flutings, Sacral Dimples* and *The Piety of Fans*. These seem mad, but there is one which seems madder. It is *Tender Buttons* by Gertrude Stein.

The Claire Marie Publishing Company hopes that these will be "books for people who are tired of bestsellers and of the commonplace, who are eager for the sincerely exotic, the tomorrow of literature. The poets and dramatists I shall publish will be men and women who have no quarrel with the existing order of things, who have no wish to teach or to tear down, who are concerned only with the beauty of life." But to anyone who gets in touch, even superficially with these writings, they seem to try to do for the art of literature what has already been done in painting, sculpture and music, that is, to express anarchy in art.

Boston has seen some of the paintings of Matisse and Picasso, the sculptures of Brancusi, which created such a stir of amazement and contempt last spring. It has heard too, perhaps, of the new symphonies, wild sounds produced on new and unmusical instruments, which originated lately in Italy. Boston has not pretended to try to understand them, nor to admit that there is anything to understand, not even the point of view of the perpetrators. So, in a way perhaps, these books which show the contemporary anarchy of art in the form of literature may serve as examples and explanations of the thing which has upset Paris and roused New York to a cynical interest.

To begin at the far frontiers, where literary expression as we know it jumps into the deep waters of unintelligible derangements of words! If you open Gertrude Stein's book *Tender Buttons,* which deals with the three simple subjects of Objects, Food and Rooms, you will find—looking at random—this: "Come and say what prints all day. A whole few watermelon. There is no pope."

Now the first thing to say—and most people say it—is that the woman is either a colossal charlatan or mad. But there is something else to know about her. She is a doctor of medicine and a doctor of philosophy, a brilliant scholar formerly at Johns Hopkins and Radcliffe and a student in whom

William James took a great interest and for whom he has prophesied a brilliant future. Furthermore, she is widely known in Europe and one of the foci of the futurist circles in Paris, where she lives. She had already done work thought remarkable, in the more usual fields of literary expression, before she turned to her "new manner."

If we consider her then as a person who is consciously working out an art form who knows what she is about, a description of her method of work may be illuminating. She will never talk of her work herself, but a friend has given the public some hints.

"She is impelling language to induce new states of consciousness, and in doing so language becomes with her a creative art rather than a mirror of history. In her impressionistic writing she uses familiar words to create perception, conditions and states of being, never quite consciously before experienced. To prevent her impressions she chooses words for their inherent quality rather than for their accepted meaning." That is, she does not create new words as Edward Lear or Lewis Carroll did, quite seriously, to create new impressions by strange sounds, but she hopes to present impressions by arrangements of sounds of familiar words which suggest an emotion rather than define a fact.

It is known that the next morning after a sound sleep she has her work of the night before read aloud to her, the only way in which she can criticize what she has done. She cannot read her own work on the written page; it means nothing to her. From this we can gather that the effect must be gained through sound alone. A page read aloud, quite apart from its sense or nonsense, is really rhythmical, a pure pattern of sound, as Picasso's canvases are pure patterns of color. Some feel a curious hypnotic effect in her sentences read aloud. By complicated repetition and by careful combinations does she get the effects she wishes for. And to some listeners there comes a perception of some meaning quite other than the content of the phrases.

There is an illuminating parallel to this in the very latest of the experiments of Picasso whom Boston derided at the exhibition of last year. He strove to present, not pictures of objects, but impressions of the emotions these objects gave him. But lately he has seemed to feel in this a certain lack of complete success. So in an exhibition to open this fall in New York he will exhibit his latest work, compositions produced by combinations of actual materials, textiles and metals, bits of wood, brass, glass, ribbons and silks, nailed and glued together to form patterns.

This seems to be a still further step. He has ceased to try to represent the emotions which certain things give him; he has determined to give the public the actual things themselves, in the combinations by which he was affected, in the hope that the beholder will get the same effect.

He still, presumably, calls himself a painter, yet he has abolished the laws of painting at one fell swoop. His idea verges on photography on the one hand, on architecture on the other. It is undoubtedly anarchistic. This may help to understand Miss Stein; instead of trying to convey her impressions of facts through words selected very subtly for their meaning, she gives the exact arrangements and sounds of words which have affected her, in the hope the reader, or the listener, will get the same impressions. Only, such an impression must always be weaker than that of the Picasso composition, since he uses the actuality and Miss Stein can only use words, in themselves symbols, and so inevitably lose something of the force of the impression.

So much for Gertrude Stein. The other people published by the Claire Marie press are much simpler; they are at least understandable. The best example, and one which can stand for the others, is the *Patagonian Sonnets* of Donald Evans. His pale green books contain eighteen sonnets of impeccable form, mostly impressionistic portraits of his friends.

These two, Evans and Gertrude Stein, then, are anarchists in literature, striving to break away from the laws which have hitherto bound—and supported— it. Evans is less ruthless than Miss Stein, of course, and less anarchic. To understand them or to approach their point of view is not possible if one considers them as separate and unrelated. They relate to each other, and not less to the men who are doing the same thing in sculpture, painting and music. They are part of a movement which is mightily interesting Europe, has touched the artistic fringe of New York and seems quite unheard of in Boston.

This is not a defense of these writers, nor of their conceptions. It is not even an explanation. It is a primer from which the reader may go on to link up these people and to see that all their ideas, expressed in different media and differently even in the same medium, are all founded on some first principle and are tending in the same general direction. And that direction is briefly, anarchy in the arts corresponding to the older and better-known idea of anarchy in society. The liberty, they would probably say, to express their own emotions in whatever way they feel best, untrammeled by any rules or conceptions of art, however long known, however well-proved.

There is one other bit of writing which is very illuminating on this point. The last number of *Camera Work* published by Stieglitz of New York, whose gallery at 291 Fifth Avenue has been the home of the Photo-Secession and the Futurist and Cubist in painting, contains a page or two of

"Aphorisms on Futurism" by Mina Loy. It applies directly to art, but no less directly to literature. It sums up what Futurism means. It is undoubtedly the conscious expression of that Anarchy I have spoken of.

The truth or falsity of these ideas does not matter for this discussion. They are quoted simply because they seem to be the best mottoes yet evolved for what is called Futurism and what is really anarchy in the arts.

Boston Evening Transcript, July 11, 1914.

"Steinese Literature."

Charles Ashleigh

When I received this book for review I noticed within it a small, cream-colored pamphlet, which, from casual observation, I judged to be an explanation of the method and object of the work.

This document, with customary carelessness, I promptly mislaid. There followed a fevered but fruitless search. Then I wrote to other publishers, asking that another booklet be sent to me immediately. Two long weeks have I waited, but it has not arrived. Therefore, I must wrestle unaided.

I confess that I am not adequate to this book. Eager as I am to know and to welcome all manifestations of the new spirit in art and letters, yet, here I must confess myself beaten.

It is said that the author was an able assistant in psychological research to the late Professor James and that she was specially engaged in the study of the idea associations. It may be, therefore, that this seemingly incomprehensible jumble of words has for the writer certain meanings, through association, which are replete with solemn interest—this I am unable to deny or affirm.

Nevertheless, there is a certain fascination in this volume. To one who loves the nonsense rhymes of Lewis Carroll, these grouped incongruities will doubtless also appeal. But such appeal is evidently not the writer's intent. Here, for instance, is a delightful little prose poem on a subject with which we are all intimate— sausages.

It was a dreadful blow to me when I found that I was so behind the times—so encased in traditional concepts that I could not respond to this. I had considered myself up-to-date. The bizarre pronouncements and chantings of the Vorticists in the first number of *Blast* were not beyond me. When, for example, Wyndham Lewis says "the violent fungi of sullen thoughts," I recognize it as a rather beautiful and apt expression. But the Vortecists' writing is as plain as a Cusack hoarding, compared to that of Miss Stein.

Yes, I admit that I am beaten! I am left behind. I resign myself sadly to sink into the murky depths of an outworn and senile Philistinism. I may only hope that, sometimes, understanding may be vouchsafed to me, even if it be at the last. I can imagine it coming upon me at my death moment; a light illumining my face and a flame in my eyes, as, with the final remnant of my strength, I raise myself and with my dying breath exclaim: "Harmonious Pudding!"

Chicago Evening Post, August 7, 1914.

"Futurist Essays."

Anonymous

We do not purpose to be mean and bitter in discussing *Tender Buttons*. It lends itself to invective and satire; it is an excellent butt for ridicule, and offers a rare opportunity for all sort of sarcasm and funniness. But we restrain ourselves, having little sympathy with those who mock and tease the foolish.

Tender Buttons may be highly recommended to the posing class which is deliberately unintelligible in the hope of being thought elusively wise. The book does not make sense. It does not pretend to make sense. It seems to be Futurism. At first we wondered if there were not some key, some intent, some cipher. There may be. We have looked for it in vain. Take the definition of "Cold Climate," not because it is worse, but because it is shorter than the others: "A season in yellow sold extra strings makes lying place."

Again, for we heartily wish to condemn this book, let the definition of "A Dog" be presented: "A little monkey goes like a donkey that means to say that means to say that more sighs last goes. Leave with it. A little monkey goes like a donkey."

The canary boards in which the book is bound are striking, the printing is very good and easily read, and has a certain outer artistic value as is always found in Claire Marie books. That is the best we can say for it. Oh, yes—it purports to be a sort of dictionary of "objects, food, rooms."

Los Angeles Times, August 9, 1914.

Reviews of *Geography and Plays* (1922)

"Medals for Miss Stein."

Carl Van Vechten

Probably few writers are better known in this country than the American Gertrude Stein, who lives in Paris but it has been the pleasant custom to smile over this lady condescendingly or to sniff at her. Young men and old ladies who compile columns for the newspapers and who probably have never read more than two or three quoted lines of Miss Stein's work are in the habit of lifting their fingers to their noses in no very pretty gesture whenever they refer to her.

Nevertheless, it is with the most complete assurance that I rest firm in the belief that I shall live to see a reversal of this attitude. When her very long masterpiece, *The Making of Americans: Being the History of a Family's Progress* (a work in eight volumes, each containing approximately 500 typewritten pages), is at last published I expect to see young intellectuals approaching on their bellies from every point in the compass to place wreaths on this noble shrine. This work was written perhaps fifteen years ago and at that time was far in advance, both in style and length, of what any publisher would conceivably accept for publication. Now, however, there is reason to believe that her imitators have paved a popular way down which this lady with her eight volumes might march triumphantly.

Gertrude Stein is not only the founder of the modern movement in English literature, she is also at the present time far ahead of her boldest follower. With the publication of *Three Lives* her gossip was disseminated. One of these lives, that of Melanctha, the Negress, is one of the finest stories in the English language. The influence of this book, published in 1909, may be traced through Dorothy Richardson on James Joyce and May Sinclair, on Virginia Woolf and Katherine Mansfield and through May Sinclair on Zona Gale. Waldo Frank and Sherwood Anderson drank from the original fountain. Whole pages in the work of the former are written in the identical style of the early manner of Miss Stein. These statements will appear axiomatic in a few years. To utter them now, however, may seem to many a little hysterical. Nevertheless, I prefer to say them now. The chorus will sing the refrain later.

The scoffers handicap themselves by not having prepared their case. They have not read Gertrude Stein, or if they have it will be found that they have perused only a few or the more famous extracts from "Mabel Dodge at the Villa Curonia" (the celebrated "green bottle" passage, for example), or from *Tender Buttons* (probably the delectable description of chicken). These, it may be admitted, savor, to the uninitiate, of dark cocoonery. If they would begin with *Three Lives* (a book, unfortunately, not readily procurable at the present moment), pass on through the studies of Matisse and Picasso in *Camera Work*, through *Tender Buttons* to *Geography and Plays*, they would perceive that the progression of this artist is singularly definite and direct.

From the beginning she was a stylist. Although *Three Lives* and *The Making of Americans* (the manuscript of which I have been permitted to read) are written in perfectly clear English, not a single sentence is formed in an imitative or echoing manner. I defy the most prying literary detective to discover a single cliché anywhere in these books. Passing through her reiterative period, in which sometimes she contrived a whole paper out of variations of one single phrase, Miss Stein entered into her third manner, which is even more alarming to the general public than the later manner of Henry James.

And yet, even to the novice, there should be nothing very disturbing about the delightful *Geography and Plays*. If the reader would permit himself to fall under the spell of this enchantress of words, just as I have often urged concertgoers to listen to Schoenberg or Ornetin without thinking of Beethoven or Liszt, he would soon find himself reading without much difficulty. Miss Stein obviously has worked under two influences: the first is that of the psychology of William James, the second of that of the post-impressionist painters. This statement must not be taken too literally. When Kenneth Burke, for instance, drags in Clive Bell's "significant form," he is a little wide of the mark. This is a facile but dangerous label. As a matter of fact, all books and pictures have significant form, *Uncle Tom's Cabin* as much as *Jude the Obscure*. It would be safer, in reference to Miss Stein's work, to speak in guarded terms of the "psychology of the unconscious." In the whole range of her published work I do not recall a single literary reference (doubtless there are a few), although references to politics, current events, personalities, etc., are constantly recurring.

It may be added that Miss Stein is rich in one quality which her disciples and followers notoriously lack—that is, a sense of humor. It is pleasant to remember that when the world stops laughing at Miss Stein it can still laugh with her. Read aloud "White Wines," one of the plays in her new book, and see if you can't agree with me.

The New York Tribune, May 13, 1923.

"Miss Stein's Stories."

Edith Sitwell

It has taken me several weeks to clarify my own feelings about Miss Stein's writings. Her work appears to have a certain amount of real virtue, but to understand or apprehend that virtue a reader would have to study Miss Stein's methods for years, and intimately; whereas this is the first book of hers that I have read. Her virtues and faults are in exact contradiction of each other. I think it is indisputable that Miss Stein has a definite aim in her work, and that she is perfectly, relentlessly, and bravely sincere. She is trying to pull language out of the meaningless state into which it has fallen, and to give it fresh life and new significance. For this purpose she uses comparatively few words, and turns them into ever-varying and new patterns till they often do, definitely, surprise us with their meaning. I imagine, however, that she was more hampered than helped by her early training. We read in the publishers' note that "she became interested in psychology and philosophy, and worked with Münsterberg and James, who both predicted a remarkable future for her .... Practical medicine did not particularly interest her, and soon she specialized in the anatomy of the brain and direction of brain tracts...." This may account for the fact that this book, at first sight, appears to be a collection of heterogeneous words, thrown together without any respect for meaning, but only a respect for the shape and rhythm of sentences. I hope I shall not be regarded as a reactionary, but I am bound to say that I prefer words, when collected into a sentence, to convey some sense. And Miss Stein's sentences do not always convey any sense—not even a new one. It is her habit to open her mind and let words float in and out regardless of each other. What, for instance, are we to make of such a sentence as: "A clever saucer, what is a clever saucer, a clever saucer is very likely practiced and even has toes, it has tiny things to shake and really if it were not a delicate blue color would there be any reason for every one to differ"? This sentence, no doubt, would throw a psychoanalyst into a frenzy of excitement; and it was probably written for this purpose; but exciting psychoanalysts is not the highest aim of literature.

In a story called "Miss Furr and Miss Skeene," the author repeats the following sentence, with very slight variations, for six pages—it is the whole of the story: "Helen Furr was gay there, she was gayer and gayer there and really she was just gay there, she was gayer and gayer there" .... Lord Tennyson could produce the same feeling of monotony with more economy of means, and with less risk of reducing his readers to the asylum.

As an example, however, of Miss Stein's method when it is successful, let us take this delicious Picasso-like landscape: "A cloud of white and a chorus of all bright birds and a sweet a very sweet cheery and a thick miss, a thick and a dark and a clean clerk, a whole succession of mantelpieces."

To sum up the book as far as is possible, I find in it an almost insuperable amount of silliness, an irritating ceaseless rattle like that of American sightseers talking in a boarding-house (this being, I imagine, a deliberate effect), great bravery, a certain real originality, and a few flashes of exquisite beauty. One feels, too, that there is a real foundation for Miss Stein's mind, somewhere deep under the earth, but that it is too deep for her to dig down to, and that she herself is not capable of building upon this hidden foundation. She is, however, doing valuable pioneer work, and I should like to take this opportunity of begging *les Jeunes* not to hamper her by imitating her, but to leave her to work out her own literary destiny.

The Nation & The Athenæum, July 14, 1923.

"Incitement to Riot."

John W. Crawford

The medium of words is at once enriched and enfeebled by its essential inexactitude; it is virtually impossible to hit upon that organization of spoken or written thought symbols which shall carry always an identical freight from mind to mind. Translation of the spoken language into written forms is particularly treacherous; the human animal has the most devilish and irrelevant mechanism for the association of ideas. Miss Stein, at least, evades this peril; indeed, she swings to the other extreme of an expression that is so little related to the content of the average mind that she is in danger of being her own most appreciative, most receptive audience. In her poem, "Black Earth," Marianne Moore writes: "I do these things which I do, which please no one but myself."

That is one of the privileges of the artist. Miss Stein's hilarious dissociations call for robust companioning. Her epigrams that dissolve into yet other epigrams, endlessly, are less wit than detonations of a subtly negating analysis. She reads aloud much better than she reads to one's self. Reading aloud from *Geography and Plays* to almost any gathering is to experience an electric charging of the room; none is able to sit quiet, none is able to keep silent. Everyone shouts at once. They become more and more angry, more and more exhilarated, more and more tickled in their larger, more internal risibles until they guffaw. She comes alive, unquestionably, when she is read aloud.

It would seem that Miss Stein's chief difficulty, as is true of much of Alfred Kreymborg, E. E. Cummings and Vachel Lindsay, is the lack of speech notation for written words, to correspond with the conventional and standardized signposts to the interpretation of written music. Perhaps the day of the oral word artist is coming back in an idiom more closely attuned to our modern consciousness. Perhaps Gertrude Stein will be found, if not among the forefront of those new singers, at least in the ranks of the pioneers that made their song possible. Perhaps in that sense, Sherwood Anderson's foreword to Miss Stein's newest book will be fulfilled:

"Would it not be a lovely and charmingly ironic gesture of the gods if, in the end, the work of this artist were to prove the most lasting and important of all the word slingers of our generation!"

What does Miss Stein say of herself? In "France" one finds what may be a revealing gesture: "They are not pieces and there is reason, there is reason in it because the whole thing shows such dissociation that all doing it for that purpose and together there can be no question but that they succeed."

New York Call, August 19, 1923.

"Miss Stein Applies Cubism to Defenseless Prose."

G. E. K.

Gertrude Stein is an addict of a non-literary ideal, incoherence. She professes the wish to recreate life in words, not in their meaning, but wholly in themselves as such. That is, her center of interest is not in what the words or sentences connote, but rather in their related sounds or that they may bring new sensations or by their jumbling or repetition awaken long-forgotten ones.

Consequently Miss Stein is a grandstand player. She permits her mentality to fatten in order to interest the pseudo-intelligentsia—the poetry clubs; the contributors to new thought magazines and their readers; incompetents who go in for futurism in painting or cubism in sculpture. Amy Lowell turned the trick before her, but Miss Lowell's Bible was the *Oxford Book of Verse* by comparison.

From cover to cover, save for an introduction by Sherwood Anderson, who has swallowed the bait as one might expect, there is nothing but colloidal shapelessness.... Now and then she wearies of "prose" and breaks out into "verse." Here is the preliminary movement of pushing "Pink Melon Joy," nude and unashamed, out into the world: "My dear what is meat. I certainly regret visiting. My dear what does it matter".... Enough's enough! As one may judge from the above, picked at random, the book is downright blather of the worst sort. Probably Miss Stein isn't to blame. Persons ready for occupational therapy usually aren't. The publishers are the ones who really belong in the stocks.

Baltimore Sun, August 25, 1923.

"The Writing of Gertrude Stein and 'Geography and Plays.'"

Kate Buss

In the preface to Gertrude Stein's new book *Geography and Plays*, Sherwood Anderson mentions he had been asked to write something "by way of an introduction." Therefore it seems warranted to approach Miss Stein by way of Mr. Anderson. At least during a few paragraphs? But are we able? His is an enigmatically incomplete statement concerning an unusual book.

I hazard that Mr. Anderson smells stronger meat in *Geography and Plays* than the quality of its vocabulary—which is neither esoteric nor unfamiliar. But vocabulary is his theme, and apparently it is the premise from which he admires. "Little housekeeping words," he says, "the swaggering bullying street-corner words, the honest working, money-saving words...." Intriguing obscurity! What we have a right to expect of Mr. Anderson is his opinion of how Gertrude Stein combines these words in a fashion which brings consternation to so many readers.

He may not have read *Geography and Plays* before he wrote its introduction, but he had specifically considered Miss Stein's preceding book *Tender Buttons*, for it was this last collection of sketches that interested him to go and see her when he was in Paris, and from which his impulse derived to write a preface to her next volume. *Geography and Plays* continues the theories experimented with in *Three Lives* and in *Tender Buttons*.

Suppose we examine Miss Stein's first book, *Three Lives*. It was published a dozen years ago. In it are three unrelated stories of three women: Lena, Anna, and Melanctha. Melanctha, as a story, is the life of a Negro girl; and was told by the usual means of action and quotation-marked conversations which were—following literary formula —explanatory. But the story juxtaposes the conscious and the unconscious minds of the girl as these nebular areas of the brain had not been expressed in earliest English literature. One means of accomplishment Miss Stein used then, and increasingly employs today, is accented repetition. She is an attentive listener. Not only has she observed that people talk and move in circles of repetition—whether they are repressed, passionate, sophisticated, or uneducated—and by such unconsciously reiterated motif establish personality and disclose the turmoil that is within them; but as a writer she has known how to employ this universal habit as a means to present her characters. The personal rhythms of repetition that are so evident in *Geography and Plays* were sufficiently obscured, in the earlier book *Three Lives*, by familiar writing technique to have escaped particular comment.

Tender Buttons was Miss Stein's next published volume—the "Portrait of Mabel Dodge at the Villa Curonia" was privately printed in Italy and is too brief to be called a book. In *Tender Buttons* objects, food, rooms, love, are the subjects; and the repetition expedient—which belongs to the rhythm of living things—is decreased for the reason that people are not its topic. In this book suggestions by the *sounds* of words in association augments as the author's intention lessens to explain her subjects in the accepted forms of syntax, of quotation-marked conversation, of Websterian definition and simile.

Pioneers have always produced historians. Occasionally they have had a contemporary George Moore or a Clive Bell at hand with immediate and apt revelation. Surely, prefacing an author's third book, Sherwood Anderson might be expected to add to the generally accepted, if scanty fact, that Miss Stein uses words with the same purpose that her friends, Pablo Picasso, Juan Gris, Henri Matisse, use paint: which is (or which has been more than it now is) to render a considered object by splitting up and distorting its parts in order to express the impression it produced upon its re-creator.

There are many tricks in reproductive processes. Jean Cocteau (in books) practices an unaccustomed "lay out" on pages to emphasize similar theories.

Avails himself of broken lines, irregular indentations, now and again a nearly blank page, and arrangements of type to form a shape or suggest a pattern. *Geography and Plays* has no type idiosyncrasy. But singularity is obvious in its grouping of words despite the book's straightforward printing.

Mr. Anderson speaks of "An entire new recasting of life, in the city of words." Stimulating phrase! but what does it mean? He explains nothing. Let us consider the painter's theory "to distort the parts as a means to express the whole." In *Geography and Plays* I find a six-page sketch called "Miss Furr and Miss Skeene." It analyzes easily to show distortion; and concerns two young women who wish to enjoy life. Words are stressed: particularly the words "cultivated," "gay," and "regularly." If you were to read these three words lined with a great many others and repeated only once or twice you would not receive the definite impression of a *definite and regular gaiety* that Miss Stein is able to give by her intensive method of accenting these qualifying parts of speech.

I have said—what any one knows who observes his neighbor—that people repeat themselves in talk and action. This representation may be caused by an "inferiority complex," a case of the gout, or a daily-to-be-dusted drawing room. Miss Furr and Miss Skeene are boring young women who live in a maze of reiteration. The search for gaiety is their repetition urge. In this story I have named the stressed words. Miss Stein has wielded some form of "cultivate" thirty-one times; "gay," one hundred and fourteen; and "regularly" thirty-three times. This is six pages! "Travel" often occurs in the beginning of the sketch to suggest activity and the restless curiosities of youth, but is not employed toward the end; its suggestion is changed to "always" which points the final fixation of this pair of young women in their habits of gaiety.

Or, examine the portrait of a living person: that of Monsieur Roché, whom one knows in Paris as a man of discrimination and unusually harmonious response. "Roché," as the sketch is called, is described in eight hundred words in which "certainly," "completely," and "listening" are the stressed words. "Certainly" is repeated thirty-three times; "completely" twenty-eight, and "listening," seventeen times; while two qualifying adjectives are "pleasant," repeated twelve, and "beautiful" repeated eighteen times. The following sentence illustrates: "This one (Roché) certainly was listening and this was a very pleasant thing, this one was certainly one going to be doing a beautiful thing if this one is one who is a complete one." The certainty of delight in, the attention to complete beauty, are what Monsieur Roché's acquaintances read in this picture. But the entire sketch should be read. It is as delicately accurate portraiture as a miniature on ivory.

Such may seem obscure writing. Many people find it so. And unquestionably certain of Gertrude Stein's sketches make obscure reading. Or, the style may not please you. Very likely; but not to the point.

As I see it, considerations of value are: how Gertrude Stein composes; whether she is sincere; what is her influence in modern literature. The first question I have attempted to answer—although I am aware that I have no more than suggested the astute receptivity of the mind behind the method. Consideration two: is Gertrude Stein a sincere writer? This for answer: she is a student of people, an intellectual, therefore not a dilettante to be amused to play a lifelong joke upon herself. Added assurance: she was trained in the means of the conscious and unconscious minds by William James and received a degree in mental science at Johns Hopkins Medical School.

What is her influence in modern literature? Immeasurable and not very tangible for it is too recent. Sherwood Anderson—particularly in his new *Many Marriages*—and Waldo Frank in *Rahab* and *City Block* show it. Also poets of a few years ago; the adaptable Imagists; many young fictionists. I believe Mr. Anderson does not deny the influence of Gertrude Stein's writing has had upon his own. In Paris people say, using an old phrase for a new fact, that Miss Stein has created a new school, and believe that she was forerunner of Dorothy Richardson, Wyndham Lewis, even for the May Sinclair of the last half dozen novels; *avant-coureur* for Jean Cocteau, and for many young Americans both in Europe and the United States. I think this is true, and know it to be unpremeditated.

Miss Stein is interested neither in "literary schools" nor, particularly, in writers: if she likes you it is never because you scrape elbows with the intelligentsia. She reads few novels. Biography and history are her preferences. With people, focal events, actuality, she makes contacts. And to write is, to her, a serious occupation—this for the nincompoop who titters. She works every day and seldom talks about it; is not concerned with critics nor unappreciative of her own increasing public.

A final paragraph about the preface to *Geography and Plays*! In it Mr. Anderson gives an exact picture of Miss Stein as an individual, and finishes it with the following—to which I have not the disagreement I very definitely have with the limitations of his other statements: "Would it not be a lovely and charmingly ironic gesture of the gods if, in the end, the work of this artist were to be proved the most lasting and important of all the word slingers of our generation!"

Voices: A Journal of Verse, 1923.

Reviews of *The Making of Americans* (1925)

"Gertrude Stein in Critical French Eyes."

Anonymous

She has been a conundrum to the literary world for a quarter of a century. Are her novels childish babble or works of genius? The answers are conflicting. And now Gertrude Stein has published in Paris a book called *The Making of Americans*—a book seven and one-half inches wide, nine and one-half inches long, and four and one-half inches thick! And the contents are as original as the format. Willis Steell, who lives in Paris, discusses this novel in the February *International Book Review*, and tells of an interesting talk with the author. Instead of beginning *The Making of Americans* in the time worn manner of "Listen, my children, and you shall hear," he says, Miss Stein introduces her novel with a page of which the following is a part: "This that I write down a little each day here on my scraps of paper for you is not just an ordinary kind of a novel with plot and conversations to amuse you, but a record of a decent family progress."

Nothing is easier than to make fun of Gertrude Stein. "Ridicule or something worse," says Mr. Steell, "has been her bitter portion for thirty years. She has borne it imperturbably; at least, there is no indication that the laughter of groundlings has affected her any more than a distant echo might. Her method remains what it was when she first set down disconnected words of one syllable, eliding all 'ifs' and 'ands,' and offered the result as poetry." But her mind has progressed. The reviewer finds proof of it in this thousand-page novel about the author's own family.

Mr. Steell, greatly daring, couples Gertrude Stein's name with that of Marcel Proust, but only by way of contrast: "Both Marcel and Gertrude find their material in personal recollection; but while the Frenchman is delicately subjective and idealizing even the evil spirits he calls to from the depths of memory, no bull in a china shop could be so destructive as Gertrude is of artistic ideals in her clumsy, objective way." *The Making of Americans* is a history of the wanderings of three generations of a prosperous middle-class family over the face of America, with diffuse accounts of the mental and soul growth of each person, and digressions to include every individual that any one of them ever met. "But now to make again a beginning," is a constantly recurring phrase throughout the first hundred pages; but one can never feel sure that a start has actually been made. "David Hersland was a big man." So the author describes the first of the family, as far back as her own knowledge goes. He had a "little unimportant wife" and three "big resentful children." On page 49 we feel that we have really pushed off and may sit down without rocking the boat .... But we are not really off .... Lest the reader of his article should likewise grow "full up with impatient feeling," Mr. Steell here takes it for granted that Miss Stein's mode of progress, "one step forward and half a dozen backward," has been sufficiently indicated; but he adds that "it is always like this in the maze of a thousand pages." Like Marcel Proust, who could stop in the midst of a tale of passion to recall his grandmother's death bed, so Gertrude Stein mixes up generations in a maddening way; but, also like the French genius, she never loses the clue which enables her to retrace her steps.

Mr. Steell visited Miss Stein in her old-fashioned Parisian apartment, where she has lived for a quarter of a century, and heard what she had to say about her literary method. One gathers that it is a method somewhat akin to that of the ultramodern "stream of consciousness" school, but with even less self-restraint than James Joyce or Dorothy Richardson or Virginia Woolf employ. Speaking of her early novel, *Three Lives*, Miss Stein admitted to the interviewer that she had been at fault in permitting that book "to write itself resistlessly." She now makes a sort of scenario or plan of a book before beginning to write, but she still chooses words for their sound rather than for their sense. As she told Mr. Steell:

"I was always tremendously interested in the volume and rhythm of words, and in my early work I wrote in long and complicated sentences which kept on until I had completely freed myself of whatever conception was in my head. Gradually I found I could create the same intensity of conception by making the sentences enormously short. Thus the stances fall in my *Americans*: 'Resisting being is one way of being,' wherein in seven simple words I have cast a thought which formerly might have seemed to me to require a long paragraph."

But, then, she read aloud a single sentence of nearly three hundred words from page 521 of the same novel, a sentence that would confuse a German philosopher and drive a grammarian mad, adding this comment of her own:

"A serious conclusion like this, drawn from recollections that fill more than five hundred pages of my book, involving a myriad of personal recollections, comprehending innumerable little sights, sounds, acts, feelings—these could not be summed up in a sentence of seven words. It is impossible .... When I was younger and determined to write, I knew nothing of the ancient Greek curse on us all, heredity; now I have seen, I have weighed, I have reflected, I know, and my *Americans* is the outcome."

In other words, Gertrude Stein has discovered heredity and written a big book about it .... As Mr. Steell says, it is easy to laugh at Gertrude Stein. But how, then, shall we explain such praise as Jean Cocteau, that many-sided genius whom French critics are still trying to place, has bestowed upon her? With childlike pleasure Miss Stein read aloud Cocteau's comment:

"I can sense her rhythm even in translation; she possesses the *métier poétique*. Her 'Portrait of Picasso' is like a bas-relief. I seem to run my fingers over it, as tho it were a piece of plastic art. Hers was the first writing which struck me as being a new thing in the English language."

If that short piece is a bas-relief, asks the *International Book Review* writer, what shall we call *The Making of Americans*? He concedes that it is a canvas as vastly stretched as that of the Sistine Chapel's *Last Judgment*, and containing perhaps as many figures, but "with the kindest spirit imaginable for the author one couldn't call it in any sense a work of art."

In spite of her twenty-five years of erratic output, which has always excited curiosity, if nothing stronger, Miss Stein remains to many literary persons what the hippopotamus was to the farmer, "no such animal."

The Literary Digest, February 6, 1926.

"Everybody is a Real One."

Katherine Anne Porter

All I know about Gertrude Stein is what I find in her first two books, *Three Lives* and *The Making of Americans*. Many persons know her, they tell amusing stories about her and festoon her with legends. Next to James Joyce she is the great influence on the younger literary generation, who see in her the combination of tribal wise woman and archpriestess of esthetic.

This is all very well; but I can go only by what I find in these pages. They form not so much a history of Americans as a full description and analysis of many human beings, including Gertrude Stein and the reader and all the reader's friends; they make a psychological source book and the diary of an aesthetic problem worked out innocently under your eyes.

One of the many interesting things about this book is its date. It was written twenty years ago, when Gertrude Stein was young. It precedes the war and Cubism; it precedes *Ulysses* and *Remembrance of Things Past*. I doubt if all the people who should read it will read it for a great while yet, for it is in such a limited edition, and reading it is anyhow a sort of permanent occupation. Yet to shorten it would be to mutilate its vitals, and it is a very necessary book. In spite of all there is in it Gertrude Stein promises all the way through it to write another even longer and put in it all the things she left unfinished in this. She has not done it yet; at least it has not been published.

Twenty years ago, when she had been living in Paris only a few years, Gertrude Stein's memory of her Midwest American life was fresh, and I think both painful and happy in her: "The old people in a new world, the new people made out of the old, that is the story that I mean to tell, for that is what really is and what I really know." This is a deeply American book, and without "movies" or automobiles or radio or prohibition or any of the mechanical properties for making local color, it is a very up-to-date book. We feel in it the vitality and hope of the first generation, the hearty materialism of the second, the vagueness of the third. It is all realized and projected in these hundreds of portraits, the death-like monotony in action, the blind diffusion of effort, "the spare American emotion," "the feeling of rich American living"—rich meaning money, of course—the billion times repeated effort of being born and breathing and eating, and sleeping and working and feeling and dying to no particular end that makes American middle-class life. We have almost no other class as yet. "I say vital singularity is as yet an unknown product with us." So she observes the lack of it and concerns herself with the endless repetition of pattern in us only a little changed each time, but changed enough to make an endless mystery of each individual man and woman.

In beginning this book you walk into what seems to be a great spiral, a slow, ever-widening, unmeasured spiral rolling itself horizontally. The people in this world appear to be motionless at every stage of their progress, each one is simultaneously being born, arriving at all ages and dying. You perceive that it is a world without mobility, everything takes place, has taken place, will take place; therefore nothing takes place, all at once. Yet the illusion of movement persists, the spiral unrolls, you follow; a closed spinning circle is even more hopeless than a universe that will not move. Then you discover it is not a circle, not machine-like repetition, the spiral does open and widen, it is repetition only in the sense that one wave follows upon another. The emotion progresses with the effort of a giant parturition. Gertrude Stein describes her function in terms of digestion, of childbirth: all these people, these fragments of digested knowledge are in her, they must come out.

The progress of her family, then, this making of Americans, she has labored to record in a catalogue of human attributes, acts and emotions. Episodes are nothing, narrative is by the way, her interest lies in what she calls the bottom natures of men and women, all man, all women. "It is important to me, very important to me, that I sometimes understand every one .... I am hoping some time to be right about every one, about everything."

In this intensity of preoccupation, there is the microscopic observation of the near-sighted who must get so close to their object they deepen not alone on vision but on touch and smell and the very warmth of bodies to give them the knowledge they seek. This nearness, this immediacy, she communicates also, there is no escaping into the future nor into the past. All time is in the present, these people are "being living," she makes you no gift of comfortable ripened events past and gone. "I am writing everything as I am learning everything," and so we have lists of qualities and defects, portraits of persons in scraps, with bits and pieces added again and again in every round of the spiral: they repeat and repeat themselves to you endlessly as living persons do, and always you feel you know them, and always they present a new bit of themselves.

Gertrude Stein reminds me of Jacob Boehme in the way she sees essentials in human beings. He knew them as salt, as mercury; as moist, as dry, as burning; as bitter, sweet or sour. She perceives them as attacking, as resisting, as dependent independent, as having a core of wood, of mud, as murky engulfing; Boehme's chemical formulas are too abstract, she knows the substances of man are mixed with clay. Materials interest her, the moral content of man can often be nicely compared to homely workable stuff. Sometimes her examination is almost housewifely, she rolls a fabric under her fingers, tests it. It is thus and so. I find this very good, very interesting. "It will repay good using."

"In writing a word must be for me really an existing thing." Her efforts to get at the roots of existing life, to create fresh life from them, give her words a stark liquid flowingness, like the murmur of the blood. She does not strain words or invent them. Many words have retained their original meaning for her, she uses them simply. Good means good and bad means bad—next to the Jews the Americans are the most moralistic people, and Gertrude Stein is an American Jew, a combination which by no means lessens the like quality in both. Good and bad are attributes to her, strength and weakness are real things that live inside people, she looks for these things, notes them in their likenesses and differences. She loves the difficult virtues, she is tender toward good people, she has faith in them.

An odd thing happens somewhere in the middle of this book. You will come upon it suddenly and it will surprise you. All along you have had a feeling of submergence in the hidden lives of a great many people, and unaccountably you will find yourself rolling up to the surface, on the outer edge of the curve. A disconcerting break into narrative, full of phrases that might have come out of any careless sentimental novel, alternates with scraps of the natural style. It is astounding, you read on out of chagrin. Again without warning you submerge and later Miss Stein explains she was copying an old piece of writing of which she is now ashamed, the words mean nothing: "I commence again with words that have meaning," she says, and we leave this limp, dead spot in the middle of the book.

Gertrude Stein wrote once of Juan Gris that he was, somehow, saved. She is saved, too; she is free of the pride and humility, she confesses to superhuman aspirations simply, she was badly frightened once and has recovered, she is honest in her uncertainties. There are only a few bits of absolute knowledge in the world, people can learn only one or two fundamental facts about each other, the rest is decoration and prejudice. She is very free from decoration and prejudice.

The New York Herald-Tribune Books, January 16, 1927.

"We Ask for Bread."

Conrad Aiken

In an article in the January *Atlantic Monthly*, Mr. B. F. Skinner contributes an analysis of Miss Gertrude Stein's work—or rather, of that part of it which has made her famous, the Gertrude Stein of *Tender Buttons*, *Geography and Plays* and of *The Making of Americans*—which, one suspects, Miss Stein must find somewhat embarrassing. Following down a reference in *The Autobiography of Alice B. Toklas*, Mr. Skinner has unearthed an undergraduate paper in psychology (published in *The Harvard Review*) in which, describing experiments in "spontaneous automatic writing," Miss Stein quotes specimens of such writing: and these specimens are startlingly like the "style" which was to be her great gift to the world a decade or so later. Miss Stein herself, in the *Autobiography*, refers to these as a "method of writing" to be afterwards developed in *Three Lives* and *The Making of Americans*; but she is also at pains to assert that she "never had subconscious reactions, nor was she a successful subject for automatic writing." Mr. Skinner points out the obvious inconsistency. The early treatise proves quite completely that she *had* had subconscious reactions, and *had* been successful in automatic writing: and the resemblance of the later style to the earlier suggests pretty convincingly that in *Tender Buttons* and *The Making of Americans* she was "developing" it only in the sense of—to use her own favorite word—"repeating."

    Mr. Skinner very tactfully concludes that when Miss Stein began, about 1912, to make a principle of what had really been an accident, she had simply forgotten, or chosen to forget, the origins of the thing. Whether we agree with him or not, the discovery is certainly an awkward one. For nearly twenty years we have been sedulously taught, by the highbrow critics, the literary left-wingers and all the masters of the subtler schools, that in Miss Stein's work we were witnessing a bold and intricate and revolutionary and always *consciously* radical experiment in style, of which the results were to be of incalculable importance for English literature. Like the splitting of the atom, or the theory of relativity, Miss Stein's destruction of meaning was inevitably going to change, if not the world, at any rate the word. By a systematic dislocation of "affects," we were to get a revivification of word, rhythm, style and meaning. From the Paris laboratory came breathless rumors of the work in progress. Distinguished authors attended the experiments and came away impressed: the influence began to spread: Mr. Van Vechten praised, Mr. Anderson and Mr. Hemingway imitated, the Sitwells took notes. Mr. Joyce was attentive—even the cautious Mr. Eliot opened the pages of *The Criterion* to this new phenomenon, though he as quickly closed them again. In short, the thing was the very finest sort of literary Inside Tip. Not to believe was simply not to belong.

    In the light of which, Mr. Skinner's article makes of the whole thing a very cruel joke. What becomes of all this precise and detached and scientific experimentation with rhythm and meaning if, after all, it has been nothing on earth but automatic writing? Is it merely one more instance of the emperor's new clothes? Have we been duped, and his Miss Stein herself, perhaps, been duped? It looks very like it—though of course it is not impossible that Miss Stein has been pulling our legs. That she can write well, even brilliantly, when she wants to, she has amply proved. "Melanctha," an early story, is a little masterpiece, but perfectly orthodox. The *Autobiography* is a witty and delightful book, again perfectly orthodox—which makes one speculate slyly as to why, at this late date, in giving us her self-portrait, she should thus abruptly abandon the subtler communicativeness of her mature "style" for a method simpler and—shall we say—more effective. Is it a concession? Is it a confession?

There remains, however, the unpleasant little problem of the more purely "automatic" books, of which *The Making of Americans* is a very good example. M. Bernard Faÿ contributes a magnificently eulogistic preface—he could hardly say more if he were prefacing the collected works of Shakespeare. Scarcely less favorable in her opinion is Miss Stein herself, who, in the *Autobiography*, refers to it as that "monumental work which was the beginning, really the beginning, of modern writing." Reassuring, also, is Miss Stein's graceful acknowledgment of Henry James as her only real forerunner. But despite a considerable charm in the opening pages (which were written when Miss Stein was an undergraduate, and for a course in composition), and a clear enough emergence, here and there, of scene and character (notably two dressmakers), the book can only be described as a fantastic sort of disaster. If there is a maximum in unreadability, *The Making of Americans* falls short of it only by the several hundred pages which, apparently, M. Faÿ has omitted from this abridged edition. In an attempt to restrict herself to the use of only the simplest words (for no matter how complicated a psychological statement), Miss Stein falls into a tireless and inert repetitiveness which becomes as stupefying as it is unintelligible. The famous "subtlety of rhythm" simply is not there: one could better find it in a tom-tom. The phrasing is almost completely unsensory, flat and colorless—or, as Mr. Skinner admirably puts it, cold. The abuse of the present participle, in a direct but perhaps simpleminded assault on "presentness," amounts in the end to linguistic murder.

In short, the book is a complete esthetic miscalculation: it is dull; and although what it seeks to communicate is interesting, the cumbersomeness of the method defeats its own end. The analysis of human types is sometimes exceedingly acute—if one has the patience to worry it out—but as here presented it sounds as if someone had attempted to paraphrase Jung's *Psychological Types* in basic English. The attempt sometimes leads Miss Stein into unintentional comedy. She is presumably making merely a *psychological* statement when she says, "She had very little bottom to her, she had a little sensitive bottom to her enough to give a pleasant sweetness to her."

It remains to say that the book is a miracle of proofreading. How the compositor could keep his eye on the right word, the right phrase, in the gradually mounting whirlwind of repetition, or the proofreader keep accurate count of the interminable series of identical statements, without falling asleep, or, on waking, find his way to the bright particular word again, transcends understanding. Merely to think of it is almost to die of exhaustion.

The New Republic, April 4, 1934.

Reviews of *Composition as Explanation* (1925)

"Hogarth Essays."

Anonymous

Miss Stein is properly concerned with language itself. She gives a history of how she came to write in the curious way of which there are one or two examples at the end of the book. This is the best description she gives of her way of writing:

"In these two books there was elaboration of the complexities of using everything and of a continuous present and of beginning again and again and again."

Unfortunately there is no such thing, surely, as a continuous present. Miss Stein's writing resembles nothing so much as that curious effect which sometimes happens when there is something wrong with a gramophone record, and the same phrase of music is repeated again and again, because the gramophone needle is somehow caught in a rut on the record and cannot progress. If when this happened the progress of time was continually stopped and repeated with the phrase of music then Miss Stein's ways of writing would certainly be justifiable.

"I did [she says] a book called *The Making of Americans*; it is a long book, about a thousand pages. Here again it was all so natural to me and more and more complicatedly a continuous present. A continuous present is a continuous present. I made almost a thousand pages of a continuous present."

How curious not to have noticed that a book a thousand pages long takes many hours to read.

But in many ways her essay is of great interest, though, as an explanation and justification of the writings which follow it, it may be deficient. She admirably describes how a work of art is at first an object of detestation, and then all at once it becomes, almost without an interval of any kind between the two stages, a classic. And how simple and profound is her explanation of why people detest a new kind of art at first. It is, she says, because to understand it would make no difference to their lives; there is really no reason at all why they should like it. "As every one is naturally indolent, why naturally they don't see." This does, indeed, seem sensible and good-tempered after the passionate denunciations of the public by most artists. But it seems a little tendencious, for surely Miss Stein is explaining what has happened to most works of art in order to show what will one day happen to her own. One would surmise that, so far from being the forerunner of a new language which is utterly to destroy all the old *clichés* … Miss Stein has really carried to its logical conclusion, beyond which it is impossible to go further, the tendency of recent writers to destroy the period, and more and more to use words to suggest an idea or a sensation, which need not therefore be stated or described. It is a curious thing that when a writer has carried a development as far as it will go, and has in fact used it up and finished it, then he is hailed as the beginner of a new school.

Times Literary Supplement, November 25, 1926.

"From a Litterateur's Notebook."

Elliot H. Paul

Before discussing "As a Wife Has a Cow A Love Story," which seems to me to approach the ideals of Miss Stein's art most closely, a word should be said regarding *Composition as Explanation*, in which she makes important contributions to the literature of aesthetics which is shockingly meager.

Critics have written libraries full of stuff about specific books of authors or groups or periods or what not, but comparatively little has been said about the fundamentals of the art of writing, still less has been expressed concerning the art of reading. The latter cannot be neglected much longer. Happily the things called and agreed upon as classic have reached a volume which precludes the possibility of their inclusion in a single brain. Consequently, cultured non-creative men need no longer talk and act alike.

Miss Stein has definite ideas as to the usefulness of the classics. They are important because they are beautiful, and for no other reason. As a guide to modern composition, they are utterly without value and the mere holding of the notion that classics might be studied with a view to perfecting technique would preclude a person from ever making a work of art, except by accident. Works of art spring from minds which appear immature sometimes because of an abnormal specialization of articulative functions. But having been created, they transcend whatever puerile ideas their creator may hold concerning them.

So a discussion of artists is nearly always unsatisfactory, dwelling upon particular works of art has a definite limit, and there is left only as a subject for study the things which beautiful creations of all periods have in common.

Hasty people are often misled by a title. Mr. Edmund Wilson, the anonymous clerk on *The Dial* who deigned to notice the book at all, and all other American reviewers decided, erroneously, that *Composition as Explanation* was merely an attempt on Miss Stein's part to explain her own work. Nothing could be farther from the point. She uses her own work and development incidentally, as illustrations, but the book is an exposition of certain fundamentals of aesthetics which needed badly to be stated. What she says would apply to Nathaniel Hawthorne or Li Po, although much more to Li Po than to Nathaniel Hawthorne.

It was left for Miss Laura Riding, American poet residing in England, to discover this and to appreciate it.

In *Composition as Explanation*, Miss Stein sets forth a few simple facts: One age differs from another because people are seeing different things, seeing different things since they are all doing different things. The authentic art of one age differs from that of all other ages because its artists are seeing and describing different things are living in a different composition. Everybody is a part of a modern composition, whether they know it or not is unimportant.

"But," she writes almost wistfully, "those who are creating the modern composition authentically are naturally only of importance when they are dead because by that time the modern composition having become past is classified and the description of it is classical. It is really too bad very much too bad for the creator but also very much too bad for the enjoyer, they all really would enjoy the created so much better just after it has been made than when it is already a classic, but it is perfectly simple that there is no reason why the contemporaries should see because it would not make any difference as they lead their lives in the new composition anyway, and as every one is naturally indolent why naturally they don't see."

It is characteristic of Miss Stein that of the twenty-odd years she has spent in writing, only a few months have been consumed in writing about writing. "No one formulates until what is to be formulated has been made," she says. "Composition is not there, it is going to be there and we are here."

The falsity of the time element in writing has occupied the attention of the best modern writers for some years, and a wide range of experiments have been performed with a view to freeing writing from the curse of chronology. In painting, no such problem exists. No one cares which part of a canvas was painted first. In music, the problem is equally acute and George Antheil, particularly, has attempted to compose in such a way that, although the music must pass the ear, as it were, in a series of points forming a line by means of memory, the effect shall be architectural and a dimension analogous to space shall be involved.

A musical composition, if properly enjoyed, is enjoyed as a whole, reconstructed *in toto* from memory after having been heard. Its beauty lies in the fact that it does not have to be rearranged but merely remembered. Miss Stein realized that a prose composition should also possess this quality and that the time in the composition, not the time consumed by the things suggesting the composition, determines its form.

Writing about a thing which has happened, which is complete and without active time, may be compared to painting. Writing in a continuous present, as Miss Stein does, of things happening and beginning again and again, is more like music, in so far as its formal problems are concerned. So her works have to be performed, and there are few trained or capable performers.

I am not attempting to summarize the contents of *Composition as Explanation*. That is unnecessary because Miss Stein has stated what she had to state. I can only indicate the book as one which is good to be studied and in which may be found many statements of things which students and enjoyers will continue to feel.

Chicago Tribune (Paris Edition), June 19, 1927.

Reviews of *Useful Knowledge* (1928)

"Nonsense."

Edmund Wilson

Gertrude Stein's new volume called *Useful Knowledge* contains one of the most amusing of her nonsense pieces .... To characterize something as nonsense is usually to throw it out of court as literature, and there are always a great many people who are ready to dispose of new and unconventional poets, playwrights and novelists in this way. Yet our ordinary use of the word "nonsense" in English, in connection with matters of literature, is based upon a complete misconception of the nature of literature, and of human expression itself.

"Nonsense" implies "sense"; and "sense" implies "reason," "rational demonstration," "logic." Yet literature depends on suggestion: it is not explicable by what we call "reason," or reducible to what we call "Logic." A work of literature, if it is successful, must superinduce in the reader a whole set of thoughts, emotions and sensations—a state of consciousness, a state of mind. And the methods by which this is accomplished do not, by any means, meet the requirements of what is ordinarily called "sense," as distinguished from "nonsense." A work of literature depends for its effectiveness upon a web of association as complex and, in the last analysis, as mysterious as our mind and body themselves.

That this is true in the case of poetry we are most easily persuaded to admit: admirers of "Ulalume" and "Kubla Khan" would find difficulty in discovering sufficient "sense" in them to account for the effect they produce. But we also have in English—something which does not exist in France, where they think more rigorously about these things—what is known as "nonsense" poetry: we have Lewis Carroll and Edward Lear. Yet the fact is, of course, that "Jabberwocky," "The Jumblies" and "The Owl and the Pussycat" do not differ in kind from "Kubla Khan" and "Ulalume." And to confess this is not in the least to outlaw Coleridge and Poe from serious literature, but to admit Carroll and Lear as the remarkable poets they are.

There is also a kind of prose which is commonly recognized as close to poetry—this is, often, precisely, the prose written by poets. I will take an example from W. B. Yeats: "We make out of the quarrel with others, rhetoric, but of the quarrel with ourselves, poetry. Unlike the rhetoricians, who get a confident voice from remembering the crowd they have won or may win, we sing amid our uncertainty, and smitten even in the presence of the most high beauty by the knowledge of our solitude, our rhythm shudders." Here, "the presence of the most high beauty" and "our rhythm shudders" are not susceptible of being explained by anything which anyone who regarded, as many people have, Yeats's poetry as "nonsense" would be willing to accept as "sense." From the point of view of Yeats himself, there is a difference between this kind of prose and certain other kinds. In *A Vision* he writes as follows of the phase of human personality to which he assigns Bernard Shaw: "Style exists now but as a sign of work well done, a certain energy and precision of movement; in the artistic sense it is no longer possible, for the tension of the will is too great to allow of suggestion."

From Yeats's point of view, then, the prose of Bernard Shaw is devoid of suggestion, and, consequently, even of style. Let us examine a typical passage from *The Intelligent Woman's Guide to Socialism and Capitalism*, certainly Shaw's masterpiece of prose exposition …. If we examine this paragraph a little, we see that it depends as much on suggestion as the passage on rhetoric and poetry which has just been quoted from Yeats. Yeats suggests a state of mind where we are preoccupied with solitude and introspection, whereas Shaw suggests a state of mind where we are preoccupied with our relation to society; but that is the only difference. With Shaw, it is not really in the least anything describable as "facts" as differentiated from "images," "sense" as differentiated from "nonsense," which makes his statement effective: it is the hypnotic influence of such metaphors as "showing that the employer's little finger was thicker than the country gentleman's loins" and "because they had no God but Mammon"; it is the rousing rhythm of the piled-up indictment. The whole passage is loaded with suggestion from beginning to end: the suggestion of calling harsh names, the suggestion of violent antithesis, the suggestion of shifting quickly from a picture of horrible conditions to a picture of attractive ones and then abruptly shifting back to another more horrible still.

Let us, however, take another passage from a work which makes no claim to be literature, and in which the utmost effort has been exerted to get as far away as possible from poetry, and to make sense as plainly, as possible—let us take a passage from the United States Courts-Martial Manual …. It will be seen that the Courts-Martial Manual also has its metaphors: "The Army is an emergent arm of the public service"; and its cumulative rhythms: "When this engagement is breached a high obligation to the nation is disregarded, a solemn oath of allegiance is violated, and the government is defrauded," etc. The author of the Courts-Martial Manual is trying, like

Bernard Shaw, to suggest a state of mind when we shall be conscious of ourselves only in our relation to society. Now let us turn back to Gertrude Stein. She is obviously attempting … to do just the opposite from the author of the Courts-Martial Manual; she is trying to superinduce a state of mind in which the idea of the Nation will seem silly, in which we shall be conscious of ourselves as something which does not lend itself to that conception. And the methods by which she accomplishes her ends are of precisely the same character: she proceeds by a kind of incantation. "The Army is an emergent arm of the public service which the Nation holds ready," etc. can be shown to be a piece of nonsense in just the way that Gertrude Stein can. The Army is not an emergent arm of anything: it is a collection of human beings. The difference between Gertrude Stein and the author of the Courts-Martial Manual is entirely a technical one: it is a difference simply of syntax and of the order in which each evokes his or her respective group of images.

What we have been dealing with here superficially is, of course, the problem of language itself—what our words actually signify, what happens when we communicate with each other. This is a problem which raises a great many other problems: it is a problem for philosophy, and a problem with which even philosophy can proceed only uncertainly and gropingly. The point is that, in our present uncertainty as to what we mean by "nonsense" and "sense," it is foolish to use "nonsense" loosely as a term of ridicule or contempt: the same thing applies to "balderdash" and "gibberish." These terms are invariably invoked against any mode of expression which seems new. But, in reality, there is only one mode of expression, and there has never been any other. The only question in connection with a work of literature is how much we enjoy the state of consciousness to which it gives rise. And in connection with this new book of Gertrude Stein's, I confess that I find most of it very tiresome. But if I had merely said that it was a book of nonsense, and left it at that, I should have created a misleading impression.

The New Republic, February 20, 1929.

"Words and Waste."

Sylva Norman

Miss Stein's latest book "has been put together from every little bit that helps to be American." America, then, is its subject, its inspiration, or excuse. It may be something or all three, but classical English has no convenient term for expressing the relation between Miss Stein's articles and their headings. Frequently the relation is purely a verbal one. We are accustomed to treat words primarily as symbols, but Miss Stein is entangled in the spell of sound. Like a piano tuner she reiterates, repeats, combines and varies, falling into rhymes or assonances or puns, all with an equal naive enchantment at finding that words, manipulated, listed, jumbled, can produce such rhythms and sonorities. "Everywhere is not there, nor is it here nor there. I declare and they declare. And the air. We do not recognize an heir. So there."

At least half this book can be discounted as sheer sound. The normal process of creation is inverted, concepts being generated by words; so that to approach Miss Stein's work expecting to find intelligibility in the classical sense of thought-sequence, is, let us say, unjust. If what Miss Stein is doing with words and thoughts is as good and effective as what we have been doing up till now, then it cannot be condemned on the mere pleas that it is strange or hard to follow, any more than we can condemn the new law of gravitation because it is built of different factors from the old. Now Miss Stein appears to work on certain principles which she has recently tried to explain. As far as one's natural conservatism permits of understanding, one would say the process was something of this sort: Select a subject; "Woodrow Wilson," "Business in Baltimore," "The Difference Between the Inhabitants of France and the Inhabitants of the United States," are some of Miss Stein's. This subject is to lie at the back of the mind, throwing out suggestive rays of sound or sense, some of which may actively strike the brain centers, but no attempt at concentration or selection must be made. The aim is rather to record the particular piece of *living* that occurs in the brain after the subject has been introduced; to record it absolutely whole, no matter what irrelevancies, according to our standards, may intrude (which is why "Woodrow Wilson" contains phrases such as "Can you wish that jelly can be eaten with cream."). Further, it is to be recorded in the exact time it takes to occur, and read in a time that is no shorter; the thought of every second being written down to represent that second (which is why one repeated phrase may occupy a page). This forms, as Miss Stein expresses it, a "continuous present." There is to be no looking back on a state of mind and then describing it. As the awareness is born, the writing is born, and though a sequence may recur continually, it is always new, because a new instant has given it birth each time.

Miss Stein, then, is aiming at stark realism after all? If so, her attempt fails utterly, because her mental picture is an artificial one. Unorganized thought is swift and subtle; she not only weights it by translation into words, but her further thought is, as indicated, governed by the words themselves. Consequently her ponderously slipshod technique conveys no recognizable atmosphere, no effect of beauty; and since it fails in all these aims it is a waste of time and space. System, symbol, and crystallization are essential to both science and literature, if meaning is to be adequately conveyed. For instance, in astronomy, a number so great that it would fill a million volumes with noughts can be written in brief as 10, 230,000,000,000. But Miss Stein writes all her literary noughts laboriously out in an extended longhand. A review composed after her own fashion would fill at least three numbers of *The Nation*, and even so it would be sheer chance if any relevant remark emerged. This is not mental freedom; it is merely a break-up of all organized purpose and discrimination. If Miss Stein's useful knowledge points out anything, it is that the loafing mind, equipped with language, can reach a triumph of chaotic imbecility. And for this information 207 pages are too much.

The Nation and Athenæum, April 13, 1929.

"Useful Knowledge."

Anonymous

A little knowledge is a useful thing, and one can make it go quite a long way if one happens to be Miss Gertrude Stein. One doesn't hesitate for synonyms like the conventionally self-repetitive writer, but, in one's character of prophet, goes chugging on, blackening page after page, producing here and there an almost intelligible sentence, but singularly awkward and ungainly.... Then falling back on one's old trick ... a device which throws the reader's faculties into a dizzy whirl, sets his ears tingling and makes him cry out: "Oh, there must be something in it—such utter and stupendous dullness can only be the result of conscientious labor, must bear the imprint of truth!" For that, no doubt, is the secret of Miss Stein's popularity. Hitherto, we have been accustomed to see charlatanism adopt modes which, though perhaps uncomfortably esoteric, were nonetheless designed to capture our interest, to excite, titillate and shock. Miss Stein knows better. She refuses every concession; she bores us mercilessly and immoderately; and for that reason and no other reaps considerable applause.

We can dislike Miss Stein without necessarily subscribing to those canons of literary criticism which assert that aesthetic expression should not be carried beyond the bounds of immediate intelligibility. We may think, for example, that Mallarmé's later experiments are not as successful as many of his earlier poems and essays; yet we recognize and salute the dominance of the writer's personality and admit his consummate skill in the handling of words. We may not enjoy *Ulysses*; but then *Ulysses,* like *Igitur*, is the work of an artist. These are books difficult, and obscure when we penetrate them, but they are not dull. Miss Stein is dull. She has no word-sense, no skill in employing words and images. We look in vain for the indication of some genuine underlying method; and, instead, we are privileged to watch Miss Stein plugging away like an indefatigable little paddle-steamer caught in an ocean of molasses. Staunchly the paddles revolve, wreathed in the treacly stuff; gamely the funnels puff out indignant cloudlets of acrid wooly smoke. "Whither, O splendid ship...?" Whither is she steering, that intrepid New-Englander at the helm? Towards what apocalyptic future, towards what towards? And, "not to the future but to the fuchsia," answers this dauntless captain through her megaphone.

The New Statesman, April 13, 1929.

Reviews of *Lucy Church Amiably* (1931)

"Books, Books, Books: A Brief Consideration of Some Aspects of Modern American Writing."

R. M. C. [Robert Coates]

I have long felt, and occasionally been bold enough to say, that a good deal of the difficultness of "modern" writing would be cleared up if we could regard it from a historical point of view. Let us then, just briefly, survey the history of the novel. Surveys are always fun—if not for the reader, at least for the writer of the survey.

When it first appeared, toward the end of the Middle Ages in our culture and in the hands of such writers as Malory, Boccaccio, and Bonaventure des Péries, the novel was practically pure plot. Its only purpose was to tell a story, and it was written in prose because its incidents were considered too trivial to merit poetic treatment. It was not until late in the 1700s that the writers of prose fiction allowed a philosophical content to creep into, and finally entirely to permeate, their simple narratives.

This second stage, it seems to me, was essentially poetic in character. The prose writer, like the poet—if we except Rudyard Kipling and E. A. Guest—was no longer primarily concerned with his story, but rather with the effect of his story on the mood of the reader.

The characterization of all this as poetic is the fulcrum of my argument, and yet I have not space to elaborate it here; you either accept the close relation of philosophy to poetry and agree with me, or deny it and disagree. It is evident, anyway, that from being solely a chronicler of dramatic incidents, the writer of prose fiction had come more and more to philosophize, or poetize, on those incidents. The plot had become less and less important; the impact of the author's imagination on its episodes more and more important. Granting this, the third stage in the novel's development, the stage through which it is passing today—and whose manifestations in the works of certain writers cause in the minds of many readers such dismay—seems to follow almost inevitably.

For the single uniting characteristic of these writers—Joyce, Gertrude Stein, Virginia Woolf, etc.—is that they have really lost interest in the plot entirely, or at least that they no longer depend on it explicitly as justification for their philosophizing or their poetizing. The plot is there, of course, implicitly (just as there is a plot discernible behind the writings of even so abstract a poet as John Donne), but these authors tend deliberately to nullify its mechanical importance, either by ironic overemphasis or, more usually, by ignoring it almost entirely. They have thus made one more move to complete the course of prose fiction in its great sweep away from, then parallel to, and now finally back toward the path of philosophic poetry—and so have reached the point where their prose, to be understood at all, must be judged by the same traditional standards as poetry.

I am not trying now to justify obscurantism, whenever it occurs, but I am convinced that a good deal of the seeming obscurity of these "modern" writers actually derives from the reader's confusion at not finding in their works something they hadn't intended to put there in the first place; that is, a hard-driving, hair-raising, double-barreled, swift-moving plot, fully equipped with suspense, heart interest, comic relief, and all the rest of it. There are plenty of books, and excellent ones too, which provide just that. On the other hand, who complains, after reading such a poem as, say, "Kubla Khan," at not being told with journalistic exactitude the who, when, what, where, how, and why of all that went on in Xanadu? All the reader knows is that there were demon lovers and underground rivers, domes, prophecies of war, and an Abyssinian maiden who played on the dulcimer and somehow was the instigator of the whole business. He knows that he has had an intensely dramatic poetic experience and, without inquiring further into details, accepts that as enough.

Kenneth Burke is the latest to join those writers who, somewhat like the manufacturers of skinless frankfurters, hope that by removing the tight little tegument of plot they'll make it easier for you to get at the meat itself. In the preface to his new book, *Toward a Better Life*, published by Harcourt, Brace, he develops a rather neater and on the whole more apt analogy than mine by comparing his chapters to sonnets in a sequence, which, while describing the separate emotional crises in the drama, tell little of its merely material processes. If one reads it in this fashion—that is, poetically —one will perhaps see the book in its best light.

The plot, however, is easily discernible. Its central character is John Neal; the book, in fact, is one long outcry on his part against his fate. The forces of his nature are all centripetal; his struggles all go on within himself. The motives of others he sees as his own and so cannot combat them, but chiefly he inveighs against the fact that, from the very nature of the struggle, the ignoble must always overcome the noble, the virtuous be conquered by the base. He sees the process at work in his own nature, how in his relations with the two women who enter his life, and in his dealings with others, his worthiest impulses emerge in distorted and frightful actions. Like a medieval zealot (and indeed his struggle seems to me to have a somewhat religious aspect), he would exorcize his devil. Instead, the devil drives him mad. The book ends with his voice coming distantly to us as if from a sort of nowhere of insanity, in random sentences, scraps of phrases, letters to his "dear dead mistress."

I may not venture to impose my own standards on Mr. Burke; it may be that he had no intention of adopting so completely the poetic principle as I have supposed. If he did so, I think he might have profitably gone a little further in that direction. You may be asking: "Why don't these people, instead of writing prose to be judged poetically, write poetry in the first place?" I think the reason is that they consider prose to be by far the richer instrument for their purpose; in any case, we ought to be grateful to them for doing away with lines written purely for the sake of the jingle, and for sparing us the eternal tyranny of rhyme.

Though they cling to prose, however, they must employ it as the poet would, choosing their words for their evocative value, seeking to produce the same sense of sparingness, of compact utterance, that poetry gives. In this respect, though but rarely, Mr. Burke fails. Particularly in his early chapters, he falls at times into sheer rhetoric, which, however much fun it may be to write, is after all only the doggerel of prose.

Of the book as a whole, however, one can have little to say but praise. It is difficult to read, surely, and one to be avoided if you are a stickler for the traditional paths of literature. But if you can risk a journey into new fields, I think you will find it stimulating and uplifting.

I need hardly remark that Gertrude Stein's latest book, *Lucy Church Amiably*, is also difficult, from the conventional standpoint; any work of hers I judge in that respect almost before it is written. She has attained the curious position of being more talked about by more people who have never read a line of hers than any other author, and if all the witlings who have mauled her name about were some day to decide to buy one of her books and see what it was actually like, her sales would put her on the bestseller lists immediately.

May I say once more, however, that I think a good part of the confusion is due to the reader's expecting to find what was, by the author's design, deliberately left out: a connected narrative? Anyone who read Miss Stein's earlier *Three Lives* must agree that she is quite able to construct a workmanlike plot and sustain its interest to its conclusion. If she now abandons all that, it must be because she has become preoccupied with other aspects of her work.

Certainly, I think no one can tell with exactitude (at least I cannot) the plot of her new book. Further, I think Miss Stein does not greatly care. The name of the book's protagonist derives from a parish church in a country town called Lucey, in France, and the story is a kind of playful parable of this sylvan creature's loves. One may read it for the intricate delicate embroidery of the style. One may read it for the peculiar evasive beauty of some of its passages, or for one's interest in the author's way of probing the oddities of words. But one should never read it—or for that matter the writings of any other of the "moderns"—for its plot.

Her book is published by Plain Edition, 27 rue de Fleurus, Paris.

The New Yorker, February 20, 1932.

"The Plain Edition of Gertrude Stein: Lucy Church Amiably, Before the Flowers of Friendship Faded Friendship Faded, How to Write, and Operas and Plays. "

Lindley Williams Hubbell

These four books are the first of the Plain Edition which is to publish "all the work not yet printed of Gertrude Stein." Until this year the public has steadfastly refused to read Miss Stein, preferring to deride her at a safe distance; but during recent months the tide has turned with a vengeance, and it is apparent that the reading public, having thoroughly digested the works of her followers and imitators, are turning their attention, at long last, to the far more impressive original. And so to review these four books of hers, which a year ago would have been a defensive and a forensic task, is now, quite simply, a pleasure.

Lucy Church Amiably is a novel without narrative. Those who are distressed by this will do well to consider the description which the author has placed upon the title page. It is, she says, "A novel of romantic beauty and nature and *which looks like an engraving.*" Now of a painter we ask only that he paint. Some apples on a plate are enough, if he knows his business. We do not ask for implications or connotations; and we turn with relief from the picture of a comely youth receiving his diploma, painted over the auditorium of the City College of New York, to an apple of Cézanne; not because the animal kingdom is less important or interesting than the vegetable kingdom, but simply because we are interested in good painting. But of a writer we do not ask only that he write. There is thus a curious duality in the art of writing, due to the accident that speech, rather than line or color, is our medium of communication. Because we use language to write to our mothers, to make engagements over the telephone, and to say "Good morning" to the janitor, we are hurt and resentful if a novel does not tell us something, does not describe something, does not say "Good morning to us." "Oh, dear, yes," says E. M. Forster in his book on the novel, "Oh, dear, yes, the novel must tell a story." But such elegiac acceptance is not for Miss Stein. She insists upon being a writer and nothing else, and those who care greatly for writing will sooner or later come to her books and read them for pleasure.

The heroine of this novel is both the church at Lucey, and a woman, Lucy Church. This ambiguous creature changes (somewhat in the manner of *Orlando*) so impertinently back and forth that her identity is never quite captured; and the other characters are as vague and androgynous as their names; John Mary, for example, and Simon Theresa. "Oh, dear, no," as Mr. Forster would say, "this novel does not tell a story." But having read it, the sensitive reader will not soon forget the nebulous reprobate who "had three illegitimate children and he had been frequently married as well." Nor will he forget that "there is a church in Lucy and it has a steeple," and for a long time he will be hearing the soft vibration of the church bells over the Rhone, where Lucy Church stood, and where " she bent her head in the direction of the falling water."

Although Miss Stein has generally devoted herself to prose, *Before the Flowers of Friendship Faded Friendship Faded* is a poem, thirty-three pages in length. The poet, unlike the prose writer, has frequently been allowed to dispense with "meaning": "Kubla Khan" is, of course, the routine example. But Miss Stein's poetry is not meaningless as so much of —for example—Swinburne's is, where the meaning is obscured under an avalanche of words; it is meaningless only because the words are themselves their own meaning. The bare branches of a tree, between us and the sky, "mean" winter more movingly than the notations in an almanac.

In *How to Write* we find Miss Stein up to her old trick of elucidating herself by example, rather than by precept. In this collection of essays she summons, as it were for review and parade, her literary resources. "Here," she might say, "are my crack troops, the participles. See how smartly their uniforms shine, how quickly they step. And here are my auxiliary forces, the prepositions. Did you ever see such discipline? And here is my first aid corps. Watch them resuscitate these wounded sentences, straighten the mangled limbs, and pump breath into the exhausted lungs," as she sits, pleased and proud, in the reviewing stand. This is no doubt a civilized diversion; but I am sure that there are more civilized men and women than are at present enjoying Miss Stein.

I have not meant to convey the idea that Miss Stein has nothing to say to us. She has a great deal to say, and she frequently says it with charm and simplicity. She can laugh at herself and at her readers. She can say, "I think the reason I am important is that I know everything," and exclaim, with mock despair, "At last I am writing a popular novel. Popular with whom?" But what she has chiefly to give us is a Bergsonian sense of the integrity and intrinsic value of things in themselves. Things, to use a favorite word of hers, are "nice"; they are tender buttons, fastening us to a pleasant and a homely world. Sometimes, she confesses, "it takes courage to buy the kind of clock or handkerchiefs you are loving when everyone thinks it is a silly thing. It is a very difficult thing to have the courage for something no one is thinking is a serious thing." But Miss Stein always has the courage. "Metaphysics," said Bergson, "is the science which claims to dispense with symbols," and Gertrude Stein is as far from a symbolist as it is possible for a writer to be.

It was Carl Van Vechten who said, some ten years ago, that when people get through laughing at Miss Stein they can still laugh with her. This is charmingly illustrated in *Operas and Plays*, which is perhaps her funniest book. In these little closet-dramas (some of which have been set to music by Virgil Thomson) people, places, and things take part in some of the most delightfully inconsequential dialogue that has been recorded since Theocritus wrote his Fifteenth Idyl. This book gives us Miss Stein in her gutsiest mood; and, quite aside from the austerities of literary taste, I am sure that no one who enjoys the drawings in *The New Yorker* could fail to be amused by it.

After many years of neglect and contumely Miss Stein bids fair to become not only widely-read but smart. Too few people have read her in the past; now it is possible that for a while too many people may read her. But that is really not important. For whether her work is read or not, it remains what it is: the mountain from which two generations have quarried for their lesser structures.

Contempo, October 25, 1933.

Reviews of *The Autobiography of Alice B. Toklas* (1933)

"A Rose is a Rose."

Bernard Faÿ

When she was a little girl in Oakland, Miss Stein spent a great deal of her time in the public library. She read Shakespeare and she read Lincoln; she read the British Encyclopedia, and she read *Les Miserables* of Victor Hugo; and it was such a pleasure for her that it became a worry after a time. What would she do when she had read all the books? The idea made her very sad and distressed. Later when she went to Radcliffe and when she went to Johns Hopkins, and when she saw all the big libraries in the East, she felt less afraid. And now she is quite happy. Though she has very good health and very good eyes and though she reads a great deal every day she feels that there will always be a great number of books she can read. She will never have to stop reading. She will never have to stop living as long as she lives.

For Miss Stein, her books and all the books are her friends and companions, and life. Other writers like well enough to write, but they don't care to read, and they are overwhelmed by the number of books published. I remember a man, a very sensitive and very gifted writer, who couldn't enter a library without fainting. He said, "How shall I ever be able to write any more when I see all these dead books of dead people?" Most authors are jealous of the books which are not their own books, because they are mostly authors. But Miss Stein likes all books because writing for her is not an acquired trade but a way of living, and life. Books of all kinds she collects around her, good books and bad books, silly books and clever books, long books and short books, books of her friends and books of her enemies. She likes the feeling of life that comes out of this great mass of literature; she enjoys this huge stream of words flowing through the ages.

When I met her in the small, queer, and cosmopolitan, literary Paris where she has her home, I was surprised to find a healthy woman of genius where most people had told me I should find an extraordinarily clever and abnormal magician. Around her I could see a great many writers young and old, who were cultivating their literary talents just as Ripley's freaks cultivate their oddities, just as in a Barnum and Bailey circus the bearded woman is careful to have her hair grow. For a great many writers of our time literature is a useful disease that keeps them alive at the same time that it keeps them sick. It obliges them to lead a rather unhealthy life, but it provides them with bread and a certain amount of fame. They feel that they are abnormal and live an abnormal existence in a world where scientific truth rules over the minds and where social duties govern the bodies and masses. They do not enjoy their abnormality any more than a fat goose enjoys carrying inside her the valuable diseased liver which will later make her glory and sell very well as *paté de foie gras.*

These men are amusing; they often do original work; they sometimes write good books; and they happen now and then to make a great piece of writing—but they are responsible for most of the unpleasant atmosphere and bad reputation that surrounds contemporary literature. I have enjoyed meeting them and seeing them and talking with them and looking at them as I look at a moving picture screen, but then it was a relief to leave them and go and breathe the fresh air and walk in the street where people allow themselves to walk and behave as they please.

And there in the street I met again Miss Stein; she had fun in looking at the literary freaks, but she wasn't one of them, and she enjoyed the fresh air of the outside and the gay noise of the street. She wasn't afraid that it might hurt her reputation, her talent, or her style. Her writings are not tricks, but life, and I have been sure of it since I met her and since I have read her books, and everybody will see it in reading the *Autobiography of Alice B. Toklas*. There has never been a more entertaining and more easy walk through life than this book.

In the *Autobiography of Alice B. Toklas*, Miss Alice Toklas, the faithful friend of Gertrude Stein, describes the life, opinions, and conversations of Miss Stein, with the help of Miss Stein's pen. She knows Miss Stein very well, and the picture is very true. Of course it is also a picture of Paris, pre-war Paris and artistic Paris, cosmopolitan Paris and Paris of Montmartre, the Americans of Paris and the Parisians of the United States, the streets of Paris and the studios of Paris. It is a picture of the birth and growth of that new art which has shocked so many people and which has become such an essential feature of our modern life. It is a very rich picture of a very rich world, and it is a big panorama where hundreds of people come and go, but of course the center of the picture and the best part of it is Miss Stein.

"Miss Stein," "Gertrude," "Mademoiselle Stein," "la Dame du Fond de la Cour," as she is known by the public, the artists, her concièrge, and the delivery boys, should rather be known by the motto which she put forth a long time on top of her paper: "A rose is a rose." It is a very good motto and one that struck me at once, because though I have seen, and met, in my life a great many roses, I knew very well that most of these roses of my experiences had not been roses. It seems that most of the time a rose tries to be something else than a rose—and unfortunately succeeds only too well. The ambition of roses nowadays is to turn orchids or carnations or peonies or anything, but very few roses indeed admit that they are roses and stick to that.

One day in Paris there were some young writers, French and American, in Miss Stein's studio, rue de Fleurus, talking and discussing; and they were talking, with indignant undertones and innuendoes, of a fellow who had just achieved a great literary success through rather doubtful methods. Miss Stein intervened in the conversation and, to their great surprise, she was not indignant at all. They insisted on knowing her mind: "Why," she said, "don't you know that all writers, good or bad, at a time try to sell themselves and sell their souls. They do, but all of them do not succeed. It is not given to everybody to be cheap." Some roses are real roses.

A good many people are able to live interesting lives, and it is not very exceptional to have a useful life. Others have a rich life or an exciting life or an intelligent life. Very few people lead their own lives—their true lives.

How could they? So few people are really interested in what they do; so few people love what they love. The insurance system seems to be the supreme rule of modern time. Whenever you do a thing, you act as if it were a mistake or as if it were going to be a failure. You insure yourself. You never gamble squarely on your choices. You try to be useful because then other people will tell you that you are useful. You try to be intelligent because other people will testify to your intelligence, or you lead an exciting life because that will make you forget everything else. But few people trust themselves enough to choose the life they like, live it, and avoid being distracted from it by precautions or excitements. Miss Stein has done it.

When she was a girl she liked books; when she grew up she liked books and literature; and later she loved books and writing. And she very aptly put aside everything else, filled her house with books, works of art and friends, and didn't bother about other things. This sincerity is a great courage, and as a matter of fact, Miss Stein is one of the most courageous human beings I know. I can prove it. There are many women who like blown glass objects, but they generally put them carefully aside and under showcases, and whenever one of their friends goes near the showcases they push him aside. Miss Stein loves blown glass figures, and she has them all over the place, and she never puts them in a showcase, and as she has also two dogs, a big, clumsy, white dog and a sweet, bold, small, black dog, and endless friends including Poles, Czechs, and Hungarians, very few of her glass things are ever unbroken or complete. But she carries on. She has never given up her glass figures for her friends; she has never given up her friends for her glass figures.

She has never apologized for being a writer, first and finally.

She is an exception. Most of our writers are social apostles, religious prophets, political propagandists, or ice cream salesmen. What we call modern art and modernistic literature is very often merely politics. I would not like to be thought to criticize Mr. Mencken, who is a powerful pamphleteer, nor Mr. Dreiser, who is a noble soul, nor Mr. Joyce, who is an immensely clever Irishman, nor M. Valéry, one of the finest *academicians* France ever had, nor M. Gide, who has written such good things about the Bible and about animals. But isn't it clear after all that Mr. Dreiser feels that the world needs his novels to know the final truth about society, that Mr. Mencken is obliged to write because he thinks America wouldn't be quite American without his teachings? As for Mr. Joyce, his metaphysic of language makes of him an excellent pedagogue, but it is seldom that such a good pedagogue can also be a writer of equal distinction. M. Valéry claims that for him writing has become impossible, and M. Gide has avowedly become the high priest of the cult to which he devoutly gives his zeal and literary talent. All of them write as you and I take a bus.

For many people contemporary literature is synonymous with political radicalism, communism, and several other "isms." And it is true that many writers who had begun by being interested in literature and literary discoveries have turned into political men, or even politicians. But if they did so, it is not because their literary achievements led them there, but because they had reached as far as they could reach in the literary field and were compelled to find something else or to acknowledge their failure. Newness in literature is not putting new wine—or supposedly new wine—in old jars but discovering new jars which will fit the wine of the year. The gospels say it somewhere, but the writers generally overlook it. After all it is so much more easy to be preaching than to write. And it is so much a safer thing to have a political following than to try to be understood and liked for what one really is. It is the great temptation of all writers after forty; they know very well that the great masses of human beings are seldom interested in ideas in literature but are interested in religion, politics, vices, and advertisements; consequently all of them try to "stabilize" their value by an alliance of some kind with a political party, a religious organization, or some branch of big business; and the so-called radicals are often those who, lacking the courage of acknowledging publicly this failure, try to cover it up by preaching theories which sound new. The worst is that quite often they are sincere. It is not even given to all great writers—to be intelligent. Victor Hugo was very stupid.

When you enter the drawing room where Miss Toklas, sitting on her little armchair, is filling out with needlework a sketch that Picasso has drawn for her, and where Miss Stein, seated between busts of George Washington and his wife made of ivory soap and the latest paintings of Sir Francis Rose, is preparing a new edition of *Three Lives*, you feel that modernity there is not a trick, but a way of living and a real life. It is not a craze; it is a pleasure, and for years it has been so; it is familiar and an everyday joy.

Miss Stein was always fond of books, but she came to writing as a choice, and, after trying sciences, she chose writing because she felt that it was the best approach to modern life and the most alive part of her life. She had first studied philosophy at Harvard under William James and obstetrics at Johns Hopkins and she had been very good at both, though in the long run she had found obstetrics a little monotonous and not as enlightening as she expected and as William James had made her think it might be. That is why she turned to Europe. She liked it very much; she became exceedingly fond of it because of what it was, because of what she made of it, and because of what it helped her to make.

Even at its best, what science enables us to do is things, while art and literature, even if they are rotten, create human types, and human minds. And man, though he may like to play with things, can never be completely taken by things, they are stiff and uniform, they lack life and after all nothing can interest man quite as much as himself. A primarily scientific civilization would be an essentially mechanistic one, and a very dull one. Science will only be interesting in the long run if it finally helps us to create, by a very roundabout way, a modern and new humanity. Up to now it has only created machines and masses, things and animals. The two dullest things in modern life are the tour of a factory and an aviation meet.

When Gertrude Stein discovered in Paris in 1903 that art was in process of creating a new human mind; and as she was herself longing to do it, she became the godmother of modern art.

For a writer is the most amusing game. Of course it is merely a game, but it is a game that does not spoil literature, as does politics or scientific activities or preaching. Preaching and politics oblige one's mind to take social problems profoundly seriously; they destroy the freedom of the mind, the ability to be interested in the universal and the individual. Science obliges the mind to get used to a rationalistic and systematic method that is no good for the artist. Science trains you to count and avoid understanding; it gives you very good means to measure things, but it insists that you should feel and react as little as possible, while art and literature require a rich and deep ability to react, feel, dream, and act freely.

In the long run there are only two games that do not spoil the writer's mind: love and art. But art is more permanent. I should not like to be quoted as speaking against love, whose great social qualities I acknowledge, and whose valuable contribution to literature I fully realize, but love in general is too much bound with exaggeration and childishness. It induces bad habits in writers and artists; even a very gifted and genial race like the Italians have finally fallen victims to overindulgence in love; and I sometimes feel afraid that the brilliant literary youth of the United States from whom I expect so much may find itself misled by this common mistake, by believing that only love affairs constitute real topics for literature.

Anyhow Miss Stein became interested in art; and her studio in Paris became the center of the group of modern painters who are known under the name of "Cubists." She bought their pictures when other people were still making fun of them, and she bought them for 200 francs while these same people ten years later bought them for 200,000 francs. She helped them when they had not yet received the legion of honor. She gave them good dinners to eat when they were still hungry, while the fashionable people later gave them good dinners when they already had fame and dyspepsia. She took them seriously at a time when everybody was making fun of them; and she never ceased laughing with them and eventually laughing at them whenever there was a good opportunity, because she knew modern art, and she was too fond of it to be scared or bluffed by it.

Most people criticize "modern art"; some love "modern art"; very few understand, even fewer enjoy it. And they praise or blame it as a whole, because they do not understand it; and of all the reasons they have not to understand it, the outstanding one is that they take it much too seriously, they damn it or extol it in a most indiscriminate manner. In fact a bad modern painter is more irritating than a bad old master, because what he does is more directly and personally offensive to us. But for the same reason a good modern painter brings into our life things that an old master would never bring. Only in the mess of everyday life, of everyday discussion of everyday worry it is difficult to distinguish the good modern painter from the bad one. It is more easy to praise or reject all of them. Of course Miss Stein could never do that, she was not born a preacher, and she has the gayest, most spontaneous, most enlightened laugh I have ever heard. It has helped her a lot. (I do not think that any American writer has been able to laugh that way since Franklin and Mark Twain, and there is not a single writer on the whole continent of Europe who can laugh like her. I do not find any other laugh like that in the whole of European literature: Voltaire's laugh was shrill, and he looked at you while he was laughing; Rabelais's laugh was boisterous and noisy and he was apt to sneeze and spit while he was laughing. Goethe's laugh came more from the throat, Dante did not laugh, and we have reason to believe that Plato had false teeth).

Miss Stein is a great relief in a world where everybody is pompous, and particularly in literary circles. It is clear, some are pompous because they are official and then they have to be pompous, others are pompous because they are not official; they are "radical," or "apostles" of some kind, and as such they feel that they have "a mission"—hence they are pompous. I know many of them, and so do you. But after all they are colleagues, let us pass over that. It happens also now and then that modern art is pompous, and that is ghastly. The value of modern art, indeed, rests in the fact that it is a new escape from a new slavery, the slavery of the crowd, of standardization, of monotony, of the overcrowded earth, of the over-organized crowd, of the over-conscious multitude. We are so many nowadays, and we live so near each other that we never have a chance to live our own life alone except through the help of religion or art. But art itself very quickly ceases to be a personal stimulation and becomes a social element if it is not constantly renewed. It has to be recreated daily to have daily a meaning for the daily soul of men.

Forms wear off, lines wear off, there is nothing that life does not spoil and wear off. The greatest things may resist death, they do not resist life indefinitely. Copies, comments, industry, the daily use of a sentence or of an image fatally debase it, and nothing, not even the Venus of Milo, the Parthenon of Athens, is immune from this dreadful scourge. Only modern art by creating constantly new forms can save art and give a new life to old art. Modern art is not a blasphemy, it is a relay; and the "social workers" who see in it progress or the achievement of a final ideal are about as enlightened as the nice old lady who sees in it all Bolshevik propaganda. Greek art was killed by the bad imitations that Romans made of it, Roman art was killed not by the barbarians (the poor fellows admired it too much and too naively), but by the silly and endless imitations made of it all over the world; and in modern times if amongst all European arts French art has been one of the more permanent it is because it was also the one where the changes of formulas have been the most frequent and the most radical.

Of course a very large part of modern art is horrible and flat and we have got to laugh it off, as Miss Stein does, but for the rest we have to realize that it is one of the few direct remedies for most of the diseases that afflict modern humanity, such as depression, democracy, telephone, equality, unemployment, and general education. But we shall not help it by indiscriminate praise or apostolic propaganda; the only way to give it its chance is by enjoying it.

Let us not be scared or bluffed by it. It is a very silly idea to believe that it destroys all the past; on the contrast it may be said that every time Picasso paints a really great modern picture, it revives one or many old pictures which would have slept in a museum, and which receive from this new life thrown on the field of painting, a renewed reality, an accrued meaning.

Nothing proves it better than the book of Miss Stein itself. During many years she wrote books of great daring and value that seemed mysterious to a large part of the public; people spoke of her as of a witch. And generally one had the idea that she was the prisoner of this queer technique, that it had destroyed in her all other possibilities. The *Autobiography* proves, on the contrary, that she was never abler to write a more fresh, pure, and acute English than she is now. It seems as if all her work, all her experiments and trials had stirred up in her a more precise appreciation of all the qualities of all the possibilities of the English language .

Gertrude Stein has lived all the adventures of modern art as adventures, and she has built a very great work on them, probably a unique work, but also she has been keenly alive through her whole life, and the English language has been the most permanent part of her life. Now in this *Autobiography* she offers the odyssey of the most intelligent American woman alive at present.

I could add many many things. But they really do not matter very much; only the book matters and the life in the book; there is so much life in it that it is the fullest and gayest book I have read for many years.

It is full and gay and queer and unexpected all along. Miss Stein says of herself: "She always says she dislikes the abnormal, it is so obvious. She says the normal is so much more simply complicated and interesting." But so few people can be fully normal and boldly normal. So few people can love and laugh, search and choose, look and live.

Miss Stein has done it.

The Saturday Review of Literature, September 2, 1933.

"Gertrude Stein, Experimenter with Words."

Louis Bromfield

Gertrude Stein has an extraordinary power of personality and it is my impression that she has the clearest intelligence I have ever encountered. It is an intelligence which has remained fresh and vigorous since the day of her birth, never having fallen into the weakness and narrowness and limitations of the intellectual. It is an intelligence straightforward and vigorous, constantly refreshed from the springs of curiosity. Like all truly bright persons she finds this real world a very exciting place and never knows the boredom and paralysis of mind which afflicts the ordinary individual of limited resources.

Consequently Miss Stein has that peculiar variety of naiveté which is the gift of the gods. It is an innocence which is quite beyond the knowledge and experience of those who are known as sophisticated. We have had a generation of sophisticated writers, but most of them are rather like the very clever children who make better designs in yarn than the other children of the kindergarten class. This is a kind of cocksure and superficial knowledge which I suspect has never come within the experience of Gertrude Stein. I rather imagine that she was born, like Julian Huxley and Virginia Woolf and one or two other writers of our time, at a stage of development already beyond sophistication, endowed with that great simplicity which is interested in the value of everything and the price of nothing.

She is a fortunate woman, and those who are her friends and may converse with her are fortunate people, for it is an exciting experience, no matter whether one discusses learning, international politics, the latest American murder mystery (in which she always has a great interest) or art. I am inclined to believe that Gertrude Stein knows what art is. I can think of no one else whose judgment I would trust as surely. At the same moment her curiosity is passionately engaged in exploration, her sense of criticism remains aloof. She has very seldom been taken in.

Throughout her life as an experimenter with words and sentences, I suspect that Gertrude Stein the writer has been plagued by being Gertrude Stein the individual, Gertrude Stein the person. She is forever becoming between her own work and her public. If you are a friend or an acquaintance the woman herself fascinates you while you are with her. You scarcely think of her as anything but an extraordinary intelligence softened by an unusual humanity. If you are a stranger reading her work you are immediately aware of the force of the person who has set down the words you are reading. For twenty-five years reviewers and journalists have neglected her work in order to consider the woman herself. I know that all this has troubled Gertrude Stein. As a person she would prefer to melt away into insignificance, leaving only Gertrude Stein the writer. This, I am afraid, will never quite come to pass. Her influence upon American writing, so much greater than is known or conceded, has always been an intensely personal one. It has been achieved as much by Gertrude Stein the person as by Gertrude Stein the writer.

The presence of her peculiar character and intelligence is excitingly strong throughout the pages of *The Autobiography of Alice B. Toklas*. It is so evident that already I have heard plaints by those who have seen the book before publication, that her opinions on art, on life, on friends, are all made flatly with an implied denial of the right of contradiction. This is not true. In conversation, in life, as in her writing, Gertrude Stein has cleared away a great amount of rubbish. She is eminently of the twentieth century and has no time for such phrases as "if I may say so," or "in my opinion," and this is extremely refreshing. It saves a great deal of time. Gertrude Stein expects you to understand all that, and so she has helped a great many American writers to clear away much rubbish which accumulated during the nineteenth century, and which may not have been rubbish at that time, but is no longer valuable or useful to a writer in our times.

Aside from the personality of Gertrude Stein, or the vitality which springs from every sentence of the book, the subject material is itself fascinating. If it were written in the dullest possible fashion, you would still be interested in Picasso and Braque, Max Jacob and Juan Gris and a hundred other personalities which appear in the pages. It is a record of nearly thirty years of life in a fantastically changing Paris and elsewhere —a life passed in the most stimulating and important society. But Gertrude Stein is Gertrude Stein and so it does not remain simply a record. It becomes exciting.

A great part of the excitement of the book comes from the ability of Gertrude Stein to make the cook, the occasional passer-by, the tenant across the court, the policeman, as vivid and as fascinating as any of the personable, gifted and celebrated figures of whom she writes. This is achieved, I think, by an approach to character and people which is touched by a kind of wonder, the result directly of that curiosity and naiveté which is far beyond tin-pot sophistication.

For thirty years or more Gertrude Stein has been laboring with words ... to create a sense of *actuality*; that is to say, a sense of absolute reality as of suspension in time. These things, with many others having to do with writing, have concerned her since she was a child. I had the interesting good fortune to read a novel, unpublished and written in an old copy book, set down when Gertrude Stein was in her early twenties. The struggle with these elements was already present. The faded writing had in it the same fierce intensity of purpose and evidence of the same battle with words and grammar and meanings which has occupied her steadily since then.

During many phases of her career she has been accused of insincerity, and she has been attacked and derided. Her sincerity is impregnable. At times in the depths of her experiments she has been a "writer's writer" and her struggles have puzzled and confused and perhaps amused many readers of the more obscure works, but in this latest book she has emerged triumphantly. She has achieved brilliantly her desire of direct emotional transference and actuality. More than any other book I ever read, I *lived* this book, page by page, sentence by sentence, through twenty-five years. I think that this will be the experience of nearly every reader.

There is, I think, no use in quoting amusing anecdotes or bits of gossip from the book. These are things which any one can put on paper when he comes to write his autobiography, whether he has ever written a word before or not. In the *Autobiography of Alice B. Toklas*, there are plenty of them, amusing, revealing, impressive, and human, but more important than the material itself is the peculiar vividness of the writing which embellishes it. I might give catalogue of all the persons of whom Gertrude Stein writes—Picasso, Picabia, Matisse, Juan Gris, Braque, Jean Cocteau, Mabel Dodge, Mildred Aldrich, Bernard Russell, Ernest Hemingway, Carl Van Vechten, Sherwood Anderson, Sylvia Beach, Madame de Claermont, Tonnerre, Natalie Barney. I might go on for a page or two making a catalogue. She has known a great many people of prominence and importance in our time. Trust me when I say that the material is fascinating and that the writing is even more so.

Even before publication the book has been a great success. It will undoubtedly have a much greater one. Gertrude Stein has always wanted to write for a large public. Being caviar never interested her, and now it appears that her desire is to be achieved. Popular recognition in France has preceded that of the reading public in her own language. It is both interesting and important that with this book the intelligent reading public will be able to discern the source of an influence which hitherto has gone almost unrecognized, an influence which has filtered down through writer and writer until it might be said with a great deal of truth that it has set aside American writing (and by that I mean words and sentences) from all others in this century. Today one can pick up a book and by the writing of a page tell whether it is written by an American or an Englishman. It seems to me that one powerful influence, emanating from 27 rue de Fleurus, is largely responsible.

The Autobiography of Alice B. Toklas is a fascinating book. It is also an historical even in American writing as well as in the history of modern art.

The New York Herald-Tribune Books, September 3, 1933.

"A Note on Gertrude Stein."

William Troy

It must be recognized, first of all, that Miss Stein's new work is the most "comprehensible" and therefore, in a sense, the least characteristic work of hers that has appeared. The reason for this is twofold: it is presumably not her book at all, but the autobiography of her secretary-companion, Miss

Toklas; and its subject matter is of a traditional kind. Although she cannot help falling into her own syntax and idiom most of the time, Miss Stein makes at least as great an effort to be faithful to the style of her narrator as Defoe in writing *Robinson Crusoe*. Such phrases as "awe-inspiringly" and "the house of our dreams" are indented to indicate Miss Toklas's sensibility rather than Miss Stein's own; and because this sensibility is a more familiar one most readers will have less difficulty in following it. The other reason that the book is so easy to read is that it can be enjoyed for its gossip, its fund of wit and anecdotes, its revelation of a "personality." Read in this way, it should provide inexhaustible fodder for the newspaper reviewers and abundant, if somewhat superficial, enjoyment for a large section of the reading public. Indeed, it is all too tempting to plunder some of its rarer bits for the purposes of this review; to repeat what Miss Stein has to say about Matisse, Picasso, Whitehead, Hemingway, among others; to destroy the reader's own pleasure in discovering these things for himself. For among books of literary reminiscences Miss Stein's is one of the richest, wittiest, and most irreverent ever written. In it she makes ridiculous all those who have ridiculed her for the last twenty-five years with the charge that she has had "nothing to say." She shows that she has a great deal to say of the sort that historians, biographers, and literary gossipers are in the habit of saying: Miss Toklas's "autobiography" is, among other things, a critical history of modern French painting and an account of the post-war generation in American letters. But if it were only this it would be an even less characteristic book by Miss Stein than it is; others could have given us these facts, but only Gertrude Stein can give us Gertrude Stein. And the deepest interest of the book lies in the insight it gives us into the genesis of the mind and sensibility reflected in Gertrude Stein's other and more characteristic books.

There have always been only two questions about Gertrude Stein: What, precisely, has she been trying to do these many years? What, if any, is the value of what she has done? The first, which has never been satisfactorily answered, is a question that has to do not only with her method, style, and processes of composition but also with her view or "vision" of experience. The second, which cannot very well be answered before the first, is a question involving all the questions of evaluation involved in discussing any artistic work. Most of the confusion in regard to Miss Stein's work has come from the attempt to answer the second question without adequately recognizing the difficulties of the first. Before disposing of her work with any real comfort it is necessary to know a great deal not only about William

James and Bergson and Whitehead but also about Cézanne and Picasso and
Juan Gris. Her so-called naive and primitive writing, moreover, represents
such a complex synthesis of these influences that the most painstaking
analysis is required to reveal them with any degree of clarity. In the end, it
is much easier to turn a "difficult" writer like Mrs. Virginia Woolf. All that
will be pointed out here is that, in the general character of her mind and in its
central orientation, Gertrude Stein is not nearly so isolated and eccentric a
figure in American letters as is so often believed.

Before Gertrude Stein went to Paris in 1903 she had been a favorite
student of James at Radcliffe, she had published a paper in the *Harvard
Psychological Review*, and she had spent four years at Johns Hopkins, where
her researches had been praised by Halstead and Osler. She did not take her
degree there because, as she says, medicine bored her. In Paris she
immediately met Matisse, Picasso, Braque, and other young painters who
were busily overthrowing the "literary" painting of the previous generation
in favor of an ever more abstract practice of their art. Under their inspiration
she appears to have done her first literary work; *Three Lives* was written,
literally, under the shadow of Cézanne. The effect of this worship of
abstraction on a mind already trained in metaphysical speculation was to
alienate its owner even farther from the concrete life of her own time and
country. In the rue de Fleurus Miss Stein settled down to the creation of a
form of writing which in style attempted to reproduce the movements of
consciousness as described by James and Bergson, in form and diction to
conform to the ideal of austere simplification followed by the new school of
plastic artists. Like them, she hated "literature" and sought "the destruction
of associational emotion in poetry and prose." Like them also, she was
indifferent to the qualitative aspects of subject; she merely "rendered"
people, landscapes, and events. And because her passion for "elemental
abstraction" appealed to a generation that had just been through the concrete
discomforts of a world war, she became a kind of High Priestess. Although
a follower like Hemingway, remaining "nine-tenths bourgeois," never got
away from the "museum smell," her non-associational prose became one of
the greatest single influences on the prose of her time.

In her detachment, her asceticism, and her eclecticism, Miss Stein can only
remind us of another American author who lived in Europe and devoted
himself more and more exclusively to the abstract. The principal difference
between Henry James (whom Miss Stein reads more and more these days)
and Gertrude Stein is that the former still kept within the human realm by
treating moral problems. (Miss Stein has a more absolute aesthetic ideal:

"the *intellectual* passion for exactitude in the description of inner and outer reality.") Moreover, what Miss Stein has in common with James she has in common with Poe, Hawthorne, Melville, and several other important and characteristic American writers: an orientation from experience toward the abstract, an orientation that has been so continuous as to constitute a tradition, if not actually *the* American tradition. Of this tradition it is possible to see in Miss Stein's writing not only a development but the pure culmination. She has pushed abstraction farther than James or even Poe would ever have dared—to the terms of literary communication itself, "Words and Sentences." The final divorce between experience and art, which they threatened, is accomplished. Not only life but the traditional means of communication in life are "simplified" to suit the patterns which she offers in substitute.

The Nation, September 6, 1933.

"Stunning Stein."

William S. Knickerbocker

Neither knew or rather neither had read or was about to read or maybe perchance if compelled to read by say-so of me or you or he or she could read the book itself but Rip after cleaving the roasted broilers mentioned at Greendays Gertrude Toklas Stein B. Toklas. Neither knew yet there were five of us perhaps only four since Charles is only eleven going on twelve or rather there was only one of us since the rest of us were older than eleven going on twelve and Charles therefore was only able to read the *Autobiography of Toklas B. Gertrude* but he neither had read or maybe if compelled perchance maybe could read the book though he was if not under then over *Captains Courageous* by Eric Kelly of Dartmouth. Dr. Knickerbocker alone was competent for genius he is none and no power for humbug having no awe for Brancusi, Epstein, Scott Fitzgerald whatever no genius or hero himself never having brains or viscera to say what he wants to say no not *Nil Admirari* no *nolo episcopari* not even aut Caesar aut Nullus but. Rip possessed *Tender Buttons* in his also *Sweet Singer of Michigan* Library of course Frances was too sensible to perceive the genius of Stein and maybe too engrossed in Galsworthy's *Candelabra* anyway Lilian smelt of Delphinium just cut in her garden of was it nasturtiums? Dr. Knickerbocker himself immolated in the pouring rain on Labor Day sitting at dinner at

Greendays never having read Gertrude Stein and though capable never intended to except excerpts of *Alice* in Atlantic hence the only one competent to comment because he is the only one living who practices what Toklas Stein preaches never to have an idea because literature is Gertrude Stein and Gertrude means something but doesn't say it but leaves critics like William Troy in *The Nation* say "her non-associational prose became one of the greatest single influences on the prose of her time."

Lilian said what she said was very non-Stein; it is easy to write like that meaning only too meaningful and so very un-Steinian unsimian that "anyone can write like Stein" because writing like that doesn't need much understeining. Much more Steining stunning was the old gag. Our age leans to Stein or is it Beer with stein. Are we too much steined stoned stunned? "Non-associational prose." O pish-tosh. Like water which isn't wet. "One of the greatest single influences on the prose of her time." O William of Troy where is your sister Helen? O Cluett Peabody! Alice B. Toklas by Gertrude Stein is not to read it though buy it. Publishers must live. Full of backgammon and spinach. But Charles aged eleven going on twelve said a mouthful when he said with the wisdom of serpents and harmlessness of doves Gertrude is like The Emperor's Clothes.

Sewanee Review, 1933.

Reviews of *Four Saints in Three Acts* (1934)

"Two Brands of Piety."

Kenneth Burke

Two new American operas: *Four Saints in Three Acts*, words by Gertrude Stein and music by Virgil Thomson, recently performed at Hartford, Connecticut, and now at the Forty-fourth Street Theater in New York; and *Merry Mount*, libretto by Richard L. Stokes and music by Howard Hanson, presented at the Metropolitan.

Superficially, the works are antipodes. The Stein-Thomson number had about it much of the alembication, the archness and mild effrontery, that has regularly gone with the Parisian cosmopolitanism of our cultural expatriates. Its seriousness was frequently overlaid with the apologetic smirks of fashion. The Stokes-Hanson work dismissed all such subterfuge: dealing with the rigors of our early Puritan morality, it was as stark and severe as it could be.

Thomson's facile associationism often led him to give a comical emphasis to Miss Stein's cryptic passages, to delve into that bag of self-protective mannerisms which was the possession of Jules Laforgue in poetry and of such musicians as Satie, Milhaud, Casella, and Rieti. Hanson, as the composer of a "Nordic" and a Romantic symphony, could not abide by this indirect approach to his material: he was as sober as Wagner or Moussorgsky, and frequently sounded like them. In his earnestness he even permitted us to hear premonitory Indian war-hoops behind the curtain before disclosing the conflagration of the Puritan village, and I confess that the literalness of this "foreshadowing" seemed to dispel the receptivity rather than awaken it. In merely waiting for the curtain to rise one was more malleable to the dramatist's wishes than after hearing these realistic yips. Frankly tuneful, Thomson treated Stein's fluid words like unrhymed jingles. He even gave us an aria constructed of vocal exercises; and in one place he managed a duet like the antiphonal announcements of a cuckoo clock and a grandfather's clock. Hanson aimed at firm, archaistic melodies based upon ancient church modes.

In setting, the Stein-Thomson performance was superb in its devices for ocular ingratiation. No revue for the glorification of the American girl could discover surer methods of awakening our delight in color and choric maneuvers than did the blended scenery and costumes of Florine Stettheimer and the constantly alert choreography of Frederick Ashton. The Metropolitan presentation relied upon the strictly naturalistic style of stage setting and those flames and smoke which are the mechanic's triumphs. In contrast with the lithe and comely nakedness of the Negro dancers in *Four Saints*, we had in *Merry Mount* the unintentionally comic semi-nudity of the unfortunate Lady Marigold, the innocent victim of Wrestling Bradford's righteously distorted lustfulness.

But for all the superficial differences, there is a common element to be noted in these two works. Thomson has previously written frankly devotional music, as well as some entertaining music for another of Stein's pieces, "Capital Capitals." In *Four Saints* he seems to have combined these two aspects of himself quite well, giving us, beneath the picturesque and the grotesque, the kinds of sound that are authentically ecclesiastical in feeling. The effect was undoubtedly enhanced to a great extent by the cast of Negroes, who are equipped by a long tradition to season their congregational expressions with sportiveness. Thomson has shown that even a burlesque of the "sacred song" can draw effectively from precisely the same wells of response as the simple article might do—and there was a passage in the manner of Bach which flowered unappealingly for the brief moment it lasted.

I should like to discourse easily and familiarly on the plot of Stein's piece, but must admit that I cannot. The words show evidence of a private playfulness which makes them much more difficult to fathom than if they were written under gas. Indeed, with our modern technique of interpretation, words spoken truly at random, in dreams or hallucination, would be much more revealing—but Miss Stein's extremely loquacious reticence shows evidence of a waking deliberation which too often makes her lines elusive rather than allusive. Is there, in a highly attenuated form, something of that ultimate confusion of birth, rebirth, marriage, love, and death which lies at the bottom of Wagnerian preoccupations, secularly in *Tristan* and ecclesiastically in *Parsifal*? One gets a "drift": that there is to be a play about saints; that Saint Therese has two selves; that one of them is quite Rotarian; that there is a dirge-like epithalamium—if epithalamium it was—a dark purple procession marching to rhymes in "ed" ("wed in dead in dead wed led in led wed dead in dead in dead in led in wed in said in," and so so) which seemed, by our lubricious way of thinking, to gravitate about the celestial omission of the word "bed"; and at the end everything seems happily settled.

The Stokes libretto, on the other hand, was unmistakable, at least if one happens to have read it, and not relied upon the muffled articulations that carried across the footlights. Wrestling Bradford is in great need of a woman, and his sleep is sorely troubled. In keeping with the ideology of his times, he attributes his discomfiture to the work of demons, who are thought to be struggling for the possession of America. Another group of settlers, having more joyous notions of the "good life," arrives—and the young minister Bradford falls in love with one of them, Lady Marigold, who asks him to marry her to a member of her own party. Bradford "rationalizes" his turbulent disappointment with the help of the fact that the newer settlers plan to erect so godless and pagan a thing as a Maypole. He instigates an attack against them as allies of evil, and Marigold's fiancé is killed. However, Marigold continues to repulse Bradford, who in a dream sells his soul to the powers of hell, thereby obtaining the lady in the dream-form of Asoreth. Upon awakening, he finds his village fired by Indians, and attributes this misfortune to his oath sworn in Hell. He confesses his unholy alliance, and seizing the swooning Marigold, he leaps with her into the flames, while the Puritans chant the Lord's Prayer in terror. Operatic opportunities: contrast of Puritan and Cavalier songs, the dance about the Maypole, the attack by the Puritans, the satanic revels in hell, Bradford's public confession of his contract with Satan.

As I had read the words of both works before seeing the performances, I had a great surprise in store for me. Stokes's text seemed to me an excellent vehicle for opera, and Stein's seemed almost negligible—yet I believe that the Stein-Thomson work is the more effective of the two theatrically—on a first hearing at least, though the fancier work might very conceivably wear thin more quickly on subsequent hearings. Stokes's text is highly respectable. But Stein's nonsense, as reinforced by Thomson, has established its great musicality. Even as nonsense it sings well: indeed, its very ambiguity may have prodded the composer to express its *quality* as utterance; if what was said was vague, *en revanche* it was said with extreme mobility of emphasis. Many modern composers, alienated by the triteness of texts, have set their scores to purely arbitrary syllables, but I believe that Thomson has profited by choosing instead the stimulus and guidance of living words, which give surer hints as to what tonal sequences—by obeying and emphasizing the natural rise and fall of spoken words—will best recommend themselves to listening.

Neither work ventures into the field of dissonance. Hanson's is largely modal. Thomson's broken fragments of tune, his continual popping forth of brief melodic figures, would probably be found on analysis to have been built about the simplest and most fundamental of chords, like the intervals of a bugle call, or like so many of the spirituals, which seem hardly more than incidental weavings about a structure of do-mi-sol. I can easily imagine him being harnessed by Broadway or Hollywood for the purposes of commerce. The Hanson orchestration was much more highly developed, Thomson being content with the barest sufficiency of instrumental background.

Hanson's work at its best is manly and imposing. At every point it is frank in a way in which the Stein-Thomson product is not. Thomson's at its worst is effete, and content with mere tonal wisecracking. But as a piece of ingratiation—and all art in the end must ingratiate itself—I believe that *Four Saints* prevails. Perhaps it is one kind of light entertainment which all the world will some day care for, when a new day has imposed the privileges and problems of leisure upon all, and the wealthy patrons of this bounteous performance will have been generously admitted into the ranks of the spectacle-loving masses.

The Nation, February 28, 1934.

"A Prepare for Saints."

Joseph Wood Krutch

Three new productions have opened since my last report. For the sake of the record I shall name them later, but as none moved me to enthusiasm and as all seem destined to disappear before this can find its way to type, I prefer to say first a word or two in favor of *Four Saints in Three Acts*, which is scheduled for a return engagement on April 2. In a previous issue Mr. Burke discussed this "opera to be sung" at some length and with a greater coherence than I shall be able to achieve, but in honesty I must report two things: first, that pure prejudice kept me away until near the end of the first engagement; and second, that when—against my will—I actually attended I was charmed and delighted.

Miss Stein's published text is far from encouraging. I shall not go as far as some who have maintained that her words contribute nothing to the pleasure of the production and that its success is due wholly to the music of Virgil Thomson, admirably sung by the all-Negro cast. Nevertheless, much of the credit for the libretto must go to whoever broke up the continuous text into dialogue, assigned it to various characters, and conceived the engagingly appropriate non sequiturs of the action. *Four Saints in Three Acts* is a success because all its elements—the dialogue, the music, the pantomime, and the sparkling cellophane *décor*—go so well with one another while remaining totally irrelevant to life, logic, or common sense. It has been said on good authority that the pleasure of being mad is one which only madmen know, but by being insane in some elusively consistent fashion Miss Stein and her collaborators have opened that pleasure to the general public.

To call the work satire as some have done is, I think, to miss the point. Even to call it funny is to run the risk of being misunderstood, for though it is certainly amusing—irresistibly so, indeed—it is not funny in any raucous or farcical way, and its charm is at least as conspicuous as its humor ever is. In the first place, all the characters—however eccentric they may be—are intensely likable. They have lightness, and grace, and courtesy, and amiability. If the audience cannot understand them, they seem at least to understand one another perfectly and to live in a delightful atmosphere of mutual esteem. When, for example, Saint Theresa paints Easter eggs or declares herself "not interested" in the proposal to kill twenty thousand Chinamen by pushing a button, both the work of art and the declaration of intention are received with an awed respect equaled only by the graciousness with which the saints treat the mere unsanctified laymen. In the second place, the grotesqueries are never of an awkward, harsh, or discordant kind. On the contrary, everything is so gentle, so kindly, and so pretty when looked at or listened to merely as a thing in itself that one tends to succumb to almost completely to the charm and to be a little surprised when one finds one's laughter bubbling out from time to time.

If it is necessary to interpret the work or to assign to it some specific "intention," then I should be inclined to say that *Four Saints in Three Acts* is a half-serious, half-playful experiment in carrying to their illogical conclusions several of the most characteristic tendencies of the more esoteric types of modern literature. One will find something of the learned allusiveness of *Ulysses* and *The Waste Land*, coupled with something of their tendency to associate, through the mere sound of a word or some other superficial connection, things not ordinarily associated. One will find also the tendency toward form without content and toward a kind of intelligibility without meaning characteristic of surrealism and the Dadaists. Yet the effect achieved by Miss Stein and her collaborators is quite different from that usually associated with such *fauves*. Her opera is not tortured, violent, despairing, or even unhappy. It is, on the contrary, graceful and distinctly *pretty* (rather than beautiful) so that her style can perhaps be best described as a kind of modern rococo. One smiles at its delicate, meaningless, but graceful convolutions as one smiles at the gimcrack charm of Spain's most trivial religious art. At times one may even think of an old-fashioned valentine wrought out of paper lace and colored celluloid. But one smiles appreciatively, as one usually smiles at such engagingly innocent prettiness. Doubtless many will regard this comparison as outrageous but I see nothing surprising in the ironic fact that Miss Stein's determination to be more sophisticated than anyone else should have led her back to a kind of childish naïveté. In any event, her opera is to be recommended to all who are ready to relish an evening of untroubled really very simple pleasure.

Returning now to the record, I must report that *The Pure in Heart* is—or rather was—John Howard Lawson's incoherent attempt to write a such-is-life-in-a-great-city sort of play about a chorus girl who kept her heart innocent in spite of the fact that she was afflicted with what I believe are called "round heels"; also that *Another Love* (Vanderbilt Theater) is a tepid, sentimental comedy-drama from the French concerning itself with a misunderstood adolescent who steals a lady away from his philandering father. *The Shattered Lamp* (Maxine Elliott's Theater) belongs in another category. It is a rather solidly written if somewhat melodramatic story of the coming of the Nazis. Nevertheless, I doubt that its virtues are conspicuous enough to overcome the public's reluctance to look at painful things.

The Nation, April 4, 1934.

"The Theatre: Stein on the Table."

George Jean Nathan

For the purposes of a final dissection and a good critical song ringing clear, let us put Gertrude Stein on the table and determine, now that her self-admitted chef d'oeuvre, *Four Saints in Three Acts,* has been delivered to us, just what is or isn't inside her. It is Miss Stein's stout contention that the meaning and sense of words placed together is of no importance; that it is only their sound and rhythm that count. This, in certain specific phases of artistic enterprise, may—for all one's initial impulse to impolite titter—be not entirely so silly as it sounds. Beautiful music often is meaningless (in the same sense of the word) and yet finds its effect and importance in sound and rhythm. Poetry, also, often finds its true reason and being in a complete lack of intelligence and in the vapors of lovely sound and lulling rhythms. Painting, too, need not have "meaning," nor "sense," but may project its power alone by form (which is rhythm) and by color (which is the equivalent of sound). Even drama itself may have little meaning and sense, yet may evoke a curious meaning-within-absence-of-meaning (regards to Dreiser) nonetheless; for example, Strindberg's *Spook Sonata* or—to go to extremes in even absurdity—something like John Howard Lawson's *The International.*

Up to this point, there conceivably may be something in Miss Stein's literary Bolshevism. But now let us see how she combines theory with practice. In demonstration and proof of her conviction that the meaning and sense of words are of infinitely less significance than their sound and rhythm she presents to us, in the chef d'oeuvre mentioned, such verbal matrimony as … "To know to know to love her so. Four saints prepare for saints. It makes it well fish. Four saints makes it well fish" .

Repressing a horse-laugh and hitching up our ear-muffs, let us meditate this arch delicatessen. That Miss Stein is absolutely correct in announcing that it has not either meaning or sense, I hope no one will be so discourteous as to dispute. But if Miss Stein argues that, on the other hand and to its greater virtue, it has rhythm and beautiful sound, I fear that I, for one, shall have to constitute myself a cad and a bounder and inform her that she is fish and it does not make it well fish either. In point of fact, any one with half an ear to rhythm and sound (whether in song, in reading, or in recitation) can tell her that any such arrangement of words—to pick at random—as "beside beside very attentively intentionally and bright" is not only lacking in rhythm and pleasant sound but that, in addition, it is painfully cacophonous. It is perfectly true that words shrewdly strung together may be meaningless and may still sound better than words strung together with some meaning—take Eddie Guest's poetry, for instance—but one fears that Miss Stein has not mastered the trick which she so enthusiastically sponsors and advocates. I am no Gertrude Stein, but I venture constructively to offer her a laboratory specimen of what she is driving at and fails to achieve. The example: "Sell a cellar, door a cellar, sell a cellar cellar-door, door adore, adore a door, selling cellar, door a cellar, cellar cellar-door." There is damned little meaning and less sense in such a sentence, but there is, unless my tonal balance is askew, twice more rhythm and twice more lovely sound in it than in anything, equally idiotic, that Gertrude ever confected.

One more point and we conclude our performance. Granting for the moment Miss Stein her premise that the rhythm and sound of words are more important than their sense and meaning, may we ask how she feels about a possibly perfect combination of the two? Does she, or does she not, believe that beautiful rhythm and beautiful sound combined with sense and meaning may constitute something finer than mere rhythm and sound wedded to meaninglessness and lack of sense? While she is pardonably hesitating to make up her mind, let us ask her to consider such things, for example, as the hauntingly beautiful Marlow speech in Conrad's *Youth*, or Caesar's parting from Cleopatra in the Shaw play, or Dubedat's from his wife in the same writer's *The Doctor's Dilemma*, or Brassbound's from Cicely in the same writer's *Captain Brassbound's Conversion*, or Candida's from the poet Eugene in the same writer's *Candida*, or Galsworthy's "To say goodbye! To her and Youth and Passion! To the only salve for the aching that Spring and Beauty bring—the aching for the wild, the passionate, the new, that never quite dies in a man's heart. Ah, well, sooner or later all men had to say goodbye to that. All men—all men!..." Or a hundred passages from Shakespeare, or a score from George Moore. Or some of the prose of Max Beerbohm, or Cabell's *Jurgen* chapter, "The Dorothy Who Did Not Understand," or Maurya's magnificent wail to the sea in the Synge play, or some such line from Sean O'Casey's *Within the Gates* as "To sing our song with the song that is sung by a thousand stars of the evening!" Or Dunsany's little two hundred word fable *The Assignation* from its beginning "Fame singing in the highways, and trifling as she sang, with sordid adventurers, passed the poet by" to her final whisper "I will meet you in the graveyard at the back of the Workhouse in a hundred years."

Come on, Gertie, let's hear what you have to say.

Vanity Fair, May 1934.

Reviews of *Portraits and Prayers* (1934)

"Books and Things."

Lewis Gannett

Gertrude Stein is a jolly, bright-eyed, wholly natural, likeable, laughing human being; I met her and liked her—and Alice B. Toklas—at Random House's party for her last week. She insisted so amiably, so without pose, so convincingly, that her prose really makes sense to any one who can read with his ears as well as his eyes, that I tried very hard to make sense of her *Portraits and Prayers.* I regret to report complete failure.

Here are strings of words titled "Cézanne," "Matisse," "Picasso," "Bernard Faÿ," "Sitwell Edith Sitwell," "Mabel Dodge at the Villa Curonia," "A Valentine to Sherwood Anderson," "Jo Davidson," "He and They Hemingway," "Carl Van Vechten," etc.; and I almost believe that to Miss Stein and the initiates they have some kind of communicable meaning. To the lay reader they will be as utterly meaningless (or as laughable, according to the lay reader's temperament) as the text of *Four Saints in Three Acts,* which, without the music and stage settings and direction, was a big, fat zero.

Why Miss Stein does it I do not know. I had believed her a poseur. I met her and lost that simple key to character. In the *Atlantic Monthly* last January B. F. Skinner exhumed an article Miss Stein wrote in 1896 for *The Psychological Review* on automatic writing, and deduced that Miss Stein had returned to automatic writing without being quite aware of what she was doing. That explanation also seemed more plausible before meeting Miss Stein than after; for she is extraordinarily aware of herself, her interlocutors, and everything that goes on about her.

Miss Stein talks well and sensibly in perfectly understandable language. She can write vigorous, communicable English, as *The Autobiography of*

Alice B. Toklas proved. She can do more than that: She writes a vigorous, emphatic prose which is her own; one or two of the portraits in *Portraits and Prayers* use the same personal yet communicated rhythms. The eccentricities, for instance, of her prose about Juan Gris have a meaning:

"He (Juan Gris) used to dwell upon the lack of trust and comradeship in Spanish life. Each one is a general or does not fight and if he does not fight each one is a general. No one that is no Spaniard can help any one because no one no Spaniard can help any one. And this being so and it is so Juan Gris was a brother and a comrade to every one being one as no one ever had been one."

But sample this opening passage of the "Portrait of Virgil Thomson": "Yes ally. As ally. Yes ally yes as ally. A very easy failure takes place. Yes ally. As ally. As ally yes a very easy failure takes place. Very good. Very easy failure takes place. Yes very easy failure takes place. When with a sentence of intended they were he was neighbored by a bean." Pooh!

I wish Gertrude Stein would do a little public laughing at herself. She laughs well. But she went off from the Random House tea with Carl Van Vechten, who talks and writes about her weirdest prose of tones of religious awe. Can it really be that she, too, takes it all seriously?

The New York Herald-Tribune, November 7, 1934.

"Cheating at Solitaire."

Henry Seidel Canby

I have never before reviewed a book I have not read. I have always tried to read Gertrude Stein since her earliest publications and I have always failed. I have tried in this book, though not so hard as before, because I anticipated failure. My eye goes on over the smooth rhythms, but my brain ceases to function. I hear but do not comprehend: I apprehend without comprehension; I feel without the registering of thought; I am pleased with sonorous variants on sound while my rational being coincidentally is first irritated, then outraged, and finally stops all traffic like a dizzy policeman in a tangle of cars pushing everywhere and nowhere on football day. Something childish in me likes the play with words; the adult in me protests against the writing back of language to the primitive or pre-human. Which is probably what Miss Stein wishes me to do, so that I can go on in this review with an easy conscience.

There may be psychological reasons for Miss Stein's avoidance of rational communication which I do not understand and with which I am not concerned. She is an intelligent and charming person who can state interesting ideas in a language which is loose but nevertheless expressive, as the excerpts from her lecture on drama published in this *Review* last week will prove. Also there may be some virtue (like Indian herbs) for professional writers, whose words are constantly going stale on them, in an experience with a style in which words become "sounds and sweet airs which give delight and hurt not." Hermit thrushes challenging each other across a dusky glade make such sounds, but they do not use words.

What is clear to me after many years of beginning to read Gertrude Stein, capped by a hearing of the *Four Saints*, and now this book, is that her admirers and critics have been on the wrong track. They have taken her both too seriously, and not seriously enough.

Her ideas have been praised. There are none communicated in any of her creative writings. Her success in imitating personality by suggestive words has been praised. There is no such imitation. The effect is purely subjective, read into the sketch which itself is a very simple (often shrewd) statement, built upon and turned over and twisted in and out, until what would have passed as a good remark in conversation becomes (to those who can keep their minds on it) impressive because it seems so difficult. She has been praised for an invigoration of language. She has not invigorated, she has debilitated it, by striking at its essence, what makes it language, by separating denotation from connotation and letting the latter run. She has used only one legitimate rhetorical device, repetition for emphasis. And this she naturally did not invent. It is the method of primitives, or in those writing of primitives, the method of Anita Loos in *Gentlemen Prefer Blondes*, as Wyndham Lewis has said. She uses it in the primitive's manner, but if her art makes it impressive to the over-rationalized, who had forgot that true things must be said twice, her whimsy makes it ridiculous by saying her say not twice but twenty times.

Her art can be summed up in a single sentence. She has a good ear. The subtle possibilities of the sounds of prose she understands. The subtle rhythms of the sounds of speech she hears and records. It was this that made the *Four Saints*, whose meaning so far as it had any was given it by composer and producer, good singing and good hearing. The sounds of its prose and verse were excellently handled. It made good libretto, better libretto than anything else, because in most opera no one listens to the libretto anyway.

She has a good ear and artfully contrives sounds in a faraway imitation of music, which can do so much better and more richly what she attempts because she is not hampered by a linguistic medium. Miss Stein is hindered by her unfortunate predilection for words. For words are not only restricted to a limited range of sounds, but also they insist on meaning something. Her art is the sophisticated development of the child's "Tiddledy-diddlety-fiddlety-doo," and she would have been much more truly successful if she also had stuck to nonsense. Once she began to use words as a medium for this primitive art of vocal sound and rhythm, she violated one of those canons of both art and commonsense whose breaking is punished by artistic suicide. The writer may live on in a halo of notoriety, like the man with the copper stomach, but as artist he is dead. For words, whatever else they do, and there is a great deal else they do, must make sense. If they do not make sense they are no longer being used as words. Dung is as beautiful a word as the couplet ding-dong, but it cannot be used for sheer beauty of sound as long as it means dung which is not beautiful. Or rather it can be made beautiful only by lifting dung to beauty, which is not what Miss Stein tries to do at all. Mark Twain had the right idea: "Punch, brothers, punch with care, Punch in the presence of the passenjare" is beautiful, but it is also comic, and he presented it as both. So does not Miss Stein. She plays with her words, pretending they are not words, and you would willingly play with her if she would keep on pretending and asked only that you should listen to the ingenious sounds she makes. But you have to be a little childish to pretend that they say something when it is quite evident that they do not. Or to listen to them as sounds merely when it is evident that they continue to mean what mankind has assigned to them. Anyone can win by cheating at solitaire. And that is what Miss Stein is doing. Anyone with a good ear (not a common possession, and Miss Stein's is excellent) can make enchanting successions of sounds if they do not bother with sense. The difficult thing is to make sense, which is precisely what all great stylists have accomplished.

No, this book is not by any definition literature. It is music of a primitive and rather fascinating kind, vitiated by the drag of meaning.... This is the art of the mockingbird, sound that means so little as not to matter.... This is an insult to the civilization that with incredible labor united, however imperfectly, sound and sense. In such a sentence, in order to win her game, whatever it was, she has pretended that her cards are not the clubs and hearts which unmistakably and irrevocably, so long as words are words, they are. She has escaped from sense, and however I admire her admirable ear I will not go with her, having troubles of my own saying all that I wish, but still not prepared to go off the deep end into nonsense in hope that my rhythmic space will have some meaning.

The Saturday Review of Literature, November 17, 1934.

Reviews of *Lectures in America* (1935)

"Gertrude Stein Comma."

Ella Winter

When all the tumult has died there is still a great deal to say about Gertrude Stein. Whether you understand what she is after or not, she is a challenging writer and a challenging figure in the literary world. A shrug of the shoulders and an attempt (usually inadequate) to imitate her still annoyingly do not end the subject.

Since her return to the country early this year Miss Stein has published several books and a careful perusal of them makes somewhat clearer to the reader who is willing to take the trouble to find out, what she is after. Particularly do her *Lectures in America* unravel some puzzles. To be understood they have to be read aloud, as all her work is written to be read aloud. Then, even if you don't get the sense, at least you get the cadences and her singing rhythm is frequently very beautiful. *Four Saints in Three Acts* abounds in these and all who saw the opera sung by Negroes with sets done in cellophane in New York agreed that it was a great experience. With so much written today that is meant to make sense and doesn't, such as reports in the Hearst newspapers, it is a relief to read something that doesn't intend to make sense in the ordinary sense and so sets you free to use some of your unused senses to make sense. Read the pigeon on the grass alas passage and see if it doesn't move you as much, a great deal more, than for instance Tennyson's "of immemorial elms and murmuring of innumerable bees."

Gertrude Stein's repetition is not just repetition. She explains what it is in the "Lecture on Portraits and Repetition" .... A frog hopping and a bird singing vary their insistence, and so do humans telling a story. Listen, consciously listen the next time a person tells you a story—not to what they are telling you but the way they are telling it. "And then I sez to him, I sez, sez I, when he asks me what I thinks of it, I sez to him, I sez ...." Just watch—I mean listen.

These lectures are all shot through with homely little illustrations from Gertrude Stein's life. She went from California when she was about seventeen to live with "a whole group of very lively little aunts" in Baltimore, and there she began to listen consciously to what anybody was saying. And there she began to notice the difference between repetition and insistence and many other things such as the need to listen and talk at the same time. "One may really indeed say that that is the essence of genius, of being most intensely alive, that is being at the same time one who is talking and listening." She keeps everything alive, intensely alive all the time. She is so concretely interested in America because she is interested in its vitality (as are most European visitors, only they aren't always so aware that that is really the thing that grips and fascinates them after their own more dying Europe). She tells you how she began to wonder about certain problems then to find answers to those and then to wonder about others ... she "bothered" while she wondered, but when she got her answers, as she got the answers to what really is the difference between prose and poetry, what did she feel about nouns, and commas, and adverbs, and descriptions of people, and the relation between the inside and the outside reality of people, when she had written a book about the thing she was wondering about that was the time when she felt she had her answer and then she would begin to wonder about something else. And the quality of her wonder and her constantly alive and moving and changing wonder she gets into these pages, so that you go through the adventure with her and are stimulated and excited and confused and then cleared up as you are when you're trying to remember something and can't and then suddenly do remember.

This is what makes Gertrude Stein a perpetually alive and stimulating writer whether you "understand" the meaning of the sentences she writes or whether you do not.

And this is what has attracted the vital American people—especially the young people the length and breadth of America—to her, as she is attracted to the young people, on this her first visit to her homeland in twenty-eight years. Their vitality calls to her and her vitality calls to them and when they get together inevitably something exciting happens and Gertrude Stein tries to express it, to say it, in sentences and phrases and words not that say it but that are it.

And when Gertrude Stein wonders she is courteous enough to her subject to wonder all around it and for a long time in and out of it, in nouns and without names really. She wonders in rhythm and in cadences and she rouses wonder in you and she never answers your wonders because that would end it, that would be death. And she made up her mind very early in life that the thing about life and the only thing about life was life.

At any rate she broke new paths. She challenged the traditional ways of writing and using punctuation and nouns and adjectives and adverbs. She was intensely alive to new combinations of words and phrases and sentences. And she could communicate her excitement to many writers who have digested and used her wonder in their own writing. The newest group of very young writers many of whom want to write about the working-class and proletarian subjects are more consciously interested just now in content than in form, thinks Gertrude Stein; but they unconsciously already use forms she has made familiar. Many of them would not write the way they are writing but for Gertrude Stein. She is wondering about narrative now and so are they. She thinks the old traditional novel form is dead and so do they. She is wondering what will become of the narrative, what form will it take, and she is experimenting with it, and they are experimenting with it. Many of them don't know she was a pathbreaker for them, she doesn't always know it and because she isn't interested in politics she tends not to bother about them. But she has influenced them and her bold challenging of existing conventions in writing match their bold challenging of existing conventions in social organization and social thinking as well as the expressing of that thinking. Only change is possible in Gertrude Stein's outlook, the only permanent and unchanging thing is change and without change it is death. "I am certain that what makes American success is American failure." Gertrude Stein wants to adapt the English language for American use: the tight little formed little island England had other uses for English than has the sprawling vital American continent. The chain of American literary innovators who have adapted English to new American purposes to her consists of Emerson, Poe, Mark Twain, Walt Whitman, Henry James and Gertrude Stein. In the past thirty years it has been Gertrude Stein. She thinks so and so why not say so. She is the next link but she is also the break in the tradition. She is the innovator.

She is explaining the aliveness of literature in the Elizabethan period .... And however obscure you may think her there is not a moment that she is not trying to make herself quite clear to you: "I am trying not to give to myself but to you a feeling of the way English literature feels inside me."

Well about the commas which is what this piece started out to talk about. Gertrude Stein early on felt they were servile and she didn't like them and because she didn't like them she would have nothing to do with them. That's why she is a revolutionary. She doesn't like a thing that most people think is necessary to life, that they think you simply can't do without, she doesn't like it so she does without it. Commas for example.

So Gertrude Stein is a pathbreaker, a revolutionary and a torch for those who feel like not using or putting up with the using of anything that to them is particularly degrading. Gertrude Stein is a revolutionary in writing and in thinking and in feeling and so she is a revolutionary.

And she is the next bridge between the last two eras: the conventional stuffy outlived Georgian era that thought you had to write the way the grammar books said and live the way the people who run things said and the era when people will write the way they see and feel and live and like, and live the way they see and feel and live and like because they see and feel and like that way and because there is no one and nothing to stop them. Gertrude Stein is a bridge and whoever has understandingly walked across that bridge can never walk back.

Pacific Weekly, April 12,1935.

"A Stone of Stumbling."

John Gould Fletcher

As a civilization becomes more and more complex, literature—and by this I mean literature in the sense of an elaborated art, resting on the aesthetic cooperation between writer and reader, not merely literature for the sake of self-expression, or ordinary commercial writing—literature itself tends to become more and more conscious of its limitations, limitations well expressed by Doctor Johnson when he said that "books were written in order to enable men to enjoy life, or to endure it." The idea that all the great world literatures have had at their beginning, that the chief aim of writing was to represent everything in the known human world along with its prototypes in the unknown supernatural world, an idea represented by Homer, Virgil, Dante, or, to some extent, by Shakespeare, gradually is abandoned, and in its place comes a self-conscious attempt to restate human emotion for emotion's sake, or to describe life for the sake of the description. Thus literature in its last phases necessarily always becomes either romantic or naturalistic, and this was just as true of the late Greek or Roman civilizations as it is of the world today. The difference between such a writer as W. B. Yeats, for example, and some of the anonymous bards of ancient pagan Ireland is that where the former poets were referring to matter within the range of common knowledge or belief, the modern poet is re-using the material of ancient myth to produce a consciously induced state of mind that is remote from our daily concerns, that is elaborately controlled by intellectual devices of stylization, that is intended to produce the effect of a self-imposed "vision." In short, where the anonymous old singer used words because they evoked in his hearers an instant recognition of certain generally held beliefs, the modern writer consciously uses them as imaginative counters to induce, as Coleridge said, "a willing suspension of disbelief," and therefore has at the same time to be less general and more exact in their use, as well as more aware of the purposes for which he is using them.

It follows, therefore, that modern literature is at once more complex and less easy to grasp in its essence than literature of the remote past; and this fact rests at the base of much recent criticism that has been made of modern literature, in the name of a revised classicism. Whether the critics who have condemned all modern romanticism along with all modern naturalism in favor of a classic ideal have ever paused to reflect that after all, the modern writer has little if any choice, in the present state of politics, ethics, economics, religion, and social life, than to be either naturalistic or romantic, is not for me to say. But one thing is certain: none of these critics has even attempted to deal with such a writer as Miss Gertrude Stein. For here is a modern writer who alike refuses to be classified as either naturalistic or romantic, and who yet insists that what she is doing is an inevitable extension and development of English literature transposed from its nineteenth-century setting in the British Isles to a new set of conditions which are essentially not British, but American. Moreover, this writer has insisted, for more than twenty years, and still insists, that what she is doing is not only clear and intelligible, but can be explained in simple terms to a modern audience.

The present volume, therefore, consisting of Miss Stein's lectures delivered during her recent triumphal progress of America, should be welcomed by critics of all parties; if it is not, the fault is either because these critics have come to the conclusion that Miss Stein does not know what she is talking about, or that they are skeptical whether what she is talking about bears any real relation to the problems that beset the modern writer in the present day. For my part, I frankly accept the latter point of view. Miss Stein knows perfectly well what she is talking about. But what she is talking about has nothing whatever to do with modern literature or indeed with anything beyond literature for the nursery. She has oversimplified her problem without clarifying it. In distinction Yeats or Joyce or Pound or any representative modern, she is clear as to what she likes and dislikes and why she likes or dislikes it. But it is a clarity achieved by ignoring the necessary relationship between writer and audience, one which emerges not out of skepticism and hesitation, but out of plain blunt straightforward naive stupidity, a stupidity which may perhaps account for her popularity at this moment with many other stupid people in the United States.

If it be argued that this criticism is unfair to Miss Stein, I can only hereby recommend the reader of this review to look at some of this remarkable woman's writing itself. I pass over the extraordinary account given in the first pages of this volume and headlined "What Is English Literature?" of how English literature began in the accurate description of the "island daily life," went on to the Elizabethan's preoccupation with new words, became confused under Milton, cleared up again in the eighteenth century, when again the "island daily life" apparently became its subject, and then degenerated in the nineteenth century, when apparently the business of "owning everything outside," and having to explain the inside "island daily living" to the outside world led the English to concentrate on phrase-making and to a transference of emotion from sentences to paragraphs. I pass over Miss Stein's favorite idea that the paragraph is emotional, while the sentence is not. I pass over the theory that the essence of American literature is precisely its lack of connection with daily living at all: "As it has to be, because in its choosing it has to be that it has not to be, it has to be without any connection with that from which it is choosing."

I pass over all this to concentrate on the next-to-the-last lecture, here called, appropriately enough, "Portraits and Repetition." To me, the following passages culled from it contain the essence of Miss Stein's thought (I have adhered to her own punctuation):

"The difference between thinking clearly and confusion is the same difference that there is between repetition and insistence. A great many think that they know repetition when they see or hear it but do they .... When I first began writing portraits of any one I was not so sure, not so certain of this thing that there is no difference between clarity and confusion. I was however almost certain then when I began writing portraits that if anything is alive there is no such thing as repetition .... As I say I had the habit of conceiving myself as completely talking and listening, listening was talking and talking was listening and in so doing I conceived what I at that time called the rhythm of anybody's personality .... In other words the making of the portrait of anyone is as they are existing as they are existing has nothing to do with resembling anyone or anything."

In other words, no one has to remember anything about *Tender Buttons, Geography and Plays, Lucy Church Amiably, Four Saints in Three Acts, The Making of Americans*, or others of Miss Stein's immortal works, in order to admire and worship and know the "rhythm of the personality" of Miss Stein. "There is no difference between clarity and confusion." If this is where the modern movement has got us to, then the sooner we stop being modern, the better. For here we have it that it is not the stone which the builders rejected, but the other stone they forgot about ("listening and talking did not presuppose resemblance") and which they later stumbled upon by accident, which has become the headstone of the corner. Whether one is to use Miss Stein's prose as something to sing in one's morning bath, or to repeat (*sotto voce*) while doing one's daily dozen, whether one can employ it for the killing of bores, or for the remorseless unhinging of one's own brain, I cannot say. But there is not doubt it is here—and Miss Stein will continue to write it, and Random House continue to publish it, so long as a nose is a nose is a nose.

The American Review, June 1935.

"The Impartial Essence."

Kenneth Burke

The repetitions and blithe blunderings that Gertrude Stein has somehow managed to work into a style make her *Lectures in America* hard for a critic to discuss. Though they have as their subject a theory of writing, they are expressed so girlishly that we are tempted not to ask how the various parts fit together.

The keystone of Gertrude Stein's literary theories seems to be her doctrine of "essence." She would get at the "essence" of the thing she is describing. She thus tends to consider literature primarily as *portraits*. She makes portraits, not only of people, but of landscapes; plays are to her little other then group portraits; and eventually people and landscapes become so interchangeable that a play can describe a landscape by assembling portraits of people. Hence let us, instead of attempting to follow the order of exposition in Miss Stein's book itself, build up her literary schema in our own way with "essence" as the starting point:

The essence of a thing would not be revealed in something that it does. It would be something that a things is. The search for essence is the attempt "to express this thing each one being that one." A thing's essence is something that makes it distinct from other things; it is, as she says at another point, a thing's "melody." Since it is something that the thing *is*, action would tend to obscure it rather than reveal it .... Suppose, now, that you held to such a doctrine of essence, and wanted in your writing to get down the absolute essence of each thing you wrote about. Consider the sort of problems, in both theory and method, that might arise. In the first place, you would have to worry about resemblance. In putting down the essence of Mr. A, you would have to guard against any tendency to think of him in terms of somebody he resembled—Mr. A1. Again, since essence is something that a thing now is, you would have to guard against the tendency to think of your subject in terms of memories (an exaction which might explain in part her tendency to feel that stories or acts obscure the perception of essence). And you would now have brought yourself to the paradoxical position wherein your knowledge of your subject's past or of people like him amounts to "confusion" (a sad state of affairs upon which Miss Stein dwells at some length).

At this point you might rebel; but if you go on, as Miss Stein did at her leisure, you will find attendant considerations arising. You will talk much about getting "inside" things (perhaps thus being led to note as the primary fact about English literature the stimulus it derived from insularity). And since you, as an *outsider*, are busied with the literary task of describing things until you get *inside* them, there will necessarily hover about your theories some hint of mystic communion. In time your doctrine of essence brings you to the metaphysical problem of the One and the Many, for if you start by trying to find wherein each one is that one, you begin to find a general intermingling; and particularly as you make that outside you to be inside you, you come, through the medium of yourself, upon a kind of universal essence .... How does this work out in practice? You start to write about something, to describe it, to makes its portrait. You have a personal style, a set of mannerisms that suit your particular essence, and as you write you gradually get into the swing of them. When you get going, you are "excited." And since your excitement arises during your description of a thing, you may call this excitement the melody or essence of the thing. You may feel that each subject has its particular essence because you have used a particular combination of words in writing about it. But you feel the "unity" of all subjects because the quality of your excitement is the same in all cases (the way you feel when you get going), and you call this melody of yours the melody of the thing.

If the essence of external things is thus identified with the qualities of your style, you may tend to think of writing (description) primarily as a monologue act, done with little direct concern for an audience. And since this stylistic circulation about an object obliges you to consider the strategy of expression, you may arrive at the thoughts on the nature of naming that Miss Stein verbalizes as a shifty distinction between prose and poetry ("that is poetry really loving the name of anything and that is not prose").

However, you are now on the verge of a change. For the strategy of expression leads into considerations of the audience. From this point, you begin to suspect the suggestive values of narrative, since narrative unquestionably has a significant appeal to audiences. But at this point, if you are Miss Stein, you simply state that you have changed your opinion—and stop. As a kind of compromise between your initial notion of essence as non-dramatic and the fully revised notion that essence might best show itself in action, you may be grateful for her halfway metaphor: the essence is something like the engine in a car—a going without a destination.

It seems to me, however, that Miss Stein should have continued her revisionary process, until all the initial visionary assertions had been similarly modified. She might have considered, for instance, the ways in which remembrance and resemblance are inevitable; the ways in which the primary fact of English literature might be called its transcendence of insularity, etc. And then, and only then, should she have begun her book. As it stands, I maintain that it is (a) the first draft of a critical credo, (b) complicated by the co-presence of its revision, (c) further vitiated by the fact that the revisionary process was not applied to all its parts. Above all, I believe, a complete revision would require her to stress (at least in this "imperfect world" of history) the *dramatic*, the *active*, the *partisan*, in direct contrast with the feature of *passivity* that is now infused through her doctrine of portrait and essence.

The New Republic, July 3, 1935.

Reviews of *Narration* (1935)

"Contemporary Criticism."

F. Cudworth Flint

The name of Gertrude Stein has long evoked wholehearted emotion of various sorts, even in persons who have read little or nothing of her work. But human nature pays unconscious tribute to sheer durability. Miss Stein is still with us; during the years she has continued "being one who is at one and the same time telling and listening to anything or everything." To be able to do both at once is, by the bye her definition of a genius. As the number of those who have had the role merely of listening to Miss Stein has grown, the earlier simpler responses to her work have been modified by curiosity. An effect sustained for so long must have notable causes; what *is* Miss Stein about? To satisfy this curiosity Miss Stein visited America in 1934-1935, delivering lectures on her literary methods and aims. One of these lectures—"Poetry and Grammar," included in her book *Lectures in America*— was delivered at the University of Chicago in November 1934. At the invitation of the University, she returned in March 1935, to give four lectures on narration, setting forth "all I know just at present about how writing is written how an audience is existing telling anything is telling that thing." In his introduction Mr. Wilder attributes to these lectures three conspicuous merits: the lectures are "models of artistic form," they are "object-lessons of the teaching method," and they are notable for "the richness and vitality of the ideas contained in them." Their artistic form "reposes upon an unerring ear for musical emphasis that is characteristic of all life," and upon an "economy of the punctuation, which has been explained by Miss Stein as being a form of challenge to a livelier collaboration on the part of the reader." They exhibit pedagogic virtue because they progress from simple to complex matters, and because "these lectures first prepare and provoke the correct questions in the listeners' minds." Then, too, "there is an almost terrifying exactness in Miss Stein's use of the very words that the rest of the world employs so loosely": for example, *anybody, anything,* and *any way,* in her fundamental definition in these lectures: "Narration is what anybody has to say in any way about anything that can happen, that has happened or will happen in any way." And, elaborating his praise of the content of the lectures, he writes, "We hear nothing of the proportion of exposition to narrative of where to place a climax, of how to heighten vividness through the use of illustrative detail .... The outstanding passages will undoubtedly be those dealing with the psychology of the creative act as the moment of 'recognition' and the discussion of the relations between the artist and the audience." So much by way of eulogy for the author of *Tender Buttons* from the author of *The Woman of Andros*.

Nothing that has been quoted from Mr. Wilder is precisely untrue; yet he defines only half of the curiously mixed impression produced by these lectures. To take up his last point first: the matters treated in them are undoubtedly important, and Miss Stein shows herself here, as elsewhere in her critical writings, to be shrewd, and lacking neither in a sense of irony nor of humor. Moreover, her incidental comments on the general effects produced by words in successive periods of English literature—a topic treated more at length in *Lectures in America*—exemplify her possibly unique sense for an aspect of language only to be adumbrated by some such phrase as "the movement of words." The meanings of words—or perhaps their sounds as conveyors of meanings, rather than these sounds as mere phonetic phenomena—seem to register themselves in her consciousness as diagrams of movement or of position. In like manner, she responds to varieties of syntactical organization as if these were varieties of visual design. Hence she is able to convey in novel terms a vivid sense of the behavior of words aligned in written groups. No other writer of whom I know has made the distinction between the quality of words in Elizabethan times and their quality in the eighteenth century so evident and even, like the vibrations of deep sounds, *tactile*, as she has done in her *Lectures in America*. In *Narration*, she employs this gift in discussing the differences of movement between English literature and American literature; she lays great stress on the legato realization of completeness in English style as contrasted with the American staccato movement toward undefined goals. But against such insights must be set the stultifying effect of one of her constant preoccupations—her attempt to *arrest* time in language, her attempt to force a temporal art to produce the effects proper to a spatial art .... Naturally, this doctrine does not manifest its consequences in a critical work like *Narration*, save as it links up with her insistence that reiteration does not involve repetition, but is a mode of emphasis and a manifestation of variety beneath uniformity. But when one turns to *The Making of Americans*—particularly in its earlier unabridged form—it is almost impossible to concentrate one's attention upon the text for any considerable time, and the results are scanty, in view of the effort expended, should one succeed in doing so.

One wonders why Miss Stein has embarked on this unpromising endeavor. She has stated (in *Lectures in America)* that she has lost all interest in music, and she does not discuss dance—which two arts, together with literature, are the arts in and of time. On the other hand, she has long professed to be a connoisseur of painting—an art in space. But these facts by themselves do not explain the extent to which she tries to render as simultaneous the necessarily successive parts of a literary composition. She grounds her practice on her observations in psychology: "How do you know anything, well you know anything as complete knowledge as having it completely in you at the actual moment that you have it. That is what knowledge is, and essentially therefore knowledge is not succession but an immediate existing." To what degree the knowledge one has can simultaneously be present to, or a determinant of, the structure of consciousness, is a question beyond my technical competence. No doubt there is an important sense in which a literary work, when the reader has finished his reading of it, creates in the reader's mind a structure representative of itself, which can be more or less present as a whole to consciousness. But no such completed structure is present while the work is being read. Miss Stein's mistake in her theory is to imply the contrary; and her mistake in practice—in some of her narrative works—is an attempt to write as if the whole work were *at each point* in the work completely present. One is driven to the conclusion that such an endeavor, in a person of Miss Stein's evident superiority of endowment and training, can proceed only from a sensibility fundamentally eccentric. By this I imply no absolute judgment on the value of her way of experience; I merely state that, to be assimilable, much of her creative practice requires, and from her disciples has received, dilution and modification.

On other matters treated in these lectures—the distinction between prose and poetry, the relation between narrative in newspapers, in history, and in fiction, and the effect of various kinds of audiences upon various kinds of writing, she has much to say that is valuable and often at the same time amusing. Her pedagogic merits may stand as noted as Mr. Wilder. As for the vexed question of her style, one may say in brief: first, that her lectures represent a mitigation of her creative practice—it is, for example, perfectly easy to understand what she states she intends to do in writing one of her "portraits," even though the portrait itself resists penetration even by Miss Stein's own analysis; and second, that much of her repetition and her incomplete syntax cease to distract the reader, and even come to justify themselves, when the reader perceives, as he is bound to do, that these proceed *in her lectures* ... from her reproduction in her written style of the cadences and idiosyncracies of her spoken style. One who has never heard Miss Stein lecture can gain from the written text a fair idea of how she would sound. Moreover, once the reader gets into the way of hearing what he reads, her omission of most punctuation will cease to distract him, for the cadences will furnish their own punctuation. Of course, the further question arises: granted that in these lectures the reader may hear the writer, how about the merits of Miss Stein's style as spoken? To this question, I can return only an answer which may seem too much like the conclusion of the second lecture:

"We will come to day, perhaps yes, perhaps no, no and yes are still nice words, yes I guess I still will believe that I will. You will perhaps say no and yes perhaps yes."

In other words, some of her repetition for emphasis justifies itself. And her casting her remarks throughout in a simple language, avoiding most technical terms even in dealing with technical matters—of psychology and philosophy, as well as of literary technique—has, notwithstanding the circumlocution involved, the merit of forcing one to consider afresh some problem which has become stale by the familiarity of the technical language currently used in its statement and solution. On the other hand, Miss Stein, though she often arrives suddenly at a new point, invariably lingers at that point just too long, and often even goes back for a new start toward the same point. The cumulative effect of all these phenomenon is to produce in a reader, and, I must believe, in a hearer, after considerable immersion in her discourse, a feeling of somewhat amused, somewhat enlightened *stupefaction.* One's mind has traveled, but at a retarded pace not one's own—a pace not unusual for intelligent minds, in spite of the expertness of Miss Stein in analyzing literary movement, one feels cramped for movement. One must regard Miss Stein as something of a sorceress—a frank sorceress, eminently agreeable to expounding, to the profit of her audience, the secrets of her sorcery; but in the long run, a person from whom one must escape. I shall perhaps say no and yes perhaps no.

Southern Review, Spring 1936.

"Books of the Quarter."

Hugh Sykes Davies

Not many years ago, Miss Stein was honorably mentioned in most lists of the leaders of modern literature, even short ones, and was often seen in the company of those greater than herself—on paper. There was some justification. She had evolved from herself, from her own sensibility, an original means of expression, and she had developed it skillfully within its rather narrow limits. Her achievement was obviously not great, but as far as it went it appeared to be genuine, and that is more than can be said for many more pretentious experiments.

Some of the most attractive minor pieces in all the arts have been produced by such talents, limited, but within their limitations real and complete. There is unfortunately the danger that an artist of this kind may some day refuse to accept his limitations honestly. For the emotional reactions which follow any genuine creative activity, even on a small scale, are often productive of spiritual pride, and spiritual pride is a great solvent of honesty. It is to be feared that something of the kind has happened to Miss Stein. Disregarding her limitations, she has attempted which she does not understand, and which she could hardly perform even if she understood them. This book on narration marks the nadir—if we are lucky—of this sad decline in honesty. There is this to be said in excuse, that the temptation to exceed herself came from others. In his introduction Mr. Thornton Wilder says that the four lectures which compose the book were delivered at the University of Chicago, and that body must take a little of the blame for issuing such an irresponsible invitation. But Miss Stein must take much more of the blame for accepting it.

Naturally enough, she has used a means of expression which is not that commonly employed in lectures, or in critical work, and which bears some relationship to the style which has made her famous. It is not the first time, of course, that she has tried to adapt it to such purposes, but never before has the critical project been so ambitious, and before we come to any opinion about the manner, it is only fair to examine the matter.

"Ambitious" seems to be the word for it, unless "pretentious" be preferred. The discussion of the subject opens with a sort of philosophy of history, justifying the conception of centuries, and goes on to develop the differences between life in England and life in America. The conclusion seems to be this: that English life is peaceful and homely, while American life is restless and full of movement. This journalistic commonplace, woven in and out of six or seven pages, iterated and reiterated into a tedious trellis-work of verbiage, composes the bulk of the first lecture. The second lecture deals with poetry and prose and the conclusion perhaps deserves quotation:

"If poetry is the calling upon a name until that name comes to be anything if one goes on calling on that name more and more calling upon that name as poetry does then poetry does make of that calling upon a name a narrative it is a narrative of calling upon that name. That is what poetry has been and as it has been that thing as it has been a calling upon a name instead of a succession of internal balancing as prose has been then naturally at the time all the time the long time after the Elizabethans poetry and prose has not been the same thing no has not been at all the same thing."

What of the syntactical resources of poetry? And of the semantic function of words in prose? But perhaps in some obscure way objections such as these are met by Miss Stein, and I have been too stupid to see them. Even so, I can feel little shame at failing to understand a passage which displays such deplorable looseness of thought. It is enough to examine the variations of meaning of the word "thing," both singly and in its compounds "anything" and "everything." Apparently it can stand for the subject matter, the object described, a proposition by Miss Stein, or the preceding sentence as a whole. No theory can be expressed clearly through such confusion, nor can it exist clearly. And unhappily the other subjects treated in the last two lectures are just as shabbily handled as this matter of prose and poetry. I see that Miss Stein has discussed the newspaper, history, the novel, biography, and autobiography, but I do not know what she has said about them. Everywhere in the *multum-in-parvo* "thing," running through the whole gamut of its nebular meanings, just as it does with children who are learning to talk, or with stupid women who try to discuss intensely subjects which they do not understand.

The confusions of thought are made worse by Miss Stein's habit of omitting all facts and illustrations. Mr. Wilder puts a very good face on it by assuring us that "Miss Stein pays her listeners the high compliment of dispensing for the most part with that apparatus of illustrative simile and anecdote that is so often employed to recommend ideas. She assumes that the attentive listener will bring, from a store of observation and reflection, the concrete illustration of her generalization." But all that is mere euphemism. It would be better to say that Miss Stein spins a web in the void, either ignorant of facts or not caring for them. Her generalizations do not perform the function of organizing our data, for we can never know which data she has in mind. Her theories are their own reward. Perhaps they merit the title of "pure theories," for they are completely untainted by facts or concrete knowledge.

As an example of this airy theorizing, this passage will serve: "I had a funny experience once, this was a long time after I had been writing anything and everything as you all more or less have come to know it, it was about five years ago and I said I would translate the poems of a young French poet …. So I began to translate and before I knew it a very strange thing had happened."

"Hitherto I had always been writing, with a concentration of recognition of the thing that was to be existing as my writing as it was being written. And now, the recognition was prepared beforehand there it had been recognized before I began my writing, and a very queer thing was happening" …. It is dreadful to think that growing minds should have had before them such an example of loose thinking and bad criticism.

So much for the matter. Of the manner nothing better can be said. Miss Stein has elected to omit most of the usual punctuation. She does this because she wishes to challenge a livelier collaboration from the reader, and because she believes that commas make things too easy, prevent us from living our life as actively as we should lead it. Morally, this argument may be compared with that recently advanced by the Chancellor of the Exchequer to justify the imposition of taxes which he had admitted were financially unnecessary. It is good for us all to pay, he said, because then we all feel that we are actively collaborating in rearmament. Technically, Miss Stein's economy of commas may be compared with a complete renunciation of the pedal in playing the piano. At best, we might have a *tour de force*, and that only if the pianist happened to be a very good one. As it happens, we do not get so much from Miss Stein, for punctuated or unpunctuated her sentences are simply bad, ill-constructed, confused and rhythmless.

In fact all Miss Stein's old virtues have forsaken her. The trick of constant repetition which gave pleasure when it was used in prose with no rational end, for purely aesthetic purposes, has adapted itself very ill in the making of statements with meaning. It is bad enough to hear a silly theory advanced once; it is agony to hear it advanced twenty times in quick succession. And the faults which have sprung up in the ground left vacant by the dead virtues are a weedy legion—the vagueness of conception, slackness of thought, the endeavor to make commonplace views impressive by gesticulation and emphasis. It is a pity.

The Criterion, July 1936.

Reviews of *The Geographical History of America, or The Relation of Human Nature to the Human Mind* (1936)

"Perspicuous Opacity."

Marianne Moore

Gertrude Stein has a theory that the American has been influenced by the expansiveness of the country and the circumstance that there are great areas of flat land where one sees few birds, flowers, or animals. There are no nightingales, she says, and the eagle is not the characteristic bird it once was; whereas "the mocking-birds ... have spread ... and perhaps they will be all over, the nation bird of the United States" —one ambiguous significance which she makes unequivocal. We owe very much to Thornton Wilder for giving us the clue to the meanings in the book, since the mind resists a language it is not used to. Realizing the laziness of the ordinary reader Mr. Wilder explains that Miss Stein, as a result of thinking about masterpieces of literature, found that in them the emergences of the Human Mind were dependent upon the geographical situations in which the authors lived—flat land conducing to the ability to escape from identity, hilly land conducing to the specific and the insistent. The Human Mind and Human Nature, as he says, are here "invented terms" of a "private language,"—the Human Mind being selfless and without identity, Human Nature insisting on itself as personality; and "it cost pain to express and think these things." Therefore sadness and tears are mentioned as connected with Human Nature and the exterior trudging we do, as opposed to felicity and the operations of the Human Mind. When an author writes as if he were alone, without thought of an audience, "for an audience never does prove to you that you are you," it is this which makes a masterpiece. "Anyone who writes anything is talking to themselves," not conversing, "and that is what Shakespeare has always done, he makes them say what he wants said," and is "everlastingly interesting."

Miss Stein likes naturalness. "Nothing I like more," she says, "than when a dog barks in his sleep"; and in giving lectures here, her attitude to pretense was calculated to make those who overanalyze a piece of straight thinking seem like the milliner's assistant in *Punch* who asks a dull patron, "Would Modom entertain a feather?" She says, "I like to look about me," "I love writing and reading." In looking about her she has detected things; in science, "well they never are right about anything"; excitement "has to do with politics and propaganda and government and being here and there and society"; the electioneering politician "has no personality but a persistence of insistence in a narrow range of ideas" and is not exciting; whereas science is exciting and so is writing. Miss Stein says, "I wish writing need not sound like writing," and sometimes she has made it sound so unlike writing that one does not see at first what is meant. Looking harder, one is abashed not to have understood instantly; as water may not seem transparent to the observer but has a perspicuous opacity in which the fish swims with ease. For example, "There is no doubt of what is a masterpiece but is there any doubt what a masterpiece is."

To like reading and writing is to like words. The root meaning, as contrasted with the meaning in use, is like the triple painting or projecting lamellae, which— according as one stands in front, at the right, or at the left—shows a different picture: "In China china is not china it is an earthen ware. In China there is no need of China because in china china is china." Definitions are pleasurable, and words can fall sweetly on the ear .... "Winning is a description of a charming persona, and "the thing about numbers that is important is that any of them have a pretty name ... Numbers have such pretty names in any language."

It is a feat of writing to make the rhythm of a sentence unmistakable without punctuation: for example, "When they said reading made easy reading without tears and someone sent me such a beautiful copy of that," or "No one knowing me knows me. I am I I." In a real writer's experimenting there can be an effect of originality as one can achieve a kind of Venetian needlepoint by fitting into each other two pieces of a hackneyed pattern of peasant edging.

The Geographical History of America is offered as a detective story— "a detective story of how to write," making use of the political situation in the United States, with allusions to the two Roosevelts and the two Napoleons—and is not propaganda, which is platitude. A detective story is a conundrum, and this one has "content without form" and is "without a beginning and a middle and an end"— Chapter I following Chapter II, and Chapter III following Chapter II. The repeatings and regressions are, as Thornton Wilder says, sometimes for emphasis, sometimes a method of connecting passages, sometimes a musical refrain, sometimes playful. And, one adds, sometimes a little inconsiderate and unaccommodating and in being willing to be so, partake of Human Nature rather than of the Human Mind. And "nobody need be triumphant about that." But the book is a triumph, and all of us, that is to say a great many of us, would do well to read it.

The Nation, October 24, 1936.

"Crossword Puzzle."

R. S.

There are two astonishing things about this new book of Miss Stein's besides the text itself. One of them has to do with the publisher—Bennett Cerf; the other has to do with the master of ceremonies, Thornton Wilder, who has contributed a preface to the volume. Taking them in the order named we find on the inside flap of the jacket a blurb written by Mr. Cerf. In this blurb Mr. Cerf freely admits that he can't understand a word of what Miss Stein is saying, but that, nevertheless, he enjoys publishing Miss Stein's books.

This is such a remarkable statement that it is worth inquiry. Does it only apply to Mr. Cerf, or does it apply to other publishers as well? Does it apply to only Miss Stein's works or to a large section of every publisher's list? Is this the reason why so many books are published that don't mean anything? These questions automatically arise from Mr. Cerf's confession. Does a publisher often publish a book just because he likes publishing, or does he publish it because he likes the book?

Of course, there is a third possibility! Does a book that has no meaning pay? The answer to this question must often be yes. Is it yes with Miss Stein's books? Cerf should answer this at some point also. Why do people buy books that have no meaning? Does a book have to have meaning? Does it make any difference to the reader whether a book has meaning or not? Don't a lot of people like to read just for the sake of reading, regardless of the contents in the same way that publishers like to publish for the sake of publishing, irrespective of the contents? Who buys such books? Who are these publishers besides Mr. Cerf?

Then, as Miss Stein might say, there is Thornton Wilder. When there is Thornton Wilder is there anything else? There never used to be. There used to be only Thornton Wilder and the *Bridge of San Luis Rey*. There used to be Thornton Wilder and a clear prose style, easy and refreshing to read, often stirring. But now there is just Thornton Wilder. There is Thornton Wilder using big words with many syllables and long sentences with many clauses. There is Thornton Wilder and confusion. When Thornton Wilder is writing about Miss Stein there is Thornstein Wilder. And it is too bad. It is altogether too bad.

Thus there are too astonishing things about this book: there is the Bennett Cerf at low tide; and there is Thornstein Wilder. As for Miss Stein herself, she is all right. She never laid any claims to intelligibility. All she was doing was establishing a new literature. She is still establishing it. But it is getting further and further away from language. What is the relationship of human literature to the human language? Miss Stein says there is none. Mr. Wilder says there used to be. Mr. Cerf says he doesn't know.

New York Sun, October 30, 1936.

"Gertrude Stein on Writing."

Joseph Alsop, Jr.

Miss Gertrude Stein is no outpensioner upon Parnassus; no crank; no seeker after personal publicity; no fool. She is a remarkably shrewd woman, with an intelligence both sensitive and tough, and a single one of her books, *Three Lives*, is her sufficient ticket of admission to the small company of writers of the last decades who have had something to say and have known how to say it. Even though you may believe that she has chosen to speak in a private language since *Three Lives*, it is rather silly that it should be necessary to begin a discussion of Miss Stein's latest work by stating what she obviously is and isn't, yet that seems to be the case.

Her new book, to get down to the real business, is an exposition of her version of the mysterious conditions which, by an odd and heavenly chance, produce good or great writing. "This whole book now is going to be a detective story of how to write," she remarks of it. It is a long and a minute study of the creative process, full of much that is rewarding, and much that is horribly puzzling. Perhaps more than a detective story of how to write, it is the story of why Miss Stein writes as she does.

Fundamental in her mechanics of literary creation is a sharp distinction between "human nature" and the "human mind." Human nature, says Miss Stein, is the element in man which *does* things. It runs about, makes warm asserts itself. And it expresses itself in all the saying and writing which requires an audience, because it is an assertion of action, a mere recapitulation of *doing*. Miss Stein's "human mind" is a rarer element. Where "human nature is what any human being will *do*," the "human mind" merely *is*, and "writes what it *is*." It is man's perceptive and creative being, with no functions beyond seeing and creation.

"The human mind can write what it is because what it is is all that it is and as it is all that it is all it can do is to write."

Miss Stein's notion that an absence of punctuation will cause the reader to take a healthy athletic exercise of the mind makes that sentence difficult to follow, but it says a rather simple thing. The human mind, says Miss Stein, can "write what it is," valuably and honestly, because it confines itself to being, and does not trouble itself with doing; and because it only *is* and never *does*, its only expression is in such creation as writing. Her "human mind," in fact, is a sort of creative core of humanity, without identity, beyond time, a fragment of the divine in man, whose creative expression allows man, as it were, to partake of the divine a little.

Miss Stein believes further that a "human mind" sufficiently whole and undisturbed to create successfully is a rare occurrence. "Only one sometimes two mostly only one sometimes none but certainly mostly one in a generation can write what goes on existing as writing." Even the number of those who can read is limited to a "certain number in any generation," but there are always some who can read, and whatever flows out of the human mind is always read, and will always be worth reading. "The human mind is the mind that writes what any human mind years after or years before can read, thousands of years or no years it makes no difference." You can see that Miss Stein allows the writer a very special importance. Miss Stein's writer, her "human mind," is by no means the simple entertainer that T. S. Eliot once thought him.

The hitch comes when Miss Stein, after having accorded the writer so high a position, quietly brushes aside the problem of communication. Perhaps because she recalls an argument we had once on the subject, she has begun her discussion of the problem, and honored your reviewer, by saying that she wants me to understand that "any word can say something but really that has nothing to do with the human mind." She develops that theme at intervals throughout her book .... The writer, Miss Stein feels, often imposes on himself the limitations of human nature (because he "can think that human nature" may be "what it," or the human mind, really "is," and therefore fails to separate the two elements in himself). And, Miss Stein argues, the writer should never do this. His writing should not "sound like writing." It should flow directly out of himself, of "the human mind." Miss Stein denies that the problem of communication exists, since she contends that the "human mind," for which you may read the creative mind, ceases to be human or creative at the point when it begins to be conscious that it has an audience; when its creation fails to flow directly out of it.

Such is Miss Stein's thesis. Supposing for the purpose of the argument, that her distinction between "human nature" and "human mind" is a wholly valid one, surely the fatal defect in her position is in her very denial of the problem of communication. For what the writer creates is not worth much unless someone can understand it. Although Miss Stein makes fun in this book of the view of identity of the old lady who said "I am I because my little dog knows me," still an unread literary masterpiece is a functionless thing. And unless the writer puts his thought in terms comprehensible to the reader, the masterpiece will go unread. "Direct" communication is impossible to imagine, unless you conceive that there can be a mental telepathy between writer and reader, which permits the reader to learn the writer's intention from his private symbols.

Whether or not you believe that Miss Stein's thesis does have the defect just set forth, her book is a fascinating one, since the thesis it expresses is her reason for her departure from the common literary forum. It is full of her peculiar dry wit, and her queer verbal music, which she composes by using words as pure sounds with faint overtones of meaning, crops up in it now and again in the intervals of argument. There is much that is shrewd in it—her comments on the character of Hamlet are admirable—and occasionally there are passages which, quite without reference to Miss Stein's special style, seem a little meaningless. Those stating her theory that there is some connection between living in a flat country and the creative mind are examples.

And at the book's close, after Miss Stein's whole theory has been passed in review, it is perhaps pardonable in one to regret that she exchanged the solid richness, the life and beauty of her work in *Three Lives* for her later style she has explained in *The Geographical History of America*.

The New York Herald-Tribune Books, January 10, 1937.

Reviews of *Everybody's Autobiography* (1937)

"Self-Confidential."

Burton Rascoe

Wallace Irwin called me up last week and asked me if I could give shelter, board, and work to his aging Japanese houseboy, Hashimura Togo, until a commotion died down. Mr. Irwin lives in the Village where, it seems, a boycott is in operation against silk stockings and Japanese houseboys. Mr. Irwin is a liberal, leftist and left-handed; and the presence of Hashimura was, for the time being, compromising to him.

Mr. Irwin assured me that there had been no perceptible decrease in Hashimura's annoying efficiency and solicitude and that, moreover, he had progressed in his education to such an extent that whereas he used to find a little red vest-pocket dictionary adequate to his English needs, he now owns and employs a Roget's *Thesaurus*. For the little words Hashimura used to use, he now looks up the synonyms in Roget and picks out the synonym that is the prettiest looking, that is, the one that has the most syllables.

Hashimura came to work and efficiently disrupted my whole plan of living very quickly; but I made use of him by asking him to read Miss Stein's *Everybody's Autobiography* and to write out what he thinks of it. That kept him from tidying up my desk in such a way that I can't find anything. His report *follows:*

"For Communist-Red Liberal Fascist Sino-Japanese boy, who aspire to make himself contagious with American genius, the most reasonable conduct is for him reading this exorbitant book. All within is simpleton so Oriental will not engage polysyllables. She are untroubled to read, these Miss Gertrude Stein and Miss Alice B. Toklas who is one persons who is two persons.

"I enthrall unparalleled, I cogitate, when one is perusing these womans autobiography of everybody, when she tell how she told the honorable gentlemen who represent the press in Richmond that Virginia was uninhabited. These honorable gentlemen of the press were petrified out of bewilderment. They inquire, 'What do you connote. WE are here.' Miss Stein is adamantine. She asseverates, 'Even so, Virginia is uninhabited.' They exhort umbrage against this remark and placard in the newspapers that Miss Stein covets a malignancy against Virginians.

"Ha.   Ha.   What a jolly rogue is this Miss Stein.   As she makes explanation in this sumptuous volume she does not intend there are no people in Virginia when she use word *uninhabited.* She fabricates a laughing stock. She tell us her mind is so empty of Virginia that all she remembers about it is there was entailed a battle there nominated The Battle of the Wilderness and she deduces a Wilderness is trees with no people among them except there was a battle there and in battles there must be people so all the people in The Battle of The Wilderness must have been annihilated so Virginia is uninhabited.   Also when Miss Stein glanced out of the railway window before she reached Richmond she observed some real estate on which no house had been erected.   That was in Virginia.   Real estate upon which no house has been erected may be said to be uninhabited. *Quid est demonstrandum,* Virginia is uninhabited.

"What exhorts me most to Miss Stein is she is self-confidential.   When she was Miss Alice B. Toklas and indicted a biography of herself she wrote there were only two geniuses in the world, Pablo Picasso and Gertrude Stein. That was superfluous.   When she is Gertrude Stein she gives the kibosh to Pablo Picasso.   Which leaves us just Miss Gertrude Stein, solitary *ingenus omne.* She is performing an exhortatory conduct for I am believing that she has successfully meditated upon the analects of the honorable exquisite philosopher, Dale Carnegie, as your humble servant has also engaged himself in his hours of leisure, but to more profit than your humble servant has yet attained.

"Miss Stein promulgates a dire accusation and because of this I must have the humility to sequester antsinthepants. She allegates she is composing an autobiography of everybody in contrariety to this I must extract the most humble exception. *Id est,* she must include me out, as the phrase goes.   Her avowal asserts that in the prolonging of thirty years incumbence in France she does not understand the French when they say it and that she does not peruse French books with aversion because there are no French books to read.   She avows that everybody cultivates a facility in his natural language and that she has done this and nobody else has and everybody else has.   If she will act pardonably to reciprocate instruction from a Sino-Japanese adorer and pupil who is only holding a Roman candlestick out of which she is a catapulting star, I crave to suggest that I write a non-indigenous language more mellifluously than she native Englishes.

"Miss Stein has the misfortune to have a very limited acquaintance.   Her publisher is so concerned about this that he believes it is obligatory to itemize them.   Thus: Dashiell Hammett, Carl Van Vechten, Charlie Chaplin, Mary

Pickford, Jean Cocteau, Pablo Picasso, Jo Davidson, Mildred Aldrich, Bennett Cerf, Marie Laurencin, Guillaume Apollinaire, Virgil Thomson, Frances Picabia, Thornton Wilder, Lord Bemers, Marianne Moore, Muriel Draper, Fanny Butcher, Donald Klopfer, Mortimer Adler, Robert M. Hutchins, Louis Bromfield, Alexander Woollcott, Katharine Cornell, Mrs. Franklin D. Roosevelt, DuBose Heyward, Sherwood Anderson, Mary Garden, Anita Loos, William Saroyan, Rouben Mamoulian, Gertrude Atherton, Bob Davis.

"Wouldn't it be educational if Miss Stein could become acquainted with Hyman, Kaplan, John Q. Smith, and Hashimura Togo?"

Mr. Togo's effort is not exactly what you might call a review. That is because he has not the benefit of reading the profound essays that have been published on the art and esoteric thought of Miss Gertrude Stein. But Mr. Togo seems to have something there. I have never read a book in my life that had more words and less in it than this one, unless it was another book by Gertrude Stein. But if you take a page at a time of her, occasionally, you may find something that strikes you as pretty damn funny.

The Saturday Review of Literature, December 4, 1937.

"Obituary of Europe and Gertrude Stein."

Samuel Sillen

The mama of dada is going gaga. The dark Cassandra of the hamburgered word foretells of the collapse of Europe, the "orientalization" of the western mind, and the decay of literature. The only novels which are possible today are detective stories, "where the only person of any importance is dead." The war in Spain "obtrudes itself in one's consciousness, but one is comforted by the reflection that many art treasures were destroyed in ancient Greece and Rome and there are, after all, plenty left for people who visit museums." It's a sour world where everybody is a father: "There is father Mussolini and father Hitler and father Roosevelt and father Stalin and father Lewis and father Blum and father France." Only England is cheerful, because the blessed English have no "fathering." The other bright hope for the world is Gertrude Stein, who admits that "I am the most important writer writing today" and brags that "my writing is clear as mud."

Self-confessedly "the creative literary mind of the century," Miss Stein is at least consistent in the bankruptcy of her values. What distinguishes man from animals, she has discovered, is money: "Money is purely a human conception and that is very important to know very very important." The trouble with Roosevelt is that he spends so much money it soon won't exist. The trouble with Communists is that they "try to live without money" and become animals. Gertrude knows better, so she follows up one bestseller autobiography with another potboiler. Her passion at present is avarice, she informs us with the disarming candor of the House of Morgan.

On her American trip she lectured at leading universities, met Dashiell Hammett and Mary Pickford, skidded through the air with Alice B. Toklas. But she didn't get to see America. She was too busy worrying about Basket—her French poodle. She loves French poodles. Unlike Spanish revolutions, they don't obtrude.

Miss Stein's passion, as she confides to us, is moving around in the bathtub water. She likes to drum the Chopin funeral march on the side of the bathtub while she worries about "identity and memory and eternity." Splashing in the metaphysical surf she concludes that "Anything is a superstition and anybody rightly believes in superstitions." As the dripping goddess emerges, brandishing towel and brush, she dictates to handmaiden Toklas the shattering news that "it is not at all interesting to take working men so seriously if by working men one means only those who work in a factory."

New Masses, December 7, 1937.

Reviews of *Picasso* (1939)

"Stein on Picasso."

Agnes Mongan

Whether one considers Gertrude Stein and Pablo Picasso as original and important artists or as very clever charlatans, there can be no denial of the fact that, for good or evil, both have powerfully and widely influenced the literary and pictorial productions of our time. When Miss Stein undertakes the interpretation of Picasso's work, as years ago Picasso in his now famous portrait of Miss Stein undertook his interpretation of the writer, the

appearance of her essay—its length is a scant fifty pages—becomes at least
a minor event in both the literary and artistic worlds.

Her opening shot is dogmatic and extravagant, partisan and prejudiced.
"Painting in the nineteenth century was only done in France and by
Frenchmen, apart from that, painting did not exist, in the twentieth century
it was done in France but by Spaniards." The effect of this statement is to
arouse immediate opposition. One reads it two or three times, making mental
lists of objections and omissions, wondering just what Miss Stein means by
"painting." I am inclined to believe that such reactions were precisely her
aim. She wished an aroused, alert, attentive reader. Having jolted him into
an active, almost angry attention, she proceeds to further statements of
doubtful accuracy. Her own good humor, however, makes itself evident and
her tone becomes both friendly and informal. Few of her familiar mannerisms
are lacking, but there is more punctuation and less repetition than formerly.

Her enthusiasm is clear and her interpretation occasionally novel. She has
little to say about technique, less about composition. Obviously she is more
interested in the emotional, psychological, and historical background which
brought a painter of Picasso's gigantic productive genius to his varied
accomplishment. She is almost preoccupied with the particular and
differentiating quality of Spanish genius and the changes in this temperament
on foreign soil. She writes occasionally nonsense, but more sense, and some
wisdom.

For Americans Miss Stein's book should have a special appeal, since she
makes the claim that in this century the Spaniards and the Americans have
a fundamental understanding of each other. This generalization is supported
by the fact that of the sixty reproductions (many in color) which illustrate the
book, at least a third of the originals are now in American collections.

The Saturday Review, March 18, 1939.

"Stein on Picasso."

Nathalie Swan

Miss Gertrude Stein gives us Picasso in a polite and charming illustrated
lecture, though the reproductions of his work seem somewhat
indiscriminately chosen. Her chronological accounting of Picasso's
development serves the author as skeletal support for her thesis. She stresses
his Spanish birth, his arrival as a youth in Paris, and the subsequent

"periods" of his versatile genius. Miss Stein observes: "Why have painters for friends when he could paint as he could paint ... so in the beginning he knew intimately Max Jacob & at once afterwards Guillaume Apollinaire & André Salmon, & later he knew me & much later Jean Cocteau & still later the Surrealists, this is his literary history." Picasso, it appears, "has not the distraction of learning." He is wholly a painter and draughtsman.

This literary portrait of Picasso is drawn in a cubist manner, certain elements are noted, others ignored; the seen elements are isolated, broken down, reassembled; and as the figure represented gradually emerges, one is not surprised to recognize a strong resemblance to Gertrude Stein (perhaps it is a mandolin in her lap, perhaps it is a Picasso).

Miss Stein makes it clear that her own problem in writing and Picasso's problem in painting are identical. She defines the pure artist as a contemporary who "understands what is contemporary when the contemporaries do not yet know it." It is the artists, sensitive and irresponsible, who grasps the significant changes before the rest of us can recognize them. He should not, however, be aware of the significance of these changes, for he cannot allow his vision to be distorted. The artist may not comment, he can only expose. Miss Stein seems to feel, moreover, that complete isolation and total lack of learning are necessary features of this hygienic regime so that the artist may approach more nearly a state of saintly but receptive idiocy.

Picasso's artistic mutations are explained in terms of the influences which different countries had upon him; the "sadness and monotony" of Spain (blue period), the "gentle poetry of France" (pink or harlequin period), the Spanish landscape again (cubism), and so on. These changes are ascribed to Picasso's recurring need of "emptying himself"—of his visions, one gathers—in order that he may be able to see the next vision truthfully. Miss Stein believes that while Picasso knows and is absorbed by the heads and bodies of human beings, the soul of people does not interest him. At one time Picasso began to concern himself with souls—to interpret them (a Russian phrase) and "the interpretations destroyed his own vision so that he made forms not seen but conceived." No longer able to empty himself, he stopped working.

Miss Stein's observations are witty and often illuminating; more illuminating perhaps in regard to her own work than to the work of her star performer. One suspects that Picasso himself may well be irritated at the esoteric role she has assigned him.

As a critical explanation of the artist's place in society, her definition is trivial and limited. It is true that an intensely personal need often impels the artists; yet it is difficult to understand why as an articulate "contemporary" he should be restricted to a statement of his primary sensory reaction. It is also true that he is sometimes forced to choose between isolation and extinction. The ivory tower has its uses but they must be differentiated from the functions of the padded cell.

The New Republic, July 5, 1939.

"Picasso."

Anonymous

Miss Stein's Picasso is an adamantine Spaniard who has constantly sought to intensify his vision of "things seen without association." At the same time there is a slight peculiar tenderness in him—almost akin to sentimentality—which makes him desire various kinds of consolation. His story, as she sees it, is a fluctuation between these two tendencies. His Blue Period (1901-4) was pure Spanish, wavering, dipped in a temperament fantastically acute and touching. His return to Paris brought his Rose Period, when he almost lost himself in grace and delicacy as such. Cubism followed and a new attack in that war which would never end for him. Then 1917 and the seduction of Italy and the theater in virtually a second Rose Period. Subsequently, in the twenties, he became realistic, painted gigantic classical women, and was cool and precise and perhaps less searching—though the sheer "writing" which figured in some of his drawing did show, says Miss Stein, the retention of Saracen elements from his homeland. Next came the period of Russian influence, due perhaps to his wife; then two years of idleness (1935-37), and finally the impressive resolutions of the last two years, induced by the Spanish War. An appealing book, just, perceptive, and close to the artist. Handsomely printed, it completes what was begun in *Portraits and Prayers* and adds an indispensable item for the appreciation of the least predictable of modern painters.

The Nation, April 29, 1939.

Reviews of *The World Is Round* (1939)

"Gertrude Stein for Children."

Louise Seaman Bechtel

Here is a new book that is a new kind of book, and I like it very much. It is rather a job to tell you why, because it has to be read aloud. You and I should be taking turns, chapter by chapter, laughing and seizing the book from each other. For of course it is fun to find out how well one reads it. Inevitably one wants to see how much better one does the next bit, in spite of the lack of punctuation; how, in fact, one produces punctuation oneself with so little trouble.

But I must not talk about style before I tell you why you will like Rose. "I am Rose my eyes are blue / I am Rose and who are you / I am Rose and when I sing / I am Rose like anything." For me, that verse is enough. And you, too, perhaps, can easily remember—or have you never lost it?—that peculiar, frightening sense of being yourself, and, at times, of being almost too much yourself. *The World Is Round*, says the title, yes, that is another appalling fact, the refrain of this book. Also the sun, moon, and alas, even the stars we once thought five-pointed, are round, and keep going round and round. Where do *I* come in? Please make some one stop it all and listen to *me*.

Taking this so obvious and simple a spiritual sensation, Miss Stein has explored it, tenderly, gaily, in her usual rhythmic flow of words. The story is subtle; to some it will seem no story at all, to others a thoughtful and entirely new exploration of the moods of childhood. Here is the child's quick apperception, his vivid sensation, his playing with words and ideas, then tossing them away forever. As for the story, Rose's part is clear. She tries to find the something that is not going round, that is always there. So at last she climbs a mountain, all alone—except, for comfort, she takes her blue chair. Willie's part is not quite so clear, but he will seem funnier to children—drowning (or almost), buying a lion, going to save Rose, and in a postscript, marrying Rose! But to an adult it does become clear, the difference between them, and Willie's sense of his apartness from Rose, yet his likeness to her.

I see I am becoming complicated, so I shall begin again, for the book page by page is ridiculously simple. Rose, we learn, had a very usual home and two dogs. She sang to herself a great deal, and it made her cry. (Her dog,

Love, cried, too, when she did). Willie, too, had a sense of himself as unique, and he too sang of it, but it didn't make him cry, it made him more excited .... Well, Rose went away to school near the mountains (and all the time the world was going round). And Willie went to stay in the country, and sang of the lizard that lost its tail, and the "frogs and pigeons, butter and crackers, flowers and windows."

"It was time Willie did something, why not when the world was all so full anywhere." So he went to a place where they sold wild animals and chose a lion which he wanted to give to Rose. After several chapters of one sentence each, recapitulating facts about this lion, there comes a floating-off-the-page picture of Rose with a drum in the middle. That was when Rose, listening to the band at the door, knew that there was a lion, but it was not a real lion. The idea made Willie laugh very much and— "Billie the lion never was anywhere. The end of Billie the lion."

Now comes Rose on her trip. Before she went, she sang: "Dear mountain, tall mountain real mountain blue mountain yes mountain, high mountain all mountain my mountain. I will with my chair come climbing and once there mountain once there I will be thinking, mountain so high, who cares for the sky yes mountain no mountain yes mountain no mountain yes I will be there."

So—she goes. And there is a night of fear, but not half so fearsome as the woods in the Snow White movie. And was she lost? "She never had been lost and so how could she be found even if everything did go around and around."

Is it all utter nonsense? Well, lots of it is purposely playful, so that the author catches herself up with a "well, anyway!" For some children it will actually ring true to their half-spoken inner feelings. For some older ones Miss Stein's real meaning, that it is all imaginary, will be clear. For some adults it will carry a deep nostalgia for the dreams and fears and never-told impressions of growing older. For others, it will be too much of a shock; they will recognize the line by line landmarks of sensation, but will be impatient of so much "stream of consciousness."

Because Miss Stein has such a personal conception of style, still others will be "put off." For me, this is the first time that her style has spoken truly and artistically as perfectly fitted to her thought .... For me, the whole is an unforgettable creative experience. It may be too esoteric to have a fair chance with the average child. But it is so new in its pattern, so interesting in its word rhythms, so "different" in its humor, that the person of any age who reads it gives several necessary jolts to his literary taste. Only a true artist could have written so charming a book as *The World Is Round*.

The publishers have tried it out on many children, all of whom were "surprised and attentive." The response was perhaps most intelligent and cordial in girls of about twelve to fourteen. But with such a style, it is true, as it has been true with so many modern artists working for children, that the actual age limit cannot be guessed and should not be defined. There may be some psychologically-minded who do not believe at all in fantasy or in the encouragement of a child's own increased self-analysis. One could assure them that such books have not any other effect than the deepening of their poetic consciousness. And, in this material age, such books come seldom in the course of their reading.

The most acutely honest comment the publishers received came from a boy of twelve: "It is more relaxing than anything I ever heard of." Another said, "It is much more *human* than most books." Another, "The use of words have you laughing till your sides ache." A thirteen-year-old girl said, "I think Rose and Willie are wonderful. I like people who really feel things inside, and I adore the way they express themselves in their wonderful songs." Another girl the same age: "The story is simple and dreamy. You can forget yourself and live in a separate world while you are reading it." A younger child writes, "I love the new style writing because it is the way I, or any other child, would think and write." Of course there also were children who thought Rose, Willie and Miss Stein were just "dumb."

The book is printed in large blue type on pink paper. Clement Hurd has done modern, flowing, symbolic pictures. His clever use of white is nicely balanced by large white numbers for each chapter. The whole make-up suits the material very well.

For a postscript may I add that it is no world-shaking matter to be "for" or "against" this book. But to those who honestly enjoy it, let me say it should be used, none too solemnly, with the most varied sorts of children. We don't want them all to write like Miss Stein! We do want to jog them out of the horribly ordinary prose that engulfs them. In the big inclusive volumes of Mother Goose we used to find strong rhythms and endless variety of word patterns, but our modern, emasculated, carefully selected and word-counted material has lost that strong tang. Miss Stein is not "tops" even in her own field; she cannot touch the Joyce of *Ulysses*, for instance, or Virginia Woolf. But she is one freeing agent who was particularly fitted to do her good piece for modern children.

The Horn Book, September 1939.

"Books for Young People."

May Lamberton Becker

It is not often that a child's book makes the front pages on the day of publication. Even Ferdinand took longer. But Gertrude Stein is spot news. The trouble is that the news is so often not so. We expected, from advance information on *Four Saints in Three Acts* to be baffled, amazed and generally stood on our heads. Instead, the simplest souls and most sophisticated, we went to it on our own money five or six times running, just for the pure delight. Pure delight, simple pleasure, is what little children will get as they listen, a chapter or so at a time, to *The World Is Round*. So will the adult who reads it to them, unless his mind is too stiff to bend with the rhythm. If so, he may be as seasick amid its rollers as those stiff-muscled people who won't go with the motion of a ship but insist on bracing against it.

How do I know? By experience; twenty-fold experience. When *The World Is Round* had just reached galleys, some twenty adults who had never seen it and knew nothing of what it was about, met to read it aloud. Each one took the proof, read at sight to a mark, and passed it on to his neighbor. It was an afternoon of the sort of happiness that cleanses the mind—a child's happiness. We found ourselves reading in natural, organic rhythm; we felt once more the abstract magic of words. We came away wondering if we had not been listening as very little children do, and getting, perhaps for the first time since we had forgotten childhood, the same results from listening. Remember the impressions you had of words in early childhood: were not certain words inexplicably funny, certain others unreasonably heavy with fear? Do you remember poems you heard, prayers you learned, when you were very young? Did you get from their words a succession of clear-cut images, as we recklessly assume that children do? Were you not somewhat amazed, coming upon these poems or prayers later in life, to find that the words had not meant what you then thought they meant? Had they not created an atmosphere rather than definitely shaped images?

No, I will not quote a word of *The World Is Round*, which is about Rose and Willie and some delicious animals wild and tame, and some beautifully impossible adventures. You cannot judge it by extracts any more than you can judge a "movie" by stills. It is printed, by Miss Stein's command, on paper of a toothsome pink. It is an awful color, and every small child will think it perfectly lovely. It is the color once given toothpaste to induce children to brush their teeth, and it worked. The book will not (I hope) set a fashion in writing for little children. Miss Stein has the track, that nobody else is likely to catch, of making them listen to *The World Is Round* in the same entranced quite with which their elders enjoyed her famous play.

The New York Herald-Tribune Books, September 24, 1939.

"Slightly Pied Pipers: 'Old Possum's Book of Practical Cats,' by T. S. Eliot and 'The World Is Round,' by Gertrude Stein."

Edmund Wilson and Chauncey Hackett

Our reviewer has found himself baffled by the assignment of reviewing these two children's books by T. S. Eliot and Gertrude Stein. He had difficulty in getting through the Stein book; and aside from the poem on "The Naming of Cats," described by Mr. Hackett below, Mr. Eliot's amusing drawings of himself disguised in whiskers and prunellas—in one of which he is roller skating in the company of what appears to be an *alter ego* in spats and a silk hat—he was rather disappointed in *Old Possum.* As a writer of sheer light verse, Mr. Eliot lacks the spontaneity and recklessness that are necessary to really keep it going. But these books are intended for children, and ought to be judged by their success with children. Your reviewer has, therefore, turned them over to Mr. Chauncey Hackett, who has children and definite ideas about children's books and who has brought in an interesting report. It is perhaps worth pointing out that there seems to be something like a general tendency on the part of the more "difficult" writers to go in for children's books. Kay Boyle has done a book about a camel; and E. E. Cummings is rumored to be engaged on a book of fairy-tales. I don't know what this means—except that they evidently do not feel at the moment that they have anything better to do.

—Edmund Wilson

The first poem in *Old Possum's Book of Practical Cats* is a versified essay on "The Naming of Cats." A cat must have three names—an ordinary name (such as Potato or Jonathan), a private peculiar name shared by a master and her cat (as Quaxo, Coricopat), and a mysterious inner name known only to the cat itself and entirely undiscoverable to the human race.

Old Possum presents a ballad about a cat named Growltiger, and a somewhat A. A. Milne-ish jingle called "The Rum Tum Tugger." Next, with the sudden vivacity of a shooting star, comes a delightful lyric by the poet

T. S. Eliot ("The Song of the Jellicles"). Score thus far: Old Possum, 3;
Children (if any), 1. Old Possum next throws himself into four ballads—
"Mungojerry" and "Rumpleteaser," "Old Deuteronomy," "Macavity" and
"Skimbleshanks"—all handled rather mincingly to the muffled beat of Mr.
Kipling's tom-tom; then into four portraits in verse cunningly flavored with
essence of Calverley and Lear; and ends finally in two pieces of pure Old
Possum; all, with one exception, being either above or below the level of a
child's unbewildered interest. Final score: Old Possum, 12; Children, 2.

It looks as if Old Possum's book was not written at all for children, or
else only for certain children peculiarly within the orbit of Mr. T. S. Eliot's
intimacy and therefore familiar with allusions and catchwords meaningless
to others: this conclusion was reached after repeated experiment had shown
that normal American children either would not or could not listen to the
greater part of *Old Possum*. They could take none of it except "The Jellicles"
(headed straight for the anthologies, I believe) and "The Old Gumbie Cat"
(merely tolerated by those over five).

One old Harvard semi-classic seems to have lain dormant in Mr. Eliot's
imagination for nearly forty years. Sometime about 1901 *The Harvard
Lampoon* printed a little cartoon of an unshaven pop-eyed Irishman hanging
in air above the Charles in a suicide attempt. Beneath the picture were these
words: [Eliot's quatrain about this Irishman named "Aloysius P. MacAvity"
describes how his "philosophy shames" the "laws of Münsterberg and
James" while also "sniff[ing]" at Newton's theories of gravity.—Ed.]

In *Old Possum's Book*, MacAvity becomes a cat: [In the revised quatrain,
MacAvity is described as having "broken every human law," including
gravity. Blessed with an ability to levitate, he can "make a fakir stare."
Whoever searches for the cat discovers that *"Macavity's not there."*—Ed.]

If *Old Possum* does not appeal strongly to American childhood, it is
because so much of the humor is foreign or unintelligible to youngsters
beyond the island where Mr. Eliot has become fixed; but there is no such
obstacle to the young mind in Gertrude Stein's artfully simple *The World Is
Round*. This is a delicious confection of a book, printed in dark blue on rose-
colored paper. The simplicity of the diction is extreme. There is almost
nothing to eat in the story (usually a serious defect in a children's book), the
lion is decidedly inferior, and the plot development is so gradual that Chapter
26 is called not without humor "Rose Does Something." (Rose is the heroine.
Rose is a Rose). None of the usual devices of children's stories is here, but
this is clearly a child's book.

Brought before a jury of five kids, this book was approved by two, rejected by three. This would seem a defeat for Miss Stein. But wait. Of the two who applauded, one was a girl of ten, herself a poet. The other, a boy of three, was clearly most *en rapport* with the source of Miss Stein's power to invoke a child's interest. She has obeyed the first precept for those who would write for children: "Except you become as a little child you shall not enter."   —*Chauncey Hackett*

The New Republic, December 20, 1939.

Reviews of *Paris France* (1940)

"History Tramps Down the Champs-Elysées."

Janet Flanner

This "century is now forty years old, too old to do what is told," writes Gertrude Stein in her new small book, *Paris France*. Yet in less than forty days since Germany's march through Western Europe, Paris, France, Brussels, Belgium, and The Hague, Holland, have all learned, despite their age, to do what they are told, as have Copenhagen, Oslo, Warsaw, Prague and Vienna before them.

Paris France is Miss Stein's *homage à la France,* to the France which was, until a month ago. It is one of her saddest and funniest, deepest and easiest books to read. It is audibly written in her clear conversational style. During her forty years in Paris when she was learning to write famously in a way few understood, she was always noted in her neighborhood as a born, commonsense, glass-clear talker. It is from these forty French years of listening and looking, asking and answering that Miss Stein draws her compendious small book, written half before and after Munich, and half during this war when it was not yet a war "not only war time" and when a Bilignin country neighbor could say that in all her eighty-eight war-ridden years, "It is the first war she has ever known that men on leave come back looking so very large and so very healthy and so very fat."

The lean, ill, present days of the courageous French soldiers and the horrifying haste of history tramping down the Champs-Elysées have changed that. But even tomorrow's news cannot alter most of what Miss Stein reports because what she talks about, better than any other American ever has done in print, is the pattern of the French mind, its civilization, logic, tradition, realism, its love and privacy, good food, family and land—those permanent national French qualities like invisible belongings millions of the French are now carrying about with them even as hapless homeless refugees.

"After all the way everything is remembered is by the writers and painters of a period," says Miss Stein and then starts remembering as a writer about painters and even other writers and how in France they're respected more than millionaires or politicians, even by the French police. "Writers have to have two countries, the one where they belong and then the one in which they live really. The second one is romantic, it is separate from themselves. The English Victorians were like that about Italy, the early nineteenth century Americans were like that about Spain, the middle nineteenth century Americans were like that about England, my generation of nineteenth century Americans was like that about France." As for the all-important twentieth century, "England," she shrewdly observed from her distant French hillside, "was consciously refusing the twentieth century, knowing full well that they had gloriously created the nineteenth century and perhaps the twentieth century was going to be too many for them .... England did refuse the twentieth century, did not believe it was really there, thought everybody had made a mistake except themselves, they who knew it was still the nineteenth century. England had the disadvantage of believing in progress, and progress really has nothing to do with civilization, but France could be civilized without having progress on her mind, she could believe in civilization in and for itself."

In pungent paradoxes or within the pressure of a single page or by a paragraphed funny or fantastic, droll or dry short story about her country neighbors on their Brillat-Savarin hillside, Miss Stein amazingly condenses what she as a foreigner saw, heard and accepted as the essential specialties of French civilized life. She signals the peculiar lasting mark of French education, the healthy lack of equality between the sexes, the adult shape of even juvenile minds, the dependence of French sons on their mothers, the intimacy of French people with the soil and their lack of intimacy with each other; their truthfulness as a form of liberty, the accuracy of their language since "the French love to say a thing and say it completely"; their liking for work, "it is a pastime for them, work is," and finally "So the most striking thing about France is the family and the terre, the soil of France." She discusses French dogs, including the one which attended a village flute concert, and the French principle of pets generically. "If the children are spoiled, one's future is spoiled; but dogs one can spoil without any thought of the future, and that is a great pleasure." As for money, "it has done a lot of changing, but there is always the hope that it will stay put sometime. Anyway, the French never take money very seriously; they save it, they certainly hoard it very carefully, but they know really it has no very great permanence. That is the reason they all want a place in the country."

She tosses in four appetizing pages on the refining history of French cooking and a four-line treatise on the revolt of the intellectuals. "It could be a puzzle why the intellectuals in every country are always wanting a form of government which would inevitably treat them badly .... That was really the trouble with the surrealist crowd, they missed their moment of becoming civilized, they used their revolt not as a private but as a public thing, they wanted publicity, not civilization, and so really they never succeeded in being peaceful and exciting."

Rather surprisingly, Miss Stein, the great Picasso collector, states, "Fashion is the real thing of abstraction" and as an indication of how styles can run out in France, adds that "Napoleon was not civilized, he was not logical and he was not fashionable." However, war itself, whether Wellington's or Bismarck's or the War of 1914 which she lived and worked through, is, tragically enough, "more like a novel than it is like real life, and that is its eternal fascination. It is a thing based on reality but invented .... It is possible America does not know the world is round because there is no threat of war. To be sure, they have had a good many wars, but not threat of war. War and threats of war are different things .... The French people do not believe that anything is important but daily living and the ground that gives it to them and defending themselves from the enemy. Government has no importance except in so far as it does that," and there, in truth, the French have finally desperately been resting their case. She dedicates her book to France and to England. Well, where else and to whom would it be dedicated now, even as an epitaph?

There are moments in history when the large and latest news of the tragedy going on seems to another the clear recollections as to why the tragedy is so grievous to begin with. History right now is made up of bulletins by the minute and geography changed by the hour. But history is only occasionally so horribly headlined; the lives which went into the forming of it made slower, securer reading, and while there is more dreadful drama in the bombing of an old town, the kind of people who dwelt in it made the real record, even as to why, it was eventually destroyed. What Miss Stein has to say in *Paris France* cannot be read in competition with news but as an anterior, integral part of it. As she herself says, the way everything about a country is remembered is by the writers. Gertrude Stein has unforgettably remembered France.

The New York Herald-Tribune Books, June 23, 1940.

"Briefly Noted: Paris France, by Gertrude Stein."

Anonymous

Charming but now melancholy recital of the customs and qualities of France by an American who has known them since 1900. Dilettante in spots, though much of the book seems fresh and sagacious. Not hard reading.

The New Yorker, July 13, 1940.

"Miss Stein and France."

Justin O'Brien

This book might be called *The Autobiography of Paris France*, since, like the other autobiographies by Gertrude Stein, it tells less about its subject than about its author. That smart-aleck remark may not be altogether fair, for as we read about Miss Stein—her dogs, her friends, the village of Bilignin, and the town of Belley near her country home—we also learn much about the French and even something about Paris. In an appallingly and delightfully confused manner which simulates a one-sided conversation Gertrude Stein does discuss fashions, cooking, latinity, the French family, the peasant, and such very French concepts as civilization and equality. As if talking on the lawn at Bilignin, she illustrates her points with amusing or pathetic anecdotes—sometimes lost on the reader because he does not belong to her coterie— and peppers her speech with quaint expressions translated literally from the French. The book is full of charm, a very personal charm, and humor. Its 120 pages overflow with sententious remarks, such as "The reason why all of us naturally began to live in France is because France has scientific methods, machines, and electricity, but does not really believe that these things have anything to do with the real business of living. Life is tradition and human nature"; or "All Frenchmen know that you have to become civilized between eighteen and twenty-three and that civilization comes upon you by contact with an older woman, by revolution, by army discipline, by any escape or by any subjection, and then you are civilized and life goes on normally in a Latin way, life is then peaceful and exciting, life is then civilized, logical and fashionable in short life is life." The trouble with the post-war generation, she says, is that war prevents the process of civilization and that the young men "missed their time for becoming civilized." But this had already been said by any number of those very young men and before them by another lost generation, that of Alfred de Musset.

To Gertrude Stein, as to many of us, Paris has meant civilization. Moreover, as she says so neatly, "Paris was where the twentieth century was." Firmly rooted in tradition, the French have been able to accept and try everything without losing their balance. Their keen sense of reality is so great that they can tolerate any degree of unreality. Yet with these qualities that she recognizes in them, and their logic and supreme degree of civilization, Miss Stein does not grant them any role, except that of the "inevitable background," in the creation of twentieth-century art. In other words, the French looked on as picturesque and indulgent bystanders while the Picassos, the Steins, the Sir Francis Roses, the Bromfields, and the Hemingways made modern art. This is a parochial point of view, the point of view of the Sixth Arrondissement. Yes, it is the point of view of the tourist. On considering all that Gertrude Stein's art owes to her immediate predecessors, one cannot but find the attitude particularly ungracious.

With all its charm and flavor and superficiality, *Paris France* is a pathetic little book. It is pathetic because, obviously designed as propaganda of the nicer sort, it fails to achieve its end. The larger public having been frightened away by the author's reputation and style, it will be read and enjoyed only by the initiates, the small minority who know both Miss Stein and France. And in view of Gertrude Stein's patronizing attitude toward her subject, this will be no loss. Written before the French capitulation, *Paris France* reflects the anguish that all civilized people felt during the spring. Like all of us, Miss Stein was worried about the possible loss of one of the most precious things in the world—an irreplaceable culture. It is unfortunate that to her that culture was important chiefly as the ideal atmosphere for the creation of expatriate art.

The Nation, July 27, 1940.

"Her France, Her Paris."

Dorothy Chamberlain

Gertrude Stein has been living in her beloved France since 1903, and her explanation is that "writers have two countries, the one where they belong, and the one in which they really live." Her book, written just before and after the outbreak of the present war, is two parts how she thinks France contributes to twentieth-century culture, and one part what happens in the provinces when France is attacked from outside her borders, if not from outside the twentieth century.

England has the disadvantage of believing in progress. But France "could believe in civilization in and for itself, and so she was the natural background" for the 1900-39 period. France was the place "everybody had to be to be free." This was possible because of the French people, or Miss Stein's idea of the French as civilized people—traditionalists and at the same time logical and realistic; polite but truthful; wary of intimacy; individual revolutionists; never cruel or brutal; kind to animals and devoted to children and to the family. All of which means that they minded their own business and let immigrant artists alone—those artists were to "create" the twentieth century. For France, though more interested in civilization itself, tolerated the "progression toward the state of being civilized."

Miss Stein is an acute, thoughtful and sympathetic observer. But no matter how well she knows her France, and no matter how much she loves it, she remains a foreigner and an intellectual of a certain type and time—that is, a specialist in words and in the daily life of a limited group, to the exclusion of general ideas and the life of the country at large. By her nationality and her type of life-in-art she is doubly limited as a spokesman for the French people. It is her Paris and her France she writes about, not theirs.

Most of the artists and writers of the international set were wholly preoccupied with art and daily living. They accepted facilely, scornfully, a government that "has pretty well done what they all think a government should do: let them alone, protected them, on the whole, from the enemy, and though it costs a good deal, this government, it might cost more if it were another government." They took war for granted: "War is more like a novel than it is like real life and that is its eternal fascination." "There is always going to be a general European war, it makes logic." "Of course it is awful to be always under the threat of war and yet does it do something about logic and fashion that is interesting." Like too many of us, they were living in a dream.

Another fatal mistake was the assumption that virtue triumphs—the French, being civilized, "will have found the way to victory and peace. And a new Europe." The shop-talk of the studios cannot be accepted as an accurate or prophetic interpretation. Too often it leads to such complacent statements as "Germany's music and musicians have been dead and gone these last two years and so Germany is dead."

But any liberal, a year ago, might have endorsed Miss Stein's dedication to England and France, "who are to do what is the necessary thing to do, they are going to civilize the twentieth century and make it be a time when anybody can be free, free to be civilized and to be." Even now that such oversimple faith has been proved wrong about France, it is still hoped that England is going to do the "necessary thing."

It should not have to be mentioned that Gertrude Stein can write sentences if she wishes to. Her admiration for the French language ("The French do love to say a thing and say it completely") might be applied to the precision of her own writing. She is shrewd and humorous; deft at anecdotes that capture generalities and words that symbolize concepts. The book is full of aphorisms: "It is false without being artificial." "One has a great deal of pleasure out of dogs because one can spoil them as one cannot spoil one's children." "A child in France is a thing of value ... and a valuable thing is always well taken care of, and the French use everything but they abuse nothing." "If you have them they are not luxuries and if you do not have them they still are not luxuries."

For its literary quality, for its nostalgic pictures of life in France, and for the lesson to be learned from the fallacies of an intellectual class and the weaknesses democracy has tolerated, *Paris France* is a book you should read.

The New Republic, July 22, 1940.

"War."

Katherine Brégy

In many ways this is the most stimulating book Miss Stein has given us—a book in which she is vastly more interested in her subject than in herself. And like everybody else, in loving something more than herself she finds all that is best in herself.

She was always a subtle observer, and now it is possible to tell with a certain simplicity just what she is observing. A few superficial eccentricities of style remain—the erratic use or disease of capitals and punctuation which go along with the "stream of consciousness" style of writing. But most of the time she is so strongly stirred that she forgets all the little exoticisms except those which have become habitual. She has come to realize, for instance, that surrealism "wanted publicity, not civilization"; and what she is concerned with is the nature of French civilization. Sometimes her comments are on the Frenchman, always interested in ideas, always dependent upon his mother or some older woman who represents civilization to him; or on the Frenchwoman who—unlike her American sister who rises magnificently to a crisis—sees that the crisis itself does not arise; or on the French farmer, tired of crises, political or otherwise, and eager to go back to his fields. There are delightfully discriminating little detours on the history of French cooking, both Parisian and provincial, and on French dogs—the native ones which are useful and the imported ones which are fashionable and can be spoiled with impunity, as children cannot. And there is a penetrating observation on the French solider, who complains of no hardship except sleeping on straw; and then "it is not the discomfort, it is the destruction of civilization that he resents."

Gertrude Stein has, of course, lived long in France and she knows whereof she speaks in describing its life and its people as at once *exciting and peaceful*. Her book, written during the days of mobilization and published the day Hitler's army entered Paris, knows whereof it speaks in declaring "The French understand war because they are logical, they do not care to go to war because they are logical, and to be logical is to be Latin." But something unforseen, yet logical enough in the twentieth century—the totality of German mechanized warfare—came upon them, and it was not civilized and they fell before it .... Even without knowing French religion very well Miss Stein can still insist: "Revolutions come and revolutions go, fashions come and fashions go, logic and civilization remain and with it the family and soil of France."

That is why those of us who know and love France not only salute her civilization in this hour of humiliation and seeming eclipse. We believe also that its gift to the world is something no war and no humiliation can extinguish.

The Commonweal, August 23, 1940.

Reviews of *What Are Masterpieces* (1940)

"What Are Masterpieces."

Anonymous

Miss Stein's celebrated Oxford-Cambridge lectures of a decade or so ago—"Composition as Explanation," "An American and France," and "What Are Masterpieces"—are here printed for the first time, together with some poems, and illustrated by two drawings by Picabia. It is perhaps superfluous at this date to say that Miss Stein's writings not only are stimulating but actually mean something.

The Nation, November 23, 1940.

"And Paris."

Jerome Mellquist

Gertrude Stein, of course, prefers the special taste of France. Justifiably so, too, because she distills from it her own fragrance. Two of her books grace her list. *Paris France*, gathered while France was still secure, has the dough-smell of a good kitchen, it glistens with the beauty of Paris, carries to us the *habitants*. Excellent reproductions (8 in number) rival her text with their color. Her more recent *What Are Masterpieces* illustrated by two supple drawings from the hand of Francis Picabia, modernist, is devoted to the Oxford-Cambridge lectures of the author, as well as to a group of her poems and portraits. Charming, but principally a Stein item.

The Commonweal, November 29, 1940.

Reviews of *Ida* (1941)

"All About Ida."

W. H. Auden

Ida is not about Ida, but about Dear Ida. Who is Dear Ida? Why, everybody knows Dear Ida, but not everybody knows whom they know. Most people call the Dear Ida they know Ida, but most people do not know Ida. Then who is Dear Ida whom everybody knows? Miss Stein knows who Dear Ida is. Dear Ida lives from day to day, but a day is not really all day to Dear Ida because she does not need all day. She does not need all day because, of course, she is mostly sitting and resting and being there. Resting is what she likes best and sitting is what she does best. That is being natural, and, of course, being natural does not take all day. That is why she can only use the part of the day and night that she chooses to sit in. She stays there as long as she can, then she goes walking. Dear Ida walks in the afternoon when she is not resting. Everything happens to Dear Ida, funny things happen, husbands happen, going away happens, and Dear Ida does not know whether they are happening slowly or not. It might be slowly, it might be not. Dear Ida does not know because she does not begin, no, never, because, as Miss Stein says, if you begin, nothing happens to you. You happen. Dear Ida does not happen, Dear Ida is not funny. The only funny thing about Dear Ida is her dislike of doors. Otherwise Dear Ida is very well, very well indeed. Does Dear Ida know Ida? No, she does not know Ida, she only knows that Ida is beside her. She cannot know Ida because she thinks Ida is like what she thinks Dear Ida is like. Dear Ida does not even know Dear Ida. Only once in her life does she know Dear Ida. That is the only time Dear Ida cries. Knowing Ida beside her, and not knowing Dear Ida, like the Dear Ida she is, she thinks that Ida is Dear Ida, my twin, my twin Winnie who is winning everything and will never make me cry. When she tries to think of Ida, she can only think of her twin Winnie. When she tries to think of Dear Ida, she can only think a dog is a dog because it is always there. If Dear Ida does not know Dear Ida, who does? Ida knows. Ida is funny and is always beginning. Nothing happens to Ida. Ida does not call Dear Ida dear Ida. But Poor Ida, Lazy Ida, Bad Ida, why do you let such funny things happen to you, why don't you begin, why don't you cry? Dear Ida, you are wrong. The first of everything is not a sign of anything. Anything can be the first of everything. Perhaps ten can be a sign of something. Yes, perhaps everything after ten is a sign. I am not your twin Winnie, Dear Ida, I am Ida. If you knew this, you would not be resting. Perhaps you would be crying, but you would know Ida, and that would be as well. Most novels are Dear Ida writing about her twin Winnie, but they do not say so. Oh dear no, they say this is Ida writing about Ida. But it is only Dear Ida writing, and what does Dear Ida know about Ida as she sits, Dear Ida, and lets funny things happen and does not cry. When she writes Ida she only says, My twin Winnie who is always winning, always counting, never sitting but always crying. There is too much winning, too much counting, too much crying, too much of not resting altogether. Ida is not Dear Ida writing about her twin Winnie. Ida is Ida writing about Dear Ida. There is not too much of anything, only one hundred and fifty pages, and Dear Ida only cries once. Ida does not pretend that Dear Ida is not resting and not thinking about her twin Winnie. Dear Ida writes very often but I do not like what she writes because it is neither about Ida nor Dear Ida, only about her twin Winnie, and that is too much. I like Ida best when she writes about Ida but she does not write about her very often. Next to Ida writing about Ida, I like Ida writing about Dear Ida.

This is what Ida is. I like Ida.

The Saturday Review, February 22, 1941.

"Two Generations."

Klaus Mann

Neither Gertrude Stein nor Carson McCullers needs an introduction to the readers of this magazine. For Miss Stein is certainly not yet forgotten—not at all!— and Miss McCullers has made a rather sensational entry into American Literature with her remarkable first novel, *The Heart Is a Lonely Hunter*.

It is not really that they resemble each other—Miss Stein and Miss McCullers —quite the contrary. But since their two slender volumes, *Ida* and *Reflections in a Golden Eye*, happen to lie side by side on my reading table, it allows me to visualize these two extraordinary women walking through the amazing scenery of their capricious imaginations. They don't look like two sisters, to be sure: the difference of age and attitude is enough to banish such an idea. Nor do they give the impression of being mother and daughter of a pair of intimate friends. Rather, they are to be taken for two individuals distantly akin to each other—a well-preserved aunt, perhaps, accompanying her niece on a walk in the darkling plain.

Says Aunt Gertrude, with a toneless laugh: "It's too funny for words. Those funny things that happened to Ida. There was nothing funny about it funny things happened to her. To Ida. So she was born and a very while after her parents went off on a trip and never came back. That was the first funny thing that happened to Ida. Then, of course, many other funny things happened. And then, of course, all her marriages. Arthur. And Andrew. Andrew never read. Of course Ida was careless but not that way. I read."

"I read quite a bit, too," observes Carson in a hollow, mournful tone.

"Oh, yes," Aunt Gertrude says, shrugging her shoulders, impatiently.

"I'm afraid," says the girl, and she silently stands still, as if petrified. "I am dreadfully scared. There is a chill in the air—"

She remains motionless, her obstinate, sylvan face bent backwards, staring into space, in the attitude of one who listens for a call from a long distance.

"Don't get excited, child," Aunt Gertrude suggests, with the mild and cruel superiority of a sage. "No matter what the day is it always ends the same way, no matter what happens in the year the year always ends one day."

"The air is full of sordid mysteries," whispers the younger one, withdrawing into her ominous trance as into a cave. "Private Williams .... The mute expression in his eyes—He had never seen a naked woman till he watched Eleonora Penderton .... The Captain's wife, you must know, feared neither man, beast, nor devil; hence all the lively gossip among the ladies of the post ."

"Oh, yes, Thank you." Aunt Gertrude seems slightly irritated. "What you just said about 'neither beast nor devil' sounds rather feeble. Oh yes. Kind of Ibsen-like. So that is the way it sounds. Reminds me of Hedda Gabler. *Femme fatale*. What a bore. Not at all the kind of thing a young person should write in the twentieth century. For the twentieth century is not the nineteenth century. Not at all. Of course not."

Young Carson, absorbed in her own vision, continues, stubborn and ecstatic: "The air is charged with age-old vices—atavistic trends .... Jealousy, hatred, desire, parricidal obsessions—you can feel them, smell them, taste them—even in the stable. Mrs. Penderton, an indomitable Amazon, is dynamic enough to master Firebird, that terrific horse. But look!—she has bitten her lower lip quite through; there is blood on her sweater and shirt. Blood—everywhere ... murder, madness, decay .... What a delightful place is the military post in peacetime!"

"Yes. Of course. Not at all." Aunt Gertrude is increasingly annoyed by the macabre vivacity of her young companion. "I prefer Ida. Of course I do. Definitely. Why should everybody talk about Ida. Why not. Dear Ida."

"Oh, those lugubrious dinner parties at the Pendertons!" the delicate niece exclaims dreamily. "The Langdons and the Pendertons, all four of them squatting around the table; all four of them doomed; on the verge of actual lunacy. Private Williams watches the whole set-up from outside. Major Langdon finally becomes nervous, leaves the room and cuts off the tender nipples of her breasts with garden shears."

"How utterly ludicrous!" cries the white-haired lady, half-irked and half-amused. "With garden shears! What a joke! Her tender nipples! Think of it! Oh yes! Thank you!"

"I will kill you," the girl says in a strangled voice, looking very pugnacious, very frail, very young. "I will do it!"

"Oh, no you won't," the white-haired one assures her, full of merriment and confidence. "Of course not. How utterly amusing. Why should you! You have so much talent. So why should you do such a foolish thing?"

"Do you think I have talent?" the young visionary asks eagerly.

"Oh course you have," shrieks the gay old girl. "Obviously so. A terrific lot of it. Undoubtedly. Silly child."

"I wonder if I ought to believe you," says the infant prodigy, wide-eyed, with a faint, musing smile. Then she gives her companion a swift, searching glance. "Of course, you are an experienced woman," she admits respectfully, though not without hesitation. "A real *femme de lettres*. Much more capable as a critic, I should say, than as a creative writer. Your little book on Picasso was full of delightful things. But *Ida* falls short of your essays. Why do you want to seem so primitive? A highly articulate person who tries to talk like a baby! Frankly, your fairy-tale trick is a trifle embarrassing."

"And how about you?" grins Aunt Gertrude. "Are you so sure that you are not embarrassing, and even more than just a trifle, with your childlike gravity and complicated inventions? An inspired youth that tries to talk like a hard-boiled psychologist! Why do you want to seem so sophisticated? You are always at your best in describing the sky, or landscape, or animals, or the emotions of very primitive beings, such as Private Williams. The Private is unforgettable but the Captain's wife is a joke. What do you know about Mrs. Penderton, or about her lover, or about her husband? But for some queer reason you *do* know something about Private Williams; just as you knew something about the deaf-mutes in your first novel. Those lovely deaf-mutes. Oh yes. There, you had an uncanny insight. Something very enchanting. Very frightening. Yes. So you should write about those enchanting and frightening things. Not about the Captain's wife. So you should write about savage things. New things. Sad things. So you should write about American things. Not this nineteenth century stuff. With the garden shears! Many funny things happened to Ida. Dear Ida. But nothing *that* ridiculous. Naturally not."

"But you have your own little mannerisms yourself," Carson quietly observes.

Aunt Gertrude has a good laugh. "Plenty of them," she admits cheerfully. "But that's a different matter. Entirely. My job is done. I have done my work. And you just begin it. So it is of course different. Of course it is. All I have to do—having done my job—is to stick to my little habits as a peasant sticks to his superstitions. To stick to familiar eccentricities. People need regularity. A certain regularity. Something they can depend on. So do I. Something trustworthy. While everything crumbles. Something cosy. In the midst of general turmoil, I am a rock of Gibraltar. I am a very conservative person. So that is the way I am. Very conservative. Oh yes."

The fragile *enfant terrible* touches the hand of the older woman with a bit of timid tenderness. "Yes, there is something infinitely cosy about you. One always knows what you are going to do next; that makes your like so wonderful. Now you will say ."

"*Thank you*," Aunt Gertrude says, bowing majestically. "But I wonder what *you* are going to say next, strange little creature you are! Kind of incalculable, I suppose…. Your next book will be a masterpiece, something overwhelming—or something completely absurd. As for *Reflections in a Golden Eye*, it is an attractive mixture of both."

"Never mind," Carson giggles, suddenly casting off her dignity and capering about like a nervous imp. "*Ida* isn't so hot either, sweet cosy Aunt! But I like you. You are lots of fun."

"I know I am." Aunt Gertrude looks more stolid than ever, half like an elderly matron, half like a wandering sorcerer; at once grim and serene, with a bovine, weather-worn, generous face. "Naturally I am. Because I am having fun always. So that is why I am fun. Because funny things happen to me. The funny things of the twentieth century. Yes."

She keeps taking vigorous, majestic strides, finding her way without difficulty in the midst of the spooky darkness. Carson, however, has transformed herself into a tiny will-o'-the-wisp, hovering, fluttering, giggling among the bushes and trees. What a wan and attractive light!—wavering and intense, oversensitive, savage, charming and corruptible. The experienced aunt watches her with apprehensive admiration. "Stop this monkey business, child!" she shouts. "You might fall! You'll break your neck! You'd better be careful, or you will go astray. This is tricky ground, kind of swampy, too and the abyss is not far! Don't take a chance, crazy kid! We still need you! Who do you think you are?" thunders the gallant veteran of so many intellectual adventures, the tireless discoverer of authentic talents and amusing fakes. "An elf? A whirlwind? A psychological problem? Not at all, darling. Of course not. You are something much more vulnerable and more important. You are a poet, Carson McCullers. So if you destroy yourself, you destroy a poet. You deprive the twentieth century of a bit of poetry—if you destroy yourself.

"So then you have the unfathomable heart of a poet. Yes. The intricate splendor. Of course. The madness. The golden eye.

"So then you have the golden eye of the poet.

"(But the title of your books sounds affected.)

"A poet.

"Yes.

"Thank you."

"Thank God."

Decision, May 1941.

Reviews of *Wars I Have Seen* (1945)

"The Importance of Being Earnest."

Ben Ray Redman

In February, 1943, Gertrude Stein was warned by a friendly lawyer in Belley that she and Alice Toklas should leave France for Switzerland if they wished to avoid a concentration camp. The frontier was closed, but it could be arranged for them to pass by fraud. Miss Stein said she would have to talk it over with her friend. They did talk it over, and Miss Stein concluded the discussion by declaring: "No, I am not going we are not going, it is better to go regularly wherever we are sent than to go irregularly where nobody can help us if we are in trouble, no I said, they are always trying to get us to leave France but here we are and here we stay." And stay they did, and they did not go to a concentration camp; and this book is the result and the story of their staying.

It is a good book, a very good book, and it would be a great pity if any readers were put off it by Gertrude Stein's reputation for willful obscurity and nonsensicality. For this book makes sense, all the way through. It makes sense sentence by sentence, paragraph by paragraph, and page by page. The only difficulty it presents arises from the lack of standard punctuation—the reader is slowed in his reading because he has to do a certain amount of punctuating that the author has refused to do— but this is a minor trouble. Whether or not Miss Stein has gained much by causing the reader this particular trouble is another matter, and debatable. At least it must be admitted that she has gained an appearance, an appearance of continuous, almost seamless prose. But there is more to this continuity than mere appearance. There is a continuity of rhythm and rhythms, a continuity that is tuneless but sometimes also a little tiring, a little soporific, like the very different rhythms of Swinburne's verse; and the reader must be on his guard against it, and be more alert with Miss Stein than he would be with an author who breathed less tirelessly, and did not go on and on, and on and on, like an indefatigable talker, a talker capable of talking down even George Moore, capable of talking him down and of talking him right out of the house. But if one is careful with these rhythms, one is repaid. One sees that Miss Stein could not have said just what she had to say, as effectively as she has said it, without these rhythms, or without the repetitions she loves and with which she emphatically scores. That she lets herself be led by the nose by rhyme, because of her fondness for rhyming prose, that she allows an easy rhyme to shape her sentences as she sometimes does, is perhaps censurable; but this too is debatable, and here too there is reason in what she does, for her trick of rhyme often punches home a thought, as did the old playwright's trick when they tagged a blank verse scene with a tight and clinking couplet.

Whatever else may be said of it, Gertrude Stein's prose is now a mature, flexible, wonderfully useful instrument. And its clarity is of crystal when she wishes it to be. It is highly individual, of course, but so is every other prose style that has ever mattered in the history of literature. When anyone asks, as people do ask, why she doesn't say what she has to say in ordinary language, one can reply only with a question and demand what is meant by ordinary language. The language of Swift? Or Carlyle? Of Hemingway or of Faulkner or of Yeats? But each of these languages, in its own way, departs from the ordinary (Miss Stein herself having assisted in the Hemingway departure). The language of Edna Ferber? Or of Louis

Bromfield? Or of the latest and slickest short story the biggest and slickest magazine has most recently published? At this point the reduction to absurdity is plain; the question ceases to have meaning. Of course, Gertrude Stein cannot write in ordinary language, any more than can any other writer who is not ordinary. She can write only in her own language, and succeed or fail in the doing of it. In the past, perhaps wilfully, she has often failed to communicate, and it was either her misfortune or her fun, depending upon her intention. In this book she does communicate, she is gravely intent on communication; her success is complete, and it is our good fortune as well as hers. Let me insist again that it is a good fortune that should be missed by no reader because of prejudice, no matter how broad the base that Miss Stein may have furnished for that prejudice.

What was it like to live in France during the German occupation? *Wars I Have Seen* does not answer that question. No single book could answer it. But this book does do perfectly the job it is meant to do. It tells us what it was like to be Gertrude Stein and to live in France, in the country, in the department of the Aix close to the border of Savoy, during the German occupation. It tells us what was like from the summer of 1943 until the coming of the Americans in the autumn of 1944. It tells us as a journal would tell us, for this is what the book really is, although it has not been printed as a journal and the dates are few. It is a journal that covers rather more than a year, with a few backward glances for the purposes of furnishing background and establishing a point of view. It is a continuous, thoughtful monologue, that keeps pace with the present as it comes into being and becomes the past; it is a monologue packed with anecdotes, with what the author herself happily calls good stories. It is always today in this book, although other days are of course mentioned from time to time. We, writer and readers, are always moving forward with today as it reaches towards, but always just fails to turn into, tomorrow. Things are always changing, thoughts are always changing; particularly ideas about the war and when it will be over, or when it will not. For example, everyone knows, in the summer of 1943, that the war will be over any day; whereas, in the winter of '43-'44, everyone knows that it will probably last forever.

The anecdotes and the stories all and each have their meaningful places in the monologue, for one by one, and together in accumulation, they tell us what it was like to be Gertrude Stein and to live under the Germans; and they also tell us what Gertrude Stein thought it was like to be someone else, many other people, and to live under the Germans. What it was to belong to the families of young men who were prisoners, for example, or to be among those whose sons were being rounded up for work-camps in Germany; or to see one's menfolk taking to the mountains. Or to be, oneself, young and French and male in the time of great troubles.

The monologue continues:—on the differences between this war and the last; on the death of the nineteenth century, that is happening only now in the 1940s (Germany is still trying to cling to the nineteenth century, but we are filling it with dead); on Jews and industrialism (since the rise of industrialism, they have been small potatoes in the world's money markets); on the efficiency of secret service agents in peacetime and their futility in wartime (Miss Stein's knowledge of this subject may be a bit limited); on the historical role of Pétain in connection with the French armistice (Miss Stein's judgment of the old Marshal will cause many red hackles of prejudices to rise in fury, but I am willing to wager that history itself will substantiate her view); on the behavior of Germans in victory and defeat; on Hitler and the theory that he willed the destruction of Germany because he was an Austrian in his heart, just as Napoleon willed the destruction of France because he was an Italian; on unconditional surrender; on the ending of belief in progress and evolution and peace (all nineteenth century credos, now dead or dying with the death of that century); on French productiveness in the matter of food and French recalcitrance in the matter of discipline, even when rules are backed by German bullets; on eating during wartime, on eating well in wartime, on having at times almost too much of everything to eat in wartime.

The monologue goes on, and now and again the words take dancing precedence of the sense, without taking leave of sense, to the obvious delight of Miss Stein, who loves words and the sounds of words and the patterns of words, and to the delight of those who are glad that she remains true to her own literary nature while doing her utmost in the matter of honest communication .... The monologue goes on, until it ends in a climax of emotional, patriotic satisfaction with the arrival of American soldiers in Belley, on the 1st of September, 1944. And as it goes on, the reader, or at least this reader, becomes increasingly sure of what he has long suspected: that the great virtue of Gertrude Stein, who is popularly known as an obscure and difficult author, is her simplicity, her amazing, utter simplicity. Few writers have ever dared to be, or have ever been able to be, as simple as she. As simple as a child, pointing straight, going straight to the heart of a subject, to its roots; pointing straight, when and where adults would take a fancier way than pointing, because they had learned not to point. Borrowing that simplicity, if only for a moment, let me say again that this is a good book, a very good book.

The Saturday Review, March 10, 1945.

"Gertrude Stein's Wars."

Delmore Schwartz

It is a long way from "Toasted Susie is my ice cream," a famous and representative example of Miss Stein's middle style, to the subject of her new book, *Wars I Have Seen*, Miss Stein's direct experience of the Nazi occupation of France. Yet Miss Stein has made the long journey without losing any of her possessions or prepossessions, her prose rhythm, her affectation, her common sense, her complacency, her fascination with herself, or her love of unqualified generalization about the inner essence of anything and everything.

This book was begun during the early part of the occupation, when the German victory seemed overwhelming, and thus there is a mounting excitement as the book continues until finally the G. I.s arrive to discuss geography with Miss Stein, to take her for a ride in a jeep, to tell her that she is read in public schools in America, and to show her how different they are from older generations in America.

In between Miss Stein's studio *obiter dicta* a clear picture of the anxiety and the terror of the occupation comes through. There is even a moment when Miss Stein feels that "this kind of war is funny it is awful but it does make it all unreal, really unreal." Miss Stein does not understand this war or the other wars she has lived through. But who does? Her mind triumphs in her effort to understand war and peace in terms of the *mystique* of the *avant-garde of* Picasso's youth. Through her anecdotes and her observations her prose rhythm asserts itself like an unbroken sea, saying more than any statement can about the beautiful serenity, wakefulness, and egotism of her being. Hence even when she performs such feats of pure irrelevance as the thought that wars may have as their cause the presence of kings named George on the British throne, she remains delightful, full of intuition and self-indulgence, full of pleasure and truth, writing as if she might write and the reader might read forever, an assumption which shows the essential bond between genius and courage.

The Nation, March 24, 1945.

"*Matron's Primer.*"

Djuna Barnes

For a number of years, Gertrude Stein has been read with considerable consternation, admiration and annoyance. This book, like the earlier *Autobiography of Alice B. Toklas* is comprehensible. I remain uneasy as to the validity of the medium.

Thrown off by the "happy idiot" simplifications, the baby-like repetition, I am come to the conclusion that, in spite of its place and its time in history, and willingly acknowledging its many acute observations, the very thing which her devotees praise, though they would be the first to deny it, is her flowing sentimentality.

It is not the sentimentality of the Irish school of Synge, who is the only other writer I can think of at the moment who is as easy to copy. Neither is it the "tough" American style that weeps with its jaw set; it is an entirely personal oil that Miss Stein has invented to make the sliding more comfortable. This book is said to be an account of the Nazi occupation; it is the occupation of Miss Gertrude Stein, technique in hand.

Now any trick which works exempts the user from the exactions of the intentional; it saves labor and it pleases, but it also makes less valuable the work so constructed. It has kept Miss Stein from being taken seriously. It has saved her from meaning the things she says. Synge was taken seriously because he was not only earnest, but he was traditional in so far as he was Irish. At this point Miss Stein might refer to her own remark that there is nothing else to be but "personal" now that the nineteenth century is dead and the twentieth not real—a second Eve placed in a dead garden. That might be well enough if Miss Stein were a new girl in a new situation. She is not, she is a matron who has written a primer which she intends to take home. A primer (for old people at least) should be a dedicated absence, an informed omission.

This same quality is responsible for what has been called her "courage and resourcefulness" in remaining in France. I might add that it is also responsible for her style, a sort of static flight—she can be nudged, she cannot be hurried. You do not feel that she is ever really worried about the sorrows of the people; her concern at its highest pitch is a well-fed apprehension. She says well-fed people—that is, people who love their food as the French do—never lose wars; the Germans lose wars because their food is awful.

And there is her lack of modesty; it makes her stubborn, as a caryatid would be had it eaten the house it was intended to support. Perhaps she was started in the direction of genius—she put her foot down on that just as she put her foot down on removal from Culoz; like elderly gentlemen out on a stroll, seeing a hoop rolling toward them, put stop to its destination. She is entirely "Oh dear and a pleasure."

She tells a great deal that one wants to know about the French people during the past years of war and of occupation: their squabbling tireless endurance—"France does so naturally rise from the ashes"; their delightful economy in managing to make the Germans feel absent by just staring through them. They go about the business of their lives even when they are not allowed to have guns to shoot the eagles in their air, the eagles that are eating their chickens up; there is their admiration for modern machinery but their wisdom about the flail: "if wheat is thrashed by flail some of it can get kept, can get hidden and get eaten .... it makes it middle ages and secret." A machine would be easily seen.

The description of nature, of animals, of birds, and of the mountains and the going up and the coming down of the mountain boys, the *Marquis,* are those of a painter. And she tells how they were all proud, and afraid and annoyed; she talks of the prophecy of Saint Odile, who did indeed seem to have everything foretold; she reflects on the status of gold: "It is the thing that has no possibility of being useful that is mystic." And she does so want to see the Americans come. And finally they do come.

These soldiers she says are better than the soldiers of the first, for they are sober and now instead of just telling stories they can converse; instead of being completely drunk all of the time they now go quietly about their business.

Later, sometime in April, at a meeting of the Red Cross Club, she takes it all back. She berates them for not laughing, not "even at the little children"—she finds it shameful. They don't even take a vacation and get a bit spotty. She even tells them that she and Picasso (she always says "me" even when bringing in Shakespeare) are geniuses. I take it she is ready to be amused, and that they have not amused her. I should like to keep the book, but she always takes her writing away.

Contemporary Jewish Record, June 1945.

Reviews of *Brewsie and Willie* (1946)

"Let Them Talk and Talk."

C. G. Paulding

Willie is all right for a name but Brewsie is a wee coy bit peculiar when you are reading *Brewsie and Willie* in the subway somebody might say to you be your age because you certainly don't look as if you were age ten and you ought to be able to spell out the words even in a newspaper. The words in a newspaper they are easy and there are no troubles in them, "my gracious, my good gracious and no worries. Oh my good gracious, oh my good gracious and no worries, my good gracious." That is Brewsie talking to Willie, to Brock, to Jo, his G. I. friends and to the "fatter and younger" Red Cross nurse who is Pauline and very "cute." She has a whole chapter to herself, Chapter Fifteen.

It has become at last possible to write about a book by Gertrude Stein because nobody in his senses thinks any more that she is a joke. Some people of course will think that Chapter Fifteen is funny and they will think that it has been put here out of context in order to make sure that they will think that it is funny, but really it is here so that whoever thinks it is funny can think so quickly without wasting time because it is so short, and then can look at it again and notice with what perfection the rhythm of this interchange is rendered. Rewrite this passage using punctuation the way it is taught in the schools and see how flat it becomes when it loses its extraordinarily sensitive and deliberate timing. The phrase, "What makes you cry, said Willie, well the way…" brought in with a capital letter for the eye, but after a comma as sufficient pause, and avoiding the reintroduction of Pauline, is as close as the ear can get, not to stenography, but to the rhythm of thought. I think this passage, selected at random, can be read again and again with growing appreciation of the masterful and musical curve it describes.

Of course that is the trouble. If you have a whole book, no matter how short (this one is only 114 pages) which has to be read as carefully as you would read a poem, you simply don't read the book that way. It is not a question of difficulty either in form or in subject matter. In some of Miss Stein's earlier work the difficulty in subject matter was simply the difficulty of finding any interest in the subject matter; there was never any difficulty in the form if once you were prepared to follow the indications of comma or period or the lack of both, if you were willing to read at the cadence clearly indicated by the punctuation. Miss Stein's thinking is not difficult in the sense that Mallarmé is difficult; when she wrote her book about the French under German occupation the subject matter and her own emotions were extremely simple; the form there was close to the action and to the description and it presented no difficulty. The difficulty, however, always remained in that book as in all her other books and it is always the same: it is most trying to have to submit to the discipline of her cadences.

In *Brewsie and Willie* there is, it seems to me, a special and very interesting difficulty which comes from the artist's choice. Gracious, goodness gracious, oh my goodness gracious how American Miss Stein has remained in her heart. This intellectual, trained in medicine, living abroad for years and years, experimenting with words, drawing her interest in words form her scientific turn of mind and from Rimbaud, Mallarmé and all sort of Frenchmen who take the technique of writing so seriously, this friend of all experimentation and of Picasso, suddenly began traveling round in airplanes and jeeps from one American army base to another, listening, listening and listening to the talk of "the boys." "G .I.s and G. I.s and G. I.s and they have made me come all over patriotic. I was always patriotic, I was always in my way a Civil War veteran, but in between, there were other things, but now there are no other things." That is what she says and it is true. So that when she wanted to write down what the G.I.s had said to her, she did not write as if she were a foreigner, she renounced every kind of clear intellectual judgment from outside, she did not make a cold description of these youth wandering round Europe after the fighting was over and not even knowing in what country they were, noticing practically nothing of what was round them. She let them do the talking; she let them do the worrying. All by themselves, without very much help from her, except that she hates industrialism and men who are employee-minded and so perhaps the G.I.s talk a little more about these subjects than they would have done if she had not been there with them.

Brewsie was the great worrier. In chapter after chapter it is Brewsie who starts out worrying about what it will be like to go home. Brewsie is the worrier for all the G.I.s in the book; he is their delegate to do the worrying.

Little by little the others get started worrying too, until at the end: "Where is the man who talks, said Pauline? They won't let him talk any more, said Willie. Who won't let them talk any more, said Janet, the officers? Oh dear no, said Willie, it's all the guys, they found out from listening to it and that is the feeling you have about this book. The themes are the themes of their worries, but they stay worried; they know that they want to say something; they know that somebody has to say something and that they had better say it before they get middle-aged because there is nothing worse than to have a country run by the middle-aged; but they don't quite know what to say in order to be each one himself. They are afraid that they will always, all their lives sound all alike. "I guess job men just have to articulate alike; they got to articulate yes or no to their bosses, and yes or no to their unions, they just got to articulate alike, and when you begin to articulate alike, you got to drop thinking out, just got to drop it out, you can go on feeling different but you got to articulate the same Gallup poll, yes you do…"

So that Miss Stein has to sum it all up in a last chapter she has kept for herself because when Brewsie or Willie, Brock or Jo, Pauline or Janey, is doing the talking it may be wonderful the way it is undoubtedly in Chapter Fifteen, but it does not get you anywhere at all—except to show what they all were worrying about and that is how, when you have to have a job, you can, or you cannot make it possible to feel as an individual and that means stay free.

In the last chapter Miss Stein has one phrase that tells what she has attempted. She is not talking about her work; she is telling one of the things Americans have to do: it was all too simple; it was all yes or no; it has always been too simple: produce until you get into prosperity and then into depression. But now, Miss Stein says "you have to really learn to express complication…" Yes you do.

The Commonweal, August 2, 1946.

"Gerty and the G. I.s"

Robert S. Warshow

The chief thing Gertrude Stein tried to do was write as if she had kept her innocence. Everything had to be seen simply and sharply, as a new thing and a wonder. If the vision was direct enough, it did not matter whether it was profound: she was not trying to make progress. That is why she could write so much that was nonsense and so much that was banal ("… the girls tend to be tall, taller than they used to be but not the boys not taller than they used to be, I suppose there is a physical reason for this, I do suppose so") and still be a fine artist.

She had to leave America, where the pressures of middle-class earnestness were too strong; she had to work very hard with the language, and cultivate her egotism to follow her own way strictly, shutting out many of the important intellectual currents of her time that meant much to others but had nothing to do with her purpose —so that when she was successful she could write like a twelve-year-old girl full of intelligent and sensitive curiosity and very brilliant, more brilliant than any girl ever was at twelve. (Twelve is about right, I think: all the essential knowledge has been gained, but the adult world of sex and misfortune and ideas is still part mystery and part stupidity).

Her relations with the people of the United States were not quite like those of any other bohemian expatriate. She aroused considerable irritation—you are not supposed to go and live your own life in France while the rest of us must stick it out with the Book-of-the-Month Club and the American Labor Party—but in the end hundreds of American soldiers who had never read her books sought her out in France and called her "Gerty" and found her a great old girl. For her part, though she could not live in America she was always very seriously concerned with America and with being American, and she was certainly very happy to see the soldiers and to find that they had heard of her.

Brewsie and Willie is the result of that curious lovers' meeting between her and the American soldiers after the invasion of France. She formed a very high opinion of the soldiers—they were sure of themselves, she wrote in *Wars I Have Seen*, no longer provincial as they were in the last war—and in *Brewsie and Willie* she tried to set down what they were like and what she herself had to say to them, in a number of conversations among soldiers, and to her countrymen in general.

Her private world here got mixed up with our public world, and it is fair to say of *Brewsie and Willie* what it would not have been fair to say of the more personal *Wars I Have Seen*: that she did not look deep enough or think hard enough.

Her soldiers are very real in the things that concern them—jobs, morals, security, the threatening of the future—and in the way they talk, outwardly relaxed and inwardly worried, fumbling earnestly for answers, painfully conscious of their own inadequacies. ("Listen, said Brewsie, you see, said

Brewsie, you see I don't think we think, if we thought we could not articulate the same, we couldn't have Gallup polls and everybody answer yes or no, if you think it's more complicated than that ... thinking is funnier and more mixed than that ... oh Willie, I get so worried, I know it is just the most dangerous moment in our history, in a kind of a way as dangerous more dangerous than the Civil War ...") But their decency is too pure, and they are more honest in their thinking and more childlike in their attitudes than most Americans really are; she saw that they sucked candy and tried hard to get things straight in their minds, but she did not see how knowing and cynical they could be also, and how acquisitive and cruel. She endowed them with her own innocence—but Gertrude Stein's innocence was a literary method for the creation of Gertrude Stein's world, and in giving her innocence to the soldiers, whom she had made quite recognizable and *public*, she was patronizing them and distorting them. "G.I.s and G.I.s and G.I.s and they have made me come all over patriotic"—she fell in love, and she allowed herself to be taken in by the myth of a special American decency and good-heartedness.

And there is her final message to Americans at this moment "most dangerous in our history": Don't forget the country's raw materials. Learn to be individuals. Find why there was a depression. Worry hard and think hard. This is sound advice—except that the raw materials seem to have preyed upon her mind unduly—but I hope it is not ill-natured to say that it doesn't help much. It was said of Gertrude Stein's art that she paid too little attention to the serious preoccupations of her time; in politics she was ill and uninformed—she could apologize for Pétain and the good-natured and unintelligent *bourgeoises*.

The funniest thing is that in reading *Brewsie and Willie* one even feels a twinge of that unreasonable philistine indignation she aroused so often when she deserved it less. For that has escaped again worry and think, she said, and then by expatriating herself so effectively this time we might hope to reach her with our murmur: yes, that's what we *have* been doing, worrying and thinking.

The New Republic, October 5, 1946.

Reviews of *Selected Writings of* Gertrude *Stein* (1946)

"A Wonderchild for 72 Years."

Leo Lerman

Once upon a time a child, Gertrude, was born in Allegheny, Pa., which later became Pittsburgh, U.S.A. And this child, Gertrude, was born in many places for seventy-two years—Vienna, Austria; Paris, France; Oakland and San Francisco, California; Boston, Massachusetts; Baltimore, Maryland; Florence, Italy. She died on July 27, 1946 in Paris, France. But doubtlessly she had died in many places before. It is almost impossible to live without dying, and Gertrude lived all the time she was living. No Gertrude was a wonderchild. She was a wonderchild in all the places in which she was born and died and lived, and she was a wonderchild in places in which she had never been and of which she had probably never heard. But they all heard of her because she was this wonderchild—oh yes. Most of all she was a wonderchild in Paris, France, where also in and about she went to live in 1903 and where she lived almost always. There and everywhere she was also an *enfant terrible*—meaning a bully. What she said went, because she knew that she knew. If you did not know that she knew, you went. She would brook no interference and not a no. Lots of people came and some stayed, but sooner or later almost everybody went. Of course, some came back. But with this child, who had the look of an ageless, very wise peasant woman, everything was forever, everything was permanent, everything was everything, but she was she and that meant she was first person singular always. Sometimes she was generous with her first person singular. But always she was so explicitly first person singular that you said yes—or else!

Once she met a girl, Alice B. Toklas. She took her into her first person singular so completely that she later wrote *The Autobiography of Alice B. Toklas*, and many people read it because it became a best seller because many people read it. And almost everyone was delighted because it was quite easy to understand and so almost everyone understood it and they were pleased because now they could be among the initiate, too. There's nothing people like so much as to be among the initiate. But ever so many who read it said which is which—which is Gertrude, which is Alice B.? And some of them never did find out, nor did it matter. And she wrote it in six weeks because she had been her whole life preparing it, because a genuinely created and creative work does not spring out just like that but has to be simmering inside for years. And she bought herself a new eight-cylinder Ford car "and the most expensive coat made to order by Hermes and fitted by the man who makes horse covers for race horses, for Basket the white poodle and two collars studded for Basket. I had never made any money before."

So the next year which was 1934 she came back to America because this was the year for her opera *Four Saints in Three Acts*, and this was the year for her lecturing and seeing America and hearing it and inhaling it and not especially feeling it more than all those years in Paris, France, and elsewhere because she always felt it intensely. She always felt America. She was America. Meaning: she had an abiding sense of fun, she was an energist; she was the biggest, the best; she was an evangelist; she was all past but even more future. She was sentimental. She was real. She was decided. She was shrewd. And, of course, she was a wonderchild. That's America. That's being an American. She wrote all about being Americans in *The Making of Americans*, which is enormous, almost one thousand pages, and there is quite a lot of it in these *Selected Writings of*. She wrote all about being American in almost everything she wrote whether it was all about Picasso or Matisse or Melanctha Herbert (which last year Richard Wright has called "the first long serious treatment of Negro life in the United States").

And so this is all about Gertrude's first person singular again but this time it is all about everyone's dream world, everyone understanding, of course, that there are two dream worlds, both real, and the problem is to coincide them and then you are adjusted. Gertrude coincided her dream worlds: she was adjusted. She was so well adjusted that sometimes people couldn't stand it, and they tried, if they dared to maladjust her, but all they did was maladjust themselves. She was as incorruptible as Gibraltar, but tone is no longer impervious, so there is nothing to compare but herself to herself. No one could distract her from herself. Not even the Nazis could dislodge her from France and not even the G.I.s could do anything except love her, so they did that. Everyone is interested in personality. She was personality. Everyone wants to partake of being alive, and the moment you heard of her or saw her you knew she was alive—living. Everyone wants to escape into a dream. She was living in a dream. She was truer than history, more like fiction. Fairytales are fiction, which means fiction and fairytales are dreams. E. M. Forster said it not thinking about her but saying it and it is about her because she was never as dim as most people are dim in "real" life.

So this source of strength, this deep well of wisdom, this grandmother was a wonderchild for seventy-two years, an authentic wonderchild. That meant she was a prodigy and she behaved accordingly and was fawned upon and never fawned. And in Paris she met and stopped meeting and met again all the great because she was she and they were great and she made them great. Paris just before 1914 and until 1938 or so was the place to meet and be great, so it was obviously the place for her to be great and American and a catalytic agent. Even people who have never heard of genius are its heirs. Then there are the ones she influenced or circumscribed directly—the ones who sat around her in her beautiful rooms, the ones who wrote because she was and the ones who painted because she was. And on and off they included all the bright young men. There was Hemingway with whom "she quarreled," and to whom she once said something like, "Remarks are not criticism, Ernest." And there was Picasso. But almost from the first there was Picasso and they were two *enfants terribles*, and they got on famously even when they did not get on and together, between them they practically invented today in literature and painting .

Now sometimes Gertrude, the wonderchild, spoke right out and it was lucid. Everyone understood immediately. But sometimes she sang away more for herself than for others. She made up rhythms and said words, holding them up individually—beautiful pebbles found accidentally on some obscure beach—even the most populated shore is obscure to eyes which do not see .... Lots laughed and laughed and said, "It's a joke! It's a racket! (Sinclair Lewis said that) She's crazy!" But some could see with their ears and smell with their eyes and taste with their whole selves. And they knew what she was saying and that it was important. What she had to say was: examine language—take up words as you would beautiful objects. Look at words. Listen to words. Have they shape, color? What do they say without context? Do you see these words. Words are words. But some people never knew what she was talking about, and, of course, sometimes they couldn't have known because when a child makes up songs or phrases you can't know what he's talking about all the time even if the child's a prodigy. Children speak a shorthand all their own. They lead curious and elaborately real interior lives. There were things published which probably shouldn't have been published until a definitive edition. But after all it's because she was difficult that everyone eventually came to hear about her.

So now she has departed but she is here and everyone who writes will be more explicit because of her writing both intelligibly and unintelligibly. An now she is historical in *Selected Writings of Gertrude Stein*. All wonderchildren love publicity and to be immortalized because they know that they deserve it—who else does? So she was very pleased when she knew that this *Selected Writings of* was happening, and she wrote to Carl Van Vechten who was doing it. "I always wanted to be historical, from almost a baby on, I felt that way about it, and Carl was one of the earliest ones that made me be certain that this was going to be." And she is. But more than historical or a force or a catalytic agent or a wonderchild or a grandmother or a semanticist or an experimental writer or a publicist or a woman, she was a philosopher being faithful to herself. William James, it is said, considered her his most brilliant pupil. And, after all, he was one of the founders of pragmatism. She studied medicine for four years at Johns Hopkins. She believed in continuity, and that everything was everything all the time. And she believed that she would inevitably get what she wanted. She did. She wanted people to see, especially to see her way. Captain Edmund Geller, her escort on her venture into Belgium at the end of this last war, said to Carl Van Vechten, "Whenever she spoke she was frank and even belligerent. She made the G. I.s awful mad, but she also made them think and many ended in agreement with her." And that's about it: she made many mad and many thought her ridiculous and a phony, but she made everyone, with any sense, think. Now I have written all about *Selected Writings of Gertrude Stein* and all the writing of Gertrude Stein this way because to write about her means to enter right into her first person singular. This is not a formal criticism nor a parody, but it is about the *Selected Writing of* which Carl Van Vechten edited so lovingly and to which he wrote such interesting notes and from which he omitted *Paris France* and the whole body of *Picasso* both of which I love. Now *Picasso* is a real omission because it says more about art and artists than any other document I know and it says it irrefutably in fifty pages. But as Gertrude wrote in her little note, "And now I am pleased here are the selected writings and naturally I wanted more, but I will and can say that all that are here are those that I wanted the most, thanks and thanks again."

The Saturday Review, November 2, 1946.

"Briefly Noted: 'Selected Writings of Gertrude Stein.'"

Anonymous

The contents of this collection of Gertrude Stein could not have been better chosen and presented. It includes *Tender Buttons*, "Melanctha," and the whole of *The Autobiography of Alice B. Toklas*, as well as some excerpts from *The Making of Americans*, the last chapter and the epilogue of *Wars I Have Seen*, and varieties of shorter pieces, some of them from books that have gone out of print. Every phase of the author's style, from the queerest to the most limpid, is represented, and every period of her career. Mr. Van Vechten has made it possible for new readers to become easily acquainted with the work of this eccentric and remarkable woman and for old readers to get a well-rounded view of it. To start at the beginning and go through this volume, skipping, if they bore you, the parts that seem opaque, might be one of the best ways to read Gertrude Stein. There is a foreword by Miss Stein, written just before her death.

The New Yorker, November 9, 1946.

"Gertrude Stein, Writer or Word Scientist?"

Malcolm Cowley

Gertrude Stein, even more than Joyce, was a writer who carried the scientific spirit and the experimental method into literature. At Radcliffe (1893-97), where she worked under Münsterberg and William James, she was much more interested in psychology than in poetry or fiction. At Johns Hopkins Medical School, under Llewelyn Barker, she learned how to sharpen a scalpel and began a comparative study of the brain tracts. She proved to be such a skillful dissector of corpses that the faculty nearly gave her a medical degree in spite of her boredom with and her ultimate refusal to learn anything about the treatment of living patients.

Almost all her writing shows the effect of her laboratory training; it is as if she continued to work in a white jacket. Her first book, *Three Lives,* which she finished in 1906 and published at her own expense three years later, is a sort of post-mortem report on three women, each of whom belonged to a different psychological and physical type. The report is a successful experiment in prose style and a masterpiece of understanding, but not of sympathy; one feels when reading it a second time that the three heroines have been carried off one after another to St. James Infirmary (I saw my baby there, stretched out on a long white table, so white, so cold, so bare).

Her second and longest book, *The Making of Americans,* which she wrote from 1906 to 1908, was intended in her own phrase to be a "history of every one who ever was or is or will be living." In somewhat clearer language we might say that she designated it as an account of the various psychological types that are embodied time and again in living persons, with examples chosen from Miss Stein's immediate family. She made some attempt at systematic classification, as in her college reports to William James; but she also made experiments in grammar that interfered with her other scientific purpose by drawing a veil of incomprehension or plain boredom between herself and the reader. *The Making of Americans* is, in fact, one of the hardest books to read from beginning to end that has ever been published.

We can trace her progress toward utter obscurity and halfway back again in the volume of *Selected Writings* that has just been edited by Carl Van Vechten. Here we find samples of all her different manners, from that of the early "Melanctha," most popular of her *Three Lives,* to a prefatory message for the present volume that is probably the last page she wrote for publication. The editor, an old friend of hers, has made a wise and—if we can apply the word to Miss Stein's writings—a rather conventional selection. It includes *The Autobiography of Alice B. Toklas* and *Tender Buttons,* both reprinted in full; long extracts from *The Making of Americans,* a dozen shorter pieces, among them "Miss Furr and Miss Skeene," *Four Saints* and "The Portrait of Mabel Dodge," and the long, almost ecstatic passage that serves as a conclusion to *Wars I Have Seen.*

The book is well bound, but printed on abominable paper. As for the text, Miss Stein approved of it. "And now I am pleased here are the selected writings," she said in her final message, "and naturally I wanted more, but I do and can say that all that are here are those that I wanted the most, thanks and thanks again." I have often wondered why no critic has made a systematic attempt to explain her, as so many critics have done with Joyce and Eliot. Perhaps those who started the task were lost in a fit of yawning. Miss Stein has written many commentaries on her own work, but these explanations badly need explaining. Mr. Van Vechten offers a few useful hints in his introduction and notes to the present volume. They are, however, nothing more than hints, and apparently he would rather admire than elucidate; they have no meaning, in the ordinary sense; they are simply words arranged into new patterns, just as an abstract painting is simply colors and forms. But other writings, even of her "difficult" period, do have a connection with her own experience, do convey, or at least conceal, meanings; and it is a pity that none of her close friends or admiring critics has tried to tell what she has meant to say.

About her method as opposed to her meaning, there is much that is fairly easy to explain. She began each of her stories or plays or portraits by having a pattern; then apparently she set down on paper anything within the pattern that happened to come into her mind. It was a method that had much in common with automatic writing; one notes with interest that during her early years she preferred to work late at night, when the subconscious mind is least repressed. Later she liked to work in crowds—for example, when sitting in an automobile parked on a busy street; that was another device for releasing the subconscious. She was sometimes unable to decipher her own rapid handwriting and had to ask her friend Miss Toklas to read it. Conscious writers rarely have that difficulty; they know and remember every word they set down.

Yet automatic writing was only one of Miss Stein's many experiments. Most of the others were not only conscious but scientific in their spirit. She worked with language as if it were a material offered for analysis in a chemical laboratory. Her two favorite technical procedures were concentration and elimination; she would concentrate on one quality of the words she used while eliminating other qualities; and she would thereby produce her effects, such as they were, in their purest chemical form.

She said in a footnote added to *Tender Buttons* when this group of prose poems was reprinted in *transition:* "It was my first conscious struggle with the problem of correlating sight, sound and sense, and eliminating rhythm; some of the solutions in it seem to me still all right, now I am trying grammar and eliminating sight and sound." At various stages in her career, she tried to eliminate from her writing not only rhythm, sight and sound, but also nouns, commas, history, philosophy and meaning in general. She has concentrated, at one time or another, on adverbs, present participles, nouns (she came back to them), words standing alone, words in patterns, repetitions, sentences—and it was a happy day for her readers when, very late in life, she rediscovered the paragraph.

Like Amy Lowell, who detested and feared her, she will live more in her remembered personality than in her works. The personality was warm, forthright, vastly conceited, but also strangely humble; the works are cold and a little arrogant in their disrespect for the reader. Even in the books she wrote for ordinary people, like *The Autobiography of Alice B. Toklas,* there is a curious absence of human emotions except vanity, a curious emphasis on what might be called the market value of the persons she describes: she weighs Matisse against Picasso against Whitehead against Gertrude Stein exactly like a diamond merchant weighing his next gem. It was only in her next-to-last book, *Wars I Have Seen,* that she had a real subject outside of herself, the captivity and liberation of a country she loved. It was only in her last book, *Brewsie and Willie*—she died with a copy of it clasped in each hand —that she desperately tried to communicate with an audience, to give them a message, and by then it was too late; her habit of being incomprehensible was too strong for her to overcome.

I think of her often not as a writer primarily but as a scientist in his laboratory working at some problem that apparently has no connection with man or society. It would be nothing so great as atomic fission; it would be something humbler like the anatomy of junebugs. Year after year he would go on working while the world outside his laboratory changed and new groups of students came to hear him lecture; then suddenly it would be found that one or more of his discoveries about junebugs could be applied to curing or prolonging human life. There is something of this unexpected effect about Gertrude Stein's researches into the qualities of words. With three or four exceptions, the books that record her experiments are unreadable; and yet they have exercised a wide influence on American writing, even in the popular magazines, because of their effect on authors who were friends of hers, like Sherwood Anderson and Ernest Hemingway. Her style is like a chemical useless in its pure state but powerful when added to other mixtures. American prose has changed its whole direction partly because of Gertrude Stein.

The New York Herald-Tribune Weekly Book Review, November 24, 1946.

2

Contemporary Commentary: Style, Influence, and the Debate over Stein's Purpose

"Speculations, or Post-Impressionism in Prose."

Mabel Dodge

Many roads are being broken today, and along these roads consciousness is pursuing truth to eternity. This is an age of communication, and the human being who is not a "communicant" is in the sad plight which the dogmatist defines as being a condition of spiritual non-receptivity.

Some of these newly opened roads lie parallel and almost touch.

In a large studio in Paris, hung with paintings by Renoir, Matisse and Picasso, Gertrude Stein is doing with words what Picasso is doing with paint. She is impelling language to induce new states of consciousness, and in doing so language becomes with her a creative art rather than a mirror of history.

In her impressionistic writing she uses familiar words to create perceptions, conditions, and states of being, never before quite consciously experienced. She does this by using words that appeal to her as having the meaning that they *seem* to have. She has taken the English language and, according to many people, has misused it, or has used it roughly, uncouthly and brutally, or madly, stupidly and hideously, but by her method she is finding the hidden and inner nature of nature.

To present her impressions she chooses words for their inherent quality, rather than for their accepted meaning.

Her habit of working is methodical and deliberate. She always works at night in the silence and brings all her will power to bear upon the banishing of preconceived images. Concentrating upon the impression she has received and which she wishes to transmit, she suspends her selective faculty, waiting for the word or group of words that will perfectly interpret her meaning, to rise from her sub-consciousness to the surface of her mind.

Then and then only does she bring her reason to bear upon them, examining, weighing and gauging their ability to express her meaning. It is a working proof of the Bergson theory of intuition. She does not go after words—she waits and lets them come to her, and they do.

It is only when art thus pursues the artist and his production will bear the mark of inevitability. It is only when the "*élan vital*" drives the artist to the creative overflow that life surges in his production. Vitality directed into a conscious expression is the modern definition of genius.

It is impossible to define or to describe fully any new manifestation in aesthetics or in literature that is as recent, as near to us, as the work of Picasso or of Gertrude Stein; the most that we can do is to suggest a little, draw a comparison, point the way and then withdraw.

To know about them is a matter of personal experience; no one can help another through it. First before thought must come feeling, and this is the first step toward experience, because feeling is the beginning of knowledge.

It does not greatly matter how the first impress affects one. One may be shocked, stunned and dismayed, or one may be aroused, stimulated, intrigued and delighted. That there has been an *approach* is what counts.

It is only in a state of indifference that there is no approach at all, and indifference reeks of death. It is the tomb of life itself.

A further consciousness than is already ours will need many new forms of expression. In literature everything that has been felt and known so far has been said as it has been said.

What more there may be for us to realize must be expressed in a new way. Language has been crystalized into four or five established literary forms that up to the present day have been held sacred and intranscendant, but all the truth cannot be contained in any one or in any limited number of molds …. This is so of all the arts, for of course what is true of one must, to be justifiable, be true of them all, even to the art of life; perhaps, first of all, to that one.

Nearly every thinking person nowadays is in revolt against something, because the craving of the individual is for further consciousness, and because consciousness is expanding and is bursting through the molds that have held it up to now; and so let every man whose private truth is too great for his existing consciousness pause before he turns away from Picasso's painting or from Gertrude Stein's writing, for their case is his case.

Of course, comment is the best of signs. Any comment. One that Gertrude Stein hears oftenest is from conscientious souls who have honestly tried—and who have failed—to get anything out of her work at all. "But why don't you make it simpler?" they cry. "Because this is the only way in which I can express what I want to express," is the invariable reply, which of course is the unanswerable argument of every sincere artist to every critic. Again and again comes the refrain that is so familiar before the canvases of Picasso—"But it is so ugly, so brutal!" But how does one know that it is ugly, after all? How does one know? Each time that beauty has been reborn in the world it has needed complete readjustment of sense perceptions, grown all too accustomed to the blurred outlines, faded colors, the death in life of beauty in decline. It has become jaded from over-familiarity, from long association and from inertia. If one cares for Rembrandt's paintings today, then how could one have cared for them at the time when they were painted, when they were glowing with life. If we like St. Marks in Venice today, then surely it would have offended us a thousand year ago. Perhaps it is not Rembrandt's paintings that one came for, after all, but merely for the shell, the ghost—the last pale flicker of the artist's intention. Beauty? One thing is certain, that is we must worship beauty as we have known it, we must consent to worship it as a thing dead. *"Une grande, belle chose—morte,"*—And ugliness—what is it? Surely, only death is ugly.

In Gertrude Stein's writing every word lives and, apart from the concept, it is so exquisitely rhythmical and cadenced, that when read aloud and received as pure sound, it is like a kind of sensuous music. Just as one may stop, for once in a way, before a canvas of Picasso, and, letting one's reason sleep for an instant, may exclaim: "It is a fine pattern!"—so listening to Gertrude Stein's words and forgetting to try to understand what they mean, one submits to their gradual charm. Huntley Carter, of the *New Age*, says that her use of language has a curious hypnotic effect when read aloud. In one part of her writing she made use of repetition and the rearranging of certain words over and over, so that they become adjusted into a kind of incantation, and in listening one feels that from the combination of repeated sounds, varied ever so little, that there emerges gradually a perception of some meaning quite other than that of the contents of the phrases. Many people have experienced this magical evocation, but have been unable to explain in what way it came to pass, but though they did not know what meaning the words were bearing, nor how they were affected by them, yet they had *begun* to know what it all meant, because they were not indifferent.

In a portrait that she has finished recently, she has produced a coherent totality through a series of impressions which, when taken sentence by sentence, strike most people as particularly incoherent. To illustrate this, the words in the following paragraph are strenuous words—words that weigh and qualify conditions; words that are without softness yet that are not hard words—perilous abstractions they seem, containing agony and movement and conveying vicarious livingness. "It is a gnarled division, that which is not any obstruction, and the forgotten swelling is certainly attracting. It is attracting the whiter division, it is not sinking to be growing, it is not darkening to be disappearing, it is not aged to be annoying. There cannot be sighing. This is this bliss."

Many roads are being broken—what a wonderful word—"broken"! And out of the shattering and petrifaction of today—up from the cleavage and the disintegration—we will see order emerging tomorrow. Is it so difficult to remember that life at birth is always painful and rarely lovely? How strange it is to think that the rough-hewn trail of today will become tomorrow the path of least resistance, over which the average will drift with all the ease and serenity of custom. All the labor of evolution is condensed into this one fact, of the vitality of the individual making way for the many. We can but praise the high courage of the fad breakers, admitting as we infallibly must, in Gertrude Stein's own words, and with true Bergsonian faith— "Something is certainly coming out of them!"

Arts and Decoration, March 1913.

"How to Read Gertrude Stein."

Carl Van Vechten

The English language is a language of hypocrisy and evasion. How not to say a thing has been the problem of our writers from the earliest times. The extraordinary fluidity and even naiveté of French makes it possible for a writer in that language to babble like a child; de Maupassant is only possible in French, a language in which the phrase, "Je t'aime" means everything. But what does "I love you" mean in English? Donald Evans, of our poets, has realized this peculiar quality of English and he is almost the first of the poets in English to say unsuspected and revolting things, because he so cleverly avoids saying them.

Miss Stein discovered the method before Mr. Evans. In fact his *Patagonian Sonnets* were an offshoot of her late manner, just as Miss Kenton's superb story, "Nicknames," derives its style from Miss Stein's *Three Lives*. She has really turned language into music, really made its sound more important than its sense. And she has suggested to the reader a thousand channels for his mind and sense to drift along, a thousand instead of a stupid only one.

Miss Stein has no explanations to offer regarding her work. I have often questioned her, but I have met with no satisfaction. She asks you to read. Her intimate connection with the studies of William James have been commented upon; some say that the "fringe of thought," so frequently referred to by that writer, may dominate her working consciousness. Her method of work is unique. She usually writes in the morning, and she sets down the words as they come from her pen; they bubble, they flow; they surge through her brain and she sets them down. You may regard them as nonsense, but the fact remains that effective imitations of her style do not exist. John Reed tells me that, while he finds her stimulating and interesting, an entity, he feels compelled to regard her work as an offshoot, something that will not be concluded by followers. She lives and dies alone, a unique example of a strange art. It may be in place also to set down here the fact that once in answer to a question Miss Stein asserted that her art was for the printed page only; she never expects people to converse or exchange ideas in her style.

As a personality Gertrude Stein is unique. She is massive in physique, a Rabelasian woman with a splendid thoughtful face; mind dominating her matter. Her velvet robes, mostly brown, and her carpet slippers associate themselves with her indoor appearance. To go out she belts herself, adds a walking staff, and a trim unmodish turban. This garb suffices for a shopping tour or a box party at the *Opéra*.

Paris is her abode. She settled there after Cambridge, and association with William James, Johns Hopkins and a study of medicine. Her orderly mind has captured the scientific facts of both psychology and physiology. And in Paris the early painters of the new era captured her heart and purse. She purchased the best of them, and now such examples as Picasso's *Acrobats* and early Matisses hang on her walls. There is also the really authoritative portrait of herself, painted by Pablo Picasso.

These two painters she lists among her great friends. And their influence, perhaps, decided her in her present mode of writing. Her pictures are numerous, and to many, who do not know of her as a writer, she is mentioned as the Miss Stein with the collection of post-impressionists. On Saturday nights during the winter one can secure a card of admission to the collection and people wander in and out the studio, while Miss Stein serves her dinner guests unconcernedly with after-dinner coffee. And conversation continues, strangely unhindered by the picture viewers.

Leo Stein happens in, when he is not in Florence, and I have a fancy that he prefers Florence to Paris. He is her brother, and their tastes in art are naturally antithetical. He believes in the painters of the "third dimension," the painters of atmosphere, and the space between objects, for thus he describes the impressionists, and he includes Peter Paul Rubens in this group. And his precise manner of grouping thought is strangely at odds with Miss Stein's piquant love of gossip, and with her strange undercurrents of ideas that pass from her through and about the place.

Mr. Stein's phrase "Define what you mean by—" is almost famous. It is well-known wherever he appears. Last I saw him in the Piazza Vittorio Emanuele. I sat at luncheon time on the terrace of the *Giubbi Rossi* with Mabel Dodge when he strode into view, sandals on his feet, a bundle over his shoulder, and carrying an alpenstock. He was on his way to the mountains, and, if I remember rightly, he asked me, in response to an invitation, to define what I meant by "cocktail," something singularly difficult to do in Italy.

Miss Stein's presence, as I have said before my parenthesis, is strangely dominant in these evenings and her clear deep voice, her very mellow laugh, the adjunct of an almost abnormal sense of humor and observation, remain very pleasant memories. At one time I saw her very frequently, but we talked little of her work, although we often read it.

Of all her books only *Tender Buttons*, the latest of them to appear, is generally procurable. Besides this I know of *Three Lives*, written in her early manner; "Portrait of Mabel Dodge at the Villa Curonia," an internationally famous monograph, published privately in Florence, and never on sale. There is a very long autobiographical work, at present, I believe, considerably longer than *Clarissa Harlowe*, which runs through her various changes of style. There are several plays, one about me, which Miss Stein very kindly entitled *One*. These are very short and in her late manner. Miss Florence Bradley wished to play them in America and she may have done so in Chicago. She is now on her way to China and she may play them there; but I have no record of performances. Miss Stein is most insistent that they be performed before they are printed, but she did allow Marsden Hartley to quote from a play about him as a foreword to his collection of pictures which was exhibited at that "little place" of Mr. Stieglitz's at 291 Fifth Avenue. There are several other short portraits, and some sketches, one of shop girls in the Gallerie Lafayette in Paris which is particularly descriptive and amusing. These, I think, are Miss Stein's main contributions to her complete works.

In *Three Lives* Miss Stein attained at a bound an amount of literary facility which a writer might strive in vain for years to acquire. Simplicity is a quality one is born with, so far as literary style is concerned, and Miss Stein was born with that. But to it she added, in this work, a vivid note of reiteration, a fascinatingly complete sense of psychology and the workings of minds one on the other, which at least in "Melanctha: Each as She May" reaches a state of perfection which might have satisfied such masters of craft as Turgenev, or Balzac, or Henry James.

The number of *Camera Work* for August, 1912, contains two articles by Miss Stein about her two friends, Henri Matisse and Pablo Picasso. To me they seem to bridge the period between *Three Lives* and "The Portrait of Mabel Dodge."

"The Portrait of Mabel Dodge" made a writer amusing for those who subscribed to the clipping bureaus. The redoubtable Romeike, whom Whistler mentions, was kept busy cutting out ideas of the scriveners in Oshkosh and Flatbush about Miss Stein. To those who know Mrs. Dodge the portrait may seem to be a true one; it has intention, that is even obvious to those who do not know what the intention is. There is nothing faint or pale about Miss Stein's authority. It is as complete in its way as the authority of Milton. You may not like the words, but you are forced to admit, after, perhaps, a struggle that no other words will do.

And now a discussion of *Tender Buttons* seems imminent. Donald Evans, who is responsible for its publication, says that it is the only book ever printed which contains absolutely no errors. I have not Miss Stein's authority for this statement. At any rate the effect on printers and proofreaders was tremendous. I believe that even yet some of them are suffering from brain storm. "The Portrait of Mabel Dodge" was set up in Florence by compositors who, I believe, did not read English. So their trouble was less.

There are several theories extant relating to *Tender Buttons*. I may say that one I upheld stoutly for a few hours, that the entire book had a physical application, I have since rejected, at least in part. The three divisions which comprise the book in a way explain the title. They are "Food; Objects;

Rooms," all things which fasten our lives together, and whose complications may be said to make them "tender."

The majestic rhythm of the prose in this book, the virtuosity with which Miss Stein intertwines her words, are qualities which strike the ear at once. And *Tender Buttons* benefits by reading aloud. Onomatopoeia, sound echoing sense, is a favorite figure of speech with Miss Stein; so is alliteration which is fatally fascinating when mingled with reiteration, and Miss Stein drops repeated words upon your brain with the effect of Chopin's B minor prelude, which is popularly supposed to represent the raindrops falling on the roof at Majorka on one of those George Sand days.

The mere sensuous effect of the words is irresistible and often, as in the section labeled "Eating," or "A Seltzer Bottle," the mere pronunciation of the words gives the effect of the act or the article. On the other hand, "A Little Called Pauline" seems to me perfect in the way of a pretty description, a Japanese print of a charming creature. "Suppose an Eyes" is similarly a picture, but more poster.

It would seem to me that the inspiration offered to writers in this book was an enormous incentive to read it. What writer after reading *Tender Buttons* but would strive for a fresher phrase, a more perfect rhythmic prose? Gertrude Stein to me is one of the supreme stylists.

In case one is not delighted, amused, or appealed to in any way by the sensuous charm of her art then, of course, there is the sense to fall back on; the ideas expressed. Here one floats about vaguely for a key to describe how to tell what Miss Stein means. Her vagueness is innate and one of her most positive qualities. I have already said how much she adds to language by it. You may get the idea of it if you close your eyes and imagine yourself awaking from the influence of ether, as you gasp to recall some words and ideas, while new ones surge into your brain. A certain sleepy consciousness. Or you may read sense through the fingers as they flit rapidly— almost word by word—through your brain. It is worthy of note that almost everyone tries to make sense out of Miss Stein just as everyone insists on making photographs out of drawings by Picabia, when the essential of his art is that he is getting away from the photographic.

Trend, August 1914.

"And She Triumphed in the Tragic Turnip Field!"

Anonymous

The Futurists in literature are with us. Through frail, pale volumes that come from the presses in covers of green, blue and orange red tints they are sounding the clarion class to the new art banners. "Try us," they call out, "and if you don't like us today then maybe you will like us tomorrow. At any rate, try us."

Careless of the hectic word, avid of the titles of purple and red import, wallowing in the gold and amber ditches of the decadent, they are strewing their souls, their loves, their thoughts and the words about so that all who run may either read or stumble.

Claire Marie Burke, who played ingenue roles in the Colonial Stock Company last summer and was later seen at the Opera House in *A Good Little Devil*, was the standard-bearer until recently and the establishment is still conducted in her name.

"We propose to bring out about one book a month or ten a year," says Claire Marie. "They will be books for people who are tired of the commonplace and the best sellers. They will be for those who are eager—sincerely eager for the exotic—the tomorrow of literature.

"The poets and dramatists I shall publish will be men and women who have no quarrel with the social order of things, who have no wish to teach or tear down, who are only concerned with the beauty of life. There are dozens of such writers in New York who are brilliant, but their works lack that horrible thing—popular appeal. I don't hope to make the Claire Marie books popular—I don't think I want to—but I think they will slowly build up a public, a small public undoubtedly, of their own, which can be counted on for steady and adequate support...."

For those who are avid for the literature of tomorrow the real sensation and satisfaction is to be found in Gertrude Stein's *Tender Buttons*, which is now on the Claire Marie press. It is one of the unique books of all times. For several years Miss Stein has been the patron saint of the new artists—the Cubists and Futurists. Their work, of course, is holding the center of the stage in every land and is creating a tremendous amount of noise.

It has affected and modified the other arts, as music and literature. In the latter field, the field of literature, Miss Stein unquestionably holds the foremost position and is one of the most puzzling figures in the literary world. Yet heretofore it has been practically impossible to obtain any of her books.

Her work privately printed has been seen by but few. Although word of her art is in every one's ears, she has been a closed door to almost all save her closest friends. Recently a literary magazine asked: "Why has no publisher brought out the work of Gertrude Stein?" The answer was simplicity itself. Gertrude Stein was the reason. She steadfastly refused to seek a wider public and it was only upon the steady urging of her friends that she has consented to publish her works.

In Paris Miss Stein enjoys a great reputation as an artist in the new use of words. Her poems, plays and essays enjoy there an extraordinary distinction that resembles the immense private fame that Rossetti, the great English poet, began with.

Whether Miss Stein's work possesses permanent value, whether it is lasting art, does not really matter. Her followers believe she has added a new dimension to literature. Scoffers, on the other hand, call her writings a mad, meaningless jumble of words. There are many who assert that with her tongue in her cheek she is having a sardonic joke at the expense of those who take her seriously. Time alone can give the verdict—just as it does in all other things.

In her latest book, *Tender Buttons*, she goes even farther than she did before. Words are used with a freedom that is anarchistic, and her friends assert that they are charged with greater pregnancy. The last shackle is struck from context and collocation and each unit, each word of the sentence, stands out independently and has no relation to its fellows.

The effect produced on the first reading is something like terror. There are no known precedents to cling to. It is like a journey in unknown seas without a pilot. The amazing Gertrude Stein, casting away the last remnant of intelligibility, finds a new intelligibility which makes one "after madness go remembering...."

Cleveland (Ohio) Leader, June 21, 1914.

"Flat Prose."

Anonymous

Some time ago a writer in the *Atlantic* protested against the taboo on "beautiful prose." He asserted that the usual organs of publication, especially in America, reject with deadly certainty all contributions whose style suggests that melodious rhythm which DeQuincey and Ruskin made fashionable for their generations, and Stevenson revived in the nineties. He complained that the writer is no longer allowed to write as well as he can; that he must abstract all unnecessary color of phrase, all warmth of connotation and grace of rhythm from his style, lest he should seem to be striving for "atmosphere," instead of going about his proper business, which is to fill the greedy stomach of the public with facts.

Unfortunately, this timely fighter in a good cause was too enamored of the art whose suppression he was bewailing. He so far forgot himself as to make his own style "beautiful" in the old-time fashion, and thus must have roused the prejudice of the multitude, who had to study such style in college, and knew from sad experience that it takes longer to read than the other kind.

But there are other and safer ways of combating the taste for flat prose. One might be to print parallel columns of "newspaper English" (which they threaten now to teach in schools) until the eye sickened of its deadly monotony. This is a bad way. The average reader would not see the point. Paragraphs from a dozen American papers, all couched in the same utilitarian dialect—simple but not always clear, concise yet seldom accurate, emphatic but as ugly as the clank of an automobile chain—why we read thousands of such lines daily! We think in such English; we talk in it; to revolt from this style, to which the Associated Press has given the largest circulation on record, would be like protesting against the nitrogen in our air.

And who wants to bring back color, rhythm, beauty, a sense of the innate value of words, to the news column, or even to the editorial page! It takes to long too read them now.

Books and magazines require a different reckoning. The author is still allowed to let himself go occasionally in books—especially in sentimental books. But the magazines, with few exceptions, have shut down the lid, and are keeping the stylistic afflatus under strict compression. No use to show them what they might publish if, with due exclusion of the merely pretty, the sing-song, and the weakly ornate, they were willing to let a little style escape. With complete cowardice, they will turn the general into the particular, and insist that in any case they will not publish *you*. Far better, it seems to me, to warn editors and the "practical public" as to what apparently is going to happen if ambitious authors are tied down much longer to flat prose.

It is not generally known, I believe, that post-impressionism has escaped from the field of pictorial art, and is running rampant in literature. At present, Miss Gertrude Stein is the chief culprit. Indeed, she may be called the founder of a coterie, if not of a school.

Her art has been defined recently by one of her admirers, who is also the subject, or victim, of the word-portrait from which I intend later to quote in illustration of my argument. "Gertrude Stein," says Miss Dodge, "is doing with words what Picasso is doing with paint. She is impelling language to induce new states of consciousness, and in doing so language becomes with her a creative art rather than a mirror of history." This, being written in psychological and not in post-impressionistic English, is fairly intelligible. But it does not touch the root of the matter. Miss Stein, the writer continues, uses "words that appeal to her as having the meaning they *seem* to have [that is, if "diuturnity" suggests a tumble downstairs, it *means* a tumble downstairs]. To present her impressions she chooses words for their inherent quality rather than their accepted meaning."

Let us watch the creative artist at her toil. The title of the particular word-picture is "Portrait of Mabel Dodge at the Villa Curonia." As the portrait itself has a beginning, but no middle, and only a faintly indicated end, I believe—though in my ignorance of just what it all means I am not sure—that I can quote at random without offense to the impressions derivable from the text....

After a hundred lines of this I wish to scream, I wish to burn the book, I am in agony. It is not because I know that words *cannot* be torn loose from their meanings without insulting the intellect. It is not because I see that this is a prime example of the "confusion of the arts." No, my feeling is purely physical. Some one has applied an egg-beater to my brain.

But having calmed myself by a sedative of flat prose from the paper, I realize that Miss Stein is more sinned against than sinning. She is merely a red flag waved by the *Zeitgeist*.

For this is the sort of thing we are bound to get if the lid is kept down on the stylists much longer. Repression has always bred revolt. Revolt breeds extravagance. And extravagance leads to absurdity. And yet even in the absurd, a sympathetic observer may detect a purpose which is honest and right. Miss Stein has indubitably written nonsense, but she began with sense. For words *have* their sound-values as well as their sense-values, and prose rhythms *do* convey to the mind emotions that mere denotation cannot give. Rewrite the solemn glory of Old Testament diction in the flat colorless prose which just now is demanded, and wonder at the difference. Translate "the multitudinous seas incarnadine" into "making the ocean red"—or, for more pertinent instances, imagine a Carlyle, an Emerson, a Lamb forced to exclude from his vocabulary every word not readily understood by the multitude, to iron out all whimseys, all melodies from his phrasing, and to plunk down his words one after the other in the order of elementary thought.

I am willing to fight to the last drop of ink against any attempt to bring back "fine writing" and ornate rhetoric into prose. "Expression is the dress of thought," and plain thinking and plain facts look best in simple clothing. Nevertheless, if we must write our stories, our essays, our novels, and (who knows) our poems in the flat prose of the news column—if editors will sit on the lid—well, the public will get what it pays for, but sooner or later the spirit of style will ferment, will work, will grow violent under restraint. There will be reaction, explosion, revolution. The public will get its flat prose, and—in addition—not one, but a hundred Gertrude Steins.

The Atlantic Monthly, October 1914.

"Posing."

Richard Burton

Was there ever in the known history of man a time when the faker and *poseur* had as good a chance as he has today? Or *she* has, for I am thinking of a woman? I think not. By "chance" I mean being taken with apparent seriousness by so many people, and given so much good space in the public print. It would be amusing, if it were not so irritating. It really makes one sad, because it implies that folk in general are so avid of something new, however asinine, as to prefer it to the sane, the wholesome and the beautiful.

The case in point is Gertrude Stein, "cubist" of literature, futurist of words, and self-advertiser of pseudo-intellectual antics. She has written a book or so of inconceivably idiotic drivel, compared with which the babble of a three-year-old child is Hegelian. Her specialty seems to be the throwing together of language absolutely meaningless and insulting alike to one's sense of taste and decency. For example, here is a sentence said to be the formula for chicken: "Alas a dirty word, alas a dirty third, alas a dirty third, alas a dirty bird."

There would be no object in drawing attention to writing like this, which belongs nowhere but in a madhouse, were it not for the rather alarming amount of space and examination given its maker. The *Boston Transcript*'s excellent English correspondent, J. P. Collins, devotes several columns to Miss Stein: that is what gives one pause. The *Transcript* believes that it should fill a good part of its valued literary page with twaddle of this kind, along with a quasi-explanation of the cubist person's intention as a thinker and writer—God save the mark! It is perfectly safe to say that this writer, willing to get a bizarre reputation in such fashion as she has, is one of two things: unbalanced, or self-consciously a *poseur* who laughs in her sleeve at the ease with which she fools misguided enthusiasts.

Her record is against the fool supposition. She has studied at Radcliffe, Johns Hopkins and Harvard, and was recognized in those institutions as a young woman of parts. She may, of course, have become daffy since, for even contact with leading colleges is no safe assurance against subsequent intellectual lapse.

But the signs are the other way, and I am of the opinion that there is method in the madness of Gertrude Stein. Looked at merely as a *poseur*, and judged as such, I take off my hat to her cleverness. She has actually talked some people into the conviction that even the tommy-rot she stands for is a sincere view, and even an interviewer goes away puzzled, affected by her seeming earnestness, though skeptical of the stuff she says and prints.

When you stop to think of it, what she did, looked at as mere advertisement, was quite clever. She saw the cubist and futurist and post-impressionist and the rest of the man-monkeys in art having their little day; and she said to herself: "Why not the parallel fake in letters? They will stand for it, for they stand for it in painting and sculpture." Whereupon, knowing that it must be done quickly if at all, since you can't fool all the public all the time, nor a part of it for more than a limited period, she gets busy and produces masterpieces called *Three Lives* and *Tender Buttons*. And when tackled by the men of the press, she talks so sensibly and seriously about it all that really you are almost converted—until you turn back and read something like this: "Come and say what prints all day. A whole few watermelon. There is no pope." Then you know again that Gertrude is a prize bamboozler, and nothing else.

To show how astute she is in talking about her work, take this. Mr. Interviewer asked how a translation would affect her writings, and she replied: "The only translation that has been done so far has been that of a young German recently, and his translation of some of my work has been quite well done. It has not the quality of the original, of course" (there's a gleam of hope in that), "but so far in French the attempt has been less successful."

Every writer has a right to be judged by her best, and Miss Stein picked this jewel as typical: "A blue coat is guided, guided away, guided and guided away, that is the particular color that is used that length and not any width not even more than a shadow."

I am no tailor, but venture to assert that as a direction for making a coat, this would not do; and as to the interest or felicity we look for in literary composition, it seems to leave something wanting.

No, it's a shrewd guess that this cubist writer is having fun with all who take her cheap, absurd eccentricity for the real thing. Most of us prefer obscurity to the kind of notoriety such posturing brings; it certainly would not be very hard to write reams of the sort of balderdash she turns out. Miss Stein had better enjoy herself "hard," while the craze is on.

If, as is possible, it should turn out that she is mentally unsound, then one's humanity will cover her esthetic and other excrescences with the proverbial mantle of charity. But whichever way it may be, the feature that remains reprehensible, even alarming, is the readiness of our time to accept and foist into the publicity which is as the very breath of their nostrils, the posturings and mouthings of the Stein *genre*. Poses of the past look admirable beside it. The *precieuses* of France may have been silly, but they did not lack brains nor literary ability. Neither did that later *poseur*, Oscar Wilde, who was a literary force, in his way, with all his faults. But Gertrude Stein and all her works—really, we have fallen on evil days when she is possible! It will not do to say that nobody takes her seriously; newspapers do, or they would no give up so much space to her. And the crack-brained enthusiasts of art do, for how can they defend cubism without defending her?

It is all very funny, and very sad. Listen to it once more: "A little lace makes boils. This is not true." This is silly, stupid maundering; and this *is* true.

Minneapolis (Minnesota) Bellman, October 17, 1914.

"Gertrude Stein—Hoax and Hoaxtress: A Study of the Woman Whose 'Tender Buttons' Has Furnished New York with a New Kind of Amusement."

Alfred Kreymborg

Suppose your wife came home after a little pilgrimage to the Mecca of department stores with some brilliant bit of insanity on her head, a bit that is madder in shape and madder in color than anything your poor mortal man's eyes had ever beheld. Naturally, being a fond, solicitous husband, you inquire with loving amazement: "Where did you get that thing?" Suppose she answered you in the following style, what would you do?

"Colored hats are necessary to show that curls are worn by an addition of blank space, this makes the difference between single lines and broad stomachs, the least thing is lightening, the least thing means a single flower and a big delay a big delay, that makes more nurses than little women really little women. So clean is a light that nearly all of it shows pearls and little ways. A large hat is tall and me and all custard whole."

(Here's to your health, oh Typesetter and Proofreader!)

Then suppose that in your despair your eyes traveled away from her hat and chanced upon the new long dress she was wearing, and your cried: "But how about this thing, dear?" and she retorted:

"What is the current that makes machinery, that makes it crackle, what is the current that presents a long line and a necessary waist. What is this current. What is the wind, what is it. Where is the serene length, it is there and a dark place is not a dark place, only a white and read are black, only a yellow and green are blue, a pink is scarlet, a bow is every color. A line distinguishes it. A line just distinguishes it."

You are beginning to hold on to your head in fear that it may blow away or crack or dance a tango with one of your feet. In fact, your pet chandelier is beginning a dance of its own. Quickly, you grab the package she has brought home and in an effort to bring her back to reason, as ever go gently: "What is this, dear?" and uncover a new cup and saucer. But your wife persists: "Enthusiastically hurting a clouded yellow bud and saucer, enthusiastically so is the bite in the ribbon."

Desperately you resolve upon an immediate change of subject. If she isn't mad you are rapidly running in the direction. Fortunately, it is dinner time, and you exclaim: "Come Anastasia, love. Let us to the dining room. It is time to eat." But she rambles on, in the same vein: "A pleasant simple habitual and tyrannical and authorized and educated and articulate separation. This is not tardy."

By this time the pesky flea has bitten you. Wild-eyed, you have dragged Anastasia into the dining room. Wild-eyed, you point at the table, that beautiful domestic animal that has made you man and wife even more than the love you whispered in the woods the Spring before your wedding day. Wild-voiced, you rant:

"A table means does it not my dear it means a whole steadiness. It is likely that a change. A table means more than a glass even a looking glass is tall. A table means necessary places and a revision a revision of a little thing it

means it does mean that there has been a stand, a stand where it did shake"
....

All is well. Your connubial relationship has been strengthened by this new excursion into aesthetic adventure-land. Eating is no longer mere eating. Sitting at the dinner table is no longer mere sitting at the dinner table. Gazing across the board at Anastasia is no longer mere gazing across the board at Anastasia. A new light shines down from the chandelier. There is a new light in what used to be your water glass. There is a light even in the eyes of the stolid cook who brings on the veal, vegetables and dessert—lo, the rhubarb itself shining with unwonted brilliance. And who has done this thing? No less an entity than Gertrude Stein, once of New York and now of Paris. A few days ago Anastasia attended a tea at Mabel Dodge's on lower Fifth Avenue. And there she learned of Gertrude Stein and of Gertrude Stein's latest creation: a little canary-covered book with a magic green ball monogram and the title, *Tender Buttons*. *Tender Buttons* has been tender indeed. You and Anastasia will never differ again. The hour of quarrels is a thing of the past—like purple suspenders and yellow spats and heliotrope shirtwaists. But who and what is Gertrude Stein?

Miss Stein is a very large, a massive lady who, thanks to the riches left to her and her family by the kindliness of this earth, has her abode in Paris, moves about in the elite circles there, inviting this and that celebrity to her home, or to her Saturday evenings, and writing books when the spirit moves. She dresses in velvet, usually a brown velvet, and on occasions when indoor life is the rule, keeps her feet protected by carpet slippers. For outdoor purposes she adds a belt or a cord or a frank, joyous turban and carries a walking stick. Her famous brother, Leo Stein, who makes Florence his abode, goes her one better, as the saying is. He wears sandals and carries an alpenstock.

Among her friends are Henri Matisse and Pablo Picasso. Of course, her home is decorated with the work of those two gentlemen. One of the most noteworthy examples is a portrait of Gertrude done in Picasso's earlier mode. Originally she lived in Cambridge, Mass., where all that that may justly lay claim to the title is born. There she knew William James and studied physical as well as psychic medicine. Traces of her indebtedness to Henry as well as William may be discovered in her work, particularly so in her earliest efforts, *Three Lives*, and the portraits of Matisse and Picasso.

Gertrude has also written a portrait of Mabel Dodge—who is one of her closest friends and holds weekly salons at her Fifth Avenue home, where the artists and literati and sundry of the I. W. W. congregate for a discussion of the value of Swiss cheese as a social worker and a medium of artistic expression.

The Dodge portrait was set up in Florence by compositors who, fortunately for their nervous systems, did not read English. Their difficulties were nil. But think of the experience of English proofreaders who have to read copy of the kind set forth in *Tender Buttons* .... Miss Stein has also written various plays, as yet unprinted and unproduced. Miss Florence Bradley has often threatened to produce some of them, but so far has not found a manager who will risk the consequences. Methinks New York is in need of a little tonic of the sort. Nor would New York run away, what with its recent experience in Cubism and Marinetti poems and the music of Schoenberg and Ornstein. New York is too sophisticated these days to mind a little fresh adventure.

Often the question has been aimed at Miss Stein: "But why don't you make it simple?" and invariable her reply is: "Because this is the only way in which I can express what I want to express." That is pretty much the retort of all artists and dilettantes to the criticism of critics and public: "This is my way. It is the easiest way out of the argument, and at the same time the only way. The greatest artists themselves would find it an impossible task to explain themselves to themselves, and even their explanation might be far from the truth. You may think you are putting down such and such an impression on paper, but the actuality can be another matter."

Camera Work was the first to publish Gertrude Stein's work here. With the publication of the Matisse and Picasso portraits, the following editorial was submitted: "It is because, in these articles by Miss Stein, the post-impressionist spirit is found expressing itself in literary form that we thus lay them before our readers .... These articles bear, to current interpretative criticism, a relation exactly analogous to that born by the work of the men of whom they treat to the painting and sculpture of the older schools.

"So close, indeed, is this analogy that they will doubtless be regarded by many as no less absurd, unintelligible, radical or revolutionary than the so-called vagaries of the painters whom they seek to interpret.

"Yet—they employ a medium in the technical manipulation of which we are all at least tyros. They are expressed in words. We wish you the pleasure of a hearty laugh at them upon a first reading. Yet we confidently commend them to your subsequent and critical attention."

So, you see there are many challenges thrown at your intelligence besides those delivered in Gertrude Stein's own language. And defense of an art, if defense it is, and if defense is necessary, may often enlighten such as are in the dark. Another of Miss Stein's worshipers, Carl Van Vechten, adds the following challenge: "Miss Stein has added enormously to the vagueness of the English language." That is true: anybody will admit without argument. "She has really turned language into music, really made its sound more important than its sense." That, of course, depends upon what one means by music. Some believe anything music that has to do with sound—a sentimental as well as ignorant bit of superficiality. Whether Gertrude Stein's *Buttons* are musical or not depends upon the particular ear and taste that is doing the listening. An additional contrary argument might be: Is music literature?

No doubt Mr. Van Vechten would retort: "But music is what Miss Stein is after." Each individual who reads her work will have additional words and phrases to offer for or against it. Argument is great fun if you can afford the time and energy. And surely any reader will have to admit there is novelty in Gertrude Stein and novelty is one of the main spices of existence.

We defy Grammarian Pedagogue's favorite pupil to parse the above sentence. Where is the subject, where the predicate and where the object? Or has the sentence no object—beyond music? In that case we call on Critic Krebbiel or Critic Henderson to parse the music of the sentence. Is the sentence more than sound? Our six-year-old daughter, Ethera, loves to bang on our piano. Ask her what she is doing and she will invariably say: "I am making music." But is it music because she thinks so? Certain folk have beautiful theories, things that are a joy as theories. But when they begin to lay these theories on paper the beauty refuses to disclose itself except for the eyes or ears of its creator. And a few charlatans or followers of the faithful or the sensation seeker.

There is another item. We have been told that Gertrude Stein is the possessor of an uproarious sense of humor. De Zayas, the eminent caricaturist, claims that she is the only woman he ever met with a sense of humor. May not the fond lady be playing a joke on the world? Mystification is one of the most delightful, one of the most secretly joyous of pastimes. Who knows whether she is not laughing up her gorgeous sleeves? And that the folk who visit her of a Saturday evening are not the most intimate side of her fun? And why not a new form of hoax as well as a new form of poem, play, novel or painting?

However, there is a serious side to Miss Stein. We are told that when she visits the Louvre and sees a painting she admires more than others, she lies flat on the carpet and, so to speak, prostrates herself to it. Incidentally she was one of the first to buy Picassos and Matisses. That in itself demonstrates serious enterprise.

In either case, serious or hoaxtress, Gertrude Stein has provided the world with a new kind of entertainment for some time past. Whether you wrinkle your brow and curl you tongue for a long, ponderous defense of her work, or whether you scowl and shoot your tongue for a venomous attack, or whether you merely lean back in your velvet easy chair and open your mouth for a good roaring laugh, Miss Stein will have benefitted you. She has given you a new sensation. And sensations are so rare, particularly in these days of warfare that you don't want to deny yourself the opportunity of one. You can always go back to sleep again.

And there is always the possibility that, like Herbert and Anastasia, you may win back your lost love. Assuredly Gertrude Stein is the nurse, the guardian angel of all households.

The New York Morning Telegraph, March 7, 1915.

"Four American Impressions."

Sherwood Anderson

One who thinks a great deal about people and what they are up to in the world comes inevitably in time to relate them to experiences connected with one's own life. The round, sharp apples in this old orchard are the breasts of my beloved, lying asleep. One cannot avoid practicing this trick of lifting people out of the spots on which in actual life they stand and transferring them to what seems at the moment some more fitting spot in one's fanciful world.

And one gets also a kind of aroma from people. They are green, healthy, growing things or they have begun to decay. There is something in this man, to whom I have just talked, that has sent me away from him smiling and in an odd way pleased with myself. Why has this other man, although his words were kindly and his deeds apparently good, spread a cloud over my sky?

In my own boyhood in an Ohio town I went about delivering newspapers at kitchen doors, and there were certain houses to which I went—old brick houses with immense old-fashioned kitchens—in which I loved to linger. On Saturday mornings I sometimes managed to collect a fragrant cookie at such a place, but there was something else that held me. Something got into my mind connected with the great, light kitchens and the women working in them that came sharply back when, last year, I went to visit an American woman, Miss Gertrude Stein, in her own large room in the house at 27 rue de Fleurus in Paris. In the great kitchen of my fanciful world in which I have, ever since that morning, seen Miss Stein standing, there is a most sweet and gracious aroma. Along the walls are many shining pots and pans, and there are innumerable jars of fruits, jellies and preserves. Something is going on in the great room, for Miss Stein is a worker in words with the same loving touch in her strong fingers that was characteristic of the women of the kitchens of the brick houses in the town of my boyhood. She is an American woman of the old sort, one who cares for the handmade goodies and who scorns the factory-made foods, and in her own great kitchen she is making something with her materials, something sweet to the tongue and fragrant to the nostrils.

That her materials are the words of our English speech and that we do not, most of us, know or care too much what she is up to does not greatly matter to me. The impression I wish now to give you of her is of one very intent and earnest in a matter most of us have forgotten. She is laying word against word, relating sound to sound, feeling for the taste, the smell, the rhythm of the individual word. She is attempting to do something for the writers of our English speech that may be better understood after a time, and she is not in a hurry. And one has always that picture of the woman in the great kitchen of words, standing there by a table, clean, strong, with red cheeks and sturdy legs, always quietly and smilingly at work. If her smile has in it something of the mystery, to the male at least, of the Mona Lisa, I remember that the women in the kitchens on the wintry mornings wore often that same smile.

She is making new, strange and to my ears sweet combinations of words. As an American writer I admire her because she, in her person, represents something sweet and healthy in our American life, and because I have a kind of undying faith that what she is up to in her word kitchen in Paris is of more importance to writers of English than the work of many of our more easily understood and more widely accepted word artists.

The New Republic, October 11, 1922.

"A Guide to Gertrude Stein: The Evolution of a Master of Fiction into a Painter of Cubist Still-Life in Prose."

Edmund Wilson

There is, perhaps, no other American writer of importance who has been so badly underestimated as Gertrude Stein. And this critical neglect would seem chiefly to be due to an unfortunate accident. The earlier half of Miss Stein's literary work has never really had a fair chance of recognition: it was one of her most advanced and most daring experiments which first attracted public attention. The first most of us heard of Gertrude Stein was when *Tender Buttons* was published in 1914 and was greeted with raucous guffaws as an example of exotic Greenwich Villagism. Yet Miss Stein had already published at this time, besides two curious and interesting brochures, one of the most distinguished works of fiction by any living author—a book which had far more claim to serious recognition than the works of most of the Hergesheimers and the Cathers which followed it and which were raised to the dignity of masters by the eagerness of the new literary generation to discover authentic American talent. It was a little as if Henry James had first attracted attention with *The Wings of the Dove* or George Meredith with *One of Our Conquerors*. No one realized that the strange looking stuff which diverted him as a form of literary lunacy was really only a comparatively late phase of a genius extraordinarily conscientious and sane, which had been working steadily for many years to express itself in prose.

Gertrude Stein's first book, *Three Lives,* appeared, in 1909, at a time when there was little audience, either popular or critical, for serious American fiction. If *Three Lives* were published today we should probably hear much more about it. Indeed, have we not done honor to Sherwood Anderson, who is essentially a disciple of Miss Stein and whose very best stories, I think, are no better than *Three Lives*?

Three Lives was a work of realism but realism of rather a novel kind. There had come to be a sort of realistic formula for writing about domestic servants, invented perhaps by Flaubert and fostered, I suppose, by the Goncourts. But Miss Stein, though she shared with these writers their ironic sense and their detachment, had discovered a technique of her own. When we read *Un Coeur Simple* of Flaubert we are continually thinking about Flaubert—of his technical virtuosity, of his *tour de force* of the imagination in being able to put before us so lowly a creature at all—his researches into her simple heart are like a last triumph of sophistication. But Gertrude Stein in her treatment of her servant girls, occupies no such acrid literary altitudes. Her portraits, though no less ruthless than Flaubert's, are far closer to the originals. Indeed they are not dazzling feats of ingenuity like Flaubert's, at all, but rather the projection of three actual human beings as complex and as complete as life. The style itself, which seems to owe nothing to that of any other novelist, takes on the very accents and the rhythms of the minds whose adventures it is recording. We have ceased to see the nurse-girl as an insect to be examined at arm's length; we find ourselves living in her own world and watching it through her own eyes. And far from proving sordid or boring, it becomes extraordinarily beautiful and noble.

In *Three Lives* the style, though extremely individual, is not yet especially eccentric—though some of the author's characteristic tricks have already begun to appear. You have the rhythmic repetitions, like the refrain of a ballad, which we find imitated in Sherwood Anderson, and you have the strange stringing together of present participles which seems at first merely an attempt to reproduce some mannerism of Negro conversation, but which was afterwards to grow on Miss Stein as a mannerism of her own. "I never did use to think I was so much on being real modest, Melanctha, but now I know really I am, when I hear you talking. I see all the time there are many people living just as good as I am, though they are a little different to me. Now with you, Melanctha, if I understand you right what you are talking, you don't think that way of no other one that you are ever knowing."

Three Lives and the gigantic *Making of Americans* constitute Miss Stein's first period. The latter found no publisher when it was first written and has remained in obscurity ever since, though those who have read it in manuscript consider it her most important work and, with the example of Proust and *Ulysses*, it is to be hoped that some publisher will undertake it. Her middle manner—a logical elaboration of the earlier style of *Three Lives*—first appears in the portraits of Matisse and Picasso, published by Mr. Stieglitz in *Camera Work*, and in a sketch of the Galeries Lafayette, in a defunct magazine called *Rogue* .... This was a little queer but still intelligible; but about this time another "portrait" appeared which presented far greater difficulties. It suddenly became evident that Gertrude Stein had abandoned the intelligible altogether.

"Portrait of Mabel Dodge of the Villa Curonia," printed privately in Florence, retained the flowing manner of the other portraits but had begun speaking in a strange and disturbing language, rather like Mallarmé's language of Symbolism; and finally, in *Tender Buttons* Miss Stein abandoned even her long limpid sentences and began expressing herself in fantastic strings of words without syntax or connection .... It appeared that Miss Stein had decided to try using words for the values which she believed them to possess apart from those inherent in their actual meanings. We are told that she used to shut herself up at night and try utterly to banish from her brain all the words ordinarily associated with the ideas she had fixed upon. Concentrating upon the given image she would make her mind a blank to its ordinary vocabulary, invoking other, more subtly relevant words to render it anew.

But the real key to understanding *Tender Buttons* is to be found in Miss Stein's preoccupation with modern painting. Long a friend of Matisse and Picasso, and one of the earliest of their admirers, she has for many years been living in Paris in the full excitement of the new movement and has accumulated a collection of modern paintings, which is one of the most remarkable in Europe. It is not surprising that she should have come to wonder whether analogous effects might not be produced in literature. We are all the more or less familiar by this time with the theory of cubism and its sister genres—that violent reaction from naturalism, which holds that by splitting up or distorting an object you can give a far truer impression of its effect on the beholder than by any literal representation—and it is not difficult to see how Miss Stein's later work attempts the same fresh rendering in prose.

"Portrait of Mabel Dodge" was merely a portrait in the manner of Picasso, and the sketches in *Tender Buttons*, of which the subtitle was *Objects, Food, Rooms* were simply a series of cubist still-lifes in the manner of Gleize or Braque. She had cut down her long repetitive ruminations to telegraphic economic strokes; instead of turning the object over and over, like the ocean lapping a pebble, she had begun dropping the pebble in a well and recording only the ripples on the surface, when the pebble itself had disappeared and sunk many yards out of sight. It is not the object which we see but the vibrations caused by the object—not a focusing of something outside the artist, but the consciousness of the artist herself.

Her next publication, a small pamphlet called, felicitously, *Have They Attacked Mary. He Giggled—A Political Satire* (1917), and her most recent book, *Geography and Plays* (1922), which contains also specimens of almost all her other manners, seem to apply the method of the still-lifes in *Tender Buttons* to more complicated subjects. You have travel, anecdotes, conversations, all splintered up, reduced to their essentials, a queer selective stenography of life. Some of this is recognizable and amusing; more is completely incomprehensible; and all is tantalizing with the suggestion of a fine artist just out of reach. For the chief strength of Miss Stein's genius still appears to be her grasp of character. In spite of her excursions into still-life, she has always been preoccupied with portraits. The three women of *Three Lives*, besides being three accurately reported individuals, achieved an almost Shakespearean significance as the representatives of certain salient human types; and the essays on the modern painters seemed excellent criticism of artistic personality. Now, in her latest writings—though with a lighter irony—we have the portrait painter again; Miss Furr and Miss Skeene are plain—and incomparable—but what of Tourtebattre and Johnny Grey? They have the feeling that we have somehow been cheated out of the masterpieces of a first-rate writer of fiction.

And is it right that we should lose Gertrude Stein? That is a difficult question to answer; but I am inclined to think we should not. It is not that I object to experiments—however bold—with language and form, nor that I deny Miss Stein's partial success—it may well be, as Mr. Anderson suggests, that she has made a contribution of importance to modern prose; but that I believe her complete literary success has been prevented by her unfortunate analogy with the plastic arts. I am told by her friends that for many years she has seen almost no literary people but only sculptors and painters; and it is a fact that there is scarcely a literary reference to be found in any of her works. It would seem that Miss Stein has cut herself off so completely from the tradition and experience of other writers that she has ceased not only to recognize the limitations of literature but even to understand its aim. I will admit as much as you please in the plastic arts one need not be representational, that one should avoid especially being "literary," as the modern painters say; but, though painting ought not to be literary, I do not see why literature should not. In painting, though you may have eliminated everything else, you have at least a shape or a pattern and this is no doubt all you need; but it seems to me that literature is inevitably founded on ideas. Human speech is a tissue of ideas—however forms and colors may not be—and it seems more or less impossible for a work of literature to be anything but an arrangement of ideas.

Compare the scene in the "pub" in *Ulysses*, in which a somewhat similar use of language is made, with one of Gertrude Stein's "plays": in the former the queer devices are effective because we know what the author is trying to describe; but in the latter they go for nothing because we do not know what the "play" is all about. Miss Stein no longer understands the conditions under which literary effects have to be produced. There is sometimes a genuine music in the most baffling of her works, but there are rarely any communicated emotions. When Gertrude Stein succeeds in her new manner it is as any other poet succeeds, through coining an idea miraculously into words. But it is not, in the long run, I believe, as a painter of cubist still-lifes after Braque. And, in any case, it is in her *thought* that we are chiefly interested, and it is precisely her thought which we now rarely get. We figure her as the great pyramidal Buddha of Mr. Jo Davidson's statue, ruminating eternally on the ebb and flow of life, registering impressions like some August seismograph. And we cannot but regret that the results of her meditations are communicated to us in oracles.

Vanity Fair, September 1923.

"The Stein Songs and Poetry."

Harold T. Pulsifer

This week a colleague of mine pokes some editorial fun at the latest work from the pen of Gertrude Stein. I am quite certain that many a good laugh can be legitimately excavated from her linguistic experiment called *Geography and Plays*, but I am not so sure that a good laugh is all that awaits the diligent digger in this particular field of sound without sense.

It might be well, first of all, to try to define the task which Miss Stein has attempted. It is difficult and probably impossible for a person like myself to make such a definition in a manner satisfactory to Miss Stein and her defenders, for I confess in advance that I am not sympathetic with what I conceive to be the ends she has in view.

The task she is attempting, as I understand it, is the use of words for the creation of sound patterns without regard to their meanings. She says to the conventional poet, or the writer of conventional prose: "What you have been attempting is of little more artistic value than the work of a musician who is trying to extract speech or incident from pure music. You are merely program writers ignorant of the subtleties which await the touch of the real artist. Ignoring all the accepted meanings, connotations, and the atmosphere of the words in our language, I will use these as sound symbols in the creation of a new medium of artistic expression." If this is not a fair statement of what Miss Stein has attempted, I stand ready for correction.

Granting for the moment the desirability of the creation of such a new form of artistic expression, it seems to me that Miss Stein is building her house of the wrong materials. The basic material she seeks is not to be found in words, but in arrangements of vowels and consonants without relation to their accepted place in a spoken language. To ask a person to assume an air of complete detachment towards familiar words and phrases is a demand which the human brain inevitably finds it difficult to grant. It is like asking a surgeon to assume an air of complete impersonality and detachment in the performance of an operation on his mother or his wife. Surgeons do not attempt such operations, because they know that there are times when even a scientist cannot put aside the fact that he is also a man. Why should we be asked to ignore the spiritual heritage of the word "mother" any more than we ask the surgeon to forget that the flesh of his mother awaits the knife?

So much for the theory; now to the practice of this new art. A scientist not so long ago published a book on the theory of poetry. One of the chief of the many unfortunate errors in this volume was the fact that the scientist attempted to prove his theories by putting them into practice. He wanted to show that poetry could be constructed by scientific methods, and he succeeded only in proving that he was not, and never could be, a poet. I would not go so far as to say that Miss Stein has made quite so miserable a failure as the scientist to whom I have referred. She has in her book passages which are rhythmical and which, if divorced from any consideration of sense, have a pleasing syllabification. Possibly if they were read aloud to some one who did not understand English they might produce as marked an effect as has been sometimes made by foreign poets who have come to America to read from their works in languages unknown to their hearers. How much of this effect has been due to the inherent beauty of the language and how much to the inherent capacity of their audience to intoxicate themselves with exotic potions it would perhaps not be wise to attempt to say. I feel certain, however, that Miss Stein has not achieved any arrangement of sound at all comparable to the work of poets who have been hampered by the restrictions of sense.

One of the best ways of arriving at an understanding of poetic construction is to take some familiar and famous passage and repeat it over and over until the too solid words resolve themselves in so far as is possible into pure sound elements. The test requires the same power of detachment which Miss Stein apparently asks of readers of her book, but it is more easily achieved through hypnotic repetition than by a deliberate dismissal of all the meaning which surrounds the elements of our speech .... There may be more to be said for Miss Stein's work than for the labor of those who are trying to catch hold of the coattails of immortality by the elimination of commas and the suppression of capital letters, but I confess that when Mr. Sherwood

Anderson asks, "Would it not be a lovely and charmingly ironic gesture of the gods if, in the end, the work of the artist were to prove the most lasting and important of all the word slingers of our generation?" I am inclined to suspect that on that distant day to which Mr. Anderson refers the gods will have something better to do with their time than to make charming ironic gestures at those of us who adhere to the proven realities of poetry.

The Outlook, 1923.

"*Communications: Gertrude Stein.*"

Mina Loy

To the editor of *The Transatlantic Review*:

Dear Sir,

> Curie
> of the laboratory
> of vocabulary
>   she crushed
> the tonnage
> of consciousness
> congealed to phrases
>   to extract
> a radium of the word

Some years ago I left Gertrude Stein's Villino in Fiesole with a manuscript she had given me: "Each is one. Each one is being the one each one is being. Each one is one is being one. Each one is being the one that one is being. Each one is being one each one is one. Each one is one. Each one is very well accustomed to be that one. Each one is one." ("Galeries Lafayette"). Compare with "Vanity of vanity, vanity of vanities, all is vanity" of Ecclesiastes.

This was when Bergson was in the air, and his beads of Time strung on the continuous flux of Being, seemed to have found a literary conclusion in the austere verity of Gertrude Stein's theme—"Being" as the absolute occupation.

For by the intervaried rhythm of this monotone mechanism she uses for inducing a continuity of awareness of her subject, I was connected up with the very pulse of duration.

The core of a "Being" was revealed to me with uninterrupted insistence.

The plastic static of the ultimate presence of an entity.

And the innate tempo of a life poured in alert refreshment upon my mentality.

Gertrude Stein was making a statement, a reiterate statement ... basic and bare ... a statement reiterate ad absurdum, were it not for the interposing finger of creation.

For Gertrude Stein obtains the "belle matière" of her unsheathing of the fundamental with a most dexterous discretion in the placement and replacement of her phrases, of inversion of the same phrase sequences that are as closely matched in level, as the fractional tones in primitive music or the imperceptible modeling of early Egyptian sculpture.

The flux of Being as the ultimate presentation of the individual, she endows with the rhythmic concretion of her art, until it becomes as a polished stone, a bit of the rock of life—yet not of polished surface, of polished nucleus.

This method of conveyance through duration recurs in her later work. As she progresses it becomes amplified, she includes an increasing number of the attributes of continuity.

The most perfect example of this method is "Italians" where not only are you pressed close to the insistence of their existence, but Gertrude Stein through her process of reiteration gradually, progressively rounds them out, decorates them with their biological insignia.

They revolve on the pivot of her verbal construction like animated sculpture, their life protracted into their entourage through their sprouting hair ... a longer finger nail; their sound, their smell.

"They have something growing on them, some of them, and certainly many others would not be wanting such things to be growing out of them that is to say growing on them.

"It makes them these having such things, makes them elegant and charming, makes them ugly and disgusting, makes them clean looking and sleek and rich and dark, makes them dirty looking and fierce looking."

How simply she exposes the startling dissimilarity in the aesthetic denouement of our standardized biology.

They solidify in her words, in ones, in crowds, compact with racial impulses. They are of one, infinitesimally varied in detail, racial consistency.

Packed by her poised paragraphs into the omniprevalent plasm of life from which she evokes all her subjects and from which she never allows them to become detached. In Gertrude Stein life is never detached from Life, it spreads tenuous and vibrational between each of its human exteriorizations and the other.

"They seem to be, and that is natural because what is in one is carried over to the other one by it being in the feeling the one looking at the one and then at the other one.

"They are talking, often talking and they are doing things with pieces of them while they are talking and they are then sounding like something, they are then sounding in a way that is a natural way for them to be sounding, they are having noise come out of them in a natural way for them to have noise come out of them."

It may be impossible for our public inured to the unnecessary nuisances of journalism to understand this literature, but it is a literature reduced to a basic significance that could be conveyed to a man on Mars.

In her second phase ... the impressionistic, Gertrude Stein entirely reverses this method of conveyance through duration. She ignores duration and telescopes time and space and the subjective and objective in a way that obviates interval and interposition. She stages strange triangles between the nominative and his verb and irruptive co-respondents.

It has become the custom to say of her that she has done in words what Picasso has done with form. There is certainly in her work an interpenetration of dimensions analogous to Cubism.

One of her finest "impressions" is "Sweet Tail. Gypsies." It begins: "Curved planes.

"Hold in the coat. Hold back ladders and a creation and nearly sudden extra coppery ages with colors and a clean gyp hoarse. Hold in that curl with the good man. Hold in cheese ..." A fracturing impact of the mind with the occupation, the complexion, the cry of the gypsies.

Cubistically she first sees the planes of the scene. Then she breaks them up into their detail. Gypsies of various ages using ladders for the construction of ... something. "A clean gyp hoarse." Hear it, see it, attribute it, that voice?

The occurrences of "Hold in" impress me as a registration of her mind dictating the control of the planes of the picture it is so rapidly and unerringly putting together; no, "choosing" together. "A little pan with a yell," is a protraction of "The clean gyp hoarse," accelerated, in her chase of sounds among solids by telescoping the "little pan" with the animation of the gypsy holding it.

Per contra in "Wheel is not on a donkey and never never," her reason disengages the donkey and cart from her primary telescopic visualization.

It is the variety of her mental processes that gives such fresh significance to her words, as if she had got them out of bed early in the morning and washed them in the sun.

They make a new appeal to us after the friction of an uncompromised intellect has scrubbed the meshed messes of traditional association off them.

As in the little phrase "A wheel is not a donkey" ... a few words she has lifted out of the ridiculous, to replace them in the sanctuary of pure expression.

"A green, a green colored oak, a handsome excursion, a really handsome log, a regulation to exchange oars." An association of nomadic recreation and rest through the idea "wood" oak, log, oars.

Again how admirably the essences of romance are collected in the following curve-course that for beauty of expression could hardly be excelled.

"The least license is in the yes which makes strange the less sighed hole which is nodded and leaves the bent tender .... It makes medium and egg-light and not nearly so much."

To obtain movement she has shaped her words to the pattern of a mobile emotion, she has actually bent the tender and with medium and egg-light and not really so much, reconstructed the signal luminous, the form, the semi-honesty of the oval eye.

But in "simple cake, simple cake, relike a gentle coat .... Seal it blessing and that means gracious, not gracious suddenly with spoons and flavor but all the same active. Neglect a pink white neglect it for blooming on a thin piece of steady slim poplars." Round the cake, the sociable center, the tempo of the gypsy feast changes ... "seal it blessing," do gypsies say grace or is blessing again the bowing pattern of feeding merging with spoons and flavor?

The "gentle coating" ... icing? ... of the cake confuses with the greater whiteness of the sky wedged between poplars that are depicted with the declivity of line of Van Gogh. "Neglect it ..." Again a direction for the mind to keep the planes of the picture relatively adjusted.

"And really the chance is in deriding coconuts real coconuts with strawberry tunes and little ice cakes with feeding feathers and peculiar relations of noting which is more blessed than replies."

In "feeding feathers" the omission of the woman between her feeding and her feathers results in an unaccustomed juxtaposition of words by associating a subject with a verb which does not in fact belong to it, but which visually, is instantaneously connected.

This process of disintegration and reintegration, this intercepted cinema of suggestion urges the reactions of the reader until the theme assumes an unparalleled clarity of aspect. Compare it with George Borrow's gypsy classic and consider the gain in time and spontaneity that such abridged associations as derision and coconuts, strawberry tints dissolving into tune and above all the snatched beauty of the bizarrerie of feeding afford us.

And these eyes, these feathers are continuously held in place by the progressive introduction of further relationships. "And nearly all heights hats which are so whiled ..." And so one comes to realize how Gertrude Stein has built up her gypsies, accent upon accent, color on color, bit by bit.

Perhaps for this reason it is not so easy for the average reader to "get" Gertrude Stein, because for the casual audience entity seems to be eclipsed by excrescence.

Truly with this method of Gertrude Stein's a good amount of incoherent debris gets littered around the radium that she crushes out of phrased consciousness.

"Like message cowpowder and sashes sashes, like pedal causes and so sashes, and pedal cause kills surgeon in six safest six, pedal sashes."

Now that's just like Gertrude Stein! Even as I type this suspect excerpt it clarifies as the subconscious code message of an accident. The sending for the surgeon. The first aid with gypsy sashes.

The cow that ... like gunpowder ... may be a cause for being killed ... but if in six minutes the surgeon arrives ... the probability of safety. The simultaneity of velocity-binding sashes-pedaling of messenger's bicycle.

The Transatlantic Review, 1923.

"Communications: Gertrude Stein (Continued)."

Mina Loy

To the Editor, *The Transatlantic Review*.

Dear Sir:

There is no particular advantage in groping for subject matter in a literature that is sufficiently satisfying as verbal design, but the point at issue, for those who are confident of their ability to write Gertrude Stein with their minds shut, is, that her design could not attain the organic consistency that it does, were there no intention back of it.

Kenneth Burke deducts from her effectiveness the satisfying climax of subject. For it is rather the debris, always significant with that rhythm he analyzes that has attracted his attention than the sudden potential, and, to a mind attuned protracted illuminations of her subject which form the very essence of Gertrude Stein's art.

Nevertheless it is disconcerting to follow with great elation certain passages I have quoted when unexpectedly time and space crash into a chaos of dislocate ideas, while conversation would seem to proceed from the radiophonic exchange of the universe. Yet you "come up for air" with the impression that you have experienced something more extensively than you have before ... but what? The everything, the everywhere, the simultaneity of function.

But these concussions become less frequent as again and again one reads her, and each time her subject shows still more coherence. One must in fact go into training to get Gertrude Stein.

Often one is liable to overlook her subject because her art gives such tremendous proportions to the negligible that one can not see it all at once. As for instance in "Handing a lizard to anyone is a green thing receiving a curtain. The change is not present and the sensible way to have agony is not precautious. Then the skirting is extreme and there is a lilac smell and no ginger. Halt and suggest a leaf which has no circle and no singular center, this has that show and does judge that there is a need of moving toward the equal height of a hot sinking surface."

To interpret her descriptions of the lizard you have to place yourself in the position of both Gertrude Stein and the lizard at once, so intimate is the liaison of her observation with the sheer existence of her objective, that she invites you into the concentric vortex of consciousness involved in the most trifling transactions of incident.

Her action is inverted in the single sentence "Handing a lizard ... etc." where the act of the subject transforms into the passivity of object.

"The change is not present ..." She has taken on the consciousness or rather the unconsciousness of the lizard in the inexplicable predicament of its transportation.

And in "The sensible way to have agony is not precautious," its struggle to retrieve its habitude.

How much beauty she can make out of so little. After the "green thing receiving the curtain," this comparison of a lizard to a leaf.

"This has that show and does judge," again the inversion. She is turning the lizard outside in, its specular aspect fuses with its motor impulses and now she represents the paw of that hand to you as a hand surveyor might a prospect.

To the advocates of Stein prohibition I must confess that the lines "then the skirting is extreme and there is a lilac smell and no ginger" is not clear to me; the immediate impression I receive is that the puffing of the frightened reptile's belly is being likened to a billowing skirt that the lilac shadow on the flesh of the hand shunts into the smell of the lizard …. But why ginger? Something suggested ginger to the author and escaped her, so she denies the ginger. The greatest incertitude experienced while reading Gertrude Stein is the indecision as to whether you are psychoanalyzing her, or she you.

There is a good deal of ginger floating around in this book of *Geography and Plays*, as are also pins stuck about. The ginger so far escapes me, the pins I accept as an acute materialization of the concentric.

Compare this lizard episode with an example of a drama animated by the projection of the intellect into the infinity of the inanimate.

"The season gliding and the torn hangings receiving mending, all this shows an example, it shows the force of sacrifice and likeness and disaster and a reason." *Tender Buttons*.

Gertrude Stein possesses a power of evocation that gives the same lasting substance to her work that is found in the Book of Job. Take the colossal verse "He spreadeth the north over the empty place and hangeth the earth upon nothing." *Job*.

Which has the same mechanism as the eye-egg light episode and the lizard-curtain episode, and the analogy to Gertrude Stein is obvious in such passages as the following:

> "Am I a sea or a whale
> Darkness itself
> Who can stay the bottles of heaven
> The chambers of heaven." *Job*.

Like all modern art, this art of Gertrude Stein makes a demand for a creative audience, by providing a stimulus, which although it proceeds from a complete aesthetic organization, leaves us unlimited latitude for personal response.

For each individual with his particular experience she must induce varying interpretations, for the logician she must afford generous opportunity for inferences entirely remote from those of the artist approaching her writings. There is a scholarly manipulation of the inversion of ideas, parallel to *Alice in the Looking Glass*, one is nonplussed by the refutation of logic with its myriad insinuations that surpasses logic, which Gertrude Stein in her *Plays* achieves through syncopation.

I point these things out in passing, to draw attention to the class of material she brings to the manufacture of her new literature. If you can come to think of a philosophy, apart from the intrication of your reason, leaving on your memory an abstract impress of its particularity as a perfume or a voice might do, you can begin to sort out the vital elements in Gertrude Stein's achievement.

She has tackled an aesthetic analysis of the habits of consciousness in its lair, prior to the traditionalization of its evolution.

Perhaps the ideal enigma that the modern would desire to solve, is, what would we know about anything, if we didn't know anything about it …. To track tellection back to the embryo.

For the spiritual record of the race is the nostalgia for the crystallization of the irreducible surplus of the abstract. The bankruptcy of mysticism declared itself in an inability to locate this divine irritation, and the burden of its debt to the evolution of consciousness has devolved upon abstract art.

The pragmatic value of modernism lies in its tremendous recognition of the compensation due to the spirit of democracy. Modernism is a prophet crying in the wilderness of stabilized culture that humanity is wasting its aesthetic time. For there is a considerable extension of time between the visits to the picture gallery, the museum, the library. It asks what is happening to your aesthetic consciousness during the long long intervals?

The flux of life is pouring its aesthetic aspect into your eyes, your ears—and you ignore it because you are looking for your canons of beauty in some sort of frame or glass case of tradition. Modernism says Why not each one of us, scholar or bricklayer pleasurably realize all that is impressing itself upon our subconscious, the thousand odds and ends which make up your sensory every day life?

Modernism has democratized the subject matter and la belle matière of art, through cubism the newspaper has assumed an aesthetic quality, through Cézanne a plate has become more than something to put an apple upon, Brancusi has given an evangelistic import to eggs, and Gertrude Stein has given us the Word, in and for itself.

Would not life be lovelier if you were constantly overjoyed by the sublimely pure concavity of your wash bowls? The tubular dynamics of your cigarette?

In reading Gertrude Stein one is assaulted by a dual army of associated ideas, her associations and your own.

"This is the sub in. This is the lamb of the lantern of chalk." Because of the jerk of beauty it contains shoots the imagination for a fraction of a second through associated memories.

Of sun worship. Lamb worship. Lamb of light of the world. (Identical in Christian symbolism). Shepherd carries lantern. The lantern=lamb's eyes. Chalk white of lamb. Lantern sunshine in chalk pit=absolution of whiteness=pastel lamb=chalk Easter toy for peasants.

All this is personal, but something of the kind may happen to anyone when Gertrude Stein leaves grammatical lacunae among her depictions and the mind trips up and falls through into the subconscious source of associated ideas.

The uncustomary impetus of her style accelerates and extends the thought wave until it can vibrate a cosmos from a ray of light on a baa lamb.

This word picture which at first glance would seem to be a lamb being led past a chalk pit by lantern at sun in (down) is revised when on reading further I must conclude that it is still day light and I discover the lamb that carries itself, is itself the lantern of chalk.

And here let me proffer my apologies to Gertrude Stein who may have intended the description for … a daisy. The sun as the center, chalk as petal white, and the lamb an indication of the season of the year.

Let us leave the ultimate elucidation of Gertrude Stein to infinity.

Apart from all analysis, the natural the debonair way to appreciate Gertrude Stein is as one would saunter along a country way wise on a fine day and pluck, for its beauty, an occasional flower. So one sees suddenly:

"He does not look dead at all.
The wind might have blown him."

The Transatlantic Review, 1923.

"The Latest Thing in Prose Style."

Donald B. Willard

A new type of literature has burst upon the more or less erudite American public. It is a variety of prose narration, featured by short sentences, unusual punctuation, frequent repetitions of ideas, and the stressing of certain words till they run through the mind of the reader like the whisperings of a guilty conscience.

Miss Gertrude Stein is the person who has let loose this new brain-teaser. Born in Allegheny, Penn, educated in California, Baltimore and at Radcliffe, she now lives in Paris, whence she sends forth writings to the press of America. Those periodicals which present recherche, bizarre, clever, and novel things have given her a good bit of attention, and one of her books has just been published in Boston by the Four Seas Company.

In one way Miss Stein's work is like the gleaming sun rising out of the ocean. It has to be seen to be appreciated. Unlike the sunrise, however, the full beauty of it is not apparent at once. It has to be read carefully, then read again, and then pondered upon. Otherwise it is totally unintelligible.

A consideration of the tale of "Miss Furr and Miss Skeene" will probably give as good an idea of this literary innovation as anything could. One thing is sure, no one can read Miss Stein's work without a feeling of helplessness and of wonderment as to the limit of his own patience.

It appears that Helen Furr and Georgine Skeene both had voices, which they were cultivating. Helen's voice was good and Georgine's was maybe a little better. The two roomed together, and they were "quite regularly gay." There came a time when they separated and did not live together any more, the assumption being, it may be supposed, that Helen was a little outshone by Georgine.

A few quotations will show wherein the story is unique. Thus it begins: "Helen Furr had quite a pleasant home...." Then 10 paragraphs tell how they were gay there. All the time they kept cultivating their voices, but nevertheless they were as gay as two little squirrels. Men entered their lives only as part of the general gaiety. Just how much the men added to the gaiety is gaily uncertain....

It may be gathered that they were gay. They kept on learning new ways of being gay, and they were as regular as the multiplication table or a lodge of Bisons. By and by Georgine went to visit her brother, and Helen philosophized to herself.... The story ends by speaking of Helen, now living alone....

That is all there is to it. No additions or corrections asked for. The style has its good points, and if the reader doesn't understand it is probably his own fault. Several repetitions of every sentence in a minstrel show make it certain that the whole audience gets the idea, and certainly it is plain that Helen and Georgine were gay.

The style may become popular and it may not. It presents interesting possibilities. Imagine President Coolidge addressing the Senate on law and order in this fashion! Try to conceive of a minister telling his congregation of the wickedness of the "regularly gay" young people of the present age, and expatiating upon "learning little ways of being good!" Imagine "Yes, We Have No Bananas" drawn to half an hour's whistle by the adoption of Miss Stein's droll manner! The thought of Jackie Coogan dancing a jig with the Statue of Liberty on Boston Common is not a more thrilling fantasy.

There seems to be no doubt that Miss Stein has evolved an original way of writing, but in spite of the fact that it is quite regularly gay, it is also quite regularly complex.

Boston Globe, October 31, 1923.

"The Virtue of Intolerance."

Anonymous

If criticism owes a duty to tolerance—and no one, we suppose, would deny that the very keystone of good criticism is open-mindedness—it has no less an obligation to intolerance. For quite as much as it must be hospitable to the new and the experimental must it be cold to the shoddy and the merely eccentric. Poise is of equal value in criticism with enthusiasm, and balance is a virtue devoutly to be courted. But balance unfortunately is one of the rarest of virtues. For it is the way of human nature if it espouses a cause to cleave to it strongly, and the more warmly it upholds it the less to be able to see its faults. Thus it is that a Gertrude Stein can become a fetish to her admirers, her banalities and dullness seem the earmarks of genius, and her cult take on the seriousness of gospel. The mere fact that to the mass of the cultured public her mannerisms seem absurdities, her repetitions and involutions atrocities, has no weight with her followers. If these qualities cannot be appreciated by the conservative, why so much the worse for the conservative. And that, in the language of the day, is that.

But it is not that, it is not by any means the whole of the matter. For Gertrude Stein and her disciples may be perfectly negligible phenomenons, but the criticism that treats them not only with respect but as of enormous importance is a serious matter. It is the kind of criticism that is by the nature of the case militant rather than persuasive, that is supercilious to tradition, and scornful of standards. It is a proselytizing criticism that is dangerous since it makes a god of novelty and attaches to the bizarre inherent merit. It is sadly lacking in the saving grace of humor, is warped out of perspective by its own heat, and is self-hypnotized into seeing aridity as simplicity, oddness as beauty, emptiness as pregnancy. Surely such writing as Gertrude Stein's could not hold attention for a day if it were not for the smokescreen of importance which the critics have thrown about it. Its own stupidity would have laughed it into oblivion.

Some time ago in a Commencement address, Professor John Livingston Lowes of Harvard, after commenting upon the delights of good reading, added: "And after one has wound up one's faculties, like Mrs. Battle, over serious things, one may indulge with propriety in what I suppose one may designate as a slumming expedition among books." And he went on to explain his statement by saying that to Maculay a slumming expedition was a journey through Kitty Cuthbertson's novels with their no less than twenty-seven fainting fits in the course of five volumes; to Dr. Johnson, a reading of John Ruttey's *A Spiritual Diary and Soliloquies,* and to himself a perusal of the tear-filled pages of Henry MacKenzie's *A Man of Feeling.* Surely it is into this category of literary slumming that forging through the pages of Gertrude Stein falls, or else is all common sense fell from literature. Place it in conjunction with an even indifferently fine piece of writing, and can such a passage as the following culled from Miss Stein's effusion in *The New Criterion* entitled "Fifteenth of November" be regarded as anything other than a slum?...

If this is literature, or anything other than stupidity worse than madness, then has all criticism since the beginning of letters been mere idle theorizing. If it is literature, then alas! for literature. Thank Heaven, that there are still Professor Lowes and Harvards to conserve tradition and guide taste, and to make the world safe for eccentricity. For the times can ill afford eccentricity.

To raise the grotesque and the absurd to the plane of the serious is to render a disservice to literature. More, it is to render an insult to intelligence and invoke a curse on criticism.

The Saturday Review of Literature, February 27, 1926.

"A Word on Gertrude Stein."

Gilbert Armitage

I may as well be honest. I have read neither *Geography and Plays*, nor *Three Lives*, nor *The Making of Americans*. And what skill is not able to conceal, simplicity is constrained to admit. Yet Miss Stein is so unmistakably as important as she is neglected, that even if one cannot send people back to her works with intenser, because more conscious, appreciation—the higher function of the critic, one is doing work of some value, if one can perform only the lower function of the critic, and increase or incite their curiosity about her writing.

When Miss Stein spoke in Christ Church last week she shattered one or two current delusions about herself pretty completely. First, by pointing to the interest maintained in her works for twenty years, she proved to those who required a demonstration that she is a genuine creative artist and no charlatan. Second, in answer to a question, she said that she used all words in their common or garden meanings: which shows that she is far too sensible to try—as some of her intrepidly "modern" admirers accused her of trying—to divorce words from meaning. She is no demented or mystical mathematician, attempting by a process of arbitrary and capricious juxtapositions of words, to build up a literature of abstract patterns.

The precious word "abstract" has been the cause of innumerable misconceptions of modern art. There is and can be no such thing as abstract art. If there is one thing common to all works of art, in what medium and of what period soever, it is their concreteness. A philosophical concept is not a work of art. A work of art is an intuitive apprehension of reality, conceived in terms of concrete form in some sensuous medium. A cubist picture consists of paint on canvas, and is appreciated through the eyes. One does not apprehend the law of excluded middle in terms of a visual or a concrete image. To speak of abstract art is, therefore, bunkum.

Even Miss Sitwell has fallen for this comprehensive and comfortable term in her article on Gertrude Stein in the early October number of last year's

Vogue. She accounts for the difficulty of Miss Stein's work by saying that we are unaccustomed to abstract patterns being built of words. She then quotes the following lines by way of illustration....

She could not have chosen a worse example. This is an easily understood passage. The continuity of the series of images which compose these lines is the obvious one of subjective associations. Why, then, employ "abstract," the smug euphemism of the baffled art critic, in describing it?

Miss Stein is like every other pioneer in the history of literature. She is not trying to invent a new style. She is not so silly. She is merely striving to find the most accurate means of expressing her own relation to her time and her environment. Accurate and, therefore, new.

Any new idiom is, as Miss Stein herself said on Monday, difficult. But Miss Stein offers greater difficulty to readers of her day than did, say, Aeschylus or Marlow or Coleridge to theirs. Why? Because she is more ruthlessly subjective. Living as she does in an age when local or national feeling in art is a thing of the past, when sophistication has made men as acutely individualized as states are widely diffuse, when it is impossible to be sincere without being subjective, Miss Stein has set herself to make a personal, as opposed to the conventional, selection (*e.g.,* of the Romantics), from her own subjective impressions. Her works may almost be said to resemble the shadows cast by the unconscious upon the conscious mind. But whether this simile be too fantastic or not, her intensive individualism sufficiently explains (not explicates) the obscure and the elliptical in her writings.

The Oxford Magazine, June 17, 1926.

"Gertrude Stein."

Blanche London

Among sophisticated writers both in America and in England, Gertrude Stein is considered the high-priestess of modernism. An American by birth, for the past twenty-five years, she has been living in Paris. In France where new tendencies in art, music, literature, and philosophy have for generations been crystallized, Gertrude Stein has studied, sorted, prepared, revealed to an aesthetically stale world new principles of beauty. Her early critiques of the art of Matisse and Picasso explained from the aesthete's point of view the virtue of modern art. Her prose and poetry published during the last two decades are examples of the same point of view in literature.

This supremely civilized woman and brave experimenter in literature finds her American prophet in the person of Mr. Sherwood Anderson. In the preface to her *Geography and Plays*, he says that Miss Stein's writing is "the most important pioneer work done in the field of literature in my time." It must be understood that Miss Stein's works are not caviar to the uninitiated. In order to enjoy reading her books, you have to be "trained." You must understand all mental vagaries. You must be able to follow with her in observing details from both the artistic and the scientific points of view. You must have a highly developed emotional and intellectual perception. Above all, you must appreciate with her, not only the value of general ideas, but the intense beauty that lies in the handling of words....

Does her Jewish origin account for her rebellion against academic language forms? We doubt it. Whenever we find rebellion in art and literature, we dare not generalize concerning its cause. Art is too subjective to reduce to vague generalizations, and so is literature. In some cases, rebellion may spring up because the creator "not belonging" socially to the group around him, unconsciously finds revenge by breaking out into a sensational art form. Rebellion, however, could not have been the motive of Gertrude Stein. She is too sincere a writer and philosopher. She creates something which is at once new and primitive and eternal.

In the deep rhythmical majesty of her prose there lies the essence of the poetry of the Book of Job. This is not because she would rebel against academic forms at all; it is because only through such a style does she most sensitively express her own complex mind. Rather than rebelling, it is she who steps in time to the march of the progress of the universe. The academic forms are leftovers from a tradition that is very slowly being washed away. No cause for immediate alarm. Academic forms wear down as slowly as the rocks at the edge of a mad coast. Eventually, after geological years, sand supersedes the rocks. Some day Gertrude Stein's writing will be classic and then all of a sudden, the world will consider her work, not irritating and stimulating, but ineffably beautiful.

In her *Composition as Explanation* she explains that she is not ahead of her time. No one is ahead of their time. Only a "different" variety of work will not be accepted by contemporaries who work in another way. Why do these contemporaries refuse to accept the other writer's work? Because they do not have to accept it, and human beings are naturally too indolent to accept anything that they are not obliged to accept. And at the same time they are too indolent to take the trouble to understand.

In *The Making of Americans*, she shows her profound insight into human behavior and human emotion. She finds full meaning in such emotions as disillusionment, sensitiveness, cowardice, courage, jealousy, stubbornness, curiosity, suspicion, hopefulness, anger, subtlety, pride, egotism, vanity, ambition. This book about the decent morality of American middle-class society is so thorough in content and so universal in application that it is an epic of ourselves in the true sense of the word....

Gertrude Stein is one of the very few modern American universal writers. Why are there not more? Because they are not big enough to understand the value, literary value, of symbols. They are too content with a photographic recording of their observations—the method of Sinclair Lewis. In order to have impressive literature, symbols are required. There are many other symbols besides words. There are symbols of atmosphere, symbols of human intent, symbols of defeat, symbols of desire. The shears of Delilah are a symbol, the Dove flying from the Ark is a symbol. The use of symbols induces strength, majesty, intellectual force, and power of suggestion. This is the only way to lift literature from realistic levels to a universal category.

This use of symbols is sensitively appreciated by Gertrude Stein. Her prose and poetry are full of unexpected words and images which prick the imagination and the intellect. And it is in this complete use of symbols, indeed, that she has influenced such creative literary forces as Ezra Pound, T. S. Eliot, E. E. Cummings, Mina Loy, Carl Sandburg, Marianne Moore, the late Elinor Wylie and Frances Newman, Archibald MacLeish, Elliot Paul, the Benet brothers, Ernest Hemingway and Sherwood Anderson.

A peculiarity of her style is that it is thoroughly natural and follows with a lovely nonchalance the dictates of her subconscious as well as her conscious mind. This makes for a great deal of repetition. But it is the sort of repetition which gives variety. It is not a futile repetition but one which becomes, as it were, embroidered in multicolored threads. Sometimes such repetition results in humor, in a better psychological or scientific understanding of the detail elaborated, in a different romantic or artistic interpretation, or in a broader philosophical compass.

The fact that a Jewish writer may feel an alien and homeless in his native country has nothing to do with the great individual Jewish writer. It may indeed influence the work of mediocre writers; they develop more completely in a homogeneous group. But a great writer is not provincial and is untouched by geographic limits. No writer warped because she was not in a homogeneous racial group has written an American Negro story like "Melanctha," nor a story of American life so astute, so universal as *The Making of Americans.* Gertrude Stein towers above racial prejudices, above criterion among groups. Her sphere, in the broad sense, is art.

The New Palestine, April 5, 1929.

"The Work of Gertrude Stein."

William Carlos Williams

Let it be granted that whatever is new in literature the germ of it will be found somewhere in the writings of other times; only the modern emphasis gives work a present distinction.

The necessity for this modern focus and the meaning of the changes involved are, however, another matter, the everlasting stumbling block to criticism. Here is a theme worth development in the case of Gertrude Stein—yet signally neglected.

Why in fact have we not heard more generally from American scholars upon the writings of Miss Stein? Is it lack of heart or ability or just that theirs is an enthusiasm which fades rapidly of its own nature before the risks of today?

The verbs auxiliary we are concerned in here, continued my father, are am; was; have; had; do; did; could; owe; make; made; suffer; shall; should; will; would; can; ought; used; or is wont ...— or with these question added to them;— Is it? Was it? Will it be? ... Or affirmatively ...—Or chronologically ...— Or hypothetically — ... If it was? If it was not? What would follow?—If the French beat the English? If the Sun should go out of the Zodiac?

Now, by the right use and application of these, continued my father, in which a child's memory should be exercised, there is no one idea can enter the brain how barren soever, but a magazine of conceptions and conclusions may be drawn forth from it.—Didst thou ever see a white bear? cried my father, turning his head round to Trim, who stood at the back of his chair. —No, an' please your honor, replied the corporal.—But thou couldst discourse about one, Trim, said my father, in case of need?—How is it possible, brother, quoth my Uncle Toby, if the corporal never saw one?—'Tis the fact I want, replied my father,—and the possibility of it as follows.

A white bear! Very well, Have I ever seen one? Might I ever have seen one? Am I ever to see one? Ought I ever to have seen one? Or can I ever see one?

Would I had seen a white bear! (for how can I imagine it!)

If I should see a white bear, what should I say? If I should never see a white bear, what then?

If I can never have, can, must, or shall see a white bear alive; have I ever seen the skin of one? Did I ever see one painted?—described? Have I never dreamed of one?

Note how the words *alive, skin, painted, described, dreamed* come into the design of these sentences. The feeling is of words themselves, a curious immediate quality quite apart from their meaning, much as in music different notes are dropped, so to speak, into repeated chords one at a time, one after another—for themselves alone. Compare this with the same effects common in all that Stein does. See *Geography and Plays,* "They were both gay there." To continue—

Did my father, mother, uncle, aunt, brothers or sisters, ever see a white bear? What would they give? ... How would they behave? How would the white bear have behaved? Is he wild? Tame? Terrible? Rough? Smooth?

Note the play upon *rough* and *smooth* (though it is not certain that this was intended), *rough* seeming to apply to the bear's deportment, *smooth* to surface, presumably the bear's coat. In any case the effect is that of a comparison relating primarily not to any qualities of the bear himself but to the words rough and smooth. And to finish—*Is the white bear worth seeing? Is there any sin in it? Is it better than a black one?*

In this manner ends Chapter 43 of *The Life and Opinions of Tristram Shandy.* The handling of the words and to some extent the imaginative quality of the sentence is a direct forerunner of that which Gertrude Stein has woven today into a synthesis of its own. It will be plain, in fact, on close attention, that Sterne exercises not only the play (or music) of sight, sense and sound contrast among the words themselves which Stein uses, but their grammatical play also—i.e. for, how, can I imagine it; did my ..., what would, how would, compare Stein's "to have rivers; to halve rivers," etc. It would not be too much to say that Stein's development over a lifetime is anticipated completely with regard to subject matter, sense and grammar— in Sterne.

Starting from scratch, we get, possibly, thatch; just as they have always done in poetry.

Then they would try to connect it up by something life—The mice scratch, beneath the thatch.

Miss Stein does away with all that. The free-versists on the contrary used nothing else. They saved—The mice, under the …

It is simply the skeleton, the "formal" parts of writing, those that make form, that she has to do with, apart from the "burden" which they carry. The skeleton, important to acknowledge where confusion of all knowledge of the "soft parts" reigns as at the present day in all intellectual fields.

Stein's theme is writing. But in such a way as to be writing envisioned as the first concern of the moment, dragging behind it a dead weight of logical burdens, among them a dead criticism which broken through might be a gap by which endless other enterprises of the understanding should issue—for refreshment.

It is a revolution of some proportions that is contemplated, the exact nature of which may be no more than sketched here but whose basis is humanity in a relationship with literature hitherto little contemplated.

And at the same time it is a general attack on the scholastic viewpoint, the medieval remnant with whose effects from generation to generation literature has been infested to its lasting detriment. It is a breakaway from that paralyzing vulgarity of logic for which the habits of science and philosophy coming over into literature (where they do not belong) are to blame.

It is this logicality as a basis for literary action which in Stein's case, for better or worse, has been wholly transcended.

She explains her own development in connection with *Tender Buttons* (1914). "It was my first conscious struggle with the problem of correlating sight, sound and sense, and eliminating rhythm;—now I am trying grammar and eliminating sight and sound" (*transition* No, 14, fall, 1928).

Having taken the words to her choice, to emphasize further what she has in mind she has completely unlinked them (in her most recent work) from their former relationships in the sentence. This was absolutely essential and unescapable. Each under the new arrangement has a quality of its own, but not conjoined to carry the burden science, philosophy and every higgledy-piggledy figment of law and order have been laying upon them in the past. They are like a crowd at Coney Island, let us say, seen from an airplane.

Whatever the value of Miss Stein's work may turn out finally to be, she has at least accomplished her purpose of getting down on paper this much that is decipherable. She has placed writing on a plane where it may deal unhampered with its own affairs, unburdened with scientific and philosophic lumber.

For after all, science and philosophy are today, in their effect upon the mind, little more than fetishes of unspeakable abhorrence. And it is through a subversion of the art of writing that their grip upon us has assumed its steel-like temper.

What are philosophers, scientists, religionists, they that have filled up literature with their pap? Writers, of a kind. Stein simply erases their stories, turns them off and does without them, their logic (founded merely on the limits of the perceptions) which is supposed to transcend the words, along with them. Stein denies it. The words, in writing, she discloses, transcend everything.

Movement (for which in a petty way logic is taken), the so-called search for truth and beauty, is for us the effect of a breakdown of the attention. But movement must not be confused with what we attach to it but, for the rescuing of the intelligence, must always be considered aimless, without progress.

This is the essence of all knowledge.

Bach might be an illustration of movement not suborned by a freight of purposed design, loaded upon it as in almost all later musical works; statement unmusical and unnecessary, Stein's "They lived very gay then" has much of the same quality of movement to be found in Bach—the composition of the words determining not the logic, not the "story," not the theme even, but the movement itself. As it happens "They were both gay there" is as good as some of Bach's shorter figures.

Music could easily have a statement attached to each note in the manner of words, so that C natural might mean the sun, etc., and completely dull treatises be played—and even sciences finally expounded in tunes.

Either, we have been taught to think, the mind moves in a logical sequence to a definite end which is its goal, or it will embrace movement without goal other than movement itself for an end and hail "transition" only as supreme.

Take your choice, both resorts are an improper description of the mind in fullest play.

If the attention could envision the whole of writing, let us say, at one time, moving over it in swift and accurate pursuit of the modern imperative at the instant when it is most to the fore, something of what actually takes place under an optimum of intelligence could be observed. It is an alertness not to let go of a possibility of movement in our fearful bedazzlement with some concrete and fixed present. The goal is to keep a beleaguered line of understanding which has movement from breaking down and becoming a hole into which we sink decoratively to rest.

The goal has nothing to do with the silly function which logic, natural or otherwise, enforces. Yet it is a goal. It moves as the sense wearies, remains fresh, living. One is concerned with it as with anything pursued and not with the rush of air or the guts of the horse one is riding—save to a very minor degree.

Writing, like everything else, is much a question of refreshed interest. It is directed, not idly, but as most often happens (though not necessarily so) toward that point not to be predetermined where movement is blocked (by the end of logic perhaps). It is about these parts, if I am not mistaken, that Gertrude Stein will be found.

There remains to be explained the bewildering volume of what Miss Stein has written, the quantity of her work, its very apparent repetitiousness, its iteration, what I prefer to call its extension, the final clue to her meaning.

It is, of course, a progression (not a progress) beginning, conveniently, with "Melanctha" from *Three Lives*, and coming up to today.

How in a democracy, such as the United States, can writing which has to compete with excellence elsewhere and in other times remain in the field and be at once objective (true to fact) intellectually searching, subtle and instinct with powerful additions to our lives? It is impossible, without invention of some sort, for the very good reason that observation about us engenders the very opposite of what we seek: triviality, crassness and intellectual bankruptcy. And yet what we do see can in no way be excluded. Satire and flight are two possibilities but Miss Stein has chosen otherwise.

But if one remain in a place and reject satire, what then? To be democratic, local (in the sense of being attached with integrity to actual experience) Stein, or any other artist, must for subtlety ascend to a plane of almost abstract design to keep alive. To writing, then, as an art in itself. Yet what actually impinges on the sense must be rendered as it appears, by use of which, only, and under which, untouched, the significance has to be disclosed. It is one of the major problems of the artist.

"Melanctha" is a thrilling clinical record of the life of a colored woman in the present-day United States, told with directness and truth. It is without question one of the best bits of characterization produced in America. It is universally admired. This is where Stein began. But for Stein to tell a story of that sort, even with the utmost genius, was not enough under the conditions in which we live, since by the very nature of its composition such a story does violence to the larger scene which would be portrayed.

True, a certain way of delineating the scene is to take an individual like Melanctha and draw her carefully. But this is what happens. The more carefully the drawing is made, the greater the genius involved and the greater the interest that attaches, therefore, to the character as an individual, the more exceptional that character becomes in the mind of the reader and the less typical of the scene.

It was no use for Stein to go on with *Three Lives*. There that phase of the work had to end. See *Useful Knowledge*, the parts on the U. S. A.

Stein's pages have become like the United States viewed from an airplane— the same senseless repetitions, the endless multiplications of toneless words, with these she had to work.

No use for Stein to fly to Paris and forget it. The thing, the United States, the unmitigated stupidity, the drab tediousness of the democracy, the overwhelming number of the offensively ignorant, the dull nerve—is there in the artist's mind and cannot be escaped by taking a ship. She must resolve it if she can, if she is to be.

That must be the artist's articulation with existence.

Truly, the world is full of emotion—more or less—but it is caught in bewilderment to a far more important degree. And the purpose of art, so far as it has any, is not at least to copy that, but lies in the resolution of difficulties to its own comprehensive organization of materials. And by so doing, in this case, rather than by copying, it takes its place as most human.

To deal with Melanctha, with characters of whomever it may be, the modern Dickens, is not therefore human. To write like that is not in the artist, to be human at all, since nothing is resolved, nothing is done to resolve the bewilderment which makes of emotion an inanity: That is to overlook the gross instigation and with all subtlety to examine the object minutely for "the truth"—which if there is anything more commonly practiced or more stupid, I have yet to come upon it.

To be most useful to humanity, or to anything else for that matter, an art, writing, must stay art, not seeking to be science, philosophy, history, the humanities, or anything else it has been made to carry in the past. It is this enforcement which underlies Gertrude Stein's extension and progression to date.

Pagany, Winter 1930.

"The Career of a Modernist: Gertrude Stein is Famous for Her Influence on Current Literature."

Blanche London

Gertrude Stein, high priestess of modernism, is one of the influential literary figures of the day. An American by birth, she was our first important writer to settle in Montparnasse and has remained in Paris for twenty-five years. She was born in Allegheny, Pennsylvania, of German Jewish parentage and was educated in this country. Because, from an artistic point of view, her writing is iconoclastic, she enjoys today the literary freedom which France has always offered to those who strive for new creative form whether it be in art, music, or literature.

When Miss Stein's family moved to California, she attended the Oakland, California public schools. Later she graduated with honors from Radcliffe College in Cambridge, Massachusetts, where, specializing in psychology, she studied under the famous German psychologist, Münsterberg, and the renowned William James.

Then she pursued this work at Johns Hopkins Medical School at Baltimore, and concentrated her attention there upon brain anatomy. However, because of her desire to express herself in writing, she abandoned research in science, and went to Pairs.

During the World War, she drove a Ford car, visiting and supplying French hospitals. In appreciation for her services she was decorated by the French government with the Reconnaissance Francaise.

The greatest tribute to a litterateur is the acknowledgment from other writers that they have received inspiration in its deepest sense. That is to be a writer's writer— as Gertrude Stein. Her influence, if not general, has sifted into and been inextricably merged with the work of such gifted literary moderns as Sherwood Anderson, Carl Van Vechten, the late Frances Newman, Ernest Hemingway, T. S. Eliot, Marianne Moore, the late Elinor Wylie, Carl Sandburg, the Benet brothers, E. E. Cummings and Amy Lowell.

In painting, music, and sculpture, Miss Stein's critical sense has always been alert. She has the power to recognize genius. Living in France within the past generation, she has seen evolved in close proximity modern music, painting, and sculpture. With her pen, she made known to a doubting public the qualities of grandeur in the musical compositions of Virgil Thomson and Henrietta Gluck; in the paintings of Matisse, Picasso, and Juan Gris; in the sculptures of Elie Nadelman. Since her appreciation of these experimenters in the arts came early in their careers, she definitely aided in making Europe and America conscious of their caliber.

Miss Stein's personality is commanding. Sisly Huddleston, in his recent book, *Paris Salons, Cafes, Studios,* writes that once seen she will never be forgotten. Her mannish face and clothes give her a resemblance to a Cistercian monk. Those under her influence call her their Master.

There have been many who mocked and parodied her style, especially her habit of repeating phrases; but such writers always leave out something that is there—the symbolic element. She can write the most delicate conventional prose as shown in *Three Lives.* Other prose sketches are really abstract patterns and have no pretense of touching reality. Into certain realistic sketches, she infuses rhythmic word play, word association to interesting extremes.

Her writings show three divisions: fiction, poetry, and criticism. In *Three Lives,* published in 1908, her story about Melanctha, a young Negress, reveals a sympathetic understanding of the emotions of the Negro. In 1913, "Portrait of Mabel Dodge," brought to us another searching study. *Tender Buttons*, a book of poems, was published in 1915. In 1918 appeared *Mary, He Giggled. Geography and Plays* followed in 1923. Her recent piece of fiction is *The Making of Americans* in which is stressed the sense of dignity of the American middle class. It is a sober history of a family's progress, and into its picture of distinctively American life is brought a psychology which is universal.

In *Composition as Explanation,* ostensibly a book of general literary criticism, she not only explains the evolution of her own literary style, but also analyzes the reason why new modernistic notes will take their permanent hold on the world of the arts. In this work her irony, directed toward the element in our era of aesthetic mental indolence, she enriched the *weltanschauung* of countless minds.

If Miss Stein has been audacious, her revolt in her sphere, like that of other Jewish rebels in the arts, has paved the way for many creative writers. In fact, according to Sherwood Anderson, her writing is the most important pioneer work done within recent years in the field of letters.

Those who can appreciate her work need no explanation of it. To others, who scoff at and cannot be persuaded to enjoy modernism in literature, all explanation is futile. However, it is generally conceded that Miss Stein has altered for the modern world the whole face and complexion of English prose.

New York Jewish Tribune, March 6, 1931.

"Has Gertrude Stein a Secret?"

B. F. Skinner

In the *Autobiography of Alice B. Toklas* Gertrude Stein tells in the following way of some psychological experiments made by her at Harvard: "She was one of a group of Harvard men and Radcliffe women and they all lived very closely and very interestingly together. One of them, a young philosopher and mathematician who was doing research work in psychology, left a definite mark on her life. She and he together worked out a series of experiments in automatic writing under the direction of Münster-berg. The result of her own experiments, which Gertrude Stein wrote down and which was printed in the *Harvard Psychological Review*, was the first writing of hers ever to be printed. It is very interesting to read because the method of writing to be afterwards developed in *Three Lives* and *The Making of Americans* already shows itself."

There is a great deal more in this early paper than Miss Stein points out. It is, as she says, an anticipation of the prose style of *Three Lives* and is unmistakably the work of Gertrude Stein in spite of the conventional subject matter with which it deals. Many turns of speech, often commonplace, which she has since then in some subtle way made her own are already to be found. But there is much more than this. The paper is concerned with an early interest of Miss Stein's that must have been very important in her later development, and the work that it describes cannot reasonably be overlooked by anyone trying to understand this remarkable person.

Since this paper is hard to obtain, I shall summarize it briefly. It was published in the *Psychological Review* for September 1896 under the title, "Normal Motor Automatism," by Leon M. Solomons and Gertrude Stein, and it attempted to show to what extent the elements of a "second personality" (of the sort to be observed in certain cases of hysteria) were to be found in a normal being. In their experiments the authors investigated the limits of their own normal motor automatism; that is to say, they undertook to see how far they could "split" their own personalities in a deliberate and purely artificial way. They were successful to the extent of being able to perform may acts (such as writing or reading aloud) in an automatic manner, while carrying on at the same time some other activity such as reading an interesting story.

In the experiments with automatic writing, a planchette of the ouija board type was originally used, but as soon as the authors had satisfied themselves that spontaneous writing movements do occur while the attention is directed elsewhere, an ordinary pencil and paper were used instead. The subject usually began by making voluntary random writing movements or by writing the letter *m* repeatedly. In one experiment this was done while the subject read an interesting story at the same time, and it was found that some of the words read in the story would be written down in an automatic way. At first there was a strong tendency to notice this as soon as it had begun to happen and to stop it, but eventually the words could be written down unconsciously as well as involuntarily. (I shall use Miss Stein's psychological terminology throughout). "Sometimes the writing of the word was completely unconscious, but more often the subject knew what was going on. His knowledge, however, was obtained by sensations *from the arm*. He was conscious that he just had written a word, not that he was about to do so.

In other experiments the subject read an interesting story as before, and single words were dictated to him to be written down at the same time. These were difficult experiments, but after considerable practice they were successful. The subject was eventually able to write down "five or six" words spoken by another person, without being conscious of either the heard sounds or the movement of the arm. If his attention were not sufficiently well distracted he might become aware that his hand was writing something. The information came form the arm, not from the sound of the dictated word. "It is never the sound that recalls us. This, of course, may be an individual peculiarity to a certain extent …. Yet, Miss Stein has a strong auditory consciousness, and sounds usually determine the direction of her attention."

In a third group of experiments the subject read aloud, preferably from an uninteresting story, while being read to from an interesting one. "If he does not go insane during the first few trials, he will quickly learn to concentrate his attention fully on what is being read to him, yet go on reading just the same. The reading becomes completely unconscious for periods of as much as a page." Automatic reading of this sort is probably part of the experience of everyone.

The fourth and last group brings out the relevance of the experiments to the later work of Gertrude Stein. I shall let Miss Stein describe the result:

"*Spontaneous automatic writing.*— This became quite easy after a little practice. We had now gained so much control over our habits of attention that distraction by reading was almost unnecessary .... A phrase would seem to get into head and keep repeating itself at every opportunity, and hang over from day to day even. The stuff written was grammatical, and the words and phrases fitted together all right, but there was not much connected thought. The unconsciousness was broken into every six or seven words by flashes of consciousness, so that one cannot be sure but what the slight element of connected thought which occasionally appeared was due to these flashes of consciousness. But the ability to write stuff that sounds all right, without consciousness, was fairly well demonstrated by the experiments" ....

Here is obviously an important document. No one who has read *Tender Buttons* or the later work in the same vein can fail to recognize a familiar note in these examples of automatic writing. They are quite genuinely in the manner that has so commonly been taken as characteristic of Gertrude Stein. Miss Stein's description of her experimental result is exactly that of the average reader confronted with *Tender Buttons* for the first time: "The stuff is grammatical, and the words and phrases fit together all right, but there is not much connected thought." In short, the case is so good, simply on the grounds of style, that we are brought to the swift conclusion that the two products have a common origin, and that the work of Gertrude Stein in the *Tender Buttons* manner is written automatically and unconsciously in some such way as that described in this early paper.

The conclusion grows more plausible as we consider the case. It is necessary, of course, to distinguish between the Gertrude Stein of *Three Lives* and the *Autobiography* and the Gertrude Stein of *Tender Buttons*, a distinction that is fairly easily made, even though, as we shall see in a moment, there is some of the first Gertrude Stein in the latter work. If we confine ourselves for the present to the second of these two persons, it is clear that the hypothetical author who might be inferred from the writing itself possesses just those characteristics that we should expect to find if a theory of automatic writing were the right answer. Thus there is very little intellectual content discoverable. The reader—the ordinary reader, at least —cannot infer from the writing that its author possesses any consistent point of view. There is seldom any intelligible expression of opinion, and there are enough capricious reversals to destroy the effect of whatever there may be. There are even fewer emotional prejudices. The writing is cold. Strong phrases are almost wholly lacking, and it is so difficult to find a well-rounded emotional complex that if one is found it may as easily be attributed to the ingenuity of the seeker. Similarly, our hypothetical author shows no sign of a personal history or of a cultural background; *Tender Buttons* is the stream of consciousness of a woman without a past. The writing springs from no literary sources. In contrast with the work of Joyce, to whom a superficial resemblance may be found, the borrowed phrase is practically lacking.

From this brief analysis it is apparent that, although it is quite plausible that the work is due to a second personality successfully split off from Miss Stein's conscious self, it is a very flimsy sort of personality indeed. It is intellectually unopinionated, it is emotionally cold, and has no past. It is unread and unlearned beyond grammar school. It is as easily influenced as a child; a heard word may force itself into whatever sentence may be under construction at the moment, or it may break the sentence up altogether and irremediably. Its literary materials are the sensory things nearest at hand—objects, sounds, tastes, smells, and so on. The reader may compare, for the sake of the strong contrast, the materials of "Melanctha" in *Three Lives*, a piece of writing of quite another sort. In her experimental work it was Miss Stein's intention to avoid the production of a true second personality, and she considered herself to be successful. The automatism she was able to demonstrate possessed the "elements" of a second personality, it was able to do anything that a second personality could do, but it never became the organized *alter ego* of the hysteric. The superficial character of the inferential author of *Tender Buttons* consequently adds credibility to the theory of automatic authorship.

The Gertrude Stein enthusiast may feel that I am being cruelly unjust in this estimate. I admit that there are passages in *Tender Buttons* that elude the foregoing analysis. But it must be made clear that the two Gertrude Steins we are considering are not kept apart by the covers of books. There is a good deal of the Gertrude Stein of the *Autobiography* in *Tender Buttons*, in the form of relatively intelligible comment, often parenthetical in spirit. Thus at the end of the section on Mutton (which begins "A letter which can wither, learning which can suffer and an outrage which is simultaneous is principle") comes this sentence: "A meal in mutton mutton why is lamb cheaper, it is cheaper because so little is more," which is easily recognized as a favorite prejudice of the Gertrude Stein of the *Autobiography*. Similarly such a phrase as "the sad procession of the unkilled bull," in *An Elucidation*, is plainly a reference to another of Miss Stein's interests. But, far from damaging our theory, this occasional appearance of Miss Stein herself is precisely what the theory demands. In her paper in the *Psychological Review* she deals at length with the inevitable alternation of conscious and automatic selves, and in the quotation we have given it will be remembered that she comments upon these "flashes of consciousness." Even though the greater part of *Tender Buttons* is automatic, we should expect an "element of connected thought," and our only problem is that which Miss Stein herself has considered— namely, are we to attribute to conscious flashes all the connected thought that is present?

There is a certain logical difficulty here. It may be argued that, since we dispense with all the intelligible sentences by calling them conscious flashes, we should not be surprised to find that what is left is thin and meaningless. We must restate our theory, in a way that will avoid this criticism. We first divide the writings of Gertrude Stein into two parts on the basis of their ordinary intelligibility. I do not contend that this is a hard and fast line, but it is a sufficiently real one for most persons. It does not, it is to be understood, follow the outlines of her works. We then show that the unintelligible part has the characteristics of the automatic writing produced by Miss Stein in her early psychological experiments, and from this and many other considerations we conclude that our division of the work into two parts is real and valid and that one part is automatic in nature.

I cannot find anything in the *Autobiography* or the other works I have read that will stand against this interpretation. On the contrary, there are many bits of evidence, none of which would be very convincing in itself, that support it. Thus (1) *Tender Buttons* was written on scraps of paper, and no scrap was ever thrown away; (2) Miss Stein likes to write in the presence of distracting noises; (3) her handwriting is often more legible to Miss Toklas than to herself (that is, her writing is "cold" as soon as it is produced); and (4) she is "fond of writing the letter *m*," with which, the reader will recall, the automatic procedure often began. In *An Elucidation*, her "first effort to realize clearly just what her writing meant and why it was as it was," there are many fitful allusions to the experimental days: "Do you understand extraneous memory," "In this way my researches are easily read," a suddenly interpolated "I stopped I stopped myself," which recalls the major difficulty in her experiments, and so on.

It is necessary to assume that when Gertrude Stein returned to the practice of automatic writing (about 1912?) she had forgotten or was shortly to forget its origins. I accept as made in perfectly good faith the statement in the *Autobiography* that "Gertrude Stein never had subconscious reactions, nor was she a successful subject for automatic writing," even though the evidence to the contrary in her early paper is incontrovertible. She has forgotten it, just as she forgot her first novel almost immediately after it was completed and did not remember it again for twenty-five years. It is quite possible, moreover, that the manner in which she writes the *Tender Buttons* sort of thing is not unusual enough to remind her of its origins or to be remarked by others. One of the most interesting statements in the excerpt quoted from her early paper is that Gertrude Stein found it sufficient distraction simply to follow what she was writing some few words behind her pencil. If in the course of time she was able to bring her attention nearer and nearer to the pencil, she must eventually have reached a point at which there remained only the finest distinction between "knowing what one is going to write and knowing that one has written it." This is a transitional state to which Miss Stein devotes considerable space in her paper. It is therefore reasonable for us to assume that the artificial character of the experimental procedure has completely worn off, and that there remains only a not-far-from-normal state into which Miss Stein may pass unsuspectingly enough and in which the *Tender Buttons* style is forthcoming.

We have allowed for the presence of any or all of these kinds of meaning by speaking only of ordinary intelligibility. I do not think that a case can be made out for any one of them that is not obviously the invention of the analyzer. In any event the present argument is simply that the evidence here offered in support of a theory of automatic writing makes it *more probable* that meanings are not present, and that we need not bother to look for them. A theory of automatic writing does not, of course, necessarily exclude meanings. It is possible to set up a second personality that will possess all the attributes of a conscious self and whose writings will be equally meaningful. But in the present case it is clear that, as Miss Stein originally intended, a true second personality does not exist. This part of her work is, as she has characterized her experimental result, little more than "what her arm wrote." And it is an arm that has very little to say. This is, I believe, the main importance of the present theory for literary criticism. It enables one to assign an origin to the unintelligible part of Gertrude Stein that puts one at ease about its meanings.

There are certain aspects of prose writing, such as rhythm, that are not particularly dependent upon intelligibility. It is possible to experiment with them with meaningless words, and it may be argued that this is what is happening in the present case. Considering the freedom that Miss Stein has given herself, I do not think the result is very striking, although this is clearly a debatable point. It is a fairer interpretation, however, to suppose in accordance with our theory, that there is no experimentation at the time the writing is produced. There may be good reason for publishing the material afterward as an experiment. For example, I recognize the possibility of a salutary, though accidental, effect upon Gertrude Stein's conscious prose or upon English prose in general. In *Composition As Explanation*, for example, there is an intimate fusion of the two styles, and the conscious passages are imitative of the automatic style. This is also probably true of parts of the *Autobiography*. It is perhaps impossible to tell at present whether the effect upon her conscious prose is anything more than a loss of discipline. The compensating gain is often very great.

We have no reason, of course, to estimate the literary value of this part of Miss Stein's work. It might be considerable, even if our theory is correct. It is apparent that Miss Stein believes it to be important and has accordingly published it. If she is right, if this part of her work is to become historically as significant as she has contended, then the importance of the document with which we began is enormous. For this first time we should then have an account by the author herself of how a literary second personality has been set up.

I do not believe this importance exists, however, because I do not believe in the importance of the part of Miss Stein's writing that does not make sense. On the contrary, I regret the unfortunate effect it has had in obscuring the finer work of a very fine mind. I welcome the present theory because it gives one the freedom to dismiss one part of Gertrude Stein's writing as a probably ill-advised experiment and to enjoy the other and very great part without puzzlement.

The Atlantic Monthly, January 1934.

"Gertrude Stein: A Literary Idiot."

Michael Gold

Gertrude Stein recently returned to America after an absence of many years. In Paris, where she lived as a forbidding priestess of a strange literary cult, Gertrude Stein accumulated a salon frequented by some of the outstanding names of the modern art world and acquired the reputation of a literary freak. People either gaped at her published writings, or laughed at her incomprehensible literary epigrams— "a rose is a rose is a rose."

She was looked upon by those who believed in her as the greatest revolutionist in the history of contemporary literature, and by those who scoffed as the perpetrator of a gigantic literary hoax.

As it happens, neither of the two opinions is wholly correct. Her "revolution" resembles a literary putsch, and if her writing is "a hoax" nevertheless she earnestly believes in it.

In essence, what Gertrude Stein's work represents is an example of the most extreme subjectivism of the contemporary bourgeois artist, and a reflection of the ideological anarchy into which the whole of bourgeois literature has fallen.

What was it that Gertrude Stein set out to do with literature? When one reads her work it appears to resemble the monotonous gibberings of paranoiacs in the private wards of asylums. It appears to be a deliberate irrationality, a deliberate infantilism. However, the woman's not insane, but possessed of a strong, clear, shrewd mind. She was an excellent medical student, a brilliant psychologist, and in her more "popular" writings one sees evidence of wit and some wisdom.

And yet her works read like the literature of the students of padded cells in Matteawan.

Example: "I see the moon and the moon sees me. God bless the moon and God bless me and this you see remember me. In this way one fifth of the bananas were bought."

The above is supposed to be a description of how Gertrude Stein feels when she sees Matisse, the French modernist painter. It doesn't make sense. But this is precisely what it is supposed to do—not "make sense" in the normal meaning of the term.

The generation of artists of which Gertrude Stein is the most erratic figure arduously set out not to "make sense" in their literature. They believed that the instincts of man were superior to the reasonings of the rational mind. They believed in intuition as a higher form of learning and knowledge. Therefore, many of them wrote only about what they dreamed, dream literature. Others practiced a kind of "automatic writing" where they would sit for hours scribbling the random, subconscious itchings of their souls. They abandoned themselves to the mystic irrationalities of their spirits in order to create works of art which would be expressions of the timeless soul of man, etc. The result unfortunately revealed their souls as astonishingly childish or imbecile.

The literary insanity of Gertrude Stein is a deliberate insanity which arises out of a false conception of the nature of art and of the function of language.

A leisure class, which exists on the labor of others, which has no function to perform in society except the clipping of investment coupons, develops ills and neuroses. It suffers perpetually from boredom. Their life is stale to them.

Tasteless, inane, because it has no meaning. They seek new sensations, new adventures constantly in order to give themselves feelings.

The same process took place with the artists of the leisure class. Literature also bored them. They tried to suck out of it new sensations, new adventures.

They destroyed the common use of language. Normal ways of using words bored them. They wished to use words in a new, sensational fashion. They twisted grammar, syntax. They went in for primitive emotions, primitive art. Blood, violent death, dope dreams, soul-writhings, became the themes of their works.

In Gertrude Stein, art became a personal pleasure, a private hobby, a vice. She did not care to communicate because essentially there was nothing to communicate. She had no responsibility except to her own inordinate cravings. She became the priestess of a cult with strange literary rites, with mystical secrets. In this light, one can see that to Gertrude Stein and to the other artists like her, art exists in the vacuum of a private income. In order to pursue the kind of art, in order to be the kind of artist Gertrude Stein is, it is necessary to live in that kind of society which will permit one to have a private income from wealthy parents or sound investments. With this as a basis, you can write as you please. You can destroy language, mutilate grammar, rave or rant in the name of the higher knowledge. Nobody will disturb you. And in time perhaps you can impress or intimidate a certain number of critics and win a kind of reputation.

Gertrude Stein has won the reputation. She returns home to America after an absence of thirty-one years to find herself an object of curious respect by book clubs and lecture societies, and front page news for the newspapers.

Which seems to me to be proof that with enough money and enough persistence a madman can convince a world of his sanity. Gertrude Stein appears to have convinced America that she is a genius.

But Marxists refuse to be impressed with her own opinion of herself. They see in the work of Gertrude Stein extreme symptoms of the decay of capitalist culture. They view her work as the complete attempt to annihilate all relations between the artist and society in which he lives.

They see in her work the same kind of orgy and spiritual abandon that marks the life of the whole leisure class.

What else does her work resemble more than the midnight revels of a stockbroker throwing a penthouse party for a few intimate friends? Would it be possible to have either of these symptoms of degeneration except in a society divided into classes? Is there not an "idle art" just as there is an "idle rich"? Both do nothing but cultivate the insanity of their own desires, both cultivate strange indulgences. The literary idiocy of Gertrude Stein only reflects the madness of the whole system of capitalist values. It is part of the signs of doom that are written largely everywhere on the walls of bourgeois society.

Change the World! 1934.

"A 1 Pound Stein."

William Carlos Williams

With my knowledge and equipment, if someone should make me Professor of American in one of our better universities, I believe that within a month I could push our literature and in consequence our culture ahead at least twenty years. I would begin by expounding the lives and works of Ezra Pound and Gertrude Stein. I would present them as phases of the same thing. This would be amusing as well as instructive since the two detest each other so heartily. But with both at work upon a fundamental regeneration of thought in our language, to which each has added a noteworthy achievement during 1934, a similarity of purpose between them is easily demonstrable.

The presentation on the New York stage of Miss Stein's *Four Saints in Three Acts*, and the appearance of Pound's *Canto XXXVII* in *Poetry: A Magazine of Verse*, constitute a dual event of such importance that were our teaching places of any account whatever to the nation the authorities concerned would declare an immediate holiday in their departments of languages until their students had thoroughly familiarized themselves with the works in question.

The fact that they have not done so is proof of the national lack of culture, not to say our servility and blockheadedness.

To me Virgil Thomson's music is of doubtful aid to Stein's prose. It even shows up the major weakness in it, adding a consecutive interest which is often lacking there. But I'm not speaking of that now.

It's the disinfecting effect of the Stein manner or better said perhaps, its releasing force, that I wish to dwell upon. It's this which gives a listener to the opera his laughs, it's the same thing which fascinates an attentive reader, especially if he knows something about the terrors of writing. The tremendous cultural revolution implied by this interior revolution of technique tickles the very heart and liver of a man, makes him feel good. Good, that is, if he isn't too damned tied to his favorite stupidities. That's why he laughs. His laugh is the first acknowledgment of liberation. He feels clean. He's had a bath. He has been in fact disinfected.

For everything we know and do is tied up with words, with the phrases words make, with the grammar which stultifies, the prose or poetical rhythms which bind us to our pet indolences and medievalisms. To Americans especially, those who no longer speak English, this is especially important. We need too often a burst of air in at the window of our prose. It is absolutely indispensable that we get this before we can even begin to think straight again. It's the words, the words we need to get back to, words washed clean. Until we get the power of thought back through a new minting of the words we are actually sunk. This is a moral question at base, surely but a technical one also and first.

But every time anyone today tries to use a word it's like trying to get a few nails out of an old box to fix something with. You have to smash and pull and straighten—and then what have you got? That's not too good a simile, similes never are. In writing you can never pull out the words from the broken wood. They carry everything over with them. Unless—

Stein has gone systematically to work smashing every connotation that words have ever had, in order to get them back clean. It can't be helped that it's been forgotten what words are made for. It can't be helped that the whole house has to come down. In fact the whole house has come down. It's been proved over and over again. And it's got to come down because it has to be rebuilt. And it has to be rebuilt by unbound thinking. And unbound thinking has to be done with straight, sharp words. Call them nails to hold together the joints of the new architecture.

When in the middle of the music there is a pause and St. Paul says clearly, "The envelopes have been tied to all the fruit trees," or whatever the devil he does say, you see the trees, you see the envelopes and you don't see anything else.

It's nonsensical? So are you, only you don't know it. You can't know it without clean words. And you haven't any.

I don't care for the effect when the boys and girls stand belly to belly and say, "Thank you very much." That's not Stein, though it's good theater.

And no man can say, and be able to defend his position, that he doesn't care a whoop in Hades about all this. He can't get away with that. It's the closest, hottest interest he has. It doesn't make any difference whether or not he can sit down to a couple of thousand pages of *The Making of Americans*, any more than it makes any difference whether or not he can read through the pages of the *Congressional Record*. But by God, the results aren't something that he can ignore. If Stein has something, and she has, and if it can be shown that the repellent nature of her page, or the fascination of her page, means a regeneration of the processes of clean thinking and feeling, then it's a man's business to pay attention even when he can't read. And he'd better say, Go to it ol' girl.

The same is true in a different way for the work of Ezra Pound. Literature is right down in among the foundations of the intelligence by its chemistry of words. Difficult to the untrained mind the lines may be. If they're important, and I say they are, the only clue to be got from that is, Learn their significance. It isn't a national matter, as such, any more than *Star Spangled Banner* was of importance to St. Theresa. But just because there is a nation is no reason why works of intelligence should be systematically excluded within its confines.

My own feeling is that Stein has all she can do in tackling the fracture of stupidities bound in our thoughtless phrases, in our calcified grammatical constructions and in the subtle brainlessness of our meter and favorite prose rhythms—which compel words to follow certain others without precision of thought. Thomson's music helps in simulating the next step.

Ezra Pound, in his way, has taken that next step, the step of obstructions which are not quite open to Stein. But he is striking, as Stein is, at the basis of thought, at the mechanism with which we make our adjustments to things and to each other. This is the significance of the term culture and an indication of literature's relation thereto.

Pound, in his studious efforts to put us on the track of a released intelligence, a released spirit, a body that can function with what might be health—has dug down into the history of the *mens sans in sorpore sano* throughout the ages.

Handball and squash players in the clubs and Y. M. C. A. gyms should take an interest in that. It's at the basis of a good life that the excellence of literature is aimed. You ball-batters don't know what kind of a moral floor you're running around on. If you had any purpose in batting a ball you'd know what excellent writing is about.

And in this latest of Pound's cantos he's come to the administrations of Andrew Jackson and Martin Van Buren. In his history courses at colleges did anyone ever hear of them? Not on your life. They were Presidents of the United States. They had battles on their hands. Oh, is zat so? The same sort of answer they would give to Gert. And if anybody has the itch and doesn't go find out what's causing it we'd call him a damn fool. Well, Jackson's fought and won! For awhile, the same kind of fight that's been going on in this country and in every country since the days of the Gracchi, that against the illegal use of private interests of the resources of the government. What of it? Nothing, except that it's the *same* fight that's going on today, the same because of the stupidity, the lack of culture, the wordless proneness of the ball-batters, the pseudo-erudite, clever guys, the dumb clucks who haven't enough sense to know what it's all about.

It may be added that both Gertrude Stein and Ezra Pound live in Europe.

Rocking Horse, Spring 1935.

"Gertrude Stein: Method in Madness."

Harvey Eagleson

One of the most curious phenomena of modern literary history is the reputation of Gertrude Stein. It has long been known that William James considered her his most brilliant woman student, that she is an intimate friend of the great English scientist-philosopher, Whitehead, that she was one of the first to appreciate the work of Picasso, Matisse, and their school of artists and to collect their paintings before it was "the thing" to do. It is known that her ideas and her compositions have had an extensive influence on such diverse writers as Sherwood Anderson, Ernest Hemingway, Scott Fitzgerald, and Bernard Faÿ. For years her name has been almost a household word, so well known that newspaper columnists could allude to her, make jokes about her, and feel confident that their thousands of readers would recognize their allusions and appreciate their jokes. Yet none of the leading publishers would publish her books, and very few persons read what poetry and prose of hers found its way into print in the esoteric magazines of small cults or form the presses of obscure publishers.

Then in 1933 Miss Stein's autobiography, *The Autobiography of Alice B. Toklas*, appeared. It became a bestseller. The Modern Library brought out her early work, *Three Lives*; *The Making of Americans*, twenty-six years after she had finished writing it, appeared in a trade edition; her opera, *Four Saints in Three Acts*, was produced on Broadway with popular success; *Time* published her portrait on its cover; *Vanity Fair* honored her with a cartoon in color as its frontispiece. The magazines bristled with reviews, reviews that for the most part discussed her work with little seriousness. Most reviewers, like Clifton Fadiman in *The New Yorker*, took the publication of her books as an occasion for making "wise-cracking" remarks at her expense. Except for an occasional essay in those esoteric magazines, an article by Sherwood Anderson, and a chapter in Edmund Wilson's *Axel's Castle*, no serious study of her work has appeared.

But Miss Stein and her work are not jokes. One may like or dislike her writing, one may consider it too obscure to be artistically sound, one may be bored by her endless repetition and her monotonous rhythms, one may judge rightly that her work will never be widely read, but her influence on the arts, both graphic and literary, has been too great and too extensive for her work to be overlooked by the critic and the historian treating our period, or to be dismissed with a casual wave of the hand as semi-humorous nonsense, beneath contempt. As Edmund Wilson wrote, "one should not talk about 'nonsense' until one has decided what sense consists of." "Would it not be a lovely and charmingly ironic gesture of the gods if, in the end, the work of this artist were to prove the most lasting and important of all the word slingers of our generation!" wrote Sherwood Anderson in his introduction to *Geography and Plays*.

Miss Stein states her artistic credo thus: "Gertrude Stein, in her work, has always been possessed by the intellectual passion for exactitude in the description of inner and outer reality." She does not believe, in spite of her reputation to the contrary, that Art is esoteric, Art for Art's sake, a thing removed from life having no practical function .... Like the great German novelist, Thomas Mann, she believes that man in his most normal and characteristic manifestation is to be found in the great middle class. It is the real core, the heart and fibre of humanity. Know the middle class and you know man. The aristocracy, both intellectual and social, and the proletariat are but excrescences, the more-or-less lunatic fringe .... Except for the "portraits" of her friends, Miss Stein's work generally deals with the ordinary matters of life, the ordinary people in life, in the language and words of those people. The first and most essential step in an approach to an understanding of Gertrude Stein's work is to read it aloud. Only in that way can one realize the rhythms and sounds which are an integral part of her work. They are the rhythms of America, of American speech. Only in that way can one understand Miss Stein's peculiar punctuation, for she places marks of punctuation not where they should be placed to indicate syntactical pauses, but where they indicate speech pauses, American speech pauses. *Three Lives* and *The Making of Americans* sound like America talking, America talking after supper on summer evenings as it sits in rocking chairs on front porches, America gossiping over back fences. The long, involved, repetitious sentences, the characteristic grammatical errors, split infinitives, dangling pronouns, the idiomatic phrases of American speech are all there.

Repetition in the work of Gertrude Stein, however, is not simply a rhythmic device, a symphonic *leitmotif*. More profoundly it is an attempt to express an intricate and difficult philosophical idea. Miss Stein, like Carlyle before her and Einstein with her, is concerned with the problem of Time, "the continuous present" as she phrases it. Time is divided into three parts, the past, the present, and the future, but of these three the only one which can be said to exist in actuality is the present. The past, which was once the present, no longer exists except as it remains in the present as memory, and the future will not exist until it becomes the present. Composition to have any validity either to contemporaries or to posterity must be a presentation, "using everything" of the present, but as the present instantaneously becomes the past and as "naturally one does not know how it happened until it is well over beginning happening," a presentation of the present involves a continues "beginning again," that is, repetition.

But that is not all. The problem is still further complicated by the necessity of "using everything." While the past and the future may be said to be non-existent as separate entities, elements of both do exist in the present. From the point of view of behavioristic psychology the full explanation of any individual's environment involves, if carried to its logical conclusion, not only an analysis of all mankind but of the cosmos as well, that is, "everything." It is the same problem which Tennyson stated succinctly in *Flower in the Crannied Wall*.

> Little flower—but if I could understand
> What you are, root and all, and all in all,
> I should know what God and man is.

If we could know *all* about one single thing we would know all about the universe. It is an attempt, then, to express this idea which has produced what Margaret Anderson calls Gertrude Stein's "house-that-Jack-built style." To give a story the atmosphere of the "continuous present ... using everything," it is theoretically necessary to repeat each outstanding characteristic of a character each time that character faces a new situation, however slight, because the manner in which the character deals with the situation arises from these outstanding and ever-present characteristics. What is more, the future can be said to exist also in this present because these same conditioning factors will function similarly when situations come from the future into the present. In a way they may be said to predetermine the future. Naturally this repetition must become more frequent in proportion to the increased complexity of the character and the greater subtlety of the psychological analysis. It is all this that Miss Stein attempts to express by the stylistic device of repetition.

And there is more. She believes that each individual is a conglomerate of given characteristics and, moving through life, he merely repeats himself. "Always from the beginning there was to me all living as repeating." Meeting an individual for the first time, one observes only the constantly repeated surface characteristics. At first one does not "hear" the repeatings which arise from "bottom being," the inner depths of character, and until one can "hear" these repeatings as well as those on the surface, the individual must remain for the observer a fragmentary or erroneously conceived personality, not a "whole one."

In sorting out, classifying, recognizing, and building into wholes these "repeatings" one is aided by the factor of universality. Miss Stein believes in a fundamental unity in the cosmos .... With eggs, butter, milk, sugar, and flour, one can make several different kinds of cake by proportioning the ingredients differently, yet each cake still retains some of the original materials, eggs, butter, milk, sugar, flour. So with man. There are a certain number of elements in nature which mixed in different proportions in men differentiate one from one's fellow but leave a fundamental commonality.

Every one then is an individual being. Every one then is like many others always living .... Consoling as the thought of man's common humanity may be, man is nevertheless not free from tragedy. Like Conrad, Miss Stein believes that man "from the cradle to the grave and perhaps beyond" is alone. Complete understanding of each other or even of one's self is not given us. Because that understanding is lacking, misunderstanding, confusion, cruelty, and tragedy occur.

To Conrad, the best way to overcome this tragedy inherent in life was for men to stand together, present a unified front to an antithetical universe, to struggle futilely but gloriously against odds which could not be overcome. To Miss Stein the solution is emotional control attained through morality. The object of life is not happiness but the dignity which comes from "feeling the sadness of pain." All this, too, Miss Stein attempts to express by the device of repetition.

These are the reasons for Miss Stein's use of repetition. The artistic effectiveness of it is another matter. Margaret Anderson has stated the usual and the not unintelligent reaction to this device when she says, "I like it when she says 'a woman who had not any kind of an important feeling to herself inside her.' This seems to me interesting and important material. But when, in a book of six hundred thousand words like *The Making of Americans*, she repeats this description every time the character appears—which is probably six hundred times—I find the system uninteresting. I don't deny that it gives weight, but to me it is the weight of boredom."

Miss Stein, engrossed in stating her ideas fully, in carrying her thesis to its logical conclusion, has suffered the fate of most innovators. In stressing the idea she has fallen short of art. To be clear she must be complete, and completeness is seldom art. As has been many times pointed out, art is a matter of omission rather than commission. James Joyce, one of the greatest innovators of our, or any other time, produced an astonishing technical *tour de force* in his *Ulysses*, but Virginia Wolfe, using his technique with omissions produced a much greater work of art in *Mrs. Dalloway*. To Joyce belongs the credit for the idea, but to Mrs. Wolfe belongs the credit for the work of art. To Joyce belongs the credit for the idea, but to Mrs. Wolfe belongs the credit for the work of art. To Miss Stein belongs the idea, but to someone else will probably belong the work of art.

It may be objected that so far in the essay I have dealt only with Miss Stein's early work and that it is with her later, more incomprehensible, writings that her popular reputation is associated. True enough. Her early work, like the early work of Henry James or James Joyce, is "easier," but her later work is not, given a key, completely beyond interpretation though there are fundamental difficulties in that interpretation which must baffle Miss Stein's most sympathetic followers and in which lies the great artistic weakness of her work. Turn, then, to *Four Saints in Three Acts*.

The thesis, advanced even by Mr. Carl Van Vechten who writes the introduction to the printed libretto, that the entire opera is pure sound and very little sense arises, I am afraid, not so much from Miss Stein's obscurity as from an ignorance of the lives of Saint Therese of Avila and Saint Ignatius. I do not wish to maintain that all the lines in the libretto make sense. "Let Lucy Lily Lily Lucy Lucy let Lucy Lucy Lily Lily Lily Lily Lily let Lily Lucy Lucy let Lily," is merely a rhythmic sound pattern. But Miss Stein was not writing a play. She was writing the libretto for an opera, and in an opera sound, musical sound, not sense is the primary object. These lily-lucy passages are not the whole opera, however. They are but the embroideries on a firm fabric of sense.

Saint Therese was a great mystic, but she was also a great organizer, and she managed her temporal affairs with no little worldly acumen. In spite of opposition she founded an order, and at her death left behind her sixteen convents and fourteen monasteries which her energy had created. Within her struggled always two natures, the spiritual and the worldly. She did not teach asceticism or flagellation for others, but she practiced them herself for she knew that the flesh cried out within her. It is this struggle which Miss Stein symbolizes by Saint Therese I and Saint Therese II, which she states in the heading for Act I, "Avila: St. Therese half indoors and half out of doors," and in lines like "Leave later gaily the troubadour plays his guitar," and using a Biblical reference, "Saint Therese might it be Martha."

Saint Therese with all her mysticism was not interested in medieval scholasticism. She had no concern with question such as, How may angels could dance on the point of a needle? So in Miss Stein's opera when Saint Therese is asked a modern scholastic question, "If it were possible to kill five thousand chinamen by pressing a button it would be done" the reply is "Saint Therese not interested."

Again, take the much quoted Act III, Scene II.

"Pigeons on the grass alas.

Pigeons on the grass alas.

Short longer grass short longer longer shorter yellow grass.

Pigeons large pigeons on the shorter longer yellow grass alas pigeons on the grass."

Saint Ignatius believed he had a vision of the Holy Ghost descending in the form of a pigeon. In this scene the characters skeptically protest his pronouncement in language which is a broad burlesque of the silly repetitions in the words of a Händel oratorio. How did Saint Ignatius know it was the Holy Ghost and not just a pigeon? How could he distinguish between the Holy Ghost as a pigeon and just a pigeon? And if the pigeon he saw was different from other pigeons, must it even then of necessity have been the Holy Ghost? Might it not have been a magpie? The friends of Saint Ignatius feel that he is not doing himself and his cause any good by insisting people should credit his vision. He himself in his own life and character is sufficient argument for his cause without bringing in the questionably supernatural to complicate matters. "He asked for a distant magpie as if they made a difference." As Saint Chavez very sensibly remarks a little later, "Saint Ignatius might be admired for himself alone and because of that it might be as much as any one could desire."

One might go further and multiply these illustrations, but it seems unnecessary here. I have given enough to demonstrate that curious and unfamiliar as Miss Stein's language forms may be, they nevertheless convey

ideas and are not all nonsense. With a knowledge of the lives and legends of
Saint Therese and Saint Ignatius one can explain the libretto for one's self.
And in that statement is implied the artistic fallacy of Gertrude Stein's work
as art. Without a knowledge of Saint Therese and Saint Ignatius, *Four Saints
in Three Acts* is incomprehensible. Miss Stein herself gives us no help or
explanation. In other words, *Four Saints in Three Acts* cannot stand alone
as a work of art. It is incomplete. It must be supplemented. It is dependent
on a second thing, knowledge of Saint Therese, for its realization. It is true
that it is the artist's privilege to demand certain knowledge on the part of his
audience for full appreciation of his work, but he should not demand
knowledge before there can be *any* appreciation of his work. A knowledge
of its harmonic structure increases one's pleasure in a Bach fugue, but it is
not essential before one can derive any aesthetic experience whatsoever from
the music. As Albert Sterner expressed it in a recent essay, "the main
purpose of all creative artists is the same one, *viz.* the lucid statement, the
concrete presentation, of a *human emotional* message within the technical
limitations of his chosen medium." The "lucid statement," the factor of
communication which must exist in all art if an object is to be worthy of that
classification, has been completely disregarded by Miss Stein.

Miss Stein might argue in her own defense that the vague impression is all
she desires to give. A great deal of her work is intended to do just that, to be
only words disassociated from meaning and arranged in patterns for the sake
of creating an impression. The theory is interesting, but the practice is
illogical. The impression must be, naturally, that of the artist who creates it
or of a character into whom the artist has projected himself. To appreciate
it the observer must be able to receive the same impression as the artist or his
character, and if the factor of communication is neglected, this is impossible
of accomplishment. The impression has no meaning except for the artist.
Some extremists of Miss Stein's school would argue that it need not have.
They carry the old slogan, Art for Art's sake, one step further and make it
Art for the Artist's sake. That, too, may be justifiable to a certain point.
Each of us can store up his impressions, turn them over, inspect them, enjoy
them, but the moment these impressions are recorded, no matter in what
form, music, literature, painting, they cease to be art for the artist's sake.
Except for the purpose of communication there is no logical reason for the
artist to record an impression which already exists for his own enjoyment in
his own mind. If he records it, he is illogical and silly, because he is
thwarting his own purpose when he neglects the factor of communication.

It is into this illogical blind alley that Miss Stein's interest in technique has led her. Her writing as a whole is like a splendid workshop. The tools are all there, sharpened, polished, arranged in shining order, but that is all. The work of art they were to make is missing, and one feels inclined to exclaim with Othello, "O, Iago, the pity of it, Iago!" for Miss Stein is unquestionably one of the great feminine minds of our time. She has a shrewdness of observation, a satiric and at the same time sympathetic humor, and a philosophical profundity that is unexcelled by any other modern writer. In a book like *The Autobiography of Alice B. Toklas* she has shown us what she might do if she would. The *Autobiography* is one of the cleverest, most subtle comic books in our time. Instead of writing a conventional autobiography Miss Stein chose to present herself as seen through the eyes of a pleasant, gentle, interested, but decidedly naïve individual, her companion, Alice B. Toklas. The problem of the book was a difficult one. Miss Stein had to project herself into the character of Miss Toklas and write as she would write, or talk, observe as she would observe a sophisticated society which is perfectly comprehensible to Miss Stein but obviously not quite comprehensible to Miss Toklas, and at the same time make comprehensible to the reader what was not comprehensible to Miss Toklas without stepping out of the assumed character of Miss Toklas. That Miss Stein accomplished this feat brilliantly the *Autobiography* is evidence that the book is a unique work of art. But alas, too little of Miss Stein's work falls into that classification. That posterity and literary historians will remember her is a foregone conclusion, for while she may neglect to use her tools herself, others who come after her undoubtedly will use them, and her influence may be far reaching. But posterity will remember her as a great technician, not as a great artist. Gertrude Stein is a monumental toolmaker—pigeons on the grass alas—no more.

Sewanee Review, April 1936.

"New Words for Old: Notes on Experimental Writing."

James Laughlin IV

There is nothing new about experimental writing. In the Second Century B. C. "Father" Ennius was making verses worthy of our own E. E. Cummings. "Saxo *cere* communuit *brum*" was a good one; a separation of the word itself to show that "the head is *visibly* split." Cummings might translate that as "with a rock (t)he *he*SM*a*SHE*d.*" Nashe and Shakespeare were quite as ready to invent a word as is James Joyce. Nashe's "Lenten Stuffe" is a fantastic treasury of neologisms, and the well-remembered "multitudinous seas *incarnadine*" is only one of the Bard's poetic inventions. Rabelais was a word-maker. So was Jeremy Bentham.

The writer, the serious writer, is rendered by his occupation most sensitive to language deficiency. It is not by accident that Stein and Joyce, that Cummings and Jolts, that Basic English and Surrealism are coeval to a major crisis of civilization. Working intimately with words, the writer becomes aware of their bad habits as well as their persuasive power. He is like the canaries kept in the trenches to warn of gas attacks, able to smell them coming before the soldiers can. The sensitive writer can feel linguistic decay long before the average man, because the average man has seldom any need to say anything that was not said before by the people who gave him his linguistic orientation, so that the inherited groupings are adequate for him, while the writer, on the other hand, the poet, is always struggling for new meanings and clear meanings, trying to disentangle words from their habitual associations in order to convey a personal perspective unadulterated by alien overtones.

The scientist has no similar problem, for science long ago broke with the common language as a carrier for its meanings and established for each field a peculiar system of signs and notation. But for the writer no such escape is possible. He must make the best of the language which, with all its imperfections, insures him communication and an audience. Yet one thing he can do, and has done for centuries: he can try to improve the language, by stylistic experiment, by semantic experimentation.

Instead of floating with the stream as the commercial writer does augmenting obscurity by further repetitions of the inbred groupings, instead of drifting into the sugar-candy land of the slick-paper magazines and hair-oil journalism, where canned language runs out of one tap and dollars out of the other—instead of accepting the "system," he can reject it. He can dare to fight back, regardless of the odds against him. He can stand his ground as an artist and fight back, wrestling with words till he bleeds heart to draw from them the purity and strength of meaning they still possess beneath their encrusted surfaces.

Naturally, there is a wide variation in the methods of experimental writing, but the cause and the desired effect is always the same, or at least, closely parallel. The experimenter is in rebellion against standardization of language and is searching with all his ingenuity for a solvent to it.

Gertrude Stein began by using in *Three Lives* a simplified vocabulary and cadences antagonistic to "smooth style," cadences which intentionally disappointed and annoyed mental sound expectancy and word-grouping expectancy: "Anna was, as usual, determined for the right. She was stiff and pale with her anger and her fear, and nervous, and all atremble as was her usual way when a bitter fight was near."

But this was not enough, and she progressed, through several stages, to a complete denial of conventional meaning, believing that a wholesale "scrambling" of the familiar, expected groupings would break down the corresponding associative linkages in the reader's mind. It was a business of much pain before pleasure. Read a few pages like this: "If she does knit and he does count how many are then in it? Five in each but unverified and beside beside unverified too and a market two and well left beside the pressure pressure of an earring." See how it will physic your verbal intestine of stereotyped expressions. Try it.

Story, December 1936.

"Letters: A Response to James Laughlin."

Maurice Zolotow

Mr. Laughlin's comments on verbal and syntactical experimentation miss the core of the problem. Of course, linguistic experiments are valuable when language has gone dead, but then no serious artist has ever been the slave of his tool; every first-rate poet has work out an indigenous vocabulary.

What is questionable is the seriousness of such a writer as Gertrude Stein. Sure, her patter is stimulating to a reader temporarily bored with more familiar forms of expression but so is the argot of a New York taxicab driver or Walter Winchell. After all, experiment is supposed to have an end in view; it's supposed to produce results or conclusions. Miss Stein has mighty little to show for thirty years of experiments ... except more experiments. So she has garnered a meager crop of figs. Purgative, perhaps—for those who need a purge, but those who need a purge have probably been feeding themselves unintelligently.

The rehabilitation of language (if it be necessary on a social scale) will not come about by repeating sounds senselessly or by jumbling three languages together at the behest of the unconscious. It will take place when the experiences and the phenomena for which words stand are felt freshly and intensely, are seen cleanly and newly, and are reinterpreted intelligently and intelligibly.

If Stein, Joyce, Jolas, *transition*, pretended to be only verbal chemists, one might, with Laughlin, hail them as the brave *avant-garde*, the alchemical Roger Bacons, of a new age of literary expression. But they *do* insist that they are interpreting reality to us, they say they are presenting images of the physical world and of human passions to us. Mr. Jolas has behind him a vivid sort of mysticism. By the "spontaneous" and "uncultured" employment of *three* (no less!) languages he proposes to get back to the "dark gods of the unconscious," to the mythy cradle of the race's infancy!

Since these writers pretend to deal with the material of human experience, we have a right to judge them by the universal standards by which we praise Shakespeare and laugh at Lyly (who was, in his day, a great experimenter, and almost as boring as Gertrude Stein). No one will deny that Stein's writings are stimulating, but I hope Mr. Laughlin has gotten past the stage when he reads for the kick of it.

As I say, what is to be doubted is the seriousness of these writers. Not that they are hoaxing the public, but that they are hoaxing themselves. They are playing games with three languages when a universe of chaos cries to the artist for intelligent interpretation. If they were serious they would use whatever they have learned from their experiments to achieve socially intelligible and effective writing. What they have achieved is an amusement for jaded minds.

A writer who excises the universe of denotation, which is the heart of every word, is depriving himself of a powerful instrument, is depriving himself almost of the word itself. Far greater skill would it take to bend the word—as it exists—to mold the connotations, even to take advantage of the "stock responses" of his audience, for his own high ends. But have they any ends? That is what I would like to know.

Story, January 1937.

"Letters: A Response to Maurice Zolotow."

Robert H. Elias

Mr. Zolotow, it seems to me, has quite unfairly challenged the sincerity of Gertrude Stein; he doubts her "seriousness." I suppose her occasionally understandable style has given credence to the idea that her usually puzzling word usage is mere hoax. However, this latter method appears not to be a change, but a further development.

Her first and probably best known book, *Three Lives*, is relatively clear and comprehensible. Yet the characters are described rather than created as they are revealed by action. In *The Making of Americans*, Miss Stein is uninterested in either story or character, but is intent on the feeling of the inner person. In *The Autobiography of Alice B. Toklas*, she merely recounts happenings, quite superficially and, as the recent *Testimony Against Gertrude Stein* revealed, quite inaccurately. And when she was here in America not so long ago, she was quite surprised and baffled by manifestations of the machine age, while a football game recalled "a real Indian dance." What has been so easily understood, then, strangely enough exhibits an appalling lack of understanding.

One clue might be found in her lectures she delivered in this country. She denied the possibility of choice, of the will, and of the intellect, and, in the recent *Geographical History of America*, reaffirmed her belief in the divorce between body and mind, action and thought. Thus, in destroying the power of rational thinking, she also destroys criticism and values. And where values do not exist, content in art is secondary while technique is all-important. That is why Miss Stein is so concerned with conjunctions, verbs, sentences, and paragraphs and leaves to intuition the problem of communication.

But the matter goes deeper than this. She has not wanted to be superficial. In *Tender Buttons* we saw a series of exercises in trying to get at truth directly, but few readers were able to meet her mind. In *Portraits and Prayers* there were more examples, to the despair of the literary critics. But are they all a joke? I, for one, am afraid not. *The Autobiography* explains that Gertrude Stein's fundamental motive is "the intellectual passion for exactitude in the description of inner and outer reality," reality divorced entirely from emotion and events. Now in this description there must be nothing associational, nothing causing the image created to be created relative to anything else. Thus the writer must not rely on the reader's previous experience or appeal to his sensual side, as in the portrayal of beauty.

Exactitude, to be artistic, must be distinguished from the mechanical, which is scientific. Miss Stein has sought to make the distinction by differentiating between repetition and insistence: the former is the mechanical, the non-personal, the individual. Now, since repetition, identified with memory, is valid from an artistic point of view, art must deal with a continuous present, which, to Gertrude Stein, is, like a landscape, uneventful.

It is to give this "landscape" significance that insistence must be created. Now this cannot be done by classification, for that involves repetition and exposes the common, which is not individual. It must be done by definition or creation: it must be immediately perceivable without relation to other things.

But now, not only does the medium defeat its intent—the use of words is a reliance on association, memory, emotional reaction, and previous experience—but the theory also turns out to be suicidal. From Miss Stein's point of view any individuality is absolute, and, with respect to other individualities, its assertion is arbitrary. However, only content can be asserted arbitrarily, for arbitrary definitions are made from points of view not implied in what is asserted, and hence can be assertions about the order of content only as that order is a logical order, that is, a class name. Thus she asserts the individual as a logical order, a class name. This denies its individuality in any except a logical sense, which is arrived at through classification. And inasmuch as Miss Stein has defined art as free from repetition and, therefore, classification, this further denies the possibility of any art at all, not to mention the artist herself. Is it any wonder that such a paradox should result in confusion?

Mr. Zolotow has implied that Gertrude Stein has no end in view. It is not that the end is lacking, however, but that the end has been systematically misconceived. Gertrude Stein's value as a writer lies in her revolt against that logical classification known as realism, where the individual is characterized by the common; but her failure is in thinking that it is possible to give an absolute individuality significance as divorced from logical order.

Story, February 1937.

"Trade Winds."

Bennett Cerf

Scarcely a day goes by at our office but somebody writes in to inquire about the safety and whereabouts of Gertrude Stein and her lifelong companion, Alice B. Toklas. Not many people even claim to understand the intricacies of Miss Stein's prose style, but millions admire her rugged and magnificent personality. I am pleased to report that she is safe, well, and reasonably happy at her villa in Bilignin in unoccupied France, a bare thirty miles from the once fashionable spa of Aix-la-Chapelle. The ladies do their own gardening, cooking, and housekeeping, but this works no special hardship on them because they never could tolerate servants getting in their way and generally ended up by doing everything themselves anyhow. My last letter from Gertrude Stein was mailed in May, 1942. She is working on a new novel which she calls *Mrs. Reynolds*. She has lost track of her famous Parisian friends, but the entire village population continues to come to her for advice and solace. That is why she flatly refused to come back home when she still had the opportunity. "I belong here and I think these people need me," she wrote. Miss Stein can write very clearly when occasion demands!

The last time that I saw Gertrude Stein was in 1936, when Jo Davidson and I flew down for a weekend at Bilignin. In accordance with her instructions, we flew to Geneva, although we discovered later that the airport at Lyons was twenty miles nearer her home, not to mention an hour and a half air time closer to Paris. Gertrude had just been reading some poetry by Pablo Picasso. "I read his poems," she told us happily, "and then I seized him by both shoulders and shook him good and hard. 'Pablo,' I said, 'go home and paint'!" Miss Stein was so pleased and engrossed in her story that we lost our way at least ten times on the way to her home. We went through one village three times. The last time the children waved to us as old friends. Arrived at long last in Bilignin, Gertrude stopped the car to greet every passerby and ask them point blank the most intimate questions about their loves and business affairs, all of which they answered cheerfully and in voluminous detail. As soon as we got home, Alice threw the cook out of the kitchen and whipped us up a soufflé that I shall never forget. The July first issue of *Vogue* reprints some excellent photographs of the ladies and their villa, taken by Therese Bonney some months after the collapse of France. Both of them look fit and ready for anything.

Gertrude Stein really won the hearts of the American public when she revisited the United States in 1934. It was just after the Dillinger case had been wound up, and Gertrude said that she was replacing Dillinger as the sensation of the moment. Reporters who came to scoff at her were charmed by her ready wit. When she made a short for the newsreels, Miriam Hopkins and Mary Pickford helped her make up. Broadway loiterers stopped her for autographs. In Washington she stayed at the White House as a matter of course. The morning that she arrived in Hollywood, she demanded that Dashiell Hammett, Charlie Chaplin, and Dorothy Parker be produced for a dinner party that evening. They not only came, but boasted about it later. Gertrude even shouted down the arrogant Mr. Woollcott. "I guess she hasn't been back long enough to know that nobody ever dares to dispute

Woollcott," he explained weakly, but he was at her feet for the rest of her stay here.

Nobody would ever have mistaken Gertrude and Alice for devotees of Bergdorf Goodman. They were not interested in ensembles. Both of them were champion dawdlers. At the last moment they would dress themselves in whatever garments happened to be handy and sally forth. In those days there was an employment agency for domestics located directly below the Random House offices. Gertrude arrived for luncheon one day a full hour late and announced cheerfully, "That fool elevator boy of yours dumped us out at the employment agency. He thought we were cooks!"

For the past two years I have even sending packages of new books to Gertrude at regular intervals—particularly detective stories, which she devours. She has always been shameless in her demands on her friends. Last fall she calmly asked for eleven books on the new Random House list. "You should be flattered," she wrote complacently, "that I want so many of your new publications!" The last package that we sent, alas, was returned, stamped "service suspended." Gertrude is going to be very angry about that.

We always print an edition of exactly twenty-five hundred copies of a new Gertrude Stein book. The demand is constant. We rarely have fifty copies left over. We never have to reprint. If the complete manuscript of *Mrs. Reynolds* ever reaches us, the manufacturing department will order the usual edition without so much as consulting us. Gertrude's last book, *Ida*, was supposed to be about the Duchess of Windsor, and I sent a copy to Government House in Nassau. "It was nice of you to send me *Ida*," wrote the Duchess, "but I must confess that I didn't understand a word of it."

The Duchess had nothing on Miss Stein's faithful publishers!

The Saturday Review, September 5, 1942.

3

Veneration and Vituperation: The Making of a Celebrity

"Our Own Polo Guide: The Game Explained à la Gertrude Stein."

Anonymous

This is Proletariat's Day. With the first international polo game on, the masses came into their own dog day, so to speak. The butcher, baker, candlestick maker, conductor, guard, Coney Island barker, longshoreman, and other notables rise en masse to the occasion; put on their red neckties and steer their course to Meadow Brook, bidding the chauffeur make his own speed.

For the benefit of this vast and enfranchised autocracy of toil and the movies, we now present our own guide to polo, explaining the technicalities of the game so that he who plays may know what it's all about and who's who in sport and the charity ball.

We have adopted the phraseology of Gertrude Stein for the purpose because it harmonizes so well with our clear understanding of the game and all its ramifications, hot or cold.

Polo, a game not a basket but nevertheless, molasses running up Woodworth but Wu Ting Fang, yes, no, no, yes, certainly, but by hakes and that which is a turnip is not a peanut not withstanding.

Polo pony, a horse though no ink in a paste not which is hold your hat, a jitney to throw but no more, pink but yellow with hoofs, that is to say malaria, east is west, north is south, though it is not my treat, but John L. Sullivan whichever is going completely and I will not the waiter.

Chukker, a free and easy chicken sandwich, one on the side, stained pickles running up and down stairs in a nightshirt, which is to say yesterday but not tomorrow, horse chestnuts with a wheeze but not seidlitz powders, a period, a space, a comma, a slug, a snail, a washout, a Chinese but, a Rumanian fish, a Hungarian radish, a painting by Rembrandt, onions.

Stick, a mallet, a barrel of nails, blows, pax vobiscum, hitchy koo but an arrangement posalutely if not absotively, chasing a cheese hound but not blutwurst, whichever not whichever, whiskers and a shave.

Ball, a roundness which is a flatness which is a squareness which is a toothache in the dark on a Sunday, which is a which, which is that, which is witch hazel, which is the Witch of Endor.

Throw-in, a movement but not a menu, goulash riding a horse but the city directory which is a porpoise but not a bear, of what not, a bottle of celery tonic coming and green music.

Knock-in, a hunch which is to say 30 cents, an arrangement in red violent, absorbing, ticklish, though to call a taxi were noise but better reduced to 98 cents and a straw hat.

Safety, a rummage sale and a bushel, tomorrow night which is to say yesterday morning, foolish, foolish and nobody home.

Foul, a herring but not what's his name, yes, why not but of course considering, put a head on it and give him the check but last Tuesday, beans and a bright sunset very dull.

Now, that it is all clear as a floorwalker's direction, let's up and at 'em.

The New York Evening Sun, June 13, 1914.

"Futurist Man's Dress to Be a One-Piece Suit With One Button and Twinkling in Colors: No Straight Lines; All Cones, Triangles, Spirals and Circles—Shirt Collar, Coat and Trousers Must Be Pointed on One Side and Round on the Other."

Marguerite Mooers Marshall

Futurist man's dress has arrived in New York.

As little Gertrude Stein would remark, "Scarlet tomatoes of a Broadway. Hope in lightning, hope in bullfights, hope in Sylvia Pankhurst, no hope in vanilla ice cream. A button sweetening into symphony. All this, and not ordinary, not coordinating with chorus girls."

Which is merely the Futurist way of writing that Futurist man's dress has arrived.

Broadway will first see the costume draped about Ralph Herz, and Broadway will realize as never before the subtle appropriateness of this comedian's name. It will be sobbed in echoing unison by strong, sane men after they have cast one terror-stricken glance at Mr. Herz's habiliments.

I had a shuddering memory of the most famous Futurist masterpiece, *The Nude Descending a Staircase*—otherwise knows as *The Staircase Descending a Nude.* Such being Futurist undress, I dreaded to think what Futurist dress must resemble. But it became necessary to learn the worst.

And this is what the Futurist man's dress will be, according to Mr. Herz: "A comfortable, unsymmetrical suit made in one piece with one button, twinkling with colors, brilliant, vivid colors, no straight lines, all cones, triangles, spirals and circles. Shirt collar, coat and trousers must be pointed on one side and round on the other. There must be no so-called good taste and harmony of tone."

It seemed to me that that latest stipulation was supererogatory, in view of the preceding requirements, but I didn't dare interrupt the ecstatic Mr. Herz.

"Boots," he went on, "may be white or black, with white spats, but they must have only one button. The hat should be soft, and black, white or gray in color. Perhaps a straw hat may be worn. Every Futurist hat should be ornamented with 'modiflants'— patches or decorations of bright colored material in place of the conventional ribbon.

"The shirt ought to be of white silk or batiste, with a soft turned down collar pointed on one side and round on the other, as I have said. We want to abolish the heavy black dress suit that has the appearance of mourning, and with it must go all neutral, pale and 'pretty-pretty' tints. But color we certainly want. Man's dress should be twinkling with bright hues, and the dress itself may be gray so long as there are vivid colors with it.

"There must be no symmetry, no stripes and straight lines. The designs must suggest energy, impetuousness and movement. No dress should be too durable, for it should be our aim to both encourage industry and to give animation and pleasure to our bodies by renewing our clothes constantly.

"The Futurist man's dress must be easy to put on and easy to throw off. A man's costume should be useful to him in moving about; not something that irritates his nerves and enchains his muscles. Also hygiene must be studied, as well as simplicity and comfort."

Isn't it an enticing vision? And there are so many possible variations. For the despised evening clothes the Futurist may substitute a "White Light" suit, all sewed over with brilliants and repeating in its patterns the illuminated signs along Broadway.

To avoid the curse of durability gentlemen might appear in shadowlace costumes, with chiffon ruffles. An admirable design for expressing energy would be patterned all over with little T. R. Faces. For his impetuous suit the well dressed Futurist man would naturally choose a "militant" model, sprinkled with hatchets, hammers and bricks and fringed with bombs.

With the Futurist wardrobe will come the Futurist shave, an individual whisker; likewise the Futurist haircut, a pyramid on one side and a tonsure on the other. Really the possibilities are unlimited. And they're all as mad and merry as the wonderful breakfast ordered by one of W. J. Locke's heroes—poached eggs, raspberry shrub and absinthe frappe.

The Toledo (Ohio) Blade, July 9, 1914.

"The Same Book from Another Standpoint (With Apologies to the Author of 'Tender Buttons')."

A. S. K.

Enough water is plenty and more, more is almost plenty enough. Enthusiastically hurting sad size, such size, same size slighter, same splendor, simpler, same sore sounder. Glazed glitter, eddy eddies discover discovered discoveries, discover Mediterranean sea, large print large. Small print small, picked plumes painters and penmen, pretty pieces Picasso, Picabia plus Plato, Hegel, Cézanne, Kandinsky, more plenty more, small print single sign of oil supposing shattering scatter and scattering certainly splendidly. Suppose oil surrounded with watery sauce, suppose spare solely inside, suppose the rest.

The Little Review, July 1914.

"Gertrude Stein's Hints for the Table."

Don Marquis

The following thoughts from an article entitled "Food," by Miss Gertrude Stein, the champion scrambler—brain, egg or word—of Futurist literature, will no doubt be of considerable assistance to those who are mobilizing against the well-known price of food .... These selections are quoted from the section of Miss Stein's article headed "Breakfast." Lunch follows, we are bound to say, in the most commonplace and conventional manner. After the usual interval comes dinner. While the thoughts expressed are in themselves profound, does not this lapse into the conventional sequence of breakfast, lunch and dinner show a growing conservatism on the part of Miss Stein?

The New York Sun, August 14, 1914.

"Gertrude Stein on the War."

Don Marquis

I asked Gertrude Stein: "Explain
Why they are fighting on the Aisne."

She mused a space and then exclaimed:
"What seal brown bobble can be
    blamed?"

It saddened me! I only asked her: "Why
Do all these guns perturb the sky?"

"Objects," she said, "and rooms and toes,
But why a trunk and not a nose?"

"From occult depths your answers come,"
I said, "more deep than I can plumb!"

And rapt, from out her trance, she cried:
"Are custards curst? Are whiskers fried?"

"Too true!" I said, "alas too true!
But is not war a grief to you?"

She plunged her inward sight adown
The gulf of time, where lord and clown,

Republics, empires, princes kings
Were running round and round in rings

Intent on making copy for
The usual well-known pomes on war,

She held her great brow in her hand

Summoned her genii to command—

(Sibyl and Secress, Priestess, Sphinx:
The stars cease choiring when she thinks!)

She paled; she swallowed hard; she spoke:
"Oh, why, why, why, an artichoke?"

I swear, I'd never thought of that!
I humbly thanked her; took my hat.

And murmured as I bade good-by:
"There's more in this than meets the eye!"

The New York Sun, October 2, 1914.

"To G. S. and E. P."

Don Marquis

Ye gods, in all these worlds of thine,
Where shall the Super-Pote be found
To wed the Thoughts of Gertrude Stein
Unto the Tunes of Ezra Pound?

When Gertrude thinks, the Thoughts of her
Down dark abysses plunge and reel;
Each is a rebel Lucifer
New-slipped on a cosmic orange-peel.

When Ezra sings, the Tunes of him
Like buzz-saws rasp among the spheres
And all the shuddering cherubim
Fold cottony wings across their ears.

Untrammeled Ones! The Commonplace

Before them slithers in retreat;
Her Thoughts have knuckles on the face,
His Verses stutter in the feet.

Free Spirits! All Conventions wheeze,
When they appear, and gasp and die!
His honey-bees make only cheese,
She sets her blacksmiths forging pie.

Oh Literetoor! Oh Bunk! Oh Art!
O Cubist Bard! O Futurist!
Here we not rent the Trite apart,
And slapped the Usual on the wrist?

Have we not looped the lyric loop
And put the language on the blink
And faked a-many a Little Group
Who love to think that they can think?

Oh, much-appealed-to Muses Nine!
Where shall the Super-Fake be found
To put the Thoughts of Gertrude Stein
Into the Verse of Ezra Pound?

The New York Sun, October 3, 1914.

"Thoughts of Hermione, a Modern Young Woman."

Don Marquis

We've taken up Gertrude Stein—our little group of serious thinkers, you know—and she's wonderful; simply *wonderful*.

She Suggests the Inexpressible, you know.

Of course, she is a Pioneer. And with all Pioneers—don't you think?—the Reach is greater than the Grasp.

Not that you can tell what she means.

But in the New-Art one doesn't have to mean things, does one? One strikes the chords, and the chords vibrate.

Aren't Vibrations just too perfectly lovely for anything?

The loveliest man talked to us the other night about World Movements and Cosmic Vibrations.

You see, every time the Cosmos vibrates it means a new World Movement.

And the Souls that are in Tune with the Cosmos are benefitted by these World Movements. The other souls will get harm out of them.

Frightfully interesting, isn't it?—the Cosmos, I mean.

I have given so much thought to it! It has become almost an obsession to me.

Only the other evening I was thinking about it. And without realizing that I spoke aloud I said, "I simply could *not do without* the Cosmos!"

Mamma—poor dear Mamma!—she is so terribly unadvanced, you know!— Mamma said: "Hermione, I do not know what the Cosmos is. But this I do know—not another Sex Discussion or East Indian Yogi will never come into *this* house!"

"Mamma," I said to her. "I will not give up the Cosmos. It means everything to me; simply *everything!"*

I am always firm with Mamma; it is kinder, in the long run, to be quite positive. But what I suffer at home from objections to the advanced movements, nobody knows.

My plans for my Salon are well under way.

I am having my Costumes for it designed.

The Symbolical Note will be very strong in them. Different notes for different evenings, you know. And the lower part of the house—I'm having that done over again.

Environment means so much to me! It means so much. Environment does, in fostering the Personality, don't you think?

Though, of course, in spite of Environment Temperament will triumph.

My Costumes for my Salon will be Symbolical of my Temperament.

The New York Sun, October 13, 1914.

"Gertrude Is Stein, Stein Gertrude: That is All Ye Know on Earth, and All Ye Need to Know."

Don Marquis

New York, October 13.
To the Editor of *The Sun Dial*:—Sir: Who is Gertrude Stein?
          —Puzzled Reader

Who is Meredith? And Hardy? Who is Conrad? Who is James?
We might crush you, if you choose to, under tons of modern names!
Who is Dryden? Who is Goethe? Who is Hugo? Who is Pope?
We might spoof you, did we wish to, with a heap of classic dope!

Who is Schiller? Who is Shelley? Who is Byron? Who is Keats?
We'd consume you, were we peevish, in the hottest of white heats!
Who is Balzac? Who is Dickens? Who is Kipling? Who is Poe?
We'd assume, if we were nasty, they are names you do not know!

But preferring to be honest, to adopt the candid line,
All we know of Gertrude—really—is that she is Gertrude Stein!
'Tis enough for us we have her—(she, the subtle Theban Sphinx:
All the spheres swoon into silence when she stutters out her thinks!)

Robert Browning, major leaguer, with a wondrous batting eye,
One time walloped out this bingle—scoring many—"Never pry!"
Let us, Brother, thank the heaven for the careless gifts they send,
Be incurious and humble, be the flattered little friend—

Let us search not, seek not, ask not, why the blessing has been sent—
Little Groups, we have our Gertrude: worship her, and be content!

The New York Evening Sun, October 14, 1914.

"Taking Up Music in a Serious Way."

Don Marquis

Sir: The Faircrofts recently gave an informal dinner in their huge studio uptown. Hermione and Mater were there, and the Cunningham-Vallys and Aunty Eise and Pussy Moniker, together with most of our set and quite a little group of one of Hermione's Groups of Serious Thinkers. Mrs. Faircroft thinks serious with great enthusiasm when she is not seriously socially active. The headliner of this particular affair was one Lionel Wandress, who is a Pianist and Composer of some note, according to Hermione. Pater says a composer of some notes.

After dinner we had coffee 'round the big open fire in the studio, and our hostess grew seriously thoughtful and spilled a few remarks about watching the Fire being so like watching the Sea, and how Waves were like Thoughts, and how Flames were like Thoughts, and that Sparks were like Foam, and it now was all so analogous that by and by when telepathy was really perfected we should be able to tell what the Wild Waves are saying! Lionel Wandress waded into the talk right about here, and said that the Sea and Fire had always meant Beautiful *Musical* Thoughts to him. "There are sonatas in the Sea," he said, "and fugues in the Fire: and the Sparks and Spray are arpeggios," and a lot more of the same.

Well, of course, he was asked to play after that.

"I will do a little thing of my own," he announced, "a musical setting of Miss Gertrude Stein's *Tender Buttons*."

There was a murmur of approbation from the lofty browed ones.

Now the very grand piano stands in an alcove sort of place just off the main studio. Those seated at the fire can hear, but cannot see the piano or pianist. I happened to sit back so that I saw him perfectly. Poyntz, the Faircroft mastiff pup, was in the alcove doing an imitation of a fur rug and sighing occasionally like a Serious Thinker.

On top of the piano was a large bowl filled with chocolates, one of which Lionel grabbed before running a preliminary scale: he bit it and placed the other half within ready reach on a black key. Poyntz had been doing his imitation with one eye open, and when he spied that bit of candy made a hungry leap, landing with octave stretching paws on that keyboard. There was a brilliant burst of sound, and say! No one at the fire guessed that it was other than Wandress! *He* was a real sport; twigged immediately, and seizing a handful of chocolates placed them deftly along the keys. Poyntz gobbled them, filling the place with such a din that his scuffling footsteps were not to be heard.

When the chocolates were gone Wandress made a conventional finish on the piano, and came forward modestly, followed by the dog, who licked his hand frantically. There was a tremendous burst of applause: Hermione said it was wonderful, simply *wonderful!*

Mrs. Faircroft beamed. "It was *superb*, Mr. Wandress. *So* modern! So distinctively dissonant! So—er—transcendental. The fingering in the staccato passages was exquisite! Such a command of the keyboard! *Please* play some more for us. But Poyntz!! Charge, sire. *Charge!* I hope he didn't bother you, Mr. Wandress. I *didn't* know he was there!"

"Thank you," said the musician with elaborate bows; "let the dog stay near me, please. Have you a few more chocolate creams? Thank you. Now, Poyntz, let us orient our minds to the Sea—to the wavelike Flames—to fiery Thoughts that break into the Foam; let us render them as only a cacophonophilist can!"

And he got away with it!

The New York Sun, January 18, 1915.

"Thoughts of Hermione."

Don Marquis

Don't you think Gertrude Stein is wonderful, just simply *wonderful?*

We—our little group of serious thinkers, you know—have been giving an entire week to her, and the more we study her the more esoteric she seems and the more esoteric the more fascinating.

A great many people, you know, pretend they are understanding her when they really aren't. The way to tell is to give them a test sentence, and then watch them as they say it over and over.

If they're only faking they try to *act* emotions—to put expressions on their faces, and look delighted, and all that.

But if they really *get* the message, their faces just simply get wooden, and you can see that while their lips are repeating the words their Souls have Gone on a Journey. Like the poor dear Swami V.'s soul, you know, when he is in the silences.

We took a test sentence the other evening, and every one in the little group repeated it over and over—and to watch the way Gertrude Stein's soul influenced each ego was fascinating; just simply fascinating!

The sentence was: *Sunshine catapults and a gnawing a proving the crumpled cow beanpoles exact.*

Fothergil Finch read it over and over before the message caught him, and then he said: "It means music to me, strong, red, virile music, and a cave man killing a dinosaur with the jawbone of a mastodon, while the hurricane chants *vers libre* poems to a cowering sea."

That's the way it acted on Fothy's soul.

But it took Aurelia Gammon's soul entirely different. Don't you know Aurelia? She is a harpist, and wears the loveliest, clingy, silvery things, and lives in a made-over stable near Washington Square, and was the first woman who ever wore a purple wig to the Metropolitan Opera House, but she doesn't harp much because she has to have a sympathetic audience, and they are so hard to find.

"I myself am the harp," she says, "the harp hung in the wind—the Æolian harp!—and the sound of my audience must breathe upon me kindly, or I cannot vibrate."

Well, it took Aurelia's soul, Miss Stein's sentence did, quite differently the way it took Fothy's. It got her quicker; she went part way into the silences and said: "It means music to me, too: but music struck out of the silver strings of a harp by the wings and feet of angels, and the harp is a ladder that leads up to Heaven, and the strings are the rounds of a ladder."

That's the way it worked on Aurelia's soul.

Freddy Dane, Fothy's new friend, who does stuff for *The Lower Classes*, said it meant blood to him: "Blood and skulls and powdersmoke, and the anti-Christ of capitalism bayonetting the babies of the poor," said Freddy.

Lucia Darling, who is founding a new art cult—Lucia paints Cubist paintings as if they were Futurist sculptures, and sculpts Futurist sculptures as if they were Cubist paintings, and has combined two great arts—said:

"I see orchids, orchids, orchids! Orchids upon a sarcophagus!"

The Swami V.—Oh, yes, didn't you know?—the poor dear Swami is out of prison. Something about a parole, you know. I *hope* he won't forget and marry before his parole is up—but one can never tell about these dreamy, spiritual souls, you know. No, he wasn't rearrested again when he got out. The woman who was going to have him rearrested never had married him, it turned out. The Swami thought maybe she had, but he wasn't sure; he married so many times, you know, and it was always such a—er—well, such a detail to him, you know, that he never could remember whom he had married and whom he hadn't—the childlike old dear!

Well, anyhow, the Swami went into a trance and said something in Sanskrit—or is it Sanscrypt?—anyhow, it's wonderfully Oriental; one of the most Oriental of all languages, you know—and something none of us could understand. Then he moved his hand like he had caught something between his thumb and finger and then watched what he had caught get away and fly right through the ceiling. And when he was quite waked up all he would say was:

"It was the Golden Butterfly of Buddha."

Fothy Finch, who can be horribly slangy at times, said he rather thought the Swami had flivvered.

And then they all said, "What does it mean to *you,* Hermione?"

For a while, you know, it didn't mean anything to me. Because I felt a kind of antagonism—a challenge, you know—in the room, and unless the psychic conditions are right, you know—that is to say, if I feel any disharmony—why, you know what I mean, don't you? I mean if any one prevents me from getting into tune with the infinite I can't vibrate. But after a while I did vibrate in spite of them all, and I said:

"It makes me see the ghost of Heinrich Heine standing barefoot in the dew beside the grave of Oscar Wilde."

We are going to take up the newest Irish mystics next week—our little group of serious thinkers, you know.

The New York Evening Sun, March 13, 1915.

"The Golden Group."

Don Marquis

"Peppercorns and purple sleet
Enwrap me round from head to feet,
Wrap me around and make me thine,"
Said Amy Lowell to Gertrude Stein.

"Buzz-saws, buzzards, curds and glue
Show my affinity for you,
You are my golden sister-soul,"
Said Gertrude Stein to Amy Lowell.

"Brainstorms, bricks and amber blocks
And little mice that dwell in clocks.
I am your brother, I'll be bound,"
Said the gooey frere, the Ezra Pound.

"Stewed unicorns and rampant prunes
And piebald gnats and plenflumes,
Bind me to you as with a cinch.—
I'm nuts myself," said Fothergil Finch.

"Curried sharks on a golden plate
And psychic ants that cerebrate.—
My love for you all what tongue can tell?"
Cried the Swami V. from his padded cell.

And Hermione harked to them, rapt, elate:
And aren't they all of them simply great!
Of course, the bourgeois can't understand—
But aren't they wonderful? Aren't they grand!"

The New York Evening Sun, March 26, 1915.

"Dr. Lowes Finds 'Tender Buttons' Poetic Asparagus: Puzzled Lecture Audience Listens to 'Whow Whow Muncher Muncher' Lines.

Anonymous

Some "terrible examples" of the Futurist and Imagist movement in poetry were cited by Dr. John L. Lowes, professor of English literature in Washington University, in a lecture on "Literary Futurists" at the University Medical School last night, under the auspices of the Washington University Association.

Assuring the audience that he had not lost his senses, Prof. Lowes read a few passages from Gertrude Stein's new book, *Tender Buttons*. This author, he said, had renounced meaning and "would banish from poetry all lines that embody a recognizable idea." From her "poem," entitled "Rhubarb," he quoted the following:

"Rhubarb is susan not susan not seat in bunch. Toys not wild and laughable not in little places not in neglect and vegetable not in fold coal age not please."

From "A Substance in Cushion," by the same writer, Prof. Lowes quoted the following: "The band of it is black and white, the band has a green string. A sight a whole sight and a little groan grinding makes a trimming and a red thing not a round thing but a white thing, a red thing and a white thing."

"The trouble is," Prof. Lowes commented, "that although Miss Stein can banish meaning, she can't banish our expectation of it. When she sings, 'A curving example makes righteous fingernails,' or 'the sight of no pussy-cat is so different that a tobacco zone in white and cream,'—across our tranced wonder flits, 'like noises in a swound,' memories that disturb us with a sense of actual fingernails and tobacco and pussy-cats that we have known, and the magic spell is snapped.

"Miss Stein is consistent only in masterpieces like the poem which begins, 'Aider, why aider why whow, whow stop the muncher muncher munchers.' That is absolute music, the ultimate dim song without words. And one may take leave of Miss Stein in the felicitous vocables with which *Tender Buttons* ends: 'All this makes a magnificent asparagus, and also a fountain.'"

Prof. Lowes compared the "poetry" of *Tender Buttons* to the attempts of some futurist composers to produce music without sound. He told of the "experimental perfume concert," given in the Carnegie Lyceum, New York, "which included among its attractions 'a trip to Japan in 16 minutes,' conveyed to the audiences by a series of odors."

Illustrating further the style of the extreme imagists, he quoted two lines describing the emotions of two young persons attending a moving picture show: "We thrill to the rush and clatter/ And spatter the night with our souls." This spattering, he remarked, was merely tit for tat, since it was stated in the beginning of the same poem that "the void turns, and creaks, and spatters me with spume of gaunt fatuity." He added that "no one spattered with the spume of gaunt fatuity can be blamed for spattering back."

Another imagist, quoted by Prof. Lowes, admits that he has thoughts, and describes these thoughts as "Little silver fishes jumping in a row, Little fishes leaping upon a black cloth / With a shark behind them / O yellow eyes in the black sea!" The speaker read a recent poem, entitled "Houses," which seemed to make rather better sense than the other matter he had quoted, and then he informed his hearers that he had played a trick upon them, by reading the poem backward, line by line, beginning with the last line, ending with the first.

"The scraps that I have just been quoting," said Prof. Lowes, "have been frankly chosen as terrible examples. For carried to its extreme, the Imagist doctrine, like most things human, leads to absurdities. The essential point is the fatal facility with which the Imagists slip into just this particular excess. The distortion of images is the inevitable result of making images do duty for everything.

"The poet has absolute freedom to write his poems about the external apparatus of the life of his own day—its motor cars, and submarines, and aeroplanes, and all the rest. But these are usually obsolete before his epitaph is carved, and his poem is carried to the junk shop with them. 'It is poetry's job to catch up,' says Ezra Pound. Perhaps; but when poetry has caught up with a 1916 model, what doth it profit in the year 1917? Did you ever read William Mason's poem, published in that notable year 1776, entitled, 'Ode to Mr. Pinchbeck on His Newly Invented Patent Candle Snuffers'? No, life is made up of what endures. It is perilous, in poetry, to be up to date."

Prof. Lowes read some of the better examples of recent free verse, including passages from Amy Lowell's writings, and then read passages from two prose writings by Fiona Macleod and Maurice Hewlett. Without the change of a word in the prose matter, he shredded it into short lines, arbitrarily, in the free verse style, and showed that it was as beautiful and as rhythmic as anything that the free versifiers have done.

"The attempt to telescope prose and verse is symptomatic," he declared. "It is only one phase of a tendency, epidemic at the present time, to obliterate the dividing line between all the arts." He remarked that free verse, in the hands of artists, is susceptible of delicate effects, but declared that it was too largely in the hands, not of artists, but of artisans.

He went back into the history of poetry to show that the present movement in poetry was no new thing, and that it had its forerunners in French and Italian literature as far back as the middle ages.

Prof. Lowes said the most significant thing about the new movement in poetry is the fact that it exists, and that more people are buying and reading poetry today than in many years past. This is proven, he said, by publishers' bulletins. "That in itself," he remarked, "is a fact of happy omen. You can't steer a boat that isn't moving. Once let it gather headway, and the rudder will do its part."

St. Louis Post Dispatch, March 29, 1916.

"We Nominate for the Hall of Fame: Gertrude Stein."

Anonymous

Because she is entitled to write both L.L.D. and M.D. after her name; because she was instrumental in promoting the early fame of Matisse and Cézanne; because her Parisian salon is one of the most serious and interesting in the city of famous salons; and finally, because her experiments in style have already had an influence on the younger French writers.

Vanity Fair, August 1922.

"Literary Survey."

Editor's Note: We have had so many symposiums lately on the "ten greatest books in the last fifty years," "ten books one has most enjoyed reading" that *Vanity Fair* found it interesting to reverse the investigation and ask a number of prominent literary experts to name the ten greatest writers whom they find most thoroughly boring—whom they find that, in spite of all moral and intellectual temptations to plough through or pretend to admire, they absolutely cannot read. Here they are:

H. L. Mencken:

"It is hard for me to make up a list of books or authors that bore me insufferably, for the simple truth is that I can read almost anything. My trade requires me to read annually all the worst garbage that is issued in belles lettres; for recreation and instruction, I read such things as the Congressional Record, religious trades, Mr. Walter Lippmann's endless discussions of the Simon-Bing tests, works on molecular physics and military strategy, and the monthly circulars of the great bond houses. It seems to me that nothing that gets into print can be wholly uninteresting; whatever its difficulties to the reader it at least represents some earnest man's efforts to express himself. But there are some authors of course who try me more than most, and if I must name ten of them, then I name:

      1. Dostoevsky
      2. George Eliot
      3. D. H. Lawrence
      4. James Fenimore Cooper
      5. Eden Philpotts
      6. Robert Browning
      7. Selma Lagerlof
      8. Gertrude Stein
      9. Bjornstjerne Bjornson
     10. Goethe

As a good German, I should, I suppose, wallow happily in *Faust*. I can only report that, when I read it, it is patriotically, not voluptuously. Dostoevsky, for some reason that I don't know, simply stumps me; I have never been able to get through any of his novels. George Eliot I started to read too young, and got there by a distaste for her that has never left me; it is unsound but incurable. Against Cooper and Browning I was prejudiced by schoolmasters who admired them. Philpotts seems to me to be the worst novelist now in practice in England; certainly no small eminence. As for

Lawrence and Miss Stein, what makes them hard reading for me is simply the ineradicable conviction that beneath all their pompous manner there is nothing but tosh. The two Scandinavians I need not explain.

Vanity Fair, August 1923.

"Two Futile Attempts to Rival the Style of Gertrude Stein."

Anonymous

A bright young critic has submitted to *The News* a review of Gertrude Stein's *Geography and Plays*, saying that it is written after her own style. He is mistaken. What he says, though a bit queer, is intelligible, and therefore is utterly unlike the style of Gertrude Stein. Stuart P. Sherman, in a discussion of this book for the literary review of the *New York Evening Post*, tells of an interesting experiment he made with words in order to arrive at the secret of Gertrude Stein's style. He wrote out on slips of paper equal numbers of nouns, adjectives, conjunctions, prepositions, verbs and adverbs, and laid them off in separate piles, face downward. Then he manipulated the words somewhat at random, and on turning them up got the following result:
"Red stupidity: but go so slowly. The hope slim. Drink gloriously! Dream! Swiftly pretty people through daffodils slip in green doubt. Grandly fly bitter fish: for hard sunlight lazily consumes old books. Up by a sedate sweetheart roar darkly loud orchards. Life, the purple flame, simply proclaims a poem."
He drew back in astonishment at the results of his mechanical manipulation. Yet after all, he found, he had missed the goal. He had not discovered Gertrude Stein's process. "It seems almost impossible," he remarks, "by any unimpeded mechanical process to assort words in such a fashion that no glimmer of mind will flash out from their casual juxtapositions. The thing can be done only by unremitting intelligence of the first order—if it can be done at all."
Here is an example of the application of that kind of intelligence taken from Miss Stein's book, a quotation the like of which can easily be found anywhere in the 419 pages, Mr. Sherman assures us:

"The whole place has that which it has when it is found and it is there where there is more room. Room has not that expression. It has no change in a place."

In view of the foregoing, the young critic should not feel greatly humiliated in failing at his effort at imitation Miss Stein's style. For it is imbecilic, impossible. That is *Geography and Plays* and that, that is Gertrude Stein. Words of one or two syllables or words of more syllables that mean meaningless thoughts. Thoughts that are thought to be thoughts by those who think they think.

"That is Gertrude Stein and *Geography and Plays.*

"Modernistic, they say, and artistic, say they, because it is thought to be an intelligent thing to think. But an interesting thing to read because it is not necessary to think. It is not possible to think. A psychopathic symptom idiotically expressed. An anthology of anthropoidal imagining, Refutation of Mr. Bryan. Oh, literature, what crimes are done in they name!

"That is Gertrude Stein and *Geography and Plays*.

"Dangerous, perhaps not, because sanity will not tolerate too much and insanity is proof against insanity. Hope springs eternal from eternal springs. Hope that springs that fadism will remain impotent beyond the set that sets the pace, the intellectual pace.

"Forty-one lunatics escaped from jail, escaped their hospital jail. Lunatics, they say, are dangerous. Perhaps they are, perhaps they are not. Some of them are and some of them are not. And some of them are not in jail.

"*Geography and Plays* by Gertrude Stein!

"But that is because there is no law against that. There should be a law against that because there is no escape from things like that. Intelligent selection in reading is a privilege that most humans have. But book critics must read Gertrude Stein. Help!"

Indianapolis (Indiana) News, August 15, 1923.

"When Helen Furr Got Gay with Harold Moos: A Narrative Written in the Now Popular Manner of Gertrude Stein."

K. D.

When Georgine Skeen went away to stay two months with her brother, and left Helen Furr at the place they had been regularly living when they had been so gay there together, Helen Furr went on being gay there. She was quite gay and a little more gay than she had been when she and Georgine Skeen had been gay there together. This was because she received visits regularly from Harold Moss. Harold Moos was not a gay man but he was a very dark man, and a very heavy man and a very bald man, and of all the regularly dark men and the regularly heavy men and the regularly bald men who sat regularly there then with Helen Furr, Harold Moss was the darkest man and heaviest man and the baldest man who regularly sat with her.

Harold Moos was living regularly in the same place where Helen Furr and Georgine Skeen were living when they were being gay there. Harold was cultivating painting still-life, which was very heavy cultivating then. He was not at all gay, because he was cultivating still-life. It was not very gay still-life, it was not even such gay still-life as he was cultivating when he first sat regularly with Miss Skeen and Miss Furr when they were living regularly there then. The still-life which Harold Moos cultivated was quite pleasant when he first regularly cultivated it.

It was melons!

And it was just a shade gay when he was first painting it in that place where Helen Furr was being gay in all the big and little ways she had of being gay, but when he had been painting it three or four weeks it was not so gay as it had been when he was first painting it. It did not have such a gay smell as when he was first painting it there then. When Harold Moos's still-life did not smell so very gay he would go and sit regularly with the dark men and the heavy men and the bald men who sat with Helen Furr while she was being gay alone while Georgine Skeen had gone away to stay two months with her brother. Helen Furr was very gay whenever Harold Moos came to sit regularly with her.

She was always gay when dark men or heavy men or bald men, or men that were heavy and not so dark and bald, sat regularly with her, but she was more gay when Harold Moos sat regularly with her than when other dark and heavy and bald men sat with her, and she was very much more gay than she had been when Georgine Skeen was living there then.

Helen Furr knew all the big ways of being gay and all the little ways of being gay and she was gay in all the ways that dark men and heavy men and bald men, who sit regularly with girls, like in girls who are being gay. She knew all the old ways of being gay, and she thought up lots of new ways of being gay and particularly ways that Harold Moos would like to see her use in being gay. When Harold Moos, who was not at all gay, would come to sit regularly with her in the place where she was living, she would go up behind him and put her hands over his eyes and say "Guess who this is!" and would be very gay there then.

And she would be gay in talking baby-talk to him, and she would be gay with a Southern accent and be very gay then and she would pull Harold Moos's chair away from him when he would be sitting down and would be very gay regularly in all the big and little ways there are of being gay with dark and heavy and bald men like Harold Moos.

And she would straighten his tie and be very gay then, and she would pick threads off his coat, and be very gay then, and she was often being gay in putting on his hat, and always being gay in knocking it off.

One day when Helen Furr was being gay and Harold Moos was feeling very dark and very heavy and very bald and not at all gay they were married—regularly there then. Harold Moos who was not gay then thought Helen Furr would not be so gay when they were married regularly, but she went on being gay in all the big and little ways she had of being gay with dark and heavy and bald men before she had married Harold Moos. She could not think up any new way of being gay, so she kept on being gay in her old ways. Every day she would be gay in going up behind Harold Moos and putting her hands over his eyes and saying "Guess who this is," and she would be gay in baby-talk then, and she would be gay in lisping then, and she would straighten his tie, being gay, and she would pick white threads off the collar of his coat, being gay.

But she could not think up any new way of being gay.

One day, when they had been married regularly for a year, she again went up behind Harold Moos and put her hands over his eyes, saying "Guess who this is!" Then Harold Moos, who was not feeling regularly gay, said to Helen

Furr, "I have been thinking up a way of making you less gay and of making myself more regularly gay and in a *wholly new way*; and, with that end in view, I hereby hit you three times regularly on the head with this walking stick—One!!?x, Two x?!, Three ? X ! —and, now that I have regularly brained you, I already feel a little more gay; but, in order to make myself regularly *extraordinarily* gay, I am going to subscribe regularly to the gayest magazine in the world, which (if you had not been knocked regularly senseless) you would know is *Vanity Fair*."

Vanity Fair, September 1923.

"A Visit from St. Nicholas: As it Might Be Converted into Prose By Gertrude Stein."

Ruth Lambert Jones

If there were a Christmas there would be a Christmas mouseless dreaming in stocking and couchant red riots in the heavens jangled and pawed appellations uprisings not without chimneys and recognitions partridge-seeming pouter-pigeon perhaps floral fruition how else fillings until nasal-gesturing-accent of departure and vociferation. If there were a Christmas there would be a Christmas unless there were not.

The New York City Evening Post, December 22, 1923.

"Gertrude Stein Interprets Accurately the National Political Situation."

Anonymous

For some time we have been suffering, with many of our countrymen, from doubts. We have felt that some things were not as they should be, and that others were more, or less, than they might be. We have been torn between tendencies to bemoan commissions and omissions as noted in the daily mail from Washington, and equally insistent tendencies to hope for the best. In particular we have wondered about Daugherty, professional and habitual attorney-general. We have looked in many directions seeking light;

and have found none. We have sought to interpret some things we found lately at Washington; we have searched for an authoritative voice, but found it silent. We now know what the country needs. It needs a national poet. We nominate for the position Gertrude Stein.

We have no information leading us to assert that Miss Stein has been lately at Washington, or that she is concerning herself with the inertia of Daugherty; but we find in lines by her in the poem noted this obvious reference to the case:

"Was there was there was there what was there was there what was there was there was there. Whether and in there. As even say so."

Did Miss Stein attend the Chicago convention in 1920? If so, maybe she was in subtly reminiscent mood when she wrote:

"One. I land.

Two. I land.

Three. The land."

As for the prospects at Cleveland next November nothing could be more prophetic:

"As a so. They cannot.

A note. They cannot.

A float. They cannot....

Let me recite what history teaches.

History teaches."

We feel sorry about that last line. It is not like Miss Stein. It is obscure. It lacks the translucency of the rest. It is almost commonplace. But the rest is clear. All the rest is clear. Is clear as clear a clear clearing. One clear. Two clear. A star. Two kerosene lamps. Light. Lightning as lighter in the lightly as first as second when and why. That's the style; but we can't keep it. If we could, everything would be clear at Washington. If we could. If they could. If Washington, D.C. Washington. George. Washington Booker. Exactly as attorney-general. Exactly attorney-generals. As exactly as exactly as attorney-generals. He does. When he does. Will he do. Att- orneys-generals out.

As for the general line-up at Washington Miss Stein's lines in portraiture of Pablo Picasso are eloquent:

"He he he he and he and he and and he and he and he and and as and as he."

There, in the skillful construction and spreading vocabulary of our most courageous poet, we have the political gallery of who's who. All the conventions now have to do is to ratify from the list.

We want Gertrude Stein for the national poet. We want to know that there is in some official position someone equipped and inclined to let loose all the facts presented in a way that shall be intelligible, and Miss Stein qualifies. We want to hear from Washington something like this:

"Investigation goes as goes going. Investment when investiture. As in invitation.

When as in Walsh. Words.

When as in Wheeler. Words.

When as in Lenroot. Plants.

When as in Dill. Pickles."

If there is no possibility of making Miss Stein national poet, then we want her elected to the Senate.

Boston Herald, March 25, 1924.

"The True Story of My Break with Gertrude Stein."

Ernest Hemingway

The real story of my break with Gertrude Stein may be interesting. For a long time I had noticed that when I would come to the door of Gertrude Stein's house and ring the bell nobody would answer. Sometimes a window would open and someone would look out and then the window would shut again.

Occasionally a maid would come to the door and say, "No, Miss Stein (or *Mademoiselle Stein*, as the maid called her in French) is not home (*pas chez elle*)." I felt, though, that Miss Stein liked me and wanted to see me. So I took to dropping in informally. I would drop in during dinner and stay for dessert. (In French, *entremets* or more often, *fromage*). Or I would drop in for tea when I saw other people going in and I felt sure Miss Stein must be at home. Miss Stein was always charming.

"Hemingway, why do you always come here drunk?" she asked me one afternoon.

"I don't know, Miss Stein," I answered. "Unless it's to see you."

Another time Miss Stein said, "Hemingway, why do you come here at all?" I was at a loss for an answer.

I tried to talk about literature to Miss Stein. "I am trying to form my style on yours, Miss Stein," I said one rainy afternoon. "I want to write like you, like Henry James, like the Old Testament and—" I added, "like that great Irishman, James Joyce."

"All you young men are alike," Miss Stein said. Frankly, I was hurt. As I left, three young Russian painters entered. "All you young men are alike," Miss Stein greeted them. The young Russians broke into eager chatters. It was an exciting statement. They hoped it was true. What times we would all have then.

The next time I came to Miss Stein's house the maid struck me with a bicycle pump.

"Pardon," I said, speaking French, "that's a bicycle pump."

"*Connais bien*," she said. ("I know it," in Fr.)

"And I am Ernest Hemingway—the writer," I added.

"*Allez-vous en*," the maid replied. ("I have my orders," in Fr.)

I went back several times but the door was always locked. One day the door was nailed shut, and there was a surly looking bloodhound (*chien du sangre*) that growled as I came near, and a large sign, KEEP OUT—THIS MEANS YOU! (N'ENTREZ PAS—C'EST TOI). Miss Stein had written the sign (in French) herself.

It was then that I broke with Miss Stein. I have never ceased to feel that I did her a great injustice and, needless to say, I have never ceased to regret it.

The New Yorker, February 27, 1927.

"As a Critic Has a Headache: A Review in Synthetic Form of the Works of Gertrude Stein, Past, Present and to Come."

Isaac Goldberg

Babble.
A tower, a tow-wow-er of Babble.

Babble, baa, baa, Bull.

Baa, baa, black sheep have you any manuscripts to sell?

Baa bell, bell-wether, *Bon jour!*

Sheep wool, and a yard wide, and thus a Woolworth Tower with a Baa Bell, well worth ringing. As a sheep has a ewe, a love story.

Baa, bull.

Bull in a china shop, amok. A mocking Gertrude amok in the vocabulary, vo-babble-airy, vo-baa-bull-airy, bull, bulbul singing to Baal. This has, it has, a meaning, meaning to signify, as signification. Airy bull, fairy bull, will you, won't you, will you, won't you, will you talk with me? Bulletin, bull-it in. This bull pen, penned in syntax, taxes the ancient rhetoric with sin and kicks against the pricks against the prongs of chaos masked as order. Order emerging as chaos, K.O.'s ancient order and orders a new O.K. Gershwin, *geschwind!* Call me up by saxophone at half-past Sex. The half is not past, and the past, passing, is not; is naught; *en passant*, we shall order salad for sad Alice.

As a critic has a headache. A Review.

There are writers who write and there are readers reading, and there are writers reading and that, too, is something. Then there are somethings that write and somethings that read, and that, too, is a book. A book also is something that is read and a reading that is written. There are books that are written and there are books that are read and every beginning has a being ended, as every end has a being begun. As a typesetter has a headache; a pi.

In America are readers and are writers who live in Paris. In Paris is a city, too. There are Paris readers and there are American readers and to be a reader is something, too; another thing. There are printers and each printer in printing a writing is a reader and a printer and a critic with a headache and a tower of lead Babel. And maybe you'll not believe it, but that is something again, although being a baby is a something was a nothing and will be a nothing once more.

As a critic has a review. A Headache.

Bebble.

A tower, a tow-Wow, a two-woe, a tow-Whee!-er of Babble.

Haldeman Julius Weekly, October 1, 1927.

"A Letter to Gertrude Stein."

Lindley Williams Hubbell

The roots have struck deep; tree-root and flower-root and the small absurd
   weed nourished by dust;
In this rich soil a whole generation that would have found death in the
   wind and the black ice,
But the roots were fast, the loam was packed tightly about them, the serried
   stalks were secure,
The earth was stronger than the deep ice, the earth gave back laughter to
   the laughter of the wind, the ice cracked.

In cities it was the same: people leaned out of windows and sniffed
   the air and laughed,
Children flew past in a clatter of roller skates, children screamed, their
   voices louder than the clatter of their skates,
The older ones played ball in the streets, chairs were brought out on the
   pavements, women rocked back and forth,
In all the cities it was like this, and in the little towns no one stayed in the
   houses when work was done.

The miracle was this: that a man could look at his friend and say without
   shame,
"It is better to be dead than to laugh at a perfectly simple thing. To do
   that is worse than death."
The miracle was that sweetness was not gone out of the sap, that the stem
   was not ashamed to bear blossoms,
That the roots were glad of the rain, that the slow wind was permitted
   gladly, that the boughs were fed willingly.

Love, the bright flower, and homage, the proud spear-head of the tall
   flower,
And laughter, a spike of mullein, whatever is simple and without harm,
   whatever is unashamed of the dust it wears on its leaves,
And the sanity of the grass, the wide cool sanity of the grass that asks one

inch, two inches of earth, and one inch, two inches of air,
These shall be plaited into a sign to be given from hand to hand as a token
    and a remembrance.

Pagany, Spring 1930.

"The Autobiography of Alice B. Sullivan"

Frank Sullivan

I got the idea for writing this autobiography from a very interesting series of articles now appearing in *The Atlantic Monthly*, called *The Autobiography of Alice B. Toklas*. My name being also "Alice B.," I naturally read them. One of the many interesting things about *The Autobiography of Alice B. Toklas* is that it was not written by Alice B. Toklas at all. It was written by Gertrude Stein. Another interesting thing about the autobiography is that there is practically nothing in it about Alice B. Toklas. It is all about Gertrude Stein.

I said to myself, "Well, if Alice B. Toklas can have her autobiography written, I guess Alice B. Sullivan can, too," so I called up my very dear friend, Frank Sullivan, and asked him if he would come directly over and write my autobiography. He did, and this is my autobiography, by Frank Sullivan.

I think I have met three authentic geniuses in my life. They were Frank Sullivan, Pussyfoot Johnson, and a perfectly charming man I once met on a Number Three Fifth Avenue bus. I forget his name.

I believe I have the honor of being the first white child to be born in Nevada. I can remember, as a child—but perhaps you would prefer to hear how it was that I came to meet my dear friend, Frank Sullivan, who has meant so much to me throughout the years.

One evening I was taking a bath when the door opened and Frank walked in. He wanted to take a bath, too. Naturally, I was embarrassed, but this soon passed, because with that tact for which he is noted, Frank said, "Oh, excuse me, *sir*," and then he got into the bathtub. We had a splendid bath together and it was the beginning of a friendship which has influenced me greatly.

I shall never forget those thrilling days when I was the first white child born in Nevada. I used to try to tell Frank Sullivan about them, but he would never listen because he always wanted to be talking about himself. When I would say, "But, Frank Sullivan, one of the three authentic geniuses I have ever met, don't you realize I was the first white child born in Nevada?" he would smile tolerantly and say "Tut, I was the first white child born in our family."

This was about the time Frank was writing *The Specialist* and at this time his philosophy of art was not entirely clear, even to himself. He was confused. He was confused because of something that had happened to him in a speakeasy. This happening had influenced his point of view a great deal. He was sitting in the speakeasy when a large picture became loosened from the wall and fell on his head. The picture was *Venus Arising from the Foam*. The impact of the heavy picture upon Frank's head clarified his philosophy greatly. He bought the picture. It became the nucleus of his famous collection. He still has a great sentimental feeling for this picture, because it was the picture which fell on his head and clarified his ideas. Frank Sullivan feels that he would not be what he is today if the picture had not fallen on his head.

As a result of that incident, Frank wrote the now famous *Tender Bean*, which began like this: "Oh bean bean venus have you fallen fallen on frank-frank's bean question mark yes oh ouch cuts abrasions and contusions."

Frank wrote "Tender Bean" in chalk on the sidewalk in front of 277 Park Avenue. He was arrested for it. He wrote it in that manner because it seemed to him at the time that chalk and sidewalk were the suitable and logical vehicles for the expression of his genius. He does not think this now. Frank Sullivan changes his mind often. Tomorrow he may again think that chalk and sidewalk form the only vehicles for his artistic expression.

Now perhaps you would care to hear something about those early days of mine in Nevada. Or perhaps you would prefer to hear more about Frank. You say you would not prefer to hear more about Frank? Very well, I shall tell you something about my childhood days in Nevada. I remember that on that day when I first met Frank Sullivan, on that day when he came into my bathroom, said "Excuse me, *sir*," and got into the bathtub, I remember how surprised I was at seeing him. I had always heard he was a short, thickset man. But he was not a short, thickset man that day. I looked at him and he was not a short, thickset man. He was a tall, slender man. Later, when I got out of the tub in order to get first whack at the bath towel, I learned I was mistaken. He *was* a short, thickset man. But from where I sat in the tub, he had looked like a tall, slender man. It was from this incident that Frank derived his famous theory of perspective. No, he was not tall and slender. He was short and thickset, and very cruel to his women. This was part of his charm.

Frank Sullivan and I used to walk up and down West Fifty-second Street trying to get credit at the various speakeasies there and he used to talk to me about his theories of art. He scorned to dress like other men. He wore satin small clothes, shoes with silver buckles, a purple velvet coat heavily embroidered with gold, jewels, and passementerie, and a tremendous peruke. Taxicab-drivers frequently mistook him for Heywood Broun Quatorze.

This was the year when Frank was being ridiculed in every atelier in New York because he insisted on drawing mustaches on the girls in the cold-cream ads on the subway platforms. The Philistines said that girls in cold-cream ads should not have mustaches, at least not the great black handlebars that Frank put on them. But Frank saw them in black mustaches and he would not compromise. The subway guards threatened him but he would not compromise. He saw the girls in black mustaches. The subway guards made things so difficult for him that he could only work between two and five in the morning, when the guards were dozing. Frank did not mind this. He would not compromise.

He had to work furtively. He rarely had a chance to polish. He did not mind this, either. In his famous Pond's Extract ad (now in the Seventy-seventh Street Station of the Lexington Avenue Subway), the mustache he drew on the girl is shorter on one side than on the other. I asked Frank why this was and he said that it was because a local drew into the station and he had to run for it before he could finish the mustache. He said that he did not mind working under these conditions. He said they stimulated him.

Everybody now realizes how right Frank Sullivan was. Today there is scarcely an advertisement on an elevated or subway platform that has not got some kind of drawing on it. To this extent, Frank Sullivan has been vindicated. But he has been blamed for many things for which he is not responsible. He has been blamed for things for which his disciples are responsible. His disciples have drawn things of which he does not approve. He thinks many of them have gone too far.

In this connection, I said to Frank one day, "How would you like to hear something about my childhood days in Nevada?" He replied, "I would not like it. And I wish those disciples of mine would stick to drawing mustaches. Or at the most I wish they would content themselves with blacking the teeth on the girls in the toothpaste ads. They go too far. That is not Art. Art does not go too far."

So that, dear reader, is the autobiography of me, Alice B. Sullivan. You can see that I have not had an easy time of it. I do not know what I should have done if it had not been for my friend, Frank Sullivan.

The New Yorker, July 1, 1933.

"They Don't Speak English in Paris."

Ogden Nash

I wish that I could get in line
And shout the praise of Gertrude Stein
In any high-class hullabaloo
I rather like to holler too;
I hate like anything to miss
Swelling the roar of Ah! Boom! Siss!
And most particularly when
The cheers are led by famous men.
The fault I'm sure is solely mine,
But I cannot root for Gertrude Stein.
For Gertrude Stein I cannot root;
I cannot blow a single toot;
I must preserve a dreary silence,
Though doomed thereby to durance vilence.
I'm fond of women, also wine,
But not the song of Gertrude Stein.
No laurels can I pass, alas,
To pigeons on the grass, alas.

Oh woefully must I decline
To dance in the street with Gertrude Stein.

O Gertrude, Gertrude, is it me?
Couldn't it possible be thee?
Not in the face of all the roses
Awarded thee by them who knowses.
From Walla Walla to the Rhine
Carillons clang for Gertrude Stein,
Rung not by nitwit nincompoops
But geniuses in fervent groups.
Those pens of talent most divine
Scratch noisiest for Gertrude Stein;
Neglecting all their personal muttons,
They genuflect to *Tender Buttons*.
Why must I grunt, a lonely swine,
Rejecting the pearls of Gertrude Stein?
Why can' I praise in cataracts
Her Four such Saints in Three such Acts?
Four Saints, Three Acts, Three Acts, in fact
The Acts get a Saint and a third an act,
And Lizzie Borden took three axe
And have her mother tongue forty whacks,
And a hundred eminent artistic figures
Swallowed the woodpile, including the nigures.

I prefer to wade through Rasselas
To pigeons on the grass, alas.
The English language is better as language
Than spattered like a lettuce and mayonnaise sanguage,
So let those who will read Alice B. Toklas,
And I'll the complete works of Shakespeare and a box of chocolas.

New York American, March 22, 1934.

"Appeal to Gertrude."

Melville Cane

Gertrude—there's a good old scout!
What's it what's it all about?
Hear a tortured hemisphere
Begging you to make it clear.
Drop a clue or slip a hint
Touching on the what-you-print
What-you-print and what-there's-in't.

Abdicate the role of sibyl,
At your secret let us nibble.
Pray, divulge, reveal, disclose
In communicable prose
Why a rose a rose a rose.

Are you willfully obscure?
Are you puerile or mature?
We are anything but sure.

Are you spoofing or profound?
Is there sense within the sound?
Will you properly expound?

Is your highly Orphic text
Meant for this world or the next?
We concede we are perplexed.

Is it genius, is it sham?
Parlor game or cryptogram?
Will you answer kindly, Ma'am?

Are you hollow or a mime?
One remembers Shakespeare's line:

"Sermons lie concealed in Stein."
Gertrude answers, slightly bored:
"Gertrude is her own reward."

The New Yorker, November 3, 1934.

Richmond Times Dispatch, March 12, 1935.

"Gentlemen Prefer."

Charlotte Haldane

Who turned Anita Loos loose? I mean I have always wondered because of all we girls no one is a neater is Anita. So of all we girls I preferred Lorelei until I read a novel the other day called *The Autobiography of Alice B. Toklas*. It is all about a girl called Gertrude Stein is a Stone is a Stein is a stone which is amusing if you don't want bread but bad to the bone Stone and if not, not.

Well this girl Alice B. Toklas lives in Paris but not with gentlemen prefer gentlemen. And Paris is better there being no gentlemen but only the gentlemen friends of Gertrude B. Stein who are all well-known talkers but not otherwise like the gentlemen friends of Lorelei. The wives of the wives of their gentlemen friends Alice sat by the fire with and listened to the lives of the wives while Gertrude Sirenstein talked to their occasional husbands. Well this Alice has run Anita pretty that is because Gertrude B. Stein is really an awfully mad gal, a divine girl who even without a divining rod can beat through any girl who is no match for her. Gertrude said to Alice that she is very grateful not to have been born of an intellectual family, she has a horror of those she calls intellectual people. It has always been rather ridiculous that she who is good friends with all the women and can know them and they can know her, has always been the admired of the precious. But she always says some day they, anybody, will find out that she is of interest to them, she and her writing.

It would be strange if I turn out to be an authoress. I mean at my home near Little Rock, Arkansas, my family all wanted me to do something about my music. Because all of my friends said I had talent and they all kept after me and kept after me about practicing. But some way I never seemed to care so much about practicing. I mean I simply could not sit for hours and hours at a time practicing just for the sake of a career. So one day I got quite temperamental and threw the old mandolin clear across the room and I have never really touched it since. But writing is different because you do not have to learn or practice and it is more temperamental because practicing seems to take all the temperament out of me.

But I see I have gotten started all wrong to tell you about Alice G. Stein because something by another of our girls slipped in by mistake but any literary girl who likes writing will know at once what I mean so I will go right on telling you more about Gertrude S. Toklas. Not having any unconscience Dr. Froyd asked her what she seemed to dream about. So she told him that she never really dreamed about anything. I mean, she used her brains so much in the daytime that at night they did not seem to do anything but rest. It was also at this time that Gertrude Stein got into the habit of writing at night. It was only after eleven o'clock that she could be sure that no one would knock at the studio door. I mean a gentleman never pays for those things and a girl always pays. She realizes that in English literature in her time she is the only one.

So I suppose that most of the girls in Paris do not have such brains as we American girls. During these months after the war we were one day going down a little street and saw a man looking in at a window and going backwards and forwards and right and left and otherwise behaving quite strangely. Lipschitz, said Gertrude Stein. Yes, said Lipschitz, I am buying an iron cock. Where is it, we asked. Why in there, he said, in there it was. Gertrude Stein had known Lipschitz very slightly at one time but this incident made them friends and soon he asked her to pose. As I was saying after the return from England and lecturing we have a great many parties, there were many occasions for parties, all the Sitwells came over, Carl Van Vechten came over, Sherwood Anderson came over again. And besides there were many other occasions for parties. But I always seem to think that it is delightful to have quite a lot of girls at a party, if a girl has quite a lot of gentlemen at a party, and it is quite delightful to have all the girls from the Follies, but I really could not invite them because, after all, they were not in my set. So then I thought it all over and I thought that even if it was not etiquette to invite them to a party it really would be etiquette to invite them to a party it really would be etiquette to hire them to come to a party and be entertainers, and after they were entertainers they could mix in to the party and it really would not be a social error. We did give a great many parties in those days and the Duchess of Clermont-Tonnerre came very often. So that made the Racquet Club jealous, and one thing led to another until somebody rang for an ambulance and the police came in. Be calm madam, said my father, perhaps it is my son who has been filled. One of his axioms I always remember, if you must do a thing do it graciously. He also told me that a hostess should never apologize for any failure in her household arrangements, if there is a hostess there is insofar as there is a hostess no failure.

So you see what nice girls there all were Alice and Lorelei and Gertrude and Dorothy and if not, a gentleman is a rose is a gentleman is a rose is.

I mean, it only goes to show what a good thing it is for a girl not to have an unconscience.

The English Review, May 1936.

"To Gertrude Stein."

Maxwell Bodenheim

White, blandly isolated on the ground
Where slaughters, thievings, contradictions pour,
You twirl umbrellas, cryptograms of sounds,
Like some old princess on a wistful tour,
Abhorring nakedness and common stress,
Ignoring uproars in the ruined yards,
And fingering an old, brocaded dress
In corners of deserted boulevards.

Your mannerisms, sensitively curled,
Involved and sighing curiosities
Implore us—in the unrelenting world
Of bedlams, plottings and monstrosities—
To leave our hatreds, make the earth again
An aproned inn where subtleties can reign.

Poetry, December 1940.

"Book Is a Book."

Anonymous

There are four people in New York who have read the manuscript of Gertrude Stein's new novel. Three of the people do not matter at all well hardly at all but the fourth is us and that is a good thing because we can tell you all about Gertrude Stein's new novel. The name of the novel is *Mrs. Reynolds* but it would do you no good to go into Bretano's and ask for *Mrs. Reynolds*. Even if you had two dollars. Because Random House has decided not to print *Mrs. Reynolds* until after the war. While the war is going on Random House wants to print Quentin Reynolds alas. Bennett B. Toklas the editor of Random House may not know much but he knows that much. He knows that Quentin Reynolds will sell better than *Mrs. Reynolds* not Mrs. Quentin Reynolds but Gertrude Stein's *Mrs. Reynolds*. Paper is scarce but there are still plenty of pigeons.

"*Mrs. Reynolds* is not all about roses, it is more about Tuesdays than about roses. Mrs. Reynolds had many kinds of Tuesdays." That's what Gertrude says in her book, and she also says, "Mrs. Reynolds was very well-born. She was born on Tuesday. And the next day was Wednesday and she was a day old on Wednesday." Quentin Reynolds looked three days old last Wednesday, probably something he ate in the Stork Club but Gertrude does not say that at least not in *Mrs. Reynolds*. She tells about a lot of people named Roger and Joseph Lane and Lydia and Eph Ell, and especially about Angel Harper. Angel Harper is a character who will make the critics sit up and take notice when *Mrs. Reynolds* is published alas. "When a little dog sticks himself on a needle on the floor he cries right away. When a little child falls down he does not cry until he is picked up. This has a great deal to do with Angel Harper. A great deal." That's what Gertrude Stein says about Angel Harper. She also says that Mrs. Reynolds' brother could not remember what Angel Harper looked like, and that Claudia thought she was married but that she was mistaken because Angel Harper was never married he did not even have a brother.

Gertrude filled up two hundred and sixty-nine pages of typewriter paper writing *Mrs. Reynolds*. She wrote it in France so it had to be smuggled out, it could have gone by pigeon if it hadn't been so heavy alas. A friend of hers not Alice B. Toklas but another friend of hers smuggled it out in the front of her dress. She had trouble getting it through the customs because the customs men thought it was in code but she told them no, it was a novel by Gertrude Stein and they all said oh.

The New Yorker, February 19, 1944.

"Gertrude Was Always Giggling."

Arnold Rönnebeck

"The days are wonderful and the nights are wonderful and the life is pleasant. Bargaining is something and there is not that success. The intention is what if application has that accident results are reappearing. They did not darken. That was not adulteration."

Gertrude Stein was rather excitedly opening a small package just received from her publisher in Florence. It was the entire edition of her slender work "Portrait of Mabel Dodge at the Villa Curonia," from which I have quoted the initial paragraphs. We were at her studio apartment at 27, rue de Fleurus, not far from the Jardin du Luxembourg. The word-portrait has eleven pages printed on water-marked "Bütten" (Firenze; Tip. Galienna). She handed me one of the hastily extracted copies, saying: "Here, keep it!"

I sat down in one of her many comfortable chairs and read, and when I suggested that I translate the booklet into French and German, she laughed one of her contagious laughs and said: "Quite a stunt! Go ahead, I am sure you can do it." I did.

She refers to these translations in *The Autobiography of Alice B. Toklas* with the comment that I "thus brought her her first international reputation." About her most entertaining "Portrait of Mabel Dodge" she said: "Well, Pablo (Picasso) is doing abstract portraits in painting. I am trying to do abstract portraits in *my* medium, *words*." At that time Gertrude Stein wrote a number of other abstract word portraits expressing in an unacademic style the personality, way of life, character of work of other un-academically creative people. In 1912 Alfred Stieglitz printed in his distinguished publication *Camera Work* two such portraits by Gertrude Stein in a special Matisse-Picasso issue. Stieglitz ends his editorial with these words: "We wish you the pleasure of a hearty laugh at them upon first reading. Yet we confidently commend them to your subsequent and critical attention."

Here is a quotation from the Matisse portrait: "Some certainly were wanting to be needing to be doing that is clearly expressing something. Certainly they were willing to be a great one. They were, that is some of them, were not wanting to be needing expressing anything being struggling, he was a great one he was clearly expressing something."

With slight subtle juggling of nouns and adjectives and conjunctives these lines repeat over three pages. And suddenly you seem to recall a Matisse painting seen at Wildenstein's in New York or at Durand-Ruelle's in Paris.

Gertrude herself was always giggling, an intellectual silver giggle, over her own stuff, sitting like a very wise Bodhisatva, legs crossed, on the Directoire sofa under her portrait by Pablo in which one eye is lower than the other and it looks out of drawing, but since she always talked with a cigarette in one corner of the mouth and the smoke bothered the eye, she lived up to the apparently distorted likeness.

Interrupting her girlish giggle I said: "Now Gertrude, there isn't anything funny about this. The other day at the opening of *Les Fauves* where Matisse is heavily represented, I heard people burst out in critical or appreciative words just as incoherent as his paintings evidently appeared to them. Your writing is not 'abstract,' it is photographic. Maybe that's why Stieglitz published your portraits in *Camera Work*."— "You certainly got the idea," she said. "People don't see with their eyes what they hear with their ears. I write just the way I talk," which was mostly true. And that was why I had used the word photographic, and she liked that.

Here are some of the last lines from the Picasso portrait:

"This one was one who was working. This one was one always having something come out of him and this thing the thing coming out of him always had real meaning. This one was one who was working. This one was one who was almost always working."

When one day at the author's studio I read my French translation to the "sitter," I did not get very far. After about the first half-page, Picasso, his coal-black eyes flashing, cried: "Assez, assez, oh mon Dieu!"—and the author and the model and Alice B. and I were as usual in convulsions of laughter and Picasso said finally: "Gertrude, I just don't like abstractions."

After general recovery I said: "Look here, Picasso, it's bound to sound strange in French because the construction of the French language is different from the construction of the English language."—Picasso: "But doesn't it seem to you that this English construction is already different from English construction?"—"Now I've got you!" I yelled. "You understand the whole thing perfectly. You're talking just like Gertrude this minute." Since Picasso didn't then know much English our conversation was in French but there was much shouting and laughter.

Always there was much intellectual shouting and laughter and mentally accelerated gaiety at Gertrude Stein's Saturday evening at home. Yes, we had a glass of Bordeaux or of Chablis with the filet mignon at dinner but nothing sparkling later, just the sparkle of her own mind and vitality and wit which seemed to be constantly bubbling over and made others feel that they themselves had ideas, but it was always she who said the unexpected and paradoxical thing, and when her round face started twitching and her eyes became slits and the corners of her mouth went up and up and suddenly a deep gurgle started that shaped itself into loud laughter, well you knew that some amusing or grotesque thought had been working inside her and she could not bear keeping it for herself any longer and when it finally came out it was always something either amusing or grotesque or witty, possibly a quotation from James Joyce or William James which exactly fitted our conversation in a slightly twisted and therefore even more amusing sense. I feel that such warm, deeply human qualities of Gertrude Stein's spirit are perhaps some of her finest creative influences on those who have personally known her during those years when what we still call "modern art" was created in Paris some thirty years ago.

I know that during the period (1912-13), Gertrude Stein used "words for words' sake" just as her friend Picasso, the great abstractionist, on canvas sued "forms for forms's sake." The meaning of both forms of expression are first understandable only to the creators while the public laughs them off as absurdities. It is amazing, however, how quickly the public caught on to all this apparent unintelligibility in painting and writing.

I have quoted from Gertrude Stein's "Portrait of Mabel Dodge at the Villa Curonia" and from her word portraits published in *Camera Work* because these short but most characteristic works of hers are hardly known. There were only 150 or so copies of "Mabel Dodge," and Alfred Stieglitz informs me in a recent letter that only a few (and I quote) "public libraries are supposed to have sets of *Camera Work*. I know the Metropolitan Museum has a set. A complete one. Such are very rare. In Chicago the John Crerar Library has a set. The San Francisco Library has a set—has? The New York Public Library has one too."

Upon inquiry Mabel Dodge Luhan writes me from Albuquerque, New Mexico: "I don't remember how many of those things, the 'Portrait of M. D. at the Villa Curonia,' I had printed in Florence. I have not one myself. But it is eagerly searched for by libraries and has in some places fetched huge sums." M. D. Is right: Only last year I noticed in a catalogue of an auction of rare books in New York one copy of these eleven pages offered to the tune of seventy-five dollars.—

One day when Gertrude Stein and Alice B. were at my Paris studio for tea, Gertrude very clearly criticized some pieces of sculpture I thought I had finished and she said: "Get that real roundness into them. This way I just don't like them. After all a form is a form is a form."

Much later she wrote: "A rose is a rose is a rose."

During my six years in Paris, until the outbreak of war in 1914, I was in the habit of keeping a diary of conversations of discussions which for some reason or other seemed to me important enough to preserve. Gertrude Stein must have had the same habit, a habit not surprising on the part of one who is evidently fascinated by the spoken or written word. In *Alice B. Toklas* (pp. 122, 123) she describes a dinner party in her studio apartment at which Alice B., Picasso, the famous English museum director and critic Berenson, Mabel Dodge and I were present. I wrote down the conversation the same night, and it checks almost verbatim with the conversation as related by Gertrude Stein in *Alice B. Toklas*. In many other instances too she seems to be quoting my own notes with the exception of an incident where she has completely misunderstood my ideals and way of research, from the point of view of an artist. However I have forgiven, thinking that innuendos are amusing additions to a chatty and gossipy book. It's a case of: *Se non è vero è ben trovato.*

Gertrude, I thought when I read it, you really don't know how truly funny you are! (*Alice B. Toklas,* pp. 124, 125). I like you for being funny Gertrude yes I do yes and I regret that we have never seen each other again since those many happy Saturday evenings in Paris yes even though you returned to these your native shores exactly ten years ago yes.—

Gertrude Stein's writing may appear easy to imitate. It is not. Imitation amounts to a shallow take-off, nothing else. I would suppose it would be easy to imitate Wordsworth or even Shelley or the bombast of Victor Hugo in type, but very difficult to imitate convincingly Gertrude Stein because her style is her *meaning* and you can't imitate meaning if it is not your own. Gertrude Stein *does* write the way she talks and she always did that thing that way. There is the same photographic rendering of an impact of a reaction as we see it in her old friend Marcel Duchamp's famous painting "Nude Descending a Staircase." Once we happened to meet in the Louvre in front of the great fifth century Greek Apollo about which Rainer Maria Rilke wrote in his moving poem *Archasicher Torso Apollos* and Gertrude Stein said: "There it all is. All is there. What else is there to be said is there?"

The final paragraph of her "Portrait of Mabel Dodge at the Villa Curonia" goes like this: "There is all there is when there is all there has where there is what there is. That what is done when there is done what is done and the union won and the division is the explicit visit. There is not all of any visit."

Books Abroad, October 1944.

"Give Me Land: Gertrude Stein Talks About the Future of G. I.s."

Sgt. Scott Corbett

A great many writers who write simple stuff come up with a bunch of double-talk when a guy with a pencil and paper comes along and starts asking for opinions. Miss Gertrude Stein is not like that. She puts her double-talk into some of her books, and leaves it out of her opinions.

In the newspapers, her opinions are usually translated into the sort of patter which has become her trademark, despite the fact that she doesn't really talk that way, but just writes that way. Miss Stein does not mind this, however. It has made her, next to George Bernard Shaw, the intellectual most often quoted in a small box on the front page under a wise-cracking headline.

She is famous more for what is written about her and her opinions than for what she herself has written. Miss Gertrude Stein, if she were merely the author of the 1934 bestseller, *The Autobiography of Alice B. Toklas*, would be moderately well-known. It is, however, Miss Gertrude Stein the Personality, the rugged individualist, who has become famous.

She is also the most famous American expatriate, having lived in France most of her life. When American G. I.s first appeared in the small French village, near Lyon, in which she lived during the German Occupation, however, they brought America back to her, and she began to feel very American and very much concerned over the future of her native land and of the Joes who were going to have to carry on that future.

She began to shoot the breeze with G. I.s whenever she saw them, getting their ideas and opinions. When she took an aerial trip through Germany for a magazine, she talked to a lot of soldiers there, and she's still at it in Paris. Many a G.I. has had a sidewalk bull session with an American woman named Gertrude Stein without even realizing she was that woman who writes that crazy poetry the newspapers sometimes talk about.

One of the things about us that worries her most is the American "employee mentality." She believes industrialism is making a mess of the U.S., and she thinks we've got to get away from big business and the employee mentality and get back to being small business individualists who stand on our own feet.

"Too many Americans are dependent for everything on a 'job.' They don't really own anything, and if the job goes, everything is gone. Every Frenchman tries to own a bit of land of his own, enough to live on and to live off of if necessary. You've got to have something of your own you know you can always fall back on before you can have peace of mind and stand on your own feet and make your own way. An industrial nation is poor, because its people don't own anything. Americans don't own their high standard of living, they only rent it, which means that they are likely to lose it suddenly as so many did during the Depression.

"Nobody has ever really explained why the Depression happened in America, because nobody dared to. It happened because our industrialism lost its greatest foreign market, the one within its own borders, in 1920 when immigration was stopped. Immigration brought millions of new consumers to America, and when immigration was stopped and that market no longer existed, America had no place to sell everything its industries produced and there was a Depression. I don't mean to say by that that not stopping immigration would have saved us from a Depression. It would only have postponed it, because we couldn't have gone on forever producing things in more quantity than anybody really wanted, which is what we were doing. Don't fool yourself, the foreign market is gone, and it's not going to come back now, and if we continue to depend on industrialism and big business we're going to be poor.

"England became a great industrial nation first. Before that she was a self-contained nation with a great specialty—the finest wool cloth in the world. She threw that away to industrialize, and now she has lost her world markets and she ends up a poor nation with nothing.

"On the other hand there is France, an agricultural, small-business nation with a specialty, which is the production of luxuries, and even now the French are rich. By rich I mean they have a little money in the bank, each of them, but more than that a place to live on, a place which will feed them and house them. That's why Frenchmen don't have to worry about losing a job the way Americans do. Even if they haven't a place of their own, all Frenchmen have connections in the country.

"In America we had a great specialty, the finest steel in the world, but we used it up by using it to make everything. Instead of saving it for the things where it really mattered, fine machines and tools, we used it for gadgets as well, and we used it up."

The era of industrialism in America, she feels, is going to have to be replaced by something entirely new, if the U.S. is to survive, something which will allow the American to get back to being the individualist he was before the country became industrialized. The leadership, if it comes, will come from the South, she believes, as she has found that the young Southerners she has met are thinking more progressively than Northerners. (No, Miss Stein is not from Georgia. She was born in Allegheny, Pennsylvania).

"This generation of Southerners is not fighting the Civil War over again. Their minds are more free and flexible than the Northerners. Because their part of the country has not been industrialized, they can see the dangers more clearly than the boys from the North.

"Because we need a completely new set-up to replace industrialism, we need a lot of pioneering done, but the question is going to be whether or not our young men have it in them to do it. Funnily enough, the only pioneering being done in the States now is being done by the Negroes. They're going here, going there, trying new things, experimenting.

"The trouble is Americans aren't land crazy anymore. That's what the pioneers were, land crazy, and that's what all Frenchmen are and always have been, because they know that owning a place of your own is what gives you independence and lets you stand on your own feet, and nobody is rich unless he owns his own soul."

The ex-serviceman's Army experience is not going to help him in the job ahead, she feels.

"The Army makes men lazy. It makes them lazy because it has eight men to do one man's job. In wartime this is necessary, this is the way it has to be, because of casualties and all the unforeseen things that can happen but naturally when eight men only have one man's job to do it means they're going to get lazy."

Her view of the Occupation being done by the U.S. in Germany is that there is a great deal of confusion and very little conception of just what to do. After her trip through Germany in July, she said concerning the Germans, "There is only one thing to be done and that is to teach them disobedience, as long as they are obedient so long sooner or later they will be ordered around by a bad man, and there will be trouble." It is obedient people, she declared, who do as they are told even if they are told to go to war in a war of conquest and aggression. "Mass obedience always finds a bad man to be its leader," she says.

During the occupation of France the Germans warned Miss Stein twice, and if they had really known what she thought about them they probably would have done worse than that. She considers them an unsuccessful people, and she gets mad when G. I.s admire Germany's ways.

To G. I.s who praise German girls she has a sharp answer. She tells them that when the Germans occupied France there was no fraternization problem, because all but the out-and-out prostitutes ignored them. Then she reminds them how the German women have acted with American soldiers during the Occupation of Germany. Then she shoots them this question: "Supposing

America were ever defeated and occupied, which would you like your American women to be like—the French women or the German women?"

"Some of them go pretty white then I ask them that," she says.

At present Miss Stein is writing a book named *Brewsie and Willie*, which is the result of her talks with countless Americans soldiers. It will, she says, be about "what worries G. I.s." When the book is published, it will probably have the flavor of Gertrude, but there will be very little of pigeons in the grass, alas, and a great deal of cards on the table.

Yank, November 11, 1945.

4

Remembrances, Memorials, and the Posthumous Reputation

"The Shape of Things."

Anonymous

Hearing that Gertrude Stein is dead is like hearing that Paul Bunyan has been eaten by his ox Babe. Certainly she is not really dead: legends never die, and Miss Stein has made herself into an American legend more lasting than anything Barnum himself ever created. She sat in Paris as the Pythoness used to sit at Delphi: everybody in the world, from Picasso to a sergeant of marines, came asking for a sign, and went away happy with some oracular utterance which he could finger as if it were a Chinese puzzle. (If you believe in yourself hard enough, the world will beat a path to your door—especially in Paris). An obstinate and homely shrewdness ran through everything Gertrude Stein said, and glittered at random throughout her writings, which seemed to the average reader an unusually idiosyncratic and concrete nonsense, the sort of massive whimsy a stomach would think up if it could ever stop digesting. But in our secular, commercial, and merciless age she came somehow to stand for Wisdom, which doesn't sell itself in the streets, but gives itself away at home, in cipher. Who else ever became famous by writing his own biography, or influenced dozens of writers by treating words, so far as it is possible to do so, as objects without meaning? Who else would say that a friend's one-man show was "rather epoch-making," or would gravely decide that the Americans are today the oldest nation on earth, since they entered the twentieth century ten years before anybody else did? The world will be a duller place without her; her sins harmed no one; at this moment she is sitting in Elysian Fields talking to Samuel Johnson, the only man who could ever be her match.

The Nation, August 10, 1946.

"Letter from Paris."

Janet Flanner

To Gertrude Stein's old friends here, her death was the last chapter in her private history's concordance with the important things going on in France. She had lived in France for forty years, had worked for it during its two greatest wars, and had received public acclaim during the period between them; she had met and welcomed our Army during the liberation; and she left the scene only as international statesmen began talking over the second peace. All the French newspapers, in their obituaries, mentioned the friendship she and her faithful companion, Miss Alice B. Toklas, had for Picasso and Matisse. As a matter of fact, it was the ladies' unchanging good relations with modern paintings rather than with modern painters that best demonstrated the solidity of their jointly operating critical faculties. As they frequently chorused, painters were to be admired for their paintings, not for their characters; first-class painters often had difficult characters, and only third-class painters had really good characters. Most American collectors eventually bought modern French art as they might have bought cut flowers from a florist's shop. Miss Stein pulled hers fresh from the stem, in the ateliers where they grew, four decades ago. Today, her collection is as remarkable for its ripeness as for its freshness. Miss Toklas says that she has no idea what Miss Stein wanted with her pictures; she says Miss Stein never made any plans for her art, she just enjoyed it.

A few weeks ago, Miss Toklas was prophetically moved to send off to Yale University a mass of correspondence which Miss Stein had long promised. It consisted of whatever she had received in the mails from 1906 through the early months of 1946—all the letters (and she was a lively correspondent, in her feathery, illegible script), and everything else except her bills. Miss Stein was all for including the bills, too, which she said were remarkably interesting, inasmuch as she had paid as low as fifty dollars for some of her great paintings in the old days. Because she had paid little, she never wanted to know what her pictures had grown to be worth, and, for the same reason, she felt that she had no right to sell except to buy a necessity. Then she asked for the picture whatever she and Miss Toklas had figured the necessity would cost. She sold a Manet in order to live during the first war. Cézanne's portrait of Mme. Cézanne sitting in a chair, Picasso's girl with a fan, his Blue Period girls at a bar were all sold for specific needs, such as installing electric heating, printing an edition of her books, and moving from her rue de Fleurus residence to her last domicile, in the rue Christine, on the second floor of a private hotel where Queen Christina of Sweden once lived.

An editor recently asked Miss Stein to write something on the atomic bomb. She said that she was interested in the bomb but that there was little you could say about it, because it was so complete. During her last illness, she had the satisfaction of receiving the first two copies of her latest published book, *Brewsie and Willie*, and Miss Toklas says that she read both of them with pleasure. She also received the good news that her play *Yes Is for a Very Young Man* would be produced in the fall in America. Miss Toklas, in referring to her friend, said, "Gertrude was not deep, but she could insert herself in a fissure. So she was very near to things." Miss Stein had her greatest literary influence on young Ernest Hemingway, when he was writing *In Our Time*. It is now her epitaph. She was in our time.

The New Yorker, August 10, 1946.

"A Rose for Remembrance."

Harrison Smith

Gertrude Stein's recent death at the American Hospital at Neuilly has removed a monumental and enigmatic figure from the American literary scene. That strong, almost masculine face, with its close-cropped, wiry gray hair was magnificently sculptural and timeless; she looked, someone said, "like the bust of a Roman Emperor and at the same time like a Buddhist monk." There was an earthy, peasant quality about her and at the same time a spiritual force that was somewhat bewildering to those who expected to find in her the essence of mockery. Even before the war sent home nearly all of our expatriate writers and brought to an end the summer visits of others to her celebrated flat in the rue de Fleurus, she had left her influence on our literature. For years her books had been greeted with jeers or with abstruse critical praise that left the reader almost as bewildered as did her own repetitive sentences.

Gertrude Stein had lived in France for forty-three years, with the exception of her memorable visit to this country twelve years ago when her opera *Four Saints in Three Acts* was presented with Virgil Thomson's music and when, for some reason, that charming line of poetic nonsense "Pigeons in the grass, alas, alas" captured a public that still recalls it, as it still does "Rose is a rose is a rose is a rose." Perhaps people will recall her for her poetry and not her prose; for in the first she has repeated nouns of which she liked the sound and loved the object, and in the latter she has tried to dispense with the noun as much as possible and place the emphasis on the verb. The business of art, she believed, was to live in the complete and absolute present, and she compared her work to the motion pictures in which one image flows into the next without a break in the continuity, whereas ordinary writing progressed, she said, by a series of sentences, filled with unnecessary words and separated in brackets by stupid punctuation. Why put a question mark after a question, she asked, and why interfere with motion by using semicolons and commas? "A comma by helping you along holding your coat and putting on your shoes keeps you from living your life and actively as you should live it."

These simplifications of her reasons for writing sometimes as if she were a child of eight irritatingly bewitched with the sound of words may have been invented as an afterthought, but they often made more sense than did the critics who further bewildered her readers by stating that "the capacity to appreciate her performances is indivisible from that general feeling of spirit making the American experiment a success," or that Gertrude Stein represents "that final division between experience and life that was revealed earlier by Melville, Poe, Hawthorne, and Henry James." The ordinary man, after reading of these portentous proclamations, used to scratch his head in bewilderment and read again this line, perhaps, "What is a fact. A fact is alone and display their zeal," or these verses:

> Needs be needs be needs be near
> Needs be needs be needs to
> This is where they have their
> land astray.
> Two say.

But at least Gertrude Stein forced writers to think about words, the value and weight of them, and the sound of them. Her theories as she revealed them had certainly a profound effect on Sherwood Anderson, Ernest Hemingway, and the scores of young writers who visited her in Paris in the thirties to whom she showed the utmost kindness and patience, unless she suddenly became piqued by one of them and exiled him temporarily to the outer darkness beyond her circle. She helped to obliterate millions of unnecessary words. The clipped sentence, the strong, short phrase came into fashion, so that the best of our novelists did not write, "Her eyes drooped, her cheeks were mantled with a blush as she said, 'I love you,' with a glance of ineffable tenderness"; they now wrote, "She said, 'I love you.'" Miss Stein is also responsible in some measure for the refusal of so many of the younger generation to read Walter Scott, Dickens, or Thackeray, or the translations of Hugo and Balzac or many another great writer who had not had the good fortune to live long enough to read *Tender Buttons, Portraits and Prayers,* or *The Making of Americans.*

But in her lectures, which she enjoyed delivering in a strong voice, Gertrude Stein was not in the least confusing, as you will see if you turn to *Composition as Explanation*, which contains her lectures in Cambridge and Oxford given twenty years ago, or *Narration*, four lectures delivered during her visit to America in 1934. Her early fiction, *Three Lives* for example, stories of two servant girls and a miserable Negress, is reasonably coherent. Her two autobiographies, *The Autobiography of Alice B. Toklas* and the other attributed to everybody, for its title is *Everybody's Autobiography*, are comprehensible enough to anybody's mentality. Her latest book, published just before she died, contains the essence of the conversations she had with American soldiers in her apartment during the last year; they reveal perfectly the common American idiom, the bewilderment and restlessness of our youth today.

It is not unlikely that if she had lived and had continued to write for another few years she would have disciplined her theories to meet necessities of a continued terse and lucid prose form, without wandering off into the maze of repeated words and the whimsy of sentences without punctuation. Gertrude Stein had still a great many ideas to give to America, and not only to our writers, for she has endured stoically and with hardly controlled passion the years when the German military trampled over the fields and the fair cities of France. Though she had been ill for some time, it was fitting that she should have lived long enough to see France free and Paris unspoiled, and more beautiful, they say, than she had ever been before.

The Saturday Review, August 10, 1946.

"The Literary Spotlight."

Fanny Butcher

On the front page of the paper the picture of Gertrude Stein greeted us as we had our breakfast in Colorado Springs—the latest picture of her, tired at 72 after her doubly perilous years in France during the war .... For not only was Gertrude Stein a well-known anti-Nazi, but it would have been in the Nazi tradition to have made her pay bitterly for being a Jewess .... Such a vivid personality Gertrude Stein has always been that it never occurred to me, as I saw her picture there, that the news it accompanied was that she would never again write me one of her affectionate letters in the strangely spidery hand that seemed so different from herself ... that never again would I listen to her talk with such pleasure as I remember feeling rarely at any one's conversation ... that never again would I watch her immediate bewitchment of a room full of people or of one ardently skeptical person.

Not because Gertrude Stein has been one of the most spectacular literary figures of our day, but because she has been one of the least understood, I would like to tell you what one person who has known her professionally and personally for many years feels about her .... I met Gertrude Stein as a writer first when I was a young girl .... Ada May Krecker, one of the first women editorial writers in the country, was then writing editorials for the *Chicago Tribune* .... When I met Miss Krecker at a friend's house, she rightly read the eagerness about writing in my youthful eyes and gave me a copy of a book, which, she said, had in it some brilliant experimental writing .... The book was *Three Lives*, the first book of the then wholly unknown Gertrude Stein .... Gertrude Stein was not unknown to the group around Henry James, however, for she had been that great man's favorite and most promising pupil .... *Three Lives* enchanted me, especially the story about Melanctha, and although it was a half generation before it took its logical place in critical estimates of the work of Gertrude Stein, "Melanctha" was a signpost which pointed toward Gertrude Stein's creative future .... Read it now, and it is not hard to understand that when *Three Lives* was published, Gertrude Stein as a writer was at a crossroads in her literary career.

There was one factor in her choice of turning which is not present in every young writer's life .... She had an independent income ... not one large enough to give her burdensome responsibility, but one which made it possible for her to write as she chose without having to worry about a living .... When *Three Lives* was published, although it did not become a best seller, it was a literary sensation, and Gertrude Stein might have done what many other writers have done, duplicated in her work its popular success .... She had proved that she could write beautiful and brilliant prose, that she could write what the public wanted to read, and she might have chosen the path of conventional, ever increasing popularity .... She chose experimentation.

For years Gertrude Stein wrote what was to most readers unintelligible prose .... She experimented in a form of writing of which it is far too much a simplification to quote her famous motto, "A rose is a rose is a rose," but which is characterized by rote ... by the tidal rote of the surf, advancing, receding, always in rhythm, always proceeding toward the shore of understanding, but not reaching it directly .... There is nothing of the gunshot accuracy about Gertrude Stein's experimental writing .... However, and on this point I am sure that every reader of *The Autobiography of Alice B. Toklas, Everybody's Autobiography, Wars I Have Seen,* and *Brewsie and Willie* will agree with me that, when Gertrude Stein really wishes to point the weapon of her writing toward any bull's-eye of thought, she is the world's most skilled literary Annie Oakley .... She has, more than once, said in one sentence of pellucid prose what it has taken many another writer a chapter to say.

That quality of thinking clearly and translating her thought into communication with other minds is the one for which literary history may give Gertrude Stein the greatest credit .... For no one of her generation influenced more young writers, both directly and indirectly than did Gertrude Stein .... Her immediate influence on, for instance, Ernest Hemingway has never been questioned, and Ernest Hemingway himself has acknowledged his debt ... and his influence on his own generation of writers has carried into the younger generation .... It was at the evenings in her apartment in the rue de Fleurus in Paris between the two wars that the young writers gathered to talk about their art and to listen to the proponents of other arts .... For Gertrude Stein was one of the first non-painting members of the group of artists in Paris who created the modern movement and carried it to fruition .... It was her appreciation in words of the work of such painters as Picasso and Matisse which brought their ideas and those of their followers and apostles to the attention of Americans.

My first meeting with Gertrude Stein as a person was in her home in Bilignin in the Haute Savoie, where for much of the war she and Alice B. Toklas lived right under the nose of the German occupying officers who did not even know that one of them was the Gertrude Stein whom they would have been happy to incarcerate .... We drove over the mountains from Aix les Bains for luncheon, sat on a terrace from which one had one of the most magnificent views I have ever seen, had a marvelously prepared native Savoie meal, sat again on the terrace ... and all the time Gertrude talked and I listened, bewitched by what she was saying.

But I left after a day of mental enchantment, still not certain what she was trying to do ... and I have to admit that to this day only flashes of her intent come to me as I read some of the more complicated prose .... I know that to me its form is the form of the surf ... that its power is the power of insistence, or repetition ... and I feel that if I could read it as a child reads, without preconceived ideas of what it ought to be, I could understand everything .... For the young never seem to misunderstand Gertrude Stein .... Her lectures in colleges all over the United States were fabulously successful, and I have had many a college student say that of course you can't expect the older generation to know what Gertrude Stein means .... What she means to every one who came in personal contact with her is inestimable.

Chicago Tribune, August 11, 1946.

"In Memoriam: Gertrude Stein, 1898."

L. W. S., M. L. E., L. S. E.

In the death of Gertrude Stein in Neuilly, France, on July 27, 1946, Radcliffe has lost one of its noted graduates, a legend in the world of literature and art, famous throughout the world. Because there are few facts of her two score years in France which have escaped public print and because her prodigious literary output is so well known to readers in her native America as elsewhere, the *Quarterly*, in the tribute which follows, does not attempt to present a well-rounded life history of Radcliffe's distinguished Alumna. Rather, we seek to convey, through intimate anecdotes, the impression that Gertrude Stein made on her Radcliffe friends of the 1890s, three of whom have graciously allowed us to draw this composite picture from material they submitted at the request of the Secretary of 1898, Florence Locke Lawrence.— *The Editor.*

Gertrude Stein seems to have been known by very few undergraduates of her time. She lived in a private student house with seven or eight others and was part of a small circle of brilliant men and women students who met in a Cambridge home. What set her apart from all the others was her personal quality. Knowing her intimately enhanced every interest one had. To attend a symphony concert or an opera with her was to gain new enjoyment from it. To live in that small student house with her was to feel that rare, warm, human quality which not only brought famous people to see her in Paris but made the G. I.s flock to her home when she was past seventy.

She came to Radcliffe in 1893, at the age of nineteen, to be near her brother Leo, who was studying at Harvard, and to share in the sort of education he was getting. Their parents were dead, and Gertrude and Leo, the two youngest of five children, had always been very good companions. Gertrude was admitted to Radcliffe as a special student on the strength of a letter that she wrote to the Academic Board, setting forth her reasons for wanting to study there. Her formal education had been desultory, given largely by tutors and interrupted by family sojourns in Europe. She had read enormously, and she brought with her a library of English classics, poetry, and history which filled from floor to ceiling the wall of a large room. (When she was eleven or twelve, her family thought they were headed for a financial crash, and so Gertrude and Leo had taken all the money they had and bought books as the best insurance against a dreary future. The family weathered the crisis, and they had the books, anyway, and lived in them).

As a special student, Gertrude Stein seems to have been admitted almost at once to courses designed for graduate students, and much of her work was done in small groups in laboratories at Harvard. History, philosophy, and psychology were her major interests, especially experimental psychology as it was beginning under Professor Münsterberg. She did work in association, which some think may perhaps have been the starting point for her peculiar literary style. Later she was probably also influenced by the philosophy of Henry Bergson.

William James was a great friend of hers, and it was by his advice that she decided to take the course in medicine at Johns Hopkins, as a preparation for further study of psychology. This raised the question of a B. A. degree from Radcliffe as a prerequisite and the passing of those overlooked entrance examinations. It took fifteen exams to enter Radcliffe in those days, and by 1897, when Gertrude Stein had finished her college work for a degree *magna cum laude*, she still had an entrance test in advanced Latin to take.

In her approach to the problem of learning Latin may be found one of the keys to her life. She was always doing what was most significant for her at the time. To know Latin was not significant for her, but she had to pass Latin to do what was significant—study at Johns Hopkins. She put off the real study of Latin until the last moment, carrying a Latin grammar under her arm and apparently hoping she might absorb it through her pores. One of her anxious friends taught her that *isieme esiumibus* were the endings of the third declension, but it is doubtful that she knew where the dividing lines came. She wrote a *Caesar* examination that she said was very consistent, either all right or all wrong. Then in fun she used the Bible as oracle to see if she had passed, and found her finger on a passage in *Lamentations*. The prophecy was true. *E* would have meant failure, but her mark was *F*. She spent her summer gaily in Europe and the next year learned and passed Latin.

She was awarded her degree from Radcliffe with the Class of 1898, after she had already completed one year of brilliant work at Johns Hopkins. Graduation from Johns Hopkins was not significant for her, but it was significant to protest a course in obstetrics which she thought should not be required. So she refused to take the course and got no degree.

She was absolutely indifferent to conventions. On one occasion, for instance, when she could think of no proper ending for a theme and was impatient to close, she simply wrote, "Well, good-bye, gentlemen."

She enjoyed being different, and once remarked that what she wished for was more *glorie*—a wish that seems to have been fulfilled in her later years. Just as she refused to be bound by conventionalities, she refused also to be bound by loyalties to her past associations.

She was wholly unconcerned as to what people might think of her unconventionality and refused to be governed by what they thought she should do. Already in her college days she refused to be bound by the dictates of style, though she then dressed on the whole conventionally. She clung to one particular "sailor hat" until it became so disreputable that a friend placed it deep in an ash barrel.

An active member of the Radcliffe philosophy club, she loved discussion and not infrequently was as willing to talk on one side of a subject as the other. She was sometimes rather overpowering in argument and so asserted her opinions as to leave her opponent feeling somewhat futile and flattened out, though usually of the same opinion still. Her well-developed sense of humor, her originality, her clear, active mind, quick in association, made her a brilliant conversationalist.

When her Radcliffe friends think of Gertrude Stein, it is of a good companion with a genuine warmth of interest in those about her. She knew how to enjoy life and could lead others to enjoy it with her. She has always been like a magnet to young people who loved intellectual freedom, and it is easy to understand why young writers, artists, and American G. I.s were attracted to her.

Radcliffe Quarterly, August 1946.

"Gertrude Stein: An Epilogue"

Carl Van Vechten

She who was known and loved universally as Gertrude Stein, born at Allegheny, Pennsylvania, in 1874, now rests in the cemetery of Pére Lachaise at Paris, along with Balzac, Oscar Wilde, Daumier, Beaumarchais, Delacroix, Brillat-Savarin, and countless other writers, painters, and musicians. "She has ascended to Paradise," a friend of hers and mine recently observed, "and doubtless is now engaged in puzzling God!"

In spite of advice to the contrary, it is much too early to appraise her work and its value. This is a matter which time alone can take care of. To appraise her personality is a much simpler affair. She was one of the great personages not only of her own epoch but of the seventy odd years which preceded her birth and it is unlikely that any more startling figure will shake the literary world in the 20th century. It is probable, indeed, that the vivid legend which her personality created will trail clouds of glory behind her for a long time to come. The statues, paintings and photographs of her that exist will recreate her ruggedly noble appearance for posterity. Books will be contrived in an attempt to capture her charm, her wit, her intelligence, her warm communication with the spirit of those about her. Elliott Paul has already set it down as his opinion that her talk was as brilliant as the famed talk of Oscar Wilde. Certainly the desire to listen to her was almost a universal trait so far as her friends and acquaintances were concerned, and many of these were very celebrated people indeed. Her beautiful voice in itself was hypnotic enough to give her words a special characteristic; no other voice in Paris, save that of the divine Sarah Bernhardt, has ever evoked more enthusiastic comment, but if Sarah's voice was golden, Gertrude's was somewhere between the deeper tones of a bell and a cello.

She was, it must be generally known by now, convinced that words had lost their meaning. I thought of this when I recently listened to some young people discussing the current language. "Radical" originally meant "basic," it would appear and it seemed highly probable to these boys and girls that "reactionary" in the first instance may have been employed to indicate a subject who reacted to outward stimuli. The somewhat out-of-date Thesaurus on my shelves gives communist as a synonym for mischief-maker, evildoer, oppressor, tyrant, even brute, savage, monster, and scourge of the human race! It is little wonder, considering these and cognate matters, that somebody should decide that the time had come to rename objects on a large scale. That Gertrude Stein's work, or even her design for work, was largely unintelligible to the outer world did not deter her from continuing. Very quickly she discovered (or said that she had discovered) that it was (and is) impossible to arrange words in any order whatever in which they do not make sense, absolutely impossible, and this was an important discovery inasmuch as her idea was to make sense, to be denotative constructively, not, as so many critics believe (and have written that they believe) to express the psychology of the unconscious, not to beguile her own ears and those of her readers with meaningless, even if beautiful, sounds, not, especially NOT, to use words for their associations, their connotations. This is about as much (although she has said and written cryptically a great deal more) as she has ever actually let be known about her work, for the very good reason that long ago she assured herself that her writing needs no explanation. "Read what I have written," she always said to those who demanded a key to the meaning of her work. Reading it is not such an unpleasant chore as some cynical persons would have us believe. It can be, if sympathetically approached, quite the reverse, a most agreeable exercise.

Her indirect influence on contemporary writing has been extensive as has been pointed out on innumerable occasions. She has told us how she has weighed words and studied their values until she was in complete possession of their essence and she has given some other writers the incentive to follow this procedure.

She never confused the language of conversation with the language she invented and experimented with, and there is a great body of her work based on this universal language of conversation which is open to the casual reader to understand: *Three Lives,* a classic in her own lifetime, *Wars I Have Seen, Brewsie and Willie*, much of *The Making of Americans*, and the two autobiographies, *Alice's* and *Everybody's*, all of which are most rewarding in one way or another.

Somebody has said that when Gertrude Stein wrote about herself, she easily excelled the attempts of other to write about her. It is further true that she seldom wrote about anything else but herself. One of the reasons that her "difficult" work is hard to understand is that it is almost entirely subjective.

It has been said of her that she was an actress who knew her part and played it for all it was worth. This is completely inaccurate. She has always wanted to be understood and appreciated and in the beginning suffered intensely when she was laughed at. She consoled herself by saying: "Nothing is meaningless if one likes to do it," as good a philosophy as any.

In the work of most writers distinct periods can be separated one from the other, but in the work of Gertrude Stein her conversation pieces mixed with her landscape, her gossip with her lectures. All of it was part of her, some of it, no doubt, less well done than the rest, but all of it a kind of testimony to her mind, her temperament, yes, her genius. She may one day stand in marble on a pedestal and watch Paris and the world go by, but in a sense she stood on a pedestal all her life. *Three Lives* would give her a position as a great writer; there is sufficient evidence that she was a great woman as well.

Syndicated Column, November 7, 1946.

"Gertrude Stein."

Henry Rago

The death of Gertrude Stein, on July 27, 1946, was not only a sadness but a shock to those who had seen her in her last year. That strongly driven life had been going at its old speed. She had come back to Paris early in 1945 and resumed a busy salon in the rue Christine. Her dozens of interests were immediately set in motion: the comings and goings of visitors almost every day, the endlessly growing web of correspondence which her swift handwriting spun and controlled from a powerful center, and the administration of her own corporate entity as both artist and *akademia*.

She was talking and writing the aphorisms which have gained popular currency in her little book, *Brewsie and Willie*. She had a great vogue with the soldiers and she was reveling in it. She was planning an opera, with Virgil Thomson, on the life of Susan B. Anthony. There was a remarkable new artist whom she had found, a Spaniard named Riva-Rovira; she had seen him sketching along the Quai and had taken him in hand. When I left Paris, Riva-Rovira had had two successful shows and had painted a sternly aristocratic portrait of his patroness. Finally—and this seemed to mean more to her than most things of that year—she had found a new poet in a twenty-year-old boy from Milwaukee named George W. John. The excitement of that discovery is in a note she gave him to be used as what she called a "little blurb" for a possible book and meanwhile, I think, as a kind of identity-paper. I have a copy of it and her wish that I use it for advertisement of the event:

"A great many soldiers came and one day unexpectedly a poet. He had come and left many little pieces of paper and on each piece of paper was a poem. He like all the soldiers had been in many places, Italy France Belgium Holland Germany England and then later India, as he was a field service man, and everywhere there were landscapes and all the landscapes were poems. He was the only one whom that happened and he was a poet. I was excited and thought with the poems on them and the name George John. At the end of a long week he came again, tall gentle thin and young, and I told him he was a poet but he knew that and I knew it, and now I am telling it here where the poems are printed.

George John."

I was in the studio the night that the little pieces of paper she speaks of were organized into the manuscript of a book. George John sat a little uneasily on a small chair while Gertrude Stein handled his little poems with her bold hands and directed the seating arrangements. She told John, "You sit there," and she told me, "You sit here." When Alice Toklas came in and asked us what we were doing, Gertrude Stein said, "We're going to make a book." Miss Toklas thought that we would need a table for that, so she packed a table for us, found an ashtray for me, and left to prepare some mulled wine. When we were all settled we went through the manuscript. Gertrude Stein knew quickly the ones she liked and the ones she didn't like. Sometimes she would say of a bad one, "This is bad, George. Good heavens, it's bad. No, you'd never want that." And she would laugh so heartily that George would laugh too.

Her talk, in her 72nd year, was never without that exuberance. One marveled upon the process that kept her loves and hatreds so fresh. She discoursed vigorously on the personalities in her private heaven and hell and, I imagined, was endlessly engaged weighing application from her purgatory. Apparently not many such applications were granted: she enjoyed her own invective too heartily. (She said of one banished novelist, "You know, even when he was poor the holes in his clothes were overdone.") It was striking that, whatever her vehemence, there was never any chance for bitterness to survive the clean salt air of her conversation.

In any case, her most energetic conversation still turned on the artistic problems with which she had lived so busily and so intimately and for so long; and she talked of them with her original apostolic fervor. She talked about her opponents as though she had just come from reading for the first time an unfavorable review of *The Making of Americans*. She pounced upon the word "repetition" in Edmund Wilson's review of *Wars I Have Seen* and talked zealously, as though for the first time, about the difference between repetition and "variation." She talked in the same way about the "present immediacy" in narrative, about the problem of tenses, about the need in the twentieth century to "work the whole paragraph out of its parts" instead of laying out sentences which "begin at one end of the paragraph and hope to come out at the other." All these echoes from her writings never sounded like quotations; the phrases always sounded completely fresh and they fitted into the immediate and vital argument of the moment without even the interruption of quotation marks; they were all spontaneous —the more spontaneous, I thought, for being so naturally the habit of her thought and speech.

Her talk seemed polarized in the question of time. She was interested, as she always was in her writings, in the nature of the twentieth century: its beginnings in the American civil war, its need to concentrate on "existence" rather than events, because events were too common an occurrence in our time ("It's more important to *have* four saints on the stage than to make them do anything"). She said one day that because the French have a great sense of realism, they know that the elegant is the *à la mode;* and because the English have a sentimental view of life, the elegant for them is the *démodé*. Time was the reality which she could not forgive the English for sentimentalizing.

In all this it seemed that her interest in abstraction had sometimes been used unfairly against her: she was not such an abstractionist that she was completely isolated from the consciousness which burdened other artists of her day. Time was her subject—just as it is the subject of perhaps the greatest philosopher of our century, the inseparable factor in the universe charted by our physics, and the preoccupation of what will probably endure of our literature. When she said in her *Lectures in America* that poetry has to do with the noun and prose with the verb, she was thinking of the *stasis* and *kinesis* which occupied Joyce, and of the distinction in Aristotle between what has happened and what will always happen. It was the timeless which she was seeking in her quarrel with tenses; it was basically not continuous motion she wanted in her narrative, it was the avoidance of discontinuities and perhaps it was even the neutralization of motion. Whether she laid nouns side by side in verses which were almost tactile, or made verbs almost liquid in their fluency in her prose, she wanted a pattern which would keep the beginning from being isolated from the end. She was aware somehow that the nemesis in the modern consciousness is time, the flood of particulars overwhelming the permanently significant. The major artists in our fiction have dramatized this need to control time in terms of their material, chiefly by the evocation of myth. Gertrude Stein chose a minor art, the dramatization of this tension in her *form*. Her material is created ironically; her interest is in the grammar and what can be done with it to make it move without seeming to move, or change without seeming to change—almost by sleight-of-hand.

"Everybody knows that I chose," she wrote in these pages in February, 1940, in some verses from *Two Hundred Stanzas in Meditation*. And she continued to choose: she often said that a writer should never do what he knows he can do. She applied this maxim by losing interest in anything once she saw that she could do it. If this explains many of her failures, it would be well for literature to have more of its failures issue from such wholesome intentions. But having chosen, she gave us a rich gift of fantasy and playfulness, a refreshment of our language, and a new appreciation of formal prose. Even with the reduction of its many extravagances and personal indulgences, more than enough of her work will stand to compel lasting attention to the example and achievement in which she put her confidence:

"I will be will welcome when I come.

Because I am coming."

Poetry, November 1946.

"Gertrude Stein Memorial."

Carl Van Vechten

Authors are frequently forgotten a few days after they die. They may be revived with honors much later, but immediately after death nobody talks about them. You have only to recalls the names of Henry James, George Moore, and Anatole France to understand fully what I mean. The experience of Gertrude Stein has been completely dissimilar. She is, indeed, fast becoming a legend. Born in 1874, she died in a hospital in Paris at the end of July 1946, not quite a year ago, and was presently buried in Père Lachaise Cemetery along with Balzac, Oscar Wilde, Beaumarchais, Daumier, and Delacroix.

About a month after she died, *Selected Writings of Gertrude Stein* appeared. A little later, a publisher in Dublin issued *Gertrude Stein's First Reader*. A pamphlet by Deseuilles, *Une Fervente de la Repetition*, appeared in Paris. In this month of May, only ten months after her death, the three principal stage works of Gertrude Stein have been or will be presented in New York. *The Mother of Us All*, Miss Stein's tribute to Susan B. Anthony, with a musical score by Virgil Thomson, was given nine performances here a week or two ago. *Yes is for a Very Young Man* will be read to you this evening, for the most part by the cast which appeared in the original production of the play in Pasadena. And next Sunday afternoon at three o'clock the Stein-Thomson opera *Four Saints in Three Acts* will be sung by the original Negro cast over the radio.

Last Monday I visited the Yale University Library at New Haven to inspect the exhibition in Miss Stein's honor on view there now. As I looked over the specimens of her own manuscripts, the letters she had received from Matisse, Braque, Picasso, Hemingway, Thornton Wilder, Scott Fitzgerald, Sherwood Anderson and many others, as I examined the photographs made of her from childhood on, it seemed to me that Gertrude Stein is more alive than she has ever been before. The librarian at Yale informs me that this show has drawn a larger attendance than any other similar exhibition ever held in that library. In the fall the Yale University Press will publish a book of hers, *Four in America*, with a preface by Thornton Wilder. And four distinct writers are at present engaged on her biography, each on his own.

Aside from her writing, Gertrude Stein was a warm and wise personality. She possessed, I should think, the most beautiful voice I have ever listened to and when she used it her purpose was to say something. Elliott Paul has described her conversation as being as brilliant as the famed conversation of Oscar Wilde. Her curiosity, her good humor, her endless interest in what was going on in the world, were qualities which brought many young men to her side and made many of them her friends for life. At this moment she probably has more disciples among the veteran G. I.s. Or the United States Army than any other single person. When she visited America in the fall of 1934, Virgil Thomson's opera, *Four Saints*, having enjoyed a New York season, was playing in Chicago. We, Gertrude, Alice and I, planned to go there to hear it performed. I suggested flying. Gertrude had never flown but she was easily persuaded to try it. We did fly. Almost as soon as we were in the air we skimmed our way above the clouds, the bright sun beating down on them as it would have done on the ice fields the clouds resembled. "The air is solid," she exclaimed and from then on she was a devotee of the plane.

In examining her work one is irresistibly reminded of the painters who were her friends, particularly Picasso. As Picasso painted Cubistic pictures or distorted his images in order to invent new realms for the artist to enter, so she experimented with words, finding it indeed impossible to arrange words so that they would be meaningless, until she was completely their mistress and she could command them. She began with a conscious use of repetition which she has explained was a device employed for the sake of emphasis. A toad, she has written, never hops the same hop twice, not the same distance or the same height: every hop is a little different from every other one. Beginning then with repetition, she went on to make other experiments, until she had created her own style and was in complete control of the English language. Words obeyed her; she was no longer their slave. Her influence on other writers, too, has been marked. In the hundreds of letters written to her during her lifetime, which have been presented to the Yale Library, there is much enthusiastic and grateful evidence to this effect.

Remarks delivered at the Gertrude Stein Memorial meeting of the YMHA Poetry Center, New York, May 22, 1947.

"Proper and Improper Subject Matter: Time and Identity Is What You Tell About."

B. L. Reid

The truth is that in examining those procedures that for her were not pure creativity, Gertrude Stein denounces most of what we are accustomed to consider the "proper" matter and manner of art. Kenneth Burke, in writing of what he sees as Miss Stein's preoccupation with form at the expense of subject matter, says that she is attempting to achieve an "art by subtraction" (410). The phrase is pithy and much more broadly applicable than Mr. Burke makes it in his essay. In a very real sense, subtraction in the field of the arts is her most characteristic activity. She dismisses and strips away the traditional until all that is left, finally, is her own very personal, very narrow art—the thin result of a complex and frequently impressive aesthetics.

In order to clarify these ramified corollary portions of Miss Stein's aesthetics, I will subsume them under the headings of "matter" and "manner," and attempt to answer the questions of what is proper and improper subject matter, what is proper and improper technique for the genuine creative artist. At once we have to "begin again" with Miss Stein, recalling one of the capital statements of her creed:

"Gertrude Stein ... has always been possessed by the intellectual passion for exactitude in the description of inner and outer reality. She has produced a simplification by this concentration, and as a result the destruction of associational emotion in poetry and prose. She knows that beauty, music, decoration, the result of emotion should never be the cause, even events should not be the cause of emotion nor should they be the material of poetry and prose. Nor should emotion itself be the cause of poetry and prose. They should consist of an exact reproduction of either an inner or an outer reality" (*Autobiography* 174).

When we add to these sweeping dismissals the whole vast area of the "imagination," which Gertrude Stein has already allocated to "minor" or "precious" writers, and reflect abruptly that we have catalogued here virtually all that centuries of writers have taught us is their real province, the full iconoclasm of her thinking becomes quickly apparent.

We are told, too, that we would have been mistaken to assume, as we might well have been tempted, that Miss Stein's definition of the creative state is Plato's "ecstasy" of creation with its fringe of madness. Hers is a far soberer thing; its main components are *gravitas* and absence of passion. "Exact reproduction" is her end, and her means begins with the subtraction of that extraneousness in which other writers have found their content. What we have here is something very close to the so-called "reduction" process of the Phenomenologists, and one cannot help wondering whether Miss Stein had encountered Husserl or his followers. I am inclined to suspect that this process, too, goes back to her association with William James, but to James as psychologist rather than as philosopher. It was, after all, at the psychological-laboratory level that she knew James most intimately, and one may conclude, uncharitably but justly, that the important thing Gertrude Stein took away from that association was not the philosophical large-mindedness, the broad humaneness of James, but the much narrower and more bloodless ideal of scientific "objectivity." If this impression is as sound as it seems, it helps to explain a great deal of Gertrude Stein's direction. It is almost as if she had taken James' injunction to "keep your mind open" (*Autobiography* 67) as the whole of the man and assumed that the mind is never to be allowed to close upon a truth. She leaves James at this point and retreats into a barren cavern of her own making; it is surgically clean and hospitable to objectivity, but there is not much life there.

At any rate, the passage seems to give us a fairly complete summary answer to our questions. Along with imagination, Miss Stein lists beauty, music, decoration, events, and emotion as improper subject matter; proper subject matter is "inner and outer reality." Beauty, music, and decoration have no place in the artist's proper technique; proper technique consists of "description" or "reproduction"—the latter is closer to her final position—of proper subject matter, and it will proceed by "simplification" and "concentration" toward the "destruction of associational emotion." This much is clear. But the connotations of these terms for her and the route by which she arrived at this position need a good deal of tracing and amplification for sharp definition.

With this goal in mind, we should remind ourselves of the primacy of the time problem by recalling other dicta of Gertrude Stein:

"The business of Art ... is to live in ... and to completely express ... the complete actual present" ("Plays" 104-105).

" ... the human mind knows what it knows and knowing what it knows it has nothing to do with seeing what it remembers" (*Geographical History* 27).

"Master-pieces ... are knowing that there is no identity and producing while identity is not" ("What Are Masterpieces" 90-91).

These statements, it will be readily seen, are central to Miss Stein's notion of the true creative state: a condition of almost mystical union of subject-artist-time in one magical bundle of "knowing." One thinks of such terms as *Aufklärung,* or even of the principle of "epiphany" in the early Joyce; but the added element of time, in the form of the necessary ongoing presentness of the "knowing," makes it less a bundle than a rolling ball of knowing, and our earlier metaphor is finally more satisfying.

On the basis of these dicta, we can logically conjecture that "beauty, music, decoration, events, emotion" are unwelcome to Gertrude Stein because they conflict with the ideal creative state. Indeed, this is the case; in various ways, as she sees it, they do conflict, and they must be cast into hell-fire. Although her attitude is thus sweepingly iconoclastic, it is at least all of a piece, part of a single coherent body of thought. Most of our conventional subject materials are herded together and damned by Miss Stein for the cardinal sins of pastness—remembering and identity—thereby cutting off the mind laboring to create from the ideal presentness of knowledge and forcing upon it the consciousness of the historical process of its knowing and hence the fatal consciousness of self.

From one point of view, however, "events" are improper subject matter in a somewhat different sense, and we can isolate that aspect for separate treatment. Events, as noted earlier, are improper matter because they are anachronistic; they are not part of the true "composition" of our time: "To the Twentieth Century events are not important" ("How Writing Is Written" 11). This conviction led Miss Stein into some very curious attitudes, into some of those frequent specious, perverse opinions that so sadly mar the total picture of her aesthetics and make it so difficult to weigh. On this basis she was able, for example, to rationalize a great admiration for the detective story as "the only really modern novel form ... the hero is dead to begin with and so you have so to speak got rid of the event before the book begins" ("What Are Masterpieces" 87). She was even moved to attempt the genre herself, although the result, *Blood on the Dining Room Floor,* resembles the conventional detective story only in its title.

At any rate, the consequences of removing events from the possible subject matter of a writer are clear: he cannot deal with happenings, with a course of events put together along a story line in the way that makes up what we usually call plot. It is significant that only the three earliest of Miss Stein's "creative" books, *Three Lives, The Making of Americans,* and the "forgotten" first novel, posthumously published as *Things as They Are,* contain a recognizable story line, and in *The Making of Americans,* it is merely rudimentary. She justifies this exclusion on the grounds of the anachronism of narrative and blows it up into a trend in which she is among the great figures: "... in the three novels written in this generation that are the important things written in this generation, there is, in none of them a story. There is none in Proust in *The Making of Americans* or in *Ulysses*" ("Portraits and Repetition" 184).

This, however, is another of her half-truths. Many writers, enough to constitute a major trend, have felt that a narrative method is not consonant with the subtler, more ramified "knowledge" of ourselves gained from twentieth-century science and psychology, and have therefore modified or suppressed the classical narrative line. But all, even Joyce, have retained enough rudiments of narrative to keep us roughly posted in space and time; it simply is not true that there is "no" story in Proust or even the Joyce of *Finnegans Wake.* Gertrude Stein, on the other hand, has sought obliteration of the narrative line, and her work, on these grounds as well as others, is not strictly comparable to anything in the main stream of literature in our century.

Events, in addition to committing the private sin of anachronism, share in what is for Miss Stein a deadlier sin, that of forcing memory and identity upon the writer: "I wrote a story as a story, that is the way I began, and slowly I realized this confusion, a real confusion, that in writing a story one had to be remembering…. It is this element of remembering that makes novels so soothing. But and that was the thing I was gradually finding out … realizing the existence of living being actually existing did not have in it any element of remembering and so the time of existing was not the same as in the novels that were soothing." ("Portraits and Repetition" 181). Here, "realizing the existence of living being actually existing" represents another of Miss Stein's synonyms for the familiar concept of the ongoing present knowledge, the pragmatist reality.

"Nor should emotion itself be the cause of poetry or prose," says Gertrude Stein, and the flaw in emotion as in events, is that emotion contributes to identity and consciousness of self: "The pleasures that are soothing all have to do with identity and the pleasures that are exciting all have to do with identity and moreover there is all the pride and vanity which play about master-pieces … and these too all have to do with identity" ("What Are Masterpieces" 91). To make the picture absolute: "The human mind has nothing to do with sorrow and with disappointment and with tears" (*Geographical History* 31).

On the topic of sex as subject matter Miss Stein gives a very curious performance indeed. At one point she writes that "sex and jealousy is not the human mind" (*Geographical History* 67) and are therefore improper matter, but in another context she reverses herself categorically; John Hyde Preston quotes her as saying to him: "Sex and death are the springs of the most valid of human emotions … creative literature unconcerned with sex is inconceivable" (191). Whatever her true opinion, the absence of a sexual element is one of the inescapable impressions one takes from her writings. If it is there, it is so successfully sublimated that it is nowhere visible. At least one could say this until the publication in 1950 of *Things as They Are,* a book with a curious history. It was Gertrude Stein's first work of any length, but apparently she never wanted to publish it. She says in *The Autobiography of Alice B. Toklas* that she put the manuscript in a drawer after finishing it and "forgot" it until she came across it by chance in later life. But Gertrude Stein was not one to withhold anything publishable without very good reason, and one doubts the story of her forgetfulness in this case. Eventually, at any rate, the manuscript came into the possession of

Carl Van Vechten, and he authorized its publication four years after Miss Stein died.

Things as They Are is sexual with a vengeance. It presents the young Gertrude Stein, transparently disguised as Adele (to whom she applies the epithets she liked to apply to herself—"impetuous and slow-minded," "commonplace and middle-class," full of "inertia" [30, 10, 6]), coquetting about the fringes of an established lesbian relationship between two other "college bred American women of the wealthier class" (4), Helen and Sophie. Adele's performance in this affair, like that of Gertrude Stein the writer on sex, is strange and equivocal. There is nothing equivocal about the lesbian attachment between Helen and Sophie, however. As far as one can tell, Adele never quite takes the complete plunge. There are "kisses" and "passionate embraces," but for Adele they seem to be mainly exploratory, tentative and still basically maidenly dippings into an area of life that both fascinates and repels her. Adele as a lover is dilettante and perverse. As Helen says to her, "After all you haven't a nature much above passionettes. You are so afraid of losing your moral sense that you are not willing to take it through anything more dangerous than a mud puddle." (12).

Adele's virginal and intellectualized flirting becomes rather tedious to the reader, and to the other principals it must have been trying in the extreme. She seems to have had little real feeling for either of the other girls and to have used their more genuine passions ultimately only as touchstones for the trying out of her own fundamentally Puritan "morality" and her rather low-keyed "instincts." The book conveys little more at last than that Adele was incapable of complete commitment, although capable of tentative, intermittent, usually delayed response. At the end one is bored with Adele because of her indecisiveness and the blithe way in which she complicates and saddens an already tense relationship.

Although it is hard to believe that Gertrude Stein did not have some such experience as that of Adele—the book is tinged with that degree of intimacy which always suggests autobiographical sources—one cannot, of course, impugn her sexuality. Dark suspicions are certainly possible, but I am more inclined to attribute her literary attitude toward sex to that pathological ability to compartmentalize her mind that I have called near schizophrenic. For some reason, to be sure, overt sex was distasteful to Gertrude Stein, seemingly in both life and literature. Bravig Imbs, for example, could attribute his fall from grace in the Stein salon only to the fact that he had discussed the pregnancy of his wife with Miss Stein and Miss Toklas (216). She impressed W. G. Rogers, significantly, as "a kind of dynamic neuter ... no more carnal than a portly abbot" (43). Finding sex distasteful, she ignored it, and then, by a manipulation of a very manageable mind and conscience, convinced herself that she had written "creative literature concerned with sex." In this way she was able to comfort her vagaries of sensibility and to retain undamaged her conviction of her "contemporaneousness."

There are a good many subjects other than events and emotion which Miss Stein does not mention in her statement of creed, but which she denounces emphatically in other portions of her writing. In this process she gradually fills out an attitude one can only call sweepingly anti-moral and anti-intellectual. Thus the true creator, she insists, cannot concern himself with "causes," with moral distinctions of right and wrong, with learning, with meanings, or with relationships or generalizations or problems of cause and effect. Although her statement of these opinions is often fragmentary and unclear, one must not think that she held them any the less strongly.

Her unconcern with the things we have loosely called "causes" is shown, for example, in *The Geographical History of America:* "...the writing that is the human mind does not consist in messages" (80). Less esoterically, she tells a friend from college days that she "does not at all mind the cause of women or any other cause but it does not happen to be her business" (*Autobiography* 69). It is not difficult to see the tremendous reaches of passionate human concern here quarantined by an arbitrary act. Gertrude Stein's most characteristic gesture, subtraction, continues to work.

Her private brand of realism enjoins her also to remain aloof to meanings in the phenomena she observes. "Anything that is," she says, "is quite enough if it is." Again, "the minute it means anything it is not concerned with the human mind" (*Everybody's Autobiography* 6). The artist, with his "intellectual passion for exactitude in the description of reality," is barred by the absoluteness of that preoccupation from reflecting upon the implications of his experience; its implications are no part of his "business." That this tendency is extendible to specifically moral problems is also clear, for "the human mind ... is not concerned with being or not being true" (*Geographical History* 110). One begins to harbor the nasty suspicion that Gertrude Stein, whether she knows it or not, is really involved in a colossally elaborated, intricately rationalized process of evasion, which is likely to lead, finally, to an arrant escape literature.

The full anti-morality and anti-intellectualism of her position are made abundantly clear in the following passage, which serves also to remind us that we are still entirely under the discipline of the parent problems of time and creativity: "It is only in history government, propaganda that it is of any importance if anybody is right about anything. Science well they never tire right about anything not right enough so that science cannot go on enjoying itself as if it is interesting, which it is.... Master-pieces have always known that being right would not be anything because if they were right then it would be not as they wrote but as they thought and in a real master-piece there is no thought, if there were thought then there would be that they are right and in a master-piece you cannot be right, if you could it would be what you thought not what you do write. Write and right. Of course they have nothing to do with one another. Right right left right left he had a good job and he left, left right left" (*Geographical History* 198-99). To bring the matter back to the real problem of the description of "reality": "As I say it makes no difference because although I am always right is being right anything ... there is something so much more pleasing and that is what is what. And what is what is what is what" (*Geographical History* 201-202).

Gertrude Stein's eyes-fixed concentration on the present "reality" has a further, very serious consequence that is yet another facet of her anti-intellectualism. She rejects, because of its inevitable dependence on the past and hence its tendency to rely on memory and identity, man's very faculty for learning, for absorbing intellectually the data of his senses, ordering them into relationships, generalizing upon them, and advancing thereby to new intellectual frontiers—the faculty, in a word, that we have always fondly believed separated us from the lower animals. These capacities, being rooted in the past, have no validity for the true creator. "What is the use of being a little boy," Miss Stein asks pungently, "if you are going to grow up to be a man?" (*Geographical History* 22). She develops the aphorism further in "What Are Masterpieces": "The boy and the man have nothing to do with each other, except in respect to memory and identity, and if they have anything to do with each other in respect to memory and identity then they will never produce a master-piece" (90).

But we are not yet done with the matter, and we should not leave Miss Stein's anti-intellectualism without noting the full preciosity, the distastefully hermetic quality of her position. We find her saying "the master-piece has to do with the human mind and the entity that is with a thing in itself and not in relation. The moment it is in relation it is common knowledge and anybody can know it and it is not a master-piece ... master-pieces exist because they came to be as something that is an end in itself and in that respect it is opposed to the business of living which is relation and necessity" (*Geographical History* 88). Real art, then, is opposed to the business of living, and a realist, a pragmatic thinker, has made a curious progress. James and Whitehead have taken leave of her long ago.

To be absolutely fair to Miss Stein, we must remark that her enmity is clearly not directed toward learning per se or toward learning as a respectable activity of the human animal. She would insist merely, with her aptitude for schizophrenic separations, that it is a category of the mind insulated from the mind's creative compartment—and inferior to it.

A kind of primitivism certainly reveals itself in Miss Stein's desire to keep the artist a perpetual naif. If she were advocating primitivism alone, her position would be easier to respect, but she has refined upon primitivism and added to it something very old and very tired: art-for-art. The view that art and the artist himself are the final repositories of value is the inevitable outcome of Miss Stein's "something that is an end in itself ... opposed to the business of living."

In surveying Miss Stein's theory of improper subject matter, I have shown that her art by subtraction has subtracted imagination, events, emotion, "causes," "meanings," moral distinctions, and learning in its elements of generalization, relationships, and logical causation. What is left, one asks, as the artist's proper matter? Pitifully little, one may well fear. In exploring this poverty, we will find ourselves involved in at least seeming paradox on the one hand and in extreme abstraction on the other, for this is one of Gertrude Stein's ultimate lairs; trapped within it, she uses her ultimate weapons of defense.

We can point up both the paradox and the abstraction, and at the same time their essential oneness, with single brief quotation from Miss Stein: "And yet time and identity is what you tell about as you create only while you create they do not exist " (*Geographical History* 92). The paradox lies in the fact that the artist's improper subject matter is at the same time his inevitable subject matter. "Time and identity is what you tell about"; that is, all those things that make you know time and identity—emotion, events, learning, and so on—are your inevitable subject matter. The abstraction enters in the artist's effort to insure that "while you create they do not exist." To achieve this end the artist must disguise his subject, not only from the reader, but more importantly from himself. But patently obliviousness to subject matter is not possible as long as vestiges of its "time and identity" remain; to disguise it is therefore not enough. Gertrude Stein was driven finally to an abstract art that would destroy her subject: the self-defeating absurdity of total abstraction. This is a crucial truth of her work.

In addition, however, to improper subject matter sterilized by abstraction, Miss Stein has another important resource. Here we can be scarcely more clear or concrete than she allows us to be, and she is neither clear nor concrete in her explication. It is perhaps best to call this the doctrine of "essence"—a term she herself uses on occasion in discussing it—the principle that the "essence" of people and objects and even events provides proper material for the descriptive realist. One must suppose, though she never says this in so many words, that "essence" is really synonymous with that "inner reality" she refers to in her creed (*Geographical History* 65). "Essence," Miss Stein intimates, is that which makes a person or a thing what he or she is, the motivating, defining truth under the surface: "I have of course always been struggling with this thing, to say what you nor I nor nobody knows, but what is really what you and I and everybody knows … in my portraits I had tried to tell what each one is without telling stories and now in my early plays I tried to tell what happened without telling stories so that the essence of what happened would be like the essence of the portraits, what made what happened be what it was" ("Plays" 121). Again she says of her purpose in a particular play, "I wanted still more to tell what could be told if one did not tell anything" ("Plays" 119).

In order to relate these particular researches to her continuing concerns and to testify once more to the fact that she is still thinking coherently of the artist's duties to live "contemporaneously" and to strive for true creativity, we may cite one further passage: "I had to find out inside everyone what was in them that was intrinsically exciting and I had to find out not by what they said not by what they did not by how much or how little they resembled any other one but I had to find out by the intensity of movement that there was inside in any one of them…. I must find out what is moving inside them that makes them them, and I must find out how I by the thing moving excitedly inside in me can make a portrait of them" ("Portraits and Repetition" 183).

In the characteristic "composition" of our time, essence proves to be "intensity of movement inside," a phrase difficult to pursue to a more tangible clarification. In perfect charity, however, it is vaguely possible to assume that Gertrude Stein may be seeking the same thing that a great artist must always seek: the ultimately unknowable truth that is historically and psychologically the "essence" of men and the combining of men into events. But I do not really think so. What she is after is an abstractly satisfactory "present knowing" of her subject, and that kind of knowing is in the first place perfectly subjective and in the second place almost perfectly incommunicable in Miss Stein's particular terms. At any rate, the textual difficulty here, as in so much of Miss Stein's theorizing, lies in her stubborn habit of defining her aims in the private language and logistics of idiosyncratic "genius."

Donald Sutherland applies what is probably his most impressive chapter, the third, to a spirited justification of these attitudes toward subject matter that I have been denouncing. The problem, as Mr. Sutherland treats it, is partly one of subject matter per se—what is proper matter for a writer after all—and partly one of the method of "expressing" that matter—in what manner is the writer to reduce his experience of his subject to the shape and language that makes it literature? The latter sense of the problem is more relevant to the subject matter of my next three chapters, and I will deal with it there at greater length. Mr. Sutherland centers his explication around the so-called "crazy book" of 1914, *Tender Buttons.* The volume is a set of still-life squibs in cubist language, divided into three compartments of "Objects Food Rooms," and it may be taken as fairly representative of that vein of radical abstraction which finally becomes Gertrude Stein's most characteristic metier.

Her great effort in *Tender Buttons*, as Donald Sutherland sees, was to apply the pragmatist concept of reality, "the direct sense of things as unique and unclassified" (74) to the "Objects Food Rooms" that were her current units of experience. As we have seen, she wanted to immunize the "memory and identity" which she felt sentimentalized all conventional literary apprehension of a subject, and one way to accomplish this was to assault the name and the customary descriptive vocabulary of an object by rendering it into a private abstract language. Thus "much of the effort in *Tender Buttons* is to replace or shock the name of anything in order to restore the sense of immediate unprepared experience" (75).

Our immediate question is: What is the function of a given subject for Gertrude Stein and what becomes of it for the reader as she handles it? The answer is, in outline, very simple: a subject for Gertrude Stein is a stimulus, or a diving board, for a plunge into a new reality; the subject comes to the reader in the form of a difficult abstract art in which the original has been replaced by a "new reality" that is sometimes penetrable, sometimes not, sometimes interesting, sometimes perfectly dull. Gertrude Stein would argue, and Donald Sutherland agrees, that the artist has no real responsibility to his subject; he can do with it anything he chooses. I think that is true, but I think it follows as well that everything he may do with it will not be of equal value. Thus while we cannot demand that a painter or a writer be as faithful to the camera sense of his object as, say, the Dutch genre painters, we can demand that the subjective sense which is his substitute be as interesting as the camera sense; we may very well ask that the "new reality" be as interesting as the old, the "sentimental" one.

It is perfectly true, as Mr. Sutherland says, that the artist's "initial vision of the subject matter is not the standard or practical vision of their contemporaries, and they are further governed by the impulse to make something of it, so that what may still be recognizable in the result is only an incident or a circumstance." I also agree that "the appreciation and enjoyment of the result" (79) is that part of the artistic process which is the reader's province and responsibility. We must agree, that is, that any departure from an original subject or any degree of abstraction in vision or technique is justifiable, but only if we feel it as a functional process, one that adds to our knowledge or our understanding or our simple enjoyment of experience. I can only send the reader to Gertrude Stein's own abstract work for a decision. For me, generally, the subjective new reality I find there is no better than the camera sense and is infinitely inferior to the sense I receive from Joyce or Proust or Virginia Woolf, who work at a level of abstraction that seems to me beautifully functional because it is electric and illuminating.

There is the further intricate question of whether Gertrude Stein is justified in applying to people, as she does, the same technique of extreme subjective abstraction that she applies to "Objects Food Rooms." I doubt it. In the conduct of life, the still-life elements are never of more than passing concern—or should not be. One cares little, after all, how one is directed to apprehend a Cutlet, a Cloak, a Cold Climate, or a Carafe; only a great master such as Cézanne or Picasso can rouse us to more than a sybaritic pleasure in objects on a table. But human beings are something else. We care passionately how human beings are disposed about the universe and how they are seen and how described. The technique that in *Tender Buttons* is intermittently interesting and generally tiresome, when applied to humanity in *The Making of Americans,* in the portraits and plays, in a "novel" like *Ida,* becomes thoroughly misleading and repugnant; the matter grows serious. Great writing teaches us about ourselves by displaying the race as mythic or heroic or satanic or simply commonplace and "true," but Gertrude Stein's technique takes life from her people. If they move at all, they walk like somnambulists; we cannot know them or know ourselves from them.

The great sin of Gertrude Stein's theory and the sin of Donald Sutherland's apology, as I see it, is that they tend to reduce life to a momentary and subjective sensation, to an elaborated dilettantism. They deny literature as a function of life aimed at complementing life by interpreting it to our intelligence and our emotions, to our conviction that we can know it and perhaps make it richer. When Mr. Sutherland says, "We know that literature is a different reality from life, and that it is differently organized" (80), we can only agree with him. But we do not have to agree that "the world may be reasonably taken as a fair" (90), which is to say that its meaning is sensation and that value judgments are unnecessary, or agree to respect art that "exists in and for itself" (91), which is simply to reassert the respectability of art-for-art.

I, for one, cannot agree with Donald Sutherland's value structure when he says: "That an intonation does not last as long as the outline of the Sierra Nevada is not relevant to the immediate and final present. All the little things that in a longer perspective of time look trivial and transient and so negligible suddenly become as real as the president of the republic or original sin or the Rock of Gibraltar, and it is quite as delightful and urgent to the mind to define these little things, any group of them given together, as to articulate a political or a theological or an imperial system"(88). More "delightful," I am sure, but to any but a dilettante mind, surely less "urgent." Mr. Sutherland is being silly. For aren't we more serious than this about literature? Don't we want it to supply us with a longer and larger truth than the momentary, private, and idiosyncratic? Not that we can ask literature to be life or to be uniformly serious and solemn and self-consciously moralistic; that is not the point. But I think we must, if we are serious about living, ask literature to be that part of life which observes life conceptually in search of usable truth, that it somehow interpret experience, that it supply us with data for generalization about our nature and our motives, and finally that it do these services in terms we can understand and, if we choose, apply.

We must also remember that Gertrude Stein carries the art-for-art position to its extreme, farther even than Donald Sutherland bothers to follow her. There is at last no real defense for this kind of aesthetics. Real art, she would have it, is not only a "different reality" from living, as we would all agree, but "an end in itself and in that respect it is opposed to the business of living." This, I think, very few would care to accept; there really is no time for an art that is opposed to the business of living.

Works Cited

Burke, Kenneth. "Engineering With Words." *Dial* 74 (April 1923): 408-12.

Imbs, Bravig. *Confessions of Another Young Man*. New York: Henkle-Yewdale, 1936.

Preston, John Hyde. "A Conversation." *Atlantic Monthly* 156 (August1935): 187-94.

Rogers, William G. *When This You See, Remember Me: Gertrude Stein in Person*. New York: Rinehart, 1948.

Stein, Gertrude. *The Autobiography of Alice B. Toklas*. New York: Harcourt Brace, 1933.

_____. *Everybody's Autobiography*. New York: Random House, 1937.

_____. *The Geographical History of America, or the Relation of the Human Nature to the Human Mind*. New York: Random House, 1936.

_____. "How Writing Is Written." *How Writing Is Written*. Ed. Robert Bartlett Hass. San Francisco: Black Sparrow P, 1973.

_____. *Lectures in America*. New York: Random House, 1935.

_____. "What Are Masterpieces and Why Are There So Few of Them." *What Are Masterpieces*. London: Pitman, 1940.

Sutherland, Donald. *Gertrude Stein: A Biography of Her Work*. 1951. Westport CT: Greenwood, 1971.

Art By Subtraction: A Dissenting Opinion of Gertrude Stein, 1958.

"Gertrude Stein and the Lesbian Lie."

Catharine R. Stimpson

Gertrude Stein began to write seriously around 1903. A decade later, she had a reputation, especially but not exclusively in avant-garde circles. As that reputation expanded to ever larger publics, it divided against itself. In a repetitive binary opposition, two "Steins" competed for attention in an arena that Stein herself could at best partially control. One "Stein" was the "Good Stein," whom the public liked. In 1933, it made a best-seller of her *jeu d'esprit*, *The Autobiography of Alice B. Toklas*. After passing through the market, *The Autobiography* went on to please a second set of cultural gatekeepers: doyens of the syllabi, denizens of the college curriculum. If Stein appears in the United States classroom, *The Autobiography* or *Three Lives* usually represents her.

The second "Stein" was the "Bad Stein," whom the public hated and ridiculed. The Bad Stein was guilty of a double transgression: first, and more blatantly, she subverted generic and linguistic codes; next, and more slyly, she subverted sexual codes. Both her word and flesh violated normalities. Since the 1970s, a mélange of audiences has inverted Stein's reputations. The Old Good Stein is the New Bad Stein. She is too obedient to convention. The Old Bad Stein is the New Good Stein. Her transgressions are exemplary deeds.[1]

The Autobiography of Alice B. Toklas and a companion text, *Everybody's Autobiography*,[2] mingle the two, pre-1970 Steins. So doing, they undercut, sometimes incisively, sometimes impotently, the binary oppositions that her reputation embodies. Skillfully, the Old Bad Stein, the transgressive Stein, is cajoling a potential reader more decorous than she into accepting a story about the Old Good Stein. Indeed, that story will establish the Old Good Stein. In a complex act of deception, confession and assertion, a misunderstood, under-published author is giving the public what she calculates it can take. Her gift demands that she handle a subgenre we insufficiently understand: the lesbian lie. This lie insists that no lesbians abed here. To imagine erotics is to fall victim to cognitive erotics. The author respects, indeed shares, a reader's sense of decorum. At its finest, such decorum construes all sexuality as private and then begs private things stay in private. At its worst, such decorum is repression's etiquette. Stein's lie, then, is at once manipulative and courteous. The author delicately refuses to stir her readers up too much. Proper manners prevail. So, less fortunately for post-Stonewall sensibilities, will ignorance.[3] Not surprisingly, the tact that renders sexuality invisible also renders money invisible. *The Autobiography* is genteel about Stein's income. The circulation of her desire and that of her dollars/francs are each veiled.

An effect of Stein's lesbian lie is to permit us to regard the Old Good Stein as if she were a "character" in the colloquial sense of "What a

---

[1] I discuss Stein's reputations more fully in "Humanism and its Freaks."

[2] In part because it deals with fewer celebrities, in part because it deals with a less celebrated setting (Stein's American lecture tour rather than Bohemian Paris), in part because it is more intellectually tiring, *Everybody's* has lacked the popularity of *Alice B. Toklas*.

[3] Heilbrun recalls her first readings of *Toklas*. She and her mother interpreted Stein as an image of freedom. She adds, "We did not, of course, recognize them as lesbians; I'm not sure we even knew the word." When her husband suggested Stein and Toklas might be a lesbian couple, Heilbrun "snorted" in disbelief.

character!" and a literary character in an autobiographical gesture. This is an ironic turn for a cultural analyst who believed that the mass media now spew out personalities in such profusion that these manufactured personalities have driven the character from fiction's dreamy stage. Indeed, *Everybody's Autobiography* shrewdly mediates on the distinctions among having a sense of personal identity, no matter how momentarily, creating a literary identity, and being a mass media personality. As character and literary character, Stein is a jolly, bluff, discreet celebrity who plays with crowds of famous men: Picasso, Matisse, Hemingway. Each of these attributes—jolliness, bluffness, discretion, fame, the company of men— is vital to her appeal. She has her anxious moments, but they test, rather than damage, the bulkhead of her cheer. Moreover, this character exists within a readable narrative. Such readability attracts two audiences that perhaps would agree only about the readable: a heterosexual audience generally suspicious of transgression, and a homosexual audience that longs to celebrate sexual, but not literary, differences.

In brief, Stein's lesbian lie pins up an accessible star, a brilliant amalgam of democratic openness, spirited realism, and enchantment. Her modulation of subversion into entertainment both follows and refines a homosexual method of seeking acceptance in modern heterosexual culture.[4] *La Cage aux Folles* is a commercially triumphant example. Camp is a complex, wickedly self-conscious extreme. Because this modulation of subversion into entertainment is often for profit, for financial as well as psychological and physical security, it is part of the *packaging* of homosexuality. Stein's estranged brother Leo hated *The Autobiography*. "God, what a liar she is," he grumped.[5] Leo was wounded because he thought his sister was being untruthful about him and perhaps vengeful as well. In his narcissism, he was fully sharpening a real point: *The Autobiography* does lie. What packaging does not? What packaging cannot? If only through omission?

In the package of *The Autobiography of Alice B. Toklas*, a woman is apparently putting down the story of a feminine life as if it were a sparkling wine. She seems to be artless and spontaneous. She is also a lady, "gently bred." Neither striving career woman, nor raving anarchist, she behaves properly in drawing rooms. (Elsewhere, Stein gives us drawing and

---

[4] Leibowitz calls *Toklas* a "cagy performance" (219).

[5] "Supplement: Testimony Against Gertrude Stein …" also accuses Stein of being a liar, a poseur, and a fool.

quartering rooms). Born in San Francisco, Alice has cared dutifully for her father and brother after her mother's death. Combining responsibility with delight, she plays the piano. She reads Henry James. She says lightly, "I myself have had no linking for violence and have always enjoyed the pleasures of needlework and gardening. I am fond of paintings, furniture, tapestry, houses and flowers and even vegetables and fruit-trees" (4).

Modern narratives of femininity demand some revolt, no matter how gently bred or in-bred. In 1907, bored, restless, Alice goes abroad. Nature itself seems to endorse her quest, for the catastrophe of the San Francisco earthquake helps her. It has brought back some traveling members of a local family, the Steins. They tell her about Europe and inspire her to go. In Paris, Alice meets their relative, the great Stein, a stoutish woman with a strong laugh and temper. In a much-repeated line, Alice declares, "I may say that only three times in my life have I met a genius and each time a bell within me rang and I was not mistaken" (5).

The Autobiography has a number of techniques with which to stress Stein's genius: the sheer steadiness of Toklas's admiration; anecdotes about people of talent and the other people of genius (Whitehead and Picasso) who respect Stein; Stein's own self-esteem. Underwriting her doubts, overwriting her pride, *The Autobiography* extols her as the most creative literary figure of the twentieth century.

The focus on Stein's genius is as crucial to the packaging of lesbianism as it was to the Stein/Toklas "marriage." As Stein's genius justifies Toklas's devotion, so it defuses the erotic threat of that marriage. Genius watchers need not fear that the habits of the genius will become a common part of daily life. Moreover, because the genius transcends ordinary intellectual and artistic categories, she or he can rationalize an escape from ordinary social and moral judgments.[6]

Simultaneously, as Stein is using the sign of "genius" to reassure her readers, she is using the sign of "art," which genius produces, to deflect her reader's attention from sexuality itself. The maneuver is weirdly crystallized in *Everybody's Autobiography*. Stein and Toklas are at Bryn Mawr College where Stein is to lecture. They are given "Miss [Carey] Thomas' old room

---

[6] Winston (243) suggests that the use of Toklas' voice permits the representation of Stein as genius to be more assured and confident than it is in *Everybody's*. Winston is exploring a problem in Stein criticism beyond the immediate scope of this essay: the relationship of the very experimental, difficult *Stanzas in Meditation* to *Toklas* as autobiographical texts.

in the Deanery" (184). Stein refuses to precede the substantive "room" with "bed" or "living" or any other qualifier, an act of self-protective vagueness. Miss Thomas, of course, is M. Carey Thomas, whose legendary rule of Bryn Mawr had ended fourteen years earlier in 1922. The Deanery had been her residence. Around 1904-5, Stein had written a novella, "Fernhurst," rooted in a Bryn Mawr scandal. Ferhurst is a women's college. Its dean, Miss Thornton, based on Thomas, is about to lose her special friend, Miss Bruce, to a married man, Philip Redfern. Yet, with tenacity and subtle skill, Miss Thornton banishes Redfern and regains "all property rights" to Miss Bruce. Now, over three decades later, Stein looks around Miss Thomas' room and notices that "it was as it was." It has the same photographs of "capital works of art." Then, a little meanly, Stein moves from art to gossip about art lovers: "Clive Bell used to be funny when he objected that Roger Fry and Miss Bell always went to see capital works of art" (184). Her gossip alludes to sexuality, the adulterous love affair between Roger Fry and Vanessa Bell. She is reminding her readers that heterosexuals can sin, too.

Unlike Oscar Wilde, Stein does not valorize the sign of "art" over "life"; the sign of "the lie" over "truth"; the sign of "artifice" over "nature." Often indulging herself in sweet pastoral, Stein prefers the green hills of her summer home, where she wrote *The Autobiography*, to green carnations. She experiments with the rhetoric of spontaneity, be it of the fragment, the paragraph, or the narrative tale. Wilde's dramatic structures and aphorisms are contributions to the rhetoric of control. Unlike Wilde, Stein never went to prison. She was far too careful. Like Wilde, Stein must ask how to write about the erotically and socially unprintable. Their theories of art and artists substitute for more explicit representations of the forbidden. Like chaff in modern weapons systems, shot out to deflect an incoming missile from its intended target, these texts distract a potentially hostile gaze from the zone of vulnerability.

In *The Autobiography*, by about 1910, Toklas and Stein have set up their home and salon together. They go out. They travel. They have lots of visitors: artists, writers, journalists, socialites. Toklas, as ostensible narrator and real homemaker, works to *familiarize* their mutual setting. It seems comfortable, close, cozy. Stein's domestication of the different is a sophisticated prophecy of *People* magazine and its vulgar television cousin, *Life Styles of the Rich and Famous*. Stein/Toklas also enjoy surrogate family members. They include the five-year-old son of the janitor, who leaps rapturously into Stein's arms when he sees a luscious Matisse, and American "doughboys" in France during World War I. For them, the couple provides the nurturing services of an exotic Welcome Wagon and warmly eccentric spinster aunts.

As Toklas chats and remembers, Stein is constructing a four-act comedy. Stein is the heroine of Act 1, her life before meeting Toklas. Act 1 ends with that staple of the women's plot marriage, Stein to Toklas. Act 2, which lasts from 1907 to 1914, is the periods of youthful innocence. Everyone is young, talented, and poor. They have fun. They think their radical thoughts and do their avant-garde work. Act 3, the periods of World War I, is the season of sorrow. Stein's characters grow up, but the maturity extracts a terrible price, which the death of Apollinaire symbolizes. Grieving for him, Toklas' voice is bleak, quiet, elegiac. However, *The Autobiography* is a comedy. Act 4 begins with peace. The cannons are carried away. Act 4 ends with the writing of *The Autobiography* itself. The young, the talented, and the poor are the middle-aged, the talented, and the no longer poor. (At his death, Picasso would leave an estate worth at least two hundred million dollars. In 1989, one of his paintings, *Pierrette's Wedding*, would bring fifty-one million at an art auction). Stein is now "Stein." Younger generation seeks admission to the salon.[7] It is a credential to be there.

Like a Hollywood movie during the Depression of the 1930s, *The Autobiography* is a fable about going from rags to riches, not from riches to rags or rags to rags. It offers a fantasy about some people who became financial successes through their commitment to the arts, to the imagination, to fantasy itself. The comic structure of *The Autobiography*, like Stein's ostensible self-confidence, makes it a buoyant text. That charm is disarming. Smile, and the world smiles with you. Weep, and you weep alone. The representation of success is even more lavish in *Everybody's Autobiography*. A best-selling author, Stein is making money. She "counts." She is a significant person with cash to think about. Her lecture tour of America is a triumph. On the boat to America, a prosperous throat doctor asks her to autograph his copy of *The Autobiography*. Both she and Toklas do so. Small wonder that the last paragraph of *Everybody*'s repeats a verb of pleasure and happiness, "I like," five times.

The charm is a refreshing contrast to two other texts that famously codify sexual ideology between 1918 and 1939. The first is *A Farewell to Arms*, which Hemingway, the lost and betraying son of *The Autobiography*, published in 1929. Set in World War I, the novel announces that

---

[7] Seigal calls this period the Americanization of the French avant-garde. Unfortunately, I find no Stein in Seigal.

heterosexual lovers may achieve a physical unity that has metaphysical strength, heroic grandeur, and mystical consolation. Hideously, they need that consolation. For the world will kill the very good and the very gentle and the very brave impartially. It will shatter strength, grandeur, and consolation into bloody parts. Catherine Barkley will die giving birth. The baby itself will be stillborn. These double deaths—the mother's hemorrhages (an awful "Hem") and the infant's suffocation—show a culture bleeding to death and strangling new life. Having said farewell to the arms of Mars, Frederick Henry must say farewell to the arms of Venus.

If *A Farewell to Arms* consolidates the myth of romantic, tragic hetero-sexuality, the second text, *The Well of Loneliness*, consolidates that of romantic, tragic homosexuality. Published in 1928, immediately found legally obscene, *The Well* is a self-conscious polemic against homophobia. However, homosexuality is as doom-laden for homosexuals, as much an urn full of ashes, as love is for Hemingway's heterosexuals. Homosexual underworlds are demonic, sordid, gloomy, ill.

When Stein does hint at a darker lesbian, she, who disdains repetition, returns to a pungent but opaque figure: a Madame Caesar, who wears trousers, the sign of the butch.[8] In *Everybody's Autobiography*, Madame Caesar seems to be "with" Madame Steiner, but she meets an "English-woman" in a tuberculosis sanatorium. The Englishwoman comes. Madame Steiner goes away. The Englishwoman returns. Then she is dead, with two bullets in her head and her Basque cap on the rock beside her. Officially, the death is a suicide. Then, the wife of an electrician moves in with Madame Caesar. Yet, Stein sends this story up. It becomes a fairy tale, a sample of black humor, and a grammatical exercise. Describing her visit with Bernard Faÿ to Madame Caesar, after the discovery of the Englishwoman's body, Stein writes: "I weep I cry I glorify but all that has nothing to do with that. / He weeps he cries he glorifies" (82).

The end of *The Autobiography*, Stein's glorification of life with Toklas, her gambol/gamble, her ludic romp, is much annotated.[9] In the last paragraphs, a reader learns that the narrator is not Toklas, but Stein. Teleological certainties and narrative conventions waver. The book's title has been illusory. The "real" autobiographer is Stein. She says nearly all of the

---

[8] Several critics have noted that "Caesar" was also a pet name for Stein in her marriage with Toklas.

[9] Schmitz (203-26) reads Stein's double narrative with great flair and plausibility.

last words to Stein: "You know what I am going to do. I am going to write it for you. I am going to write it as simply as Defoe did the autobiography of Robinson Crusoe. And she has and this is it" (252).

This joke about authorship has at least three consequences, two episte-mological. First, the ending demonstrates Stein's theory about the impossibility of autobiography if autobiography swears that it is the narrative of a unified self, a core subject; that the narrator and the subject of the narration are the same person; that the narrator's memory has been a reliable guide to his/her past; and that the person who writes about the past is at bottom the person of the past.[10] Later, Stein would shrug. "That is really the trouble with an autobiography you do not of course you do not really believe yourself why should you, you know so well so very well that it is not yourself" (*EA* 68). Next, the ending turns *The Autobiography* into a cautionary tale about the ease with which "fact" can slip into "fiction," "fiction" into "fact." The very slipperiness of these devilish categories helps to justify Stein's doubts about autobiography. So read, *The Autobiography* anticipates a prominent category of postmodern art that Linda Hutcheon has named "historiographic metafiction." Such a text "inscribes and then subverts its mimetic engagement with the world. It does not reject it ... nor does it merely accept it .... But it does irrevocably change any simple notions of realism or reference, by confronting the discourse of art with the discourse of history."[11]

A third result is to reveal a contradiction in Stein's packaging of lesbianism. On the one hand, the coda is a tribute to the lesbian couple. Its unity is at once regressive and a leap beyond individuation and its perils. The twinned voices of the women are intertwined. Indeed, the couple represents an merger-and-acquisitions policy based on feeling rather than on corporate worth. Unified, Stein/Toklas assert their rights to love as they please and work as they please. Without relying on foundational principles or master narratives, for lesbianism lacks both in any plausible form, they assert the

---

[10] Stanton (18) correctly names *Toklas* an open rejection of the autobiographical pact of "identity between a real person, the subject, and the object of enunciation." The text then cuts against strongly felt feminist notions of a female identity that an author can present and valorize.

[11] See Hutcheon 25. Although Adams lacks Hutcheon's postmodernism, he praises Stein as the inventor of the "mock autobiography," an influential subgenre that dances on the border between fiction and nonfiction.

value of their loving, working presence in the world, their capacities for breath and brain. Their story, not matter what they leave out, is the proof of their worth.[12] On the other hand, the coda maintains heterosexual roles. The husband, male-identified, has actually done the work of writing. The wife, the lady, merely speaks. Stein further placates her readers through surprising (but not shocking) them and then giving them something to do. Getting to play "Author, author, who's got the author," her readers swing their attention away from the lesbian couple and onto the game the couple is offering them, rather as if the coda were a party treat or tea cake.

The coda of *The Autobiography* recapitulates mixed messages about sexuality that Stein has tapped out throughout the text. First, the social calendar of Stein/Toklas seems to be largely heterosexual. Heterosexuals need not be monogamous. Ironically, the lesbian couple upholds the principles of monogamy. Hardly Rotarians, the friends of Stein/Toklas live out of wedlock, commit adultery, break hearts, flirt, tease. They practice the conventions of wild Western romanticism. However, they are heterosexual, even dogmatically so. Their spokesman is another genius, Picasso. He finds sexual ambiguity upsetting. He says of certain Americans, "ils sont pas des hommes, ils sont pas des femmes, ils sont des américains" (49). He does, however, approve of one American woman, a Bryn Mawr graduate, the wife of an artist. She is both beautiful and dumb, "having once fallen on her head (she) had a strange vacant expression" (49-50).

Next, Stein mentions the names of lesbians and gay men: Natalie Barney, Marsden Hartley, Stein and Toklas.[13] However, she strips these names of their sexuality. Like words themselves, the names are fleshless. Lovers become, at best, friends. *The Autobiography* prospectively half answers Ed Cohen's witty question, "What if someone wrote a novel about homosexuality and no body came?" (805). The pictures of Stein and Toklas

---

[12] Several of the most compelling feminist theories of autobiography explore women's explorations of a divided self. Martin claims that contemporary lesbian autobiography opposes "self-evidently homogeneous conceptions of identity" (82). Brilliantly, Lionnet examines the multiple self in postcolonial and African-American autobiographies by women. Because of Stein narrative devices, *Toklas* illustrates such theories. At the same time, her tributes to the lesbian couple uphold the possibilities of psychological unity and integration.

[13] Three recent explorations of the lesbian subworlds that Stein erases are Benstock; Blankley; Jay.

together are as tasteful as a middle-class Baedeker. Take, for example, a passage about Stein, Toklas, and the weather:

"Gertrude Stein adored heat and sunshine although she always says that Paris winter is an ideal climate. In those days it was always at noon that she preferred to walk. I, who have and had no fondness for a summer sun, wept but she in the sun was indefatigable. She could even lie in the sun and look straight up into a summer noon sun, she said it rested her eyes and head" (55).

In Stein's straightlaced, middle-class reticence is a double rejection of textual alternatives available to her. The first is of the romantic excesses of Natalie Barney and Renée Vivien, inseparable from her disdain for modern explorations of dreams, the irrational, and the "primitive." Stein looks straight at the sun, not into "the night." The next is of the intelligent, elegant sensuousness of Colette. In 1932, *Ces Plaisirs* evoked some of the figures that *The Autobiography* was to treat a year later. Yet, Colette gazes at the velvet of the peach, the curve of the breast, the linens of the bed of Lady Eleanor Butler and Miss Sarah Ponsonby, and then, the stone of their tomb.

However, Stein leaves a paper trail about homosexual realities. Spatially, she set *The Autobiography* in the houses that Stein/Toklas inhabited, emotionally, in their marriage. The narrative voices are theirs. A lesbian world, the water in which the fish of anecdotes swim, is so fluidly embracing that it seems both invisible and natural. Moreover, Stein refers obliquely to her more openly erotic work, to "Ada" or to her "lost" novel, *Q.E.D.* Two sorts of readers can pick up the pieces of this trail. Some, personal friends, already know the score. Others, like me, are trying to learn the score. The friends, engaged in a conspiracy of silence, will not tell how much they know. The strangers, engaged in an alternative conspiracy of revelation, insist on telling how much we have learned. Our revisionary impulse is to amplify Stein's whispers into hearty speech.

Everybody's Autobiography rambles on with an equivalent mixture of messages. However, if Toklas seems to write up *The Autobiography*, Stein writes her down in *Everybody's*. To be sure, Toklas is always there. She is Stein's companion, interpreter, housekeeper, secretary. They eat oysters and pies together. They drive around Chicago in a police car together. They are inseparable, except when Stein steps up alone to a podium. However, Stein casually and quickly dismisses Alice as the author of *The Autobiography*. So doing, she erases Alice as the gaze, the eye, that fixes Stein's identity, Stein's "I." Stein now thinks about other, less singular stabilizing gazes: her audience, her little dog, and her own. Her regard for her mirror image as "genius" is now overweening. Being straightforward about her Jewishness, she now has two names on her genius list for the twentieth century: Gertrude Stein and Albert (Ein)stein. One is female and literary; the other male and "philosophic" (21). Both are Jews.

Playfully, *The Autobiography* might seem to foreshadow postmodern theories of the death of the author, but, in another contradiction, it at once defends and defeats them. Toklas can be Stein, but only if Stein dictates that. So doing, *The Autobiography* balances an unstable subject, i.e., a Stein who can seem to be Toklas for nearly an entire book, against a stable self, a Stein who can reassert her Steinishness at will. Less ambiguously, *Everybody's Autobiography* asserts the authority of the self, especially that of the genius/author. Together, the texts exemplify Nancy K. Miller's theory that feminist critics can read women authors in ways that rewrite subjectivity without erasing it. Similarly, African-American critics can read African-American authors, postcolonial critics postcolonial authors. Miller warns us against foreclosing on the properties of agency by seeing authorship as a synecdoche for agency. She states, "The postmodernist decision that the Author is Dead and the subject along with him does not ... necessarily hold for women, and prematurely forecloses the question of agency for them. Because women have not had the same historical relation of identity to origin, institution, production that men have had, they have not, I think, (collectively) felt burdened by *too much* Self, Ego, Cogito, etc. Because the female subject has juridically been excluded from the polis, hence decentered, 'disoriginated'; deinstitutionalized, etc., her relation to integrity and textuality, desire and authority, displays structurally important differences from that universal position" (106).

As Stein packages the female lesbian subject, she also dramatizes the creation of the modern art and literature that developed simultaneously with modern sexual identities. Her lesbianism is acceptable because she either evades it or stylizes it as a joke about authorship. In a reversal, she renders modernism acceptable through turning art into life. Presenting the movers and shakers of modernism as "real people," she parcels out cultural history as anecdote and story. This technique is a prophecy of television's dominant method of conveying ideas through having a figure embody them. Watch modern physics become Einstein and Oppenheimer. Aiding Stein in her minibiographies is the myth of Bohemia, a narrative about artists that had become a well-understood formula well before 1933. Indeed, *The Autobiography* has a revealing scene. In 1907, Toklas meets Stein at an avant-garde art show in Paris. Just before Stein touches Toklas on the shoulder, she marvels, "it was indeed the vie de Bohéme just as one had seen it in the opera" (18). "Bohemia" is a space in which people have permission to be different, to be wild and crazy kids. A modern version of the rituals of misrule and of the rites of inversion, Bohemia sanctions a preference for art over commerce; feeling over reason; style over conformity; experiment over tradition.

Perhaps most crucially, both autobiographies pull back from Stein's upsetting challenges to representational codes and generic conventions. Telling her comic stories, Stein writes *of* modern art. Despite some shrewd narrative tricks, she does not write modern art itself.[14] She is a guide, not a practitioner. She is teacher, mentor, docent, not a disquieting savage on a fling. The fourth paragraph of *Everybody's* is about a Miss Hennessy's wooden umbrella. Miss Hennessy is eccentric, but Stein's prose is not. The umbrella is "carved out of wood and looks exactly like a real one even to the little button and the rubber string that holds it together" (3). In contrast, the eighth paragraph of *Tender Buttons* is also "about" Mildred's umbrella, but the prose is a riot, "A cause and no curve, a cause and loud enough, a cause and extra a loud clash and an extra wagon" (*Writings and Lectures* 164).

In deliberate retreat, Stein's autobiographies cultivate a lively, but plain and simple, style. Stein even has Toklas say that she is always "literal." *Everybody's Autobiography* obviously revises James's *The American Scene*, an earlier account of a famous expatriate's return to the landscape of origins. Far more subtle an observer of American democracy, far more sensitive to injustice, James writes much more deeply and more densely than Stein. However, her plainness and simplicity are masterstrokes in covering up and covering over her lesbianism. For her immediacies and limpidities promise that her language is a transparent window onto reality, even onto the reality that fact and fiction can blur into each other. She is direct. She tells her friends the truth, even about the trickiness of truth. In return, she takes no

---

[14] Although I stress this point, I recognize the modernity of *Toklas*. Breslin (149-62) shows how formidably Stein interrogates the formal problems of auto-biography. Among feminist critics of autobiography, Smith (175) notes how Stein invests herself with another's voice. Friedman (54-55) outlines the advantages Stein gains through the fluidity of the writing "I." Merrill reads these permeable ego boundaries through Lacanian psychoanalysis. Brodzki and Schenck (9) locate the modern in *Toklas*'s relational quality, process of defamiliarization, and drama of a self "in pieces, fragments, refractions."

chaff, no guff. How could she be such a packager? How could she lie? Deliberately, egregiously, meanly deceive?

However, a gap does exist between style's apparent promise full of disclosure and the actuality of partial disclosures. Because of that gap, the texts are not literal but ironic. Yet, the same gap makes the autobiographies mimetic. For they dramatize an actuality, the homosexual dissimulation of which Colette speaks so cleverly and respectfully. Dissimulation is a tax that homosexuals pay in order to go on being members of a society that would abhor their honesty. When Stein put her hand on Toklas's shoulder, lesbians in Paris could not wear men's clothing unless the prefect of police said they could. Stein's public silence makes much more sense when we admit the power of the legal and social codes that governed her. She efficiently chose her method of strategic dissimulation: write as if you wrote about everything and everybody. Her lie was to write as if she were incapable of lying. If she did lie, if she pretended that Alice B. Toklas wrote a book, she would reveal the trick at the end and call it a playful fiction. The creator of this Alice would show the rabbits of a literary magic trick moving from hutch to hat. If we practice pragmatics, we must note her pragmatism.

Stein's survival mechanisms, her repressions, exact their price. A passage in *Tender Buttons*, which puns on what the body and the voice can do, wryly comments on such an expense: "South, south which is a wind is not rain, does silence choke or does it not. Lying is a conundrum, lying so makes the springs restless, lying so is a reduction, not lying so is arrangeable" (200-201).

Stein's most public autobiographies lack a measure of the pleasure of many of her more radical texts. *Everybody's Autobiography* is often dogged in its descriptions of fun. Neither text has the intricate lyricism and sophisticated engagement with the naivete of "A Sonatina Followed By Another." Here, Stein retains traditional marital roles (Stein as husband, Toklas as wife), but transforms the foul into the fowls of a joyous, homey bestiary.

"And a credit to me she is sleepily a credit to me and what do I credit her with I credit her with a kiss.

1. Always sweet.
2. Always right.
3. Always welcome.
4. Always wife.
5. Always blessed.

6. Always a successful druggist of the second class and we know what that means. Who credits her with all this a husband with a kiss and what is he to be always more lovingly his missus' help and hero. And when is he heroic, well we know when.

Win on a foul pretty as an owl pretty as an owl win on a fowl. And the fowl is me and she is pretty as an owl. Battling Siki and Capridinks is pretty and winks, winks of sleep and winks of love. Capridinks. Capridinks is my lone and my Coney." (*Bee Time Vine* 32)

Moreover, Stein's public evasions of her sexual marginality and otherness help to distort her perceptions of other marginalized groups. Her comments on American blacks, for example, can be genial. They are also patronizing, inept, and foolish. She anesthetizes black history.

I am passing a judgment, at once sympathetic and truculent, on Stein's passing. The ambivalence of my judgment is related to larger, unresolved problems in feminist theory to which I can only point now. One problem is the shape of a feminist response to the lesbian lie. So far, the most influential voices have denounced the lie while exculpating the liar. In both her poem "Cartographies of Silence" and her essay "Women and Honor: Some Notes on Lying," Adrienne Rich writes eloquently of the destructive consequences of the lie, for lesbians and for all women; amnesia, "the silence of the unconscious"; madness; the erasure of trust among women (187 and elsewhere). Yet, the lesbian lie ("No lesbians here") has also been a source of courageous, jaunty, often outrageous style. The Old Bad Stein, fibbing a little about the Old Good Stein, did dash off *The Autobiography*. The liars, when they speak together, as Stein and Toklas do in Stein's more radical texts, can create a ritualistic theater. This theater's purpose is to strengthen the community of liars, to remind them that the lie is a lie, and to give the liars enough rest and relaxation to go on to further feats of linguistic inventiveness. *Their* purpose is to deceive a public that is both vigilant and unwary as it patrols the borders of permissible speech and behavior. This theatrical tongue is more apt to be spoken than written. A feature of Stein's more radical texts is their interrogation of the diglottism of conversation and conversation on the page.

Rich's argument rests on our ability to draw, finally, reliable distinctions between true and false, between language in the service of truth and language in the service of fraud. Yet feminist postmodernism questions this ability. Some of us might interpret the phrase "the lie of language" in other ways. We might ask about the lie of language in the sense of the position of language, in ways that wash away the binary distinction between "true" and "false" itself. Feminist postmodernism might then give a lesbian lie two connotations. First, it is performance that both precedes and follows a lesbian's perception of her powerlessness because of the well-muscled stigma against lesbianism. She believes that only if she merges the false ("I am not a lesbian") with the true ("I am a lesbian") can she live as a lesbian. Next, the lesbian lying might also be a parable about the inexorably secretive powers of language. Like language, the lesbian lies. Neither vicious nor exploitative, she still knows more than she overtly lets on or out. Is the Old Bad Stein inventing the Old Good Stein a paranoid story about language in operation? If so, how paranoid should we be?

Works Cited

Adams, Timothy Dow. "'She Will Be Me When This You See': Gertrude Stein's Mock Auto-biography of Alice B. Toklas." *Publications of the Arkansas Philological Association* 6.1 (1980): 1-18.

Benstock, Shari. *Women of the Left Bank: Paris, 1900-1940.* Austin: U of Texas P, 1986.

Blankley, Elyse. "Return to Mytilène: Reneé Vivien and the City of Women." *Women Writers and the City: Essays in Feminist Criticism.* Ed. Susan Merrill Squier. Knoxville: U of Tennessee P, 1984. 45-67.

Breslin, James E. "Gertrude Stein and the Problems of Autobiography." *Women's Autobiography: Essays in Criticism.* Ed. Estelle C. Jelinek. Bloomington: Indiana U P, 1980. 149-62.

Cohen, Ed. "Writing Gone Wilde: Homoerotic Desire in the Closet of Representation." *PMLA* 102 (October 1987): 801-13.

Friedman, Susan Stanford. "Women's Autobiographical Selves: Theory and Practice." *The Private Self: Theory and Practice of Women's Autobiographical Writings.* Ed. Shari Benstock. Chapel Hill: U of North Carolina P, 1988. 34-62.

Hall, Radclyffe. *The Well of Loneliness.* New York: Covici Friede, 1928.

Heilbrun, Carolyn G. *Writing a Woman's Life.* New York: Norton, 1988.

Hemingway, Ernest. *A Farewell to Arms.* 1929. New York: Modern Library, 1932.

Hutcheon, Linda. "Beginning to Theorize Postmodernism." *Textual Practice* 1 (Spring 1987): 10-31.

Jay, Karla. *The Amazon and the Page.* Bloomington: Indiana UP, 1987.

Lebowitz, Herbert. *Fabricating Lives: Explorations in American Auto-biography.* New York: Knopf, 1989.

Lionnet, Françoise. *Autobiographical Voices: Race, Gender, Self-Portraiture*. Ithaca: Cornell U P, 1989.

Martin, Biddy. "Lesbian Identity and Autobiographical Differences." In Bordzki and Schenck, 77-103.

Merill, Cynthia. "Mirrored Image: Gertrude Stein and Autobiography." *Pacific Coast Philology* 20 (November 1985): 11-17.

Miller, Nancy. *Subject to Change: Reading Feminist Writing*. New York: Columbia U P, 1988.

Rich, Adrienne. *On Lies, Secrets, and Silence: Selected Prose, 1966-78*. New York: Norton, 1979.

Schmitz, Neil. *Of Huck and Alice: Humorous Writing in American Literature*. Minneapolis: U of Minnesota P, 1983.

Seigal, Jerrold. *Bohemian Paris: Culture, Politics, and the Boundaries of Bourgeois Life, 1830-1930*. New York: Viking, 1986.

Smith, Sidonie. *A Poetics of Women's Autobiography: Marginality and the Fictions of Self-Representation*. Bloomington: Indiana U P, 1987.

Stanton, Domna C. "Autogynography: Is the Subject Different?" *The Female Autograph*. New York: Literary Forum, 1984. 3-20.

Stein, Gertrude. *The Autobiography of Alice B. Toklas*. 1933. New York: Vintage, 1960.

_____. *Bee Time Vine and Other Pieces, 1913-1927*. New Haven: Yale U P, 1953.

_____. *Everybody's Autobiography*. 1937. New York: Vintage, 1973.

_____. *Writings and Lectures, 1909-1945*. Ed. Patricia Meyerowitz. Baltimore: Penguin, 1971.

Stimpson, Catharine. "Humanism and Its Freaks." *boundary 2* 12.3-13.1 (Spring/Summer 1984): 301-19.

"Supplement: Testimony Against Gertrude Stein by Henri Matisse, Tristan Tzara, Maria Jolas, Georges Braque, Eugene Jolas, André Salmon." *transition* 23 (July 1935).

Winston, Elizabeth. "Gertrude Stein's Mediating Stanzas." *Biography: An Interdisciplinary Quarterly* 9 (Summer 1986).

American Women's Autobiography. Ed. Margo Culley. Madison: U of Wisconsin P, 1992.

"Notes from a Women's Biographer."

Linda Wagner-Martin

What appealed to me about doing a biography of Gertrude Stein, which is how [*Favored Strangers: Gertrude Stein and Her Family*] came to be, was her early life: her childhood as "Baby" of an upperclass Jewish family; her trauma while her mother, Amelia, struggled for nearly three years with abdominal (ovarian?) cancer; the collapse of the household after Amelia's death; the authoritarianism of her father Daniel and his sudden death a few years after her mother's; her four years at Radcliffe; following her old brother Leo when he transferred from Berkeley to Harvard; her disappointing years at Johns Hopkins Medical School, when she failed to graduate because of disagreements with professors over women's medicine; and her first serious love affair with May Bookstaver. At thirty, Gertrude went to live in Paris with Leo, running from a variety of family and academic pressures. I was less interested in her Paris life, I thought, assuming that that story had already been well told (it turns out that much new material exists about the later years as well). I initially wanted to do for the early years of Gertrude Stein's life what Sharon O'Brien does for her subject in *Willa Cather: The Emerging Voice*.

Unfortunately, not only was no publisher interested in Gertrude's early life—no publisher was interested in Gertrude at all. Some editors even asked who she was. So my agent suggested that I refocus the book, and it became a study of the Stein family. Since I wanted to focus on the first thirty years of Gertrude's life, this shift was workable. Her story as the baby of the family *was* a family story and the problem with much of her childhood and adolescence was the erratic behavior of her father, Daniel. I read the Stein family as thoroughly dysfunctional, the father's rigid, unpredictable edicts shaping the lives of the four younger children (Bertha and Simon were virtual drop-outs because they could never please Daniel Stein) even if the oldest, Michael, managed to escape that turmoil. Milly Stein's death, then, was particularly important because she had always been the buffer, the Angel in the House, and without her all hell broke loose. The children's fears over her very long dying were compounded because losing their mother meant that all they had left was their father. It was a double blow.

Again unfortunately for the book, the male editor who bought the project was more interested in the lives of the brother than in Gertrude. He had bought a story of the German-Jewish family who came to Baltimore almost penniless and succeeded. He wanted to hear about the strength and pride of the immigrant family and the way the boys carried on the family name. He was not expecting my discussion about women's roles in those German-Jewish families, about the way Milly was forced to become a non-entity who could not stand up to a man whose behavior suggests a manic-depressive mode, and about the problems her daughters had in that family. When I did portray the three boys, the fact that two of them were nearly non-functional as a result of their life with Daniel was, again, not the story he wanted to read.

I am describing this process in detail because it suggests how many different books are possible under one set of describers. My book was to be Gertrude's book, the story of an overweight, "homely" (in her words) but very smart Jewish girl who did not fit in either the culture of California or Baltimore, but came closer to belonging at Radcliffe, where she found a niche in the psychological laboratories of Hugo Münsterberg and William James. Nurtured, encouraged, even loved, Gertrude there found her spirit and her voice—replacing the anxiety and depression she had known in her family's household.

The resistance I encountered to my telling this story was the same I had run into with my Sylvia Plath biography, which again was bought by a male editor who was sure he knew what story I was trying to tell. "His" Sylvia was a neurotic if talented (and he wasn't so sure about that) American whose early sexual experimentation would be better left unmentioned and whose death should be the focus of the entire book. A life heading for death—what better narrative line for any story? Like the editor for the Stein biography, this one was, by temperament, a simplifier. What I have come to realize in working on these projects, although they are quite different, is that women's lives must fit into one of two plots—even in the 1990s. Either a woman is crazy and talented (at least marginally) and in that case, headed for sure suicide, or she is crazy and sexually deviant (my editor thought Stein's writing was nothing but a joke and insisted that discussion of it—or excerpts from it—not appear in the biography). In either case, the only biographies that will sell are those of the aberrant, the misfit, the sensationalized.

Even had these books been university press biographies rather than commercial, I wonder whether the expectations would have changed. Extant biographies of Gertrude Stein certainly care very little about her strength, her composed approach to writing and life, her sometimes tormented love for Alice B. Toklas. What they care about is those men Gertrude hung out with —Picasso, Hemingway, Fitzgerald, Gris, Thornton Wilder, Virgil Thomson.

The previous biographies of Stein (even the best of those, *Charmed Circle* by James Mellow) seldom explore her very close friendships with women—Mildred Aldrich, Janet Flanner, Nöel Murphy, and, later, Natalie Barney; or those with the young men that she earnestly believed she could help become better artists, writers, and people. Stein as a teacher, which was her role for most of her life, has not yet appeared in the hundreds of essays and books already published about her.

My struggle to write a biography about a normal Sylvia Plath, who inherited a genetic tendency to depression which showed up under the stresses of choosing a career and having children, and another about an equally normal Gertrude Stein, a bit shaky after her mother's traumatic and painful dying, brought me only antipathy from the editors who had bought what they thought was going to be highly sensational books. Neither was. Neither should have been. In point of fact, neither could have been.

At issue here, I have come to think, is the fact that most people who read biographies of women subjects want anything but another domestic story. They do not want six chapters on childhood and adolescent development. They do not care how the subject reached the kind of adult persona she came to have or be, or the way subsequent life events either reinforced or contradicted those early foundations. They want action, aberration, madness. They want photographs of an anorexic Plath or an obese Stein—for comic relief, never seeing that a woman's weight is often a sign of her state of health and mind. Neither editor wanted any mention of possible sexual abuse by family members unless it could be proven and documented, not drawn from the subject's writing or diaries. The "rules" of traditional biography work against the biographer's following subtle leads in texts or letters; the entire process of biography works hard to sterilize painful stories so that the reader is given orderly and conventional plotlines. Perhaps traditional biography as the world knows it has rarely dealt with the real existence of any subject—either male or female—because the most influential events often became memories to stifle instead of to voice.

My experience with Plath and Stein has led me to conclude that the conventions of traditional biography do not work for most women subjects. These conventions—that the subject has led an exemplary life, that this life is best treated chronologically and pegged on historical events external to the subject, that the subject's internal life is not intrinsically significant—may work for many men's lives, but women's lives strain against their implied narrative. The woman's biographer must attend to Woolfian "moments of being" that push through gaps in the chronology, to clusters of significant events that are often internal. Yet the power of the biographical conventions is so strong that editors, readers, and reviewers frequently assume that biographers who write something other than a conventional narrative do so not out of design but out of ignorance.

One significant cluster is puberty. Women experience the stress of menstruation, visible changes in body shape and size, and increased sexuality, experiences which are often alienating—and yet where in biography are there models for explorations of these years? Both Plath and Stein began menstruating earlier than their friends—they were ten and eleven, respectively—and they were also inarticulate (they also would not have spoken or written about such processes in either 1942 or 1885). And even in the 1990s, traditional biographic form allows gaps where such crucial explorations of self and psyche should occur ....

The account of Amelia's death [in *Favored Strangers*] uses her journal as the most important source. Gertrude was eleven when her mother's cancer was diagnosed and fourteen when she died. Using the journal is itself problematic because the entries are very short, and all previous biographers have discounted them (or worse, made snide comments about them because of their pragmatic, household-defined, and very domestic content). In relying as much as I do on them in the early sections of the biography, valuing the words of this semi-literate homebody, I am leaving myself open to all kinds of attack. In this excerpt, the connections I try to make are visibly "feminine," and, not surprisingly, my editor has asked why Gertrude's menstruation needs to be mentioned here (or needs to be mentioned at all). From the literary perspective, of course, my emphasis on the death of the mother is going to raise the charge of "sentimentality."

On the one hand, writing the parent's death has to be done because that death was so crucial to the five children's memories and their emotional lives. Whether or not this method of narrating Milly's death works better than a low-keyed, objective omniscient voice, I can no longer judge. I almost hear Milly's voice in those simple journal entries, and so my storying naturally employs her locutions, her perspective. My commitment was to use the actual words of the subjects as often and as much as possible—and in that tactic, Milly's journal seemed priceless.

In contrast to the next 500 pages of the biography, which for the most part race through years of events on both sides of the Atlantic with a clipped pace that should pull readers through the details with some finesse, this section seems slow, mournful, almost elemental—which to me felt like a suitable pace for its subject. But then, I am a woman reader, and in that role, I bring certain tastes, values, and peculiarities to any text, including this one.

Narrative, October 1993.

"Gertrude Stein's Jewishness, Jewish Social Scientists, and the 'Jewish Question.'"

Maria Damon

Two framing anecdotes can serve as case-historemes exemplifying the thicket of static buzzing around the estranged-twin subjects of Jewish social science and Gertrude Stein's Jewishness. The first is a passage from anthropologist Melville Herskovits' tribute to Franz Boas, containing a remarkable typographical error that reveals, I believe, the degree of anxiety provoked in Jewish social scientists when faced with the social scientific discourse addressing the "Jewish question." In the second, I recount an incident that highlights the ongoing critical controversies about Stein's conduct during World War II, which render her politics suspect. Here is the first:

"... as a scientist, the anthropologist studies his problem and publishes his results. With other scientists, he seeks the answer to this basic ethical problem, as yet unsolved, of how to ensure that his findings *are used* by those who would direct them toward ends *inimical* to the canons of morality of the scientific tradition within which he works" (*Franz Boas*; emphasis added).

And here is my encounter with the party line on Stein's politics:

In October 1995, "L=A=N=G=U=A=G=E" poet Charles Bernstein and I participated by telephone in a Gertrude Stein hour on WBAI radio's "Beyond the Pale," organized by Jews for Racial and Economic Justice (the gay and lesbian activist wing of the group had requested Stein as a subject of their designated special show, which fact itself was extremely interesting to me. We were the "Jews" on the panel; the other two panelists, who were present in the studio along with the JFREJ moderator, were poet Eileen Myles, who had recently co-edited *The New Fuck You Anthology of Lesbian Writing*, and Buffy Johnson, a New York painter who had known Gertrude and Alice in Paris. Charles and I came in on the second half of the hour-long show and discussed first how we did or didn't see questions of identity arising in Stein's work and how Stein's interrogation of identity through language play (as well as thematically) could itself be seen as a strong current in the Jewish intellectual tradition.

Then came the question of her politics, her survival of World War II under the auspices of Bernard Faÿ in the Vichy government. The moderator challenged any designation of Stein and Toklas as "radical" since they owed their survival to friendship with an anti-Semite whom they refused to repudiate even after Faÿ's disgrace in the wake of Allied victory. Charles and I bristled. Would it have been better that she not survive? She didn't betray anybody. People did what they had to. The whole village knew they were Jewish and protected them. I'd seen their wartime I.D. photos at the Beinecke, and they were terrified little old Jewish ladies, not callous race traitors living it up à la Nero, fiddling and diddling while their people perished. And so forth. Our vehement defense was cut off by the hour's expiration. "Thank you for being with us, but that's all the time we have." Our disembodied, miscreant Jewish voices snipped, our absence doubled. The non-Jewish artists and the political Jew wrapped it up in person.

In an earlier essay I explored Gertrude Stein's writing as "minority discourse" in the sense expressed by Deleuze and Guattari in *Kafka: Toward a Minor Literature*.[1] I had thought, before I began writing that piece, that I'd be most compelled in this direction by Stein's status as a sexual minority and as a woman. However, her Jewishness emerged as an at least equal site of creative contestation, not in opposition to those other elements of social difference, but implicated, of a piece, with them. In the present essay I want to continue that inquiry by situating the work produced during Setin's middle period (roughly, from World War I to just before the emergence of the Final Solution—primarily the works collected as *Painted Lace and Other Pieces 1914-1937*) in the discourse of Jewish social science. I will refer primarily to Otto Weininger's work but also, more cursorily, to that of Freud, Maurice Fishberg, and Melville Herskovits, all secularized Jews.

The Jewish social scientist's inquiry into systems of character, physical type, and mental processes may reflect an attempt to understand the origins of his or her socially perceived "difference" and the desire to affirm that difference. However, the inquiry may also indicate an attempt to control by intellectual mastery a system of exclusion; the anxiety of "passing" generates a search for systemic order in which one can find one's own safety zone. This essay has its autobiographical imperative: I am the daughter of an ambivalently Jewish medical anthropologist. I read my father's professional

---

[1] See "Gertrude Stein's Doggerel 'Yiddish'": Women, Dogs, and Jews."

life as an attempt to bother assert his (ethically affirmed) intelligence and efface his (socially despised) ethnicity within a larger culture which deemed his bookishness, his verbal acumen and sensitivity, his passion for Western culture unmanly even as it rewarded his achievements. Gertrude Stein's early novelistic experiments with African-American language, for example, and the novel *Q.E.D.* in which each person of the lesbian love triangle in the plot typifies a different "national" temperament, constitute a similarly problematic move to study (the other-ness of) oneself by attending to the otherness of an/other Other. Her move to Europe, in which she plunged herself into a culture alien yet somehow evocative of an older familiar world could constitute a kind of sociolinguistic fieldwork in which the real subject of study (as in most ethnographies, after all) is herself. The writing she produced in France, though less thematically concerned with "types" and character, became a practice in which language itself, in a process of experiment, undertook and underwent a dissolution of category.

Since until recently it has been assumed that an inquiry into someone's ethnicity involves establishing how she herself "felt about" being x or y, Steinians have maintained that Stein's radical anti-identitarianism foreclosed such inquiry, except to assert that "it simply wasn't important to her"; this foreclosure is exacerbated by the ongoing debates about whether Judaism/Jewishness is a religion, an ethnicity, a culture, etc. It seems indecorous to "out" Stein as a Jew, especially since it is not at all clear what that really means for someone who was not religiously observant, did not observe dietary laws (Toklas's cookbook is full of pork and shellfish recipes), and had no interest in Zionism. On the other side, staunchly ethnic Jews like the WBAI moderator from JFREG take issue with Stein's lack of public solidarity with other Jews, seeing her as an assimilationist of a worse type than the secular Jews Freud, Marx, and Emma Goldmann, the latter of whom qualify as Jews by their political engagements. Claims such as mine —that Stein's Jewishness is, arguably, a language practice—can sound vaguely Weiningerian itself, that is, essentialistic. Thus Stein's Jewishness is a topic that is best approached obliquely, as she herself does: with narrative tentativeness; with an openness toward the inclusion of fragment-clues and minutiae free-floating through her work like sidereal flotsam, as well as toward broad disciplinary inquiries into "the status of the social sciences at the end of the century" and other such currents of humanistic cliché that, when delved into, relinquish their apparent predictability and turn into discoveries perhaps intuited but nonetheless finally surprising.

For many, my subject is not a topic whose viability is immediately self-evident; I was told by another scholar whose specialty is Jewish women poets, "If you can find Jewishness in Stein you can find it anywhere." I have learned, moreover, that the editors of a forthcoming encyclopedia of Jewish American playwrights and poets almost decided to exclude Stein. Likewise, although the introduction to the very useful *Jews and Gender: Responses to Otto Weininger*, edited by Nancy Horowitz and Barbara Hyams, refers correctly to Stein as having been influenced by Weininger's writings (5), there is no essay on this subject in the book, which deals copiously with Weininger and Joyce (fully three essays dedicated to this topic), as well as Apollinaire, Heine, and German novels in general. Split into strict halves, the book addresses first the "scientific," social-context aspect of its thorny subject—Weininger as Viennese, Weininger as a liberal, Weininger and Freud, Lombroso, and Wittgenstein; the second half compromises the literary essays enumerated above. And where, indeed, given the scope of Stein's inquiry, would one "place" such an essay? Anyone wanting to investigate Stein's relationship to the forms and styles of "Jewishness" that prevailed during her long life needs to be, as she believed herself to be, both social "scientist" and "artist." These comprise a specious binarism, of course; they also express the becoming-oxymoron of the "social scientist" as that disciplinary identity took shape during Stein's era.

It is precisely this binarism to which Otto Weininger appeals in the introduction to his notorious *Sex and Character* (1903), a volume inaugurating (according to the German publisher's preface to the posthumous, post-suicide, authorized edition) the psycho-philosophical science of "characterology." Briefly, Weininger, working out of a European tradition of first religious and then scientific anti-Semitism and misogyny, proposes that "genius"—that is, the capacity to develop to the fullest extent the rational, humanistic spirituality necessary to become a fully actualized (as contemporary New Agers might say) individual—is the sole province of the Aryan male, and is inaccessible to (Aryan) women and (presumably all, though Weininger uses male pronouns exclusively) Jews. This is because characterologically (character being a combination of biological, moral, and intellectual temperament) Jews and women are incapable of self-sufficiency—that is, they have no being-in-themselves; they are reactive and parasitic, concerned only with physical survival. Weininger stresses that he is not concerned, in his scheme, with literal Jews and Aryans, with literal men and women; these are "platonic" conceptions (311), which in some measure are manifested in real individuals but function more nearly as tendencies; all Jews and Christians are combinations of Jew and Christian, all men and women are properly bisexual, with a tendency toward one pole or the other. Thus, for example, the crowning achievement of Jesus, the act that represented his genius, was that, though he was Jewish, he killed the Jew in him to found Christianity (327-28). For Weininger, this example provides the only possible solution to the Jewish question. The individual Jew must, through "steady resolution, united to the highest self-respect" (312), overcome, like Jesus, his own Judaism. Zionism is out of the question, for it does not save the Jew; it merely isolates him.

Weininger's insistence on a holistic, rational/moral individualism and on the perfectibility of society in a clear-cut and narrow teleology of values, through the self-initiated perfectibility of the individual, constitutes his liberalism. A belief in human progress along individual lines, but conforming nonetheless to a universally applicable ideal, compromises the heart of liberalism. Steven Beller has drawn a useful distinction between "intolerant" and "tolerant" liberalism (91-92); pluralism is intrinsic to the latter, but has no place in the former (we can see this distinction played out in contemporary debates about multiculturalism; will "difference" strengthen or weaken national unity? The question liberalism cannot ask is: Why should national unity be the bottom line?). Weininger clearly falls in the former camp: human rationality is defined as a single style of thinking —that of the Aryan/Christian male; human morality has one universal code —that of the Aryan/Christian male. One can also see the nature of Weininger's assimilationism, which was a strange twist on the progressive thought of his time. While many liberal Jews, sociologist Maurice Fishberg among them, advocated assimilation under the aegis of a pluralistic tolerance (that is, Jews should not be forced to be other than Jews, but they should enjoy full and egalitarian contact with the Gentile mainstream— short of intermarriage in which the offspring become non-Jewish—and have full access to rights and opportunities enjoyed by Gentiles), Weininger's solution resonates with an older model of assimilation—that is, conversion. But it is not so much a religious conversion as a characterological one, and it must, of course, be voluntary, individually undertaken, and profound, not cosmetic—the result of rigorous soul-searching and ruthless introspective asceticism. Weininger brings the Protestant work ethic to bear on the self-help project of Jewish assimilation.

However, this linear logic, meant to save Western civilization, doomed its author to suicide. Trapped in a system of thinking in which he believed himself to have found the answer, but unable to actualize it in the world (in his own being), Weininger was condemned to a certain teleological track that was self-canceling.

The overdeterminism of Weininger's binarisms—Jew/Aryan, woman/ man, Hebraism/Christianity, body/soul—articulates an almost decadently extreme dialectic—the endpoint of modernism, perhaps a line of reasoning atrophied from inbreeding. Weininger does in fact advocate letting the human race perish rather than perpetuate the immorality of coitus— immorality because it requires that man partake of woman's lack of identity by objectifying her; though she is in fact nothing but an object of man's projection, his moral integrity rests on him treating her *as if she were capable* of humanity (343*ff*). It is not hard to see how Stein may have found Weininger's ethically argued distaste for heterosexual coitus reassuring (Charlotte Perkins Gilman, an American feminist and economist, was also taken with his work); likewise, his theory of universal bisexuality, which Freud later adopted, gave philosophical permission for sexual minorities to place themselves within a continuum of social normativity. What is fascinating is how Stein's early enthusiasm for this straightforwardly misogynistic, anti-Semitic tract is later reworked; she revises its uncompromisingly unlinear premise of progress (Weininger argues that at least in theory all people can and must kill the woman and the Jew in them to become the supreme individual, the Aryan male genius) into an emergent dialogic, one that finds emancipationist possibilities in precisely the putatively unwholesome elements of character, speech, and thought in woman and Jew that Weininger contemned.

Like Stein, and other Jewish contemporaries of Weininger's, such as Freud (*Jokes and Their Relation to the Unconscious*, essentially an affectionate ethnic manifesto whose closest contemporary analogue is Henry Louis Gates's *The Signifying Monkey*), Theodore Reik, and Maurice Fishberg (*The Jews: A Study in Race and Environment,* 1911), also studied the "problem" of "Jewishness" as social scientists (Freud, unlike Fishberg, tending also toward an essayistic, humanistic model of exposition) in ways that affirmed, rather than denounced, the Jews' perceived specialness as an ethnic group. Stein, too, in her very challenge to the concept or desirability of identity, in her very claim that identity is relational rather than innate and autonomous, enacted and affirmed a kind of Jewishness that eschewed fixed categories and unlinear ways of thinking, thus instantiating Weininger's charges of Jews' faulty reasoning-cum-being-in-the-world while championing that psychic style as valid, liberating, and intellectually and aesthetically rewarding.

Sander Gilman has thoroughly documented how Weininger's ideas grow out of a history of religious and scientific anti-Semitism in Europe, in which stock indices of Jewish difference were codified into a normative discourse that influenced Jewish social scientists such as Cesare Lombroso, Arthur Schnitzler, Joseph Jacobs, Maurice Fishberg, and Freud, as well as their gentile colleagues. Jewish creativity, insofar as it existed at all (which Weininger ruled out), was intertwined with Jewish "madness" and melancholia, Jewish sexuality with Jewish pathology; Jewish "inauthenticity" was seen to be either innate (Weininger) or a result of millennia or oppression, and so on. Gilman bluntly asserts biographical detail as crucial in understanding these men's intellectual formations and conversely reads intellectual treatises as barely veiled autobiographical position papers: "The self-hating Jew Otto Weininger ... was both a baptized Jew and a repressed homosexual" (*The Jew's Body* 133). Gilman's own projections give permission to see Stein's oeuvre, if not representationally autobiographical (though that too, in some pieces), at least firmly situated within the context of debates about Jewishness that were part of the psycho-philosophical backdrop of modernist (theories and practice of) creativity.

As Gilman, again, has argued in *Jewish Self-hatred*, the emergence of the twentieth century marked the emergence not only of European and American Jews and women as political actors on their own behalf, but also of a host of sciences designed in part to contain these insurgencies through the establishment of racial, ethnic, and gender characteristics that determined immutable differences between demographic groups. For Jews placing themselves in mainstream intellectual life of the twentieth century, the challenge was to position themselves in relation to these sociobiological, psychological, sexological, and anthropological systems in a way that did not subordinate them to these discourses of classification and control but rather enabled them to participate affirmatively in the process of social definition. Unlike Weininger, many did not repudiate their own Jewishness but rather used the concept of ethnic classification to affirm what they felt to be special about their culture. Gilman has shown that Freud goes further than simple affirmation; his theory of creativity disentangles what had been articulated (by Cesare Lombroso and others) as the nexus of creativity and madness characterizing the Jewish psyche ("Weininger and Freud" 103*ff*). In Freud's view, creativity is part of everyday life and everyone's working consciousness and unconscious, rather than the special and pathological purview of one "race"; "madness" is recast as "psychopathology," a current running through everyday life— part of, one might say, "everybody's autobiography." Freud, in other words, takes what is Other and universalizes it, not as a way of robbing Jews/we Others of their specialness but instead, as the Jewish orchestrator of theory, to give the Jewish gift (in a bit of noblesse oblige) to the world, alerting it to its own unplumbed resources of wit, imagination, and magical logic.

On the other end of the century's first half, on the other side of the cultural loss comprising the Holocaust, Euro-Jewish anthropologists like Franz Boas and Melville Herskovits could no longer be naive or even fearfully premonitory about the potentially genocidal implications of their chosen science. After World War II their task became, rather than building the social sciences, rescuing the reputation of their now-tarnished-beyond-mere speculation discipline: its assumptions, methodologies, and responsibilities.

I opened this essay with the egregious typographical error that concludes anthropologist Melville Herskovits' tribute to his mentor Franz Boas, an error that reveals the anxiety that plagued Jewish social scientists of the early twentieth century. In the passage I cited earlier and repeat here, which is meant to be the climax of an appeal to ethical responsibility, he concludes that the social scientist has two duties: "As a scientist, the anthropologist studies his problem and publishes his results. With other scientists, he seeks the answer to this basic ethical problem, as yet unsolved, of how to ensure that his findings are used by those who would direct them toward ends inimical to the canons of morality of the scientific tradition within which he works." Though Herskovits writes in the 1950s, he points to the care with which progressive social scientists like Boas had to position themselves even before the Nazi decimation. Placing his ultimate faith in scientific objectivity, Herskovits describes the perversion of the "science" of anthropometry to enable rationales for fascism: the "cephalic index," the famous head-shape index, was "transmuted [from a "simple device to further the quantitative analysis of differences in physical type"] into a qualitative expression to designate a presumably superior race, first called Teutonic, then Nordic, and still later Aryan" (104). He then cites another problem, that of the destruction of indigenous cultures, a phenomenon now called "ethnicide" brought about by (Western) people with advanced technology, among whom the ethnographer can count him/herself, even with the intentions of the indigenous ones' material well-being.

Both Herskovits and Boas were towering figures in the development of American anthropology; both considered themselves firmly in the tradition of anthropoetrics and "physical anthropology," though they are now known more for their work in African-American and Native American culture respectively. Boas's influence reached across disciplines: in literary studies, he is perhaps best known for having encouraged his student Zora Neale Hurston to collect folk materials from her own ethnic group. Herskovits, whose students included Katherine Dunham, whose revolutionary choreography drew heavily on traditional Afro-Caribbean dance, is pivotal in arguing for recognition of an African diaspora culture that included preslavery, West-African elements. Though it has come under critique and revision in contemporary diaspora studies, this project is acknowledged to be a quite consciously anti-racist attempt to establish a preexisting culture for a people cast in popular discourse as atavistic and cultureless.

Chronologically, Gertrude Stein wrote the works collected posthumously as *Painted Lace and Other Pieces: 1914-1937* between the eras of Weininger's wild popularity and the postwar reckoning of the humanistic sciences and the Jews who participated in them. Though written well beyond the period of her early enthusiasm for Weininger's book (which was published when she was still living in Baltimore) and after she had definitively left the field of psychology, *Painted Lace* evinces a preoccupation with nationalism, race/religion/ethnicity, gender, and sexuality, and, most importantly, the way writing and language inform and/or "unmean" these social categories. The volume's governing metaphor, painted lace, moreover, serves as a slightly defamiliarized image of alphabetic writing on a page.

I have learned that one dear colleague, whose anthropological work treats American Jews, characterizes my work as addressing "Jews who are hated by other Jews." "Bad" Jews? Like Stein, Lenny Bruce, myself, and my dear elusive father the head-measurer? Like Weininger? Rest assured that I have no love for the latter, though the pathos of his tragic vision and life have a chrysalis-like cachet that seals him from the utter contempt he would have merited had he "successfully" "transcended" his "Jewishness." But the pathetic nature of his one saving grace (in addition, perhaps, to his theory of universal bisexuality, which Freud made famous) meets its match in Gertrude Stein's assertive appropriation of his damning characteristics of Jewish men and all women; though Stein's Jewishness has many times been dismissed as a minor aspect of her life and work, and her qualifications as a "good Jew" many times challenged, it simply cannot be argued that she was ashamed or conflicted about her status as a Jew, though often her work questions what exactly being a "Jew" means. That she, like Freud and Weininger, was a secular Jew is quite obvious; that she, like Freud and

Weininger, held a (then considered liberal) assimilationist position, could be argued for or against; that she, like Freud and unlike Weininger, enjoyed being Jewish is, I believe, palpably demonstrable.

I have written elsewhere of Stein's affirmative, though only symbolic, use of Yiddish (as I read her title "Yet Dish") as a metaphor for modernist language use and sensibility. I use the qualifying phrase "only symbolic" because Stein, as a German Jew, probably never spoke Yiddish (though Alice, as a Hungarian Jew, may have; Stein called her "my little Hebrew," indicating that she may have felt Alice to be "more Jewish" than herself), and she certainly didn't use Yiddish phrases in her work; she uses, rather, the *idea* of Yiddish as a flexible, makeshift emergency-condition collage(n) that stretches across the homelands and host lands, history and geography. To conflate Czeslaw Milosz's phrase that "language is the only homeland" and Jonathan Boyarin's image of the book as a portable homeland, Stein creates makeshift homelands in books comprised of language that is not stable, but portable, mobile, motile. In other words, language for Stein is not the safe haven it may be for Milosz, but it enacts the instability that necessarily informs a Jewish notion of home. Through this type of practice, I would claim, Stein valorizes verbal styles—repetition, circularity, "imprecision," unconventional syntactic and semantic constructions—that were despised as primitive and that were literally thought to mark the speaker or writer as less than fully human. As Daniel Boyarin has written, it is considered a religious obligation in Jewish intellectual tradition to push language—both production and interpretation of—to its limits. While Stein is not, obviously, religious, her practice demonstrates the secularization of this tenet with regard to production; Freud's oeuvre amply instantiates its interpretive aspect. (In *Q.E.D.*, the Stein character asserts, "I have the failing of my tribe. I believe in the sacred right of conversation even when it is a monologue" [57]). Also, I feel compelled to draw attention to her championing of the "Old Testament" as a model for "new" (experimental) American writing because of its stylistic tendency toward praxis in "Lecture II: Narration." Erich Auerbach makes much the same point in *Mimesis*, which is generally acknowledged to have been written in response to the Holocaust he was surviving in Turkey—and, interestingly, complicity is not a charge commonly leveled at him as it is at Stein, who made her plea for the Old Testament's centrality to Western culture in 1935.

At the same time, however, Stein's apprehension of the instability of language (and the instability of her concerted experiments in language use) and of domicile does not have the catastrophizing angst of a Weininger, who understood psycho-linguistic flux, polyvocality, multiple identity, and diffuse proliferation as atavistic and profoundly detrimental to the progress of a rational humanity. "The psychological contents of the Jewish mind are always double or multiple," writes Weininger. "There are always before him two or many possibilities, where the Aryan, although he sees as widely, feels himself limited in his choice. I think that the idea of Judaism consists in this want of reality, this absence of any fundamental relation to the thing-in-and-for-itself.... He can never make himself one with anything—never enter into any real relationships" (321-22). For him this was tragic; Jews (and women) were the ultimate negation of all that Man could and should be, and this nadir of human potential was bodied forth in language use, which is the medium of exchange in human relations. For Stein, the instability of identity, or its illusory nature, permitted community, social being-in-flux, and relationality to flourish and create new ways of apprehending reality as non-possessive: "I am I because my little dog knows me. The figure wanders on alone .... The person and the dog are there and the dog is there and the person is there and where oh where is their identity, is the identity there anywhere ("Identity A Poem" 71). Knowing that for Stein "there"-ness is a suspect category, one can understand this as a challenge rather than a plaint; the poem, the first sentence of which functions as a kind of talisman sentence for Stein, becomes a treatise on the difference between "entity" (the unfixability of an apprehended "other"/object/being) and "identity" (a need to be fixed, recognized, and given meaning by an other). For Stein, making oneself One with anything, recognizing something in and for itself (whatever that may be), would be the kiss of death—as it was for Weininger.

Dis Playst Readings

The phrase "Painted Lace" serves as title for Volume V of Stein's unpublished writings written during and after, and much affected by, World War I. It is also the name of a piece within that volume. The phrase offers a marvelous metaphor for the sense of redundancy-that-is-not-redundant, gilding the lily, "independent embroidery" (the title of another poem in the volume), a sense of performative excess that is, nonetheless, not expendable. Yet another title in that volume, "Emp Lace," combines the two phrases and simultaneously fractures the word "emplace(ment/meant)," whose militaristic positionality in untenable in a nomadic, free-range, exilic language style implied by lace, by "independent embroidery." What can "emp lace" mean? Caveat emptor: language as commodity, as excuse for word-warfare, is being "unmeant," emp-tied and untied, loosened like lace that lets the light through,

like a writing we can't read straight and shouldn't if we want in on the
shaggy dog joke, the endless yarns spun by an a-mused, Fate/fé/friend-of-
Faÿ/ lady-fairy who never cuts that thread after all. In the art of "lace,"
threads derive their aesthetic power from interplay with "negative" space,
emptiness (which Weininger claims to be the essence, insofar as there is one,
of both Jews—"the absolute Jew is devoid of a soul" [313]—and women),
just as Steinian non-sense derives its power to "unmean" from the rigidly
semantical context of most discursive forms, including that of social science,
our special concern here, and that science's relation to the "Jewish question."
In lacing language, Stein ties the "(k)not" that Herskovits forgot and that
Weininger fought.

Likewise, "Painted Lace" splits, opens, enlaces, and aerates Place by
interjecting a space and the extra lace of "ainted" letters. "Ainted"
elaborates *and* negates ungrammatically in a stage aside (P-lace is still there,
though displaced); Stein is "Arthur[/author(ing)] a Grammar" (*How to Write*
37). Decentered? You bet. Weininger's worst fears flaunted: himself, the
Jewish homosexual, in drag, camping it up, reveling in his/her effects. "I'm
a Jew, how 'bout u?" Stein teases Wein's ghost, by performing her tainted
JEWOMANISH writing in calm, experimental tones. "What happens," the
Jewoman scientist asks, "when we separate these two letters?" Oy, such cold
experimentation, treating language as if it were dead matter: Jews excel in
the field of chemistry, says Weininger, because "they cling naturally to the
matter, and expect to find the solution of everything in its properties" (315).
Unlike Goethe's, the greatest genius of Weininger's imagining, Stein's work
is not about Feelings, not about individual self-consciousness developing
ethically. *Vey iz mir!* It doesn't track like the transparent thoughts of the
male Aryan, O mighty hunter He, following the lettered spoor of The Great
Idea to its Godly punctum, a humble manger that is the origin of all meaning.
Instead, the Fat Lady's text winds around and around, has no beginning and
no end, not even any middle or edge. It's all marginalia to itself, Talmudic
bordering on borders, embroidery that has taken off from an always-already
infinite regress of no regrets and plenty of RSVPs.

As its name suggests, the section of *Painted Lace* entitled "Voice Lessons
and Calligraphy" addresses, among other subjects, writing style,
composition, the relationship between orality and graphology, domesticity
and the "feminine" arts. By presenting both media (speaking and writing) in
terms of refined, mannered mastery of a relatively old-fashioned (and thus
cosmetic/frivolous) "finishing school" type of art, Stein foregrounds the
artificiality, the *made*-ness (constructedness, as we might say now), of both

speech and writing, anticipating Derridean controversy and placing herself in the stream of the latter's argument, that is, in accord with his challenge to the supremacy and presumed anteriority of "the Voice." The section opens with "Independent Embroidery," which phrase operates, as I have suggested above, as a kind of governing trope for "Jewomanish" language use: diffuse, elaborative, inauthentic, and defective, according to Weiningerian Austro-liberal values.

Within this section, a short poem called "The Reverie of the Zionist" concludes:

"I saw all this to prove that Judaism should be a question of religion.
Don't talk about race. Race is disgusting if you don't love your country.
I don't want to go to Zion.
This is an expression of Shem." (94)

Insofar as Judaism is a race, race should be uncoupled from nationalism; the notion that countries should be the provenance or teleological punctum or particular ethnicities is abhorrent to Stein, who loves living in France and also, from a distance, at least claims to love America but has no similar feelings about Zion. Some have read this piece as Stein's repudiation of her Jewishness; however, the argument that Jews did not constitute a "race" was a popular one among progressive Jews in the interbellum period, Boas and Herskovits among them. Concerned about the anti-Semitic repercussions of how National Socialism had scientized (racialized) the Jewish question, they took the position that Jews should not be persecuted on the basis of race and, in order to argue this, attempted to demonstrate that Jews were not a racial group.

Moreover, in line with these secular Jews who on the one hand were not particularly observant but on the other hand did not want to be perceived/persecuted as a race, the last line suggests that the foregoing ought to be a legitimate opinion to hold *as a Jew*. The piece appears to be shot through with contradictions: the "reverie" of the Zionist is anti-Zion, Stein deliberately distances herself from some Jews ("Can we believe that all Jews are these") while claiming the right to speak as a Jew, and so forth. It must be remembered that the word "reverie" may have had negative overtones for Stein, who stubbornly resisted any charges of mysticism in her work, and who saw herself as a phenomenological empiricist, tracking the minutiae of the changes of human mind for the pleasure of it—a disinterested scientist. Thus the Zionist is indulging in pipe dreams; Zionism is the opiate of the Jewish masses.

The piece also has in it some of the anxiety betrayed by the error in Herskovits' book which may not have been his error at all, but that of a typesetter or a copy-editor (one Jewish colleague even suggested to me that an anti-Semitic publisher may have purposefully allowed the error to stand—this seems far-fetched to me, but the fact that someone even had the idea indicates the depth of ostensibly assimilated Jews' fears): how to "rationalize" a situation whose irrationality threatens to (and did) overwhelm and exterminate an entire culture? The apparent contradictions also enact the internal heterogeneity, the contentious pluralism that comprises the Jewish interpretive community. These concerns about the nature of race and its relation to geography run throughout the rest of the volume, particularly in "Landscapes and Geography: 1925-1934," in which the words "natural" and "national" are juxtaposed (209), and in which the ideological manipulation of social categories such as matrilineality, difference, and race/religion are subject to inquiry:

"Can a Christian father have a Christian mother.
    Yes.
    Can a Christian mother have a Christian father.
    Yes.
    It is very necessary that natural phenomena are usual.
    It is very much it is very much used it is used very much in that way.
    There are three Negroes they do not at all resemble one another.
    Moreover there are three Negroes Negroes and women five of them and they do not at all resemble one another. It is not at all astonishing that one seeing them and seeing them knows very well then that it is another thing." (202-203).

When Stein writes "Authorize natural phenomena" (215), natural phenomena are understood to be that which can be written—that is, constructed creatively, as in "arthur a grammar." Nationalism and claims of naturalism are both systems of meaning created by and not anterior to the "human mind," "never having been meant to be Natural Phenomena" (207) as commonly understood—that is, as bio-essential hardwiring. However, "Natural Phenomena" also include queer girl sex: "Aroused and dedicated to natural phenomena ... pearly and seized" (207). What has been declared deviant by racial nationalist logic is as natural a phenomenon as landscapes, geography, and writing. That is, it is all authored, all emptied, all painted lace, all vocal exercise.

One could say that Herskovits espouses Weiningerian teleology when he appeals to the twin virtues of hard science and humane citizenship, those golden sons of the Western metaphysics of unity, that Enlightenment legacy that ended, as he knew but did not want to know, in Auschwitz. Someone's typographical error that put him in the "wrong" camp was not as much of a wandering as one might have wished for. While there is, obviously, a vast difference between racist and anti-racist anthropology (and its cousins philosophy, "characterology," psychology, sociology, etc.), between Weininger and Herskovits, they have a common ideology that anxiety-induced lapses can throw into relief. Stein's language experiments eviscerate the truth claims of the modern(ist) achievements—rationalism and liberal morality—that the philosopher Weininger and the scientist Herskovits continue to cling to. Her work, however, neither collapses in despairing self-immolation nor issues prescriptives in a tinny, would-be heroic resistance to history. Relatively early in her career, it seems, Stein abandoned the idea of progress to which her two coreligionists were tightly bound—but she did not do so in a gesture of nihilism. And while thematically her writing continues to participate in their concerns—concerns about her own survival—her writing process and practice has already created an escape route, a "line of flight." Her work doesn't strive to get "there"—no landscape, nation, or race except in words, and even those words are not a place but a naughty, knotty emp lace.

Works Cited

Beller, Steven. "Otto Weininger as Liberal?" *Jews and Gender: Responses to Otto Weininger*. Ed. Nancy A. Harrowitz and Barbara Hyams. Philadelphia: Temple U P, 1995. 91-101.

Damon, Maria. "Gertrude Stein's Doggerel 'Yiddish': Women, Dogs, and Jews." *The Dark End of the Street: Margins in American Vanguard Poetry*. Minneapolis: U of Minnesota P, 1993. 202-235.

Fishberg, Maurice. *The Jews: A Study in Race and Environment*. London: Walter Scott, 1911.

Freud, Sigmund. *Jokes and Their Relation to the Unconscious*. Trans. James Strachey. New York: Norton, 1960.

Gilman, Sander. "Weininger and Freud: Race and Gender in the Shaping of Psychoanalysis." *Jews and Gender: Responses to Otto Weininger*. Ed. Nancy A. Harrowitz and Barbara Hyams. Philadelphia: Temple U P, 1995. 103-120.

_____. *The Jew's Body*. New York: Routledge, 1991.

_____. *Jewish Self-hatred: Anti-Semitism and the Hidden Language of the Jews*. Baltimore: Johns Hopkins U P, 1986.

Harrowitz, Nancy A., and Barbara Hyams. "A Critical Introduction to the History of Weininger Reception." *Jews and Gender: Responses to Otto Weininger*. Philadelphia: Temple U P, 1995. 3-20.

Herskovits, Melville. *Franz Boas: The Science of Man in the Making*. New York: Scribner's, 1953.

Stein, Gertrude. "Identity a Poem." *What are Masterpieces*. New York: Pitman, 1940. 71-79.

_____. "Lecture 2: Narration." *The Poetics of the New American Poetry*. Ed. Donald Allen. New York: Grove P, 1973. 104-12.

_____. *The Making of Americans*. New York: Harcourt Brace, 1934.

_____. *Painted Lace and Other Pieces (1914-1917)*. New Haven: Yale UP, 1955.

_____. *Q.E.D., Fernhurst, and Other Early Writings*. New York: Liveright, 1971. 51-133.

Weininger, Otto. *Sex and Character*. Authorized and anonymous translation from the 6th German edition. London: Heinneman, 1906.

Modern Fiction Studies, Fall 1996.

"Gertrude Stein and the Lost Ark."

Brenda Wineapple

Gertrude Stein is one of those renowned American authors about whom, it's commonly supposed, everything is known—and not just because she's a veritable household name in households that have never read her. A woman who fixed her eye firmly on posterity, she even saved envelope flaps she'd doodled on and, in the 1930s, began to dump a lifetime's accumulated paper into cartons to send to America, where it was sorted and deposited, through Thornton Wilder's ministration, at Yale University's Beinecke Rare Book and Manuscripts Library.

With so much available on Stein, published and unpublished, by her and about her, I hardly expected to find anything new—no biographical equivalent of the smoking gun—when I began research for a book on Gertrude and her brother Leo. A new perspective, yes, with an interpretation that differs from those of previous biographers: that was my aim, though every biographer secretly dreams of the lost ark. Nor did I expect to come upon anything concrete to help resolve what for me were key, and nagging, questions about Stein's opinion of women, herself first and foremost, or of women in general. Was she the feminist many of her supporters presume she was? And if she was, early or late, then why did she assign to Alice B. Toklas the entertainment of the wives while she gabbed with the other so-called geniuses?

Letting these questions take me where they would, I landed quite often elbow-deep in the private affairs of several other lives. And then, just when I worried most that I had crawled out on a tangent, I came upon an amazing essay written by Gertrude Stein in her youth, before she performed her feats of literature, and long before she saved her papers.

"Gertrude Gertrude remember the cause of women," one of her friends in medical school reportedly pleaded when Stein forswore the coveted Johns Hopkins degree. The cause of women was all right, said Stein in *The Autobiography of Alice B. Toklas*, it just happened not to be her cause.

When I began my research six years ago, I knew that one of Gertrude's earliest and most unmemorable writings about women is an odd tale she folded into her nine-hundred-page magnum opus, *The Making of Americans*. Originally called "Fernhurst: The History of Philip Redfern, A Student of the Nature of Women," the story is based on the tumultuous erotic career of Alfred LeRoy Hodder. The dashing Hodder, aka the Byron of Bryn Mawr College, had been an instructor of literature there when he fell in love with another celebrated teacher, Mamie Gwinn. Gwinn just happened to be the companion of the college president, Martha Carey Thomas.

To Stein aficionados, the importance of this little *roman à clef* lay mainly in its reflection of Stein's lesbian imbroglio with, coincidentally, two Bryn Mawr graduates. Beyond that, there was not much to say. Dwarfed by the huge, Talmudic novel into which it made a forgettable contribution, "Fernhurst" was apprentice work, tucked away in a corner of the Beinecke, nothing more.

But when I first read the holograph version of the story, copied neatly in Stein's hand on the pages of a tidy red notebook, I discovered a startling polemic about women and women's education. A young, preachy Stein here argues that women who cling to the "intellectual furniture obtained at their college" naively assume that their "power was as a man's." "I am for having women learn what they can," Stein was willing to concede in the early pages of "Fernhurst," "but not ... to believe that a man's work is suited to them because they have mastered a boy's education. In short ... the great mass of the world's women should content themselves with attainting to womanhood."

Such a blunt view about women's ultimate place—the home—is the most puzzling element of "Fernhurst," itself a strange amalgam of romance, diatribe, and truncated feminism. Why, for instance, did Stein spend almost one-third of this otherwise old-fashioned love story arguing against Carey Thomas and Mamie Gwinn's New Woman, the liberated creature now admitted to the colleges, professions, and equal partnerships previously closed to her? Wasn't Stein herself a New Woman? Hadn't she been an exemplary student at Radcliffe who published two articles in the *Psychological Review* before graduating and who then spent four years at Johns Hopkins Medical School readying herself for a profession in which women were absolute anomalies? Yet in "Fernhurst" she argued against all this. What's more, she used the mysterious Alfred Hodder as her protagonist, casting him as a "student of the nature of women," which is how she had characterized herself: a fledgling psychiatrist specializing in female complaints.

To date, nothing had been written about Hodder except by Gertrude's biographers, who typically suggest she had been acquainted with him at college, perhaps through her brother Leo. The files of the Harvard University archives, however, show that Hodder had left Cambridge by the time Gertrude arrived and Leo had hardly known him there. I decided to try my luck at Princeton University, where Mamie Gwinn's and Alfred Hodder's papers are kept, to determine, if I could, why he fascinated Stein, and why Gwinn and Thomas annoyed her. Warned I'd be wasting my time—there were no Steins among the Hodders—I nonetheless boarded a sweaty gray commuter train bound for southern New Jersey in the stubborn heat of June 1993.

I walked the short distance from the train station to Princeton's Firestone Library, where I plunged into dusty boxes filled with tiny sheets written in Alfred Hodder's microscopic scrawl, hundreds of letters sent to Mamie Gwinn. His was a roué's past, to be sure. Born in Ohio in 1866, Hodder as a very young man had married a dying woman in what was, he later insisted, was a "*mariage blanc*"; he claimed sexual relations would have killed her. (She died soon after, notwithstanding). Consoling himself in the arms of a modern young pianist who practiced free love, by 1889 Hodder was a member of the Colorado bar and in New York en route to Harvard University, where he'd been accepted as a doctoral student. His lover, Jessie Donaldson, sailed to Germany to study music.

A year later, Hodder abruptly left Harvard, resigning a coveted fellowship in order to work in Germany under the noted psychologist Wilhelm Wundt. Or so he said. In actuality, Jessie had written that she was pregnant, and, gentleman that he was, Hodder had rushed to her side. According to Donaldson, he married her; according to Hodder, chivalry had its limits: the pregnancy was a hoax, and common-law was all he would muster—which, in a relatively short time, produced a child anyway. And though Gertrude Stein liked to boast that she was William James's pet, only Alfred Hodder could say his daughter was born, quite literally, under a Jamesian roof.

It was a perpetually generous William James who helped Hodder land the position at Bryn Mawr, to which he went alone. When Jessie arrived eight weeks later, he consented to bring her around, albeit resentfully, since he was already smitten with Mamie Gwinn. To Gwinn, he poured out his heart in bursts of familiarity evidently unusual for Mamie, generally considered a remote and spectral figure swelling among untrodden ways, and mostly with Carey Thomas. For in their youth, these two brazen women had gone off to Europe unchaperoned, settling in Zurich while Thomas earned her Ph.D. Back in the United States, Thomas was soon appointed Bryn Mawr's first dean, and Mamie Gwinn, who shared Thomas's commitment to women's emancipation, professional opportunity, and educational attainment, was inducted as one of its first graduate students, earning her own doctorate in 1888. As a teacher, reciting Ruskin, Pater, and Swinburne, she seemed Bryn Mawr incarnate: the sovereign female scholar delivered from the affairs of vulgar men. Until, that is, she met Alfred Hodder.

It would have been easy to accept the standard interpretation, that Gertrude Stein, after learning this much about Gwinn, Thomas, and Hodder, used the story to speak of her own early love affair, another sorry triangle that involved one of Gwinn's disciples. Still, I also regarded "Fernhurst" as Stein's anser to the Bryn Mawr creed and the women representing it, with Hodder acting as the foil who brought their lofty goals to wrack. Yet appealing as it was, this theory did not mine the raw passion with which Stein condemned women's education, or at least its outcome and its aim.

Day after day, I returned to the retro-Gothic pastoral of Princeton University, sat at the long refectory-like table under a green-shaded reading lamp, and removed my bracelet (a private ritual), resting my arms before me as I prepared for another day of note taking. I read on. In 1898, Hodder left Bryn Mawr—under a predictable cloud—to settle in Greenwich Village, renting rooms in a building ironically named the Benedick (Bachelor), near Washington Square. His passion for Mamie Gwinn now fully and physically requited, he intended to write a novel, which he did, about the changing relations of the sexes. He would call it *The New Americans*; it was a book that I knew Gertrude liked.

Weary, I looked up from the table, wondering if I had strayed too far from the Steins, seduced as I was by this tangled affair. I could resolve nothing through Carey Thomas, Mamie Gwinn, or even Barnard and Mary Berenson, who were related to Carey Thomas on Mary's side. I knew there was a real Fernhurst, which was the English residence of Mary Berenson's parents, and I knew that during desultory afternoons there, Hodder was a juicy topic. Leo Stein visited Fernhurst and, later, so did Gertrude. But none of this definitively explained her reaction to the Hodder affair, never mind the New Woman or Mamie Gwinn. Yet for some reason I couldn't stop looking through those dusty boxes.

Ultimately, it was Leo Stein who provided the vital connection between his sister and Hodder, and with that established, discoveries tumbled forth. In 1899, Leo often fled Baltimore, where he was then living with Gertrude, and hung about the offices of Lincoln Steffens' newspaper, *The Commercial Advertiser*, to which Alfred Hodder contributed an occasional article. I read Hodder's journalism and then, returning to my boxes (I was by now quite proprietary), discovered that Hodder frequently whiled away his evenings in the local tap rooms on the city's back streets. He was joined by Leo's cousin Fred Stein and a man named Howard Gans—the only man in whom Hodder had trusted his secrets. And Gans and Fred Stein were Leo's best friends.

Leo quit America in 1900 for Europe. His sister, however, remained behind, shuttling more and more often between Baltimore and Manhattan, often staying with cousin Fred and Fred's sister (who later married Gans). She must have joined their merry band of friends, or so I hoped, more eager than ever for connections. For I had now arrived at a crucial but shadowy period in Gertrude's own career. She had just arranged a postgraduate internship for herself—itself an unknown fact I'd uncovered elsewhere—but in the spring of 1901, she bizarrely flunked obstetrics and could not take her degree. The event baffled those closest to her, so confident were they of her success. Imagine their surprise when she subsequently refused whatever second chance Hopkins offered and then blithely walked away, never to look back.

The reasons have remained a mystery. No original documents announce Stein's state of mind, no letters or even any second- or third-hand testimony explain Gertrude Stein's flight from medicine or the succeeding interval when she dangled between a botched medical career and a zealous literary one. All we have, really, is Stein's dismissal of the whole episode in *The Autobiography*, accompanied by her friend's dispirited entreaty, "remember the cause of women."

I took one last look at Hodder's letters and datebooks and read with a start that Gertrude Stein had indeed remembered the cause of women. This is what she told her new confidante, Hodder himself, who was so interested in what "Miss Stein" had to say that, much to my endless delight, he left a record of the conversation.

November 22, 1901. "Miss Stein" was at a "jolly" dinner last night at the Café Liberty. Miss Stein "discoursed" on Hodder's novel *The New Americans.*

In Princeton, the month was now July. It was late in the day and the temperature soared. Inside, the room seemed airless.

Stein and Hodder were each impressed enough with the other to note their meeting. Stein in "Fernhurst" and Hodder in his daily dispatch. I read on with excited, mordant fascination, sometimes catching the phrase or slang of a lost world that had, for a moment, cracked open, transporting me back ninety years. Young men and women crowded about dining tables, and, over the clank of silverware, Alfred Hodder politely told Gertrude Stein he appreciated her candor about *The New Americans*, in which she thought the women were inadequately portrayed. Gertrude Stein was talking, responding, eating dinner in a downtown restaurant, suddenly alive.

At the Benedick, Alfred Hodder sat down to write his nightly missive to Mamie Gwinn. Miss Stein was skeptical about the New Woman, he explained to Mamie, although she said that, while at Radcliffe, she and her friends had believed in the equality of the sexes as if it had been a religion. Medical school had taught her otherwise: a woman could not succeed without the help, the paternalism, in fact, of men.

I paused to imagine Gwinn's boiling reply. Later, I was able to find it, but at the time I pressed on, interested only in what Hodder recounted of Stein's conversation. I paged through more of his letters.

January 5, 1902. Another dinner, another conversation. Even if women were more intelligent, Miss Stein had insisted, men were more capable. They got things done; women just got discouraged.

February 1902. Gertrude Stein gave Alfred Hodder a typewritten essay. He was sending it to Mamie Gwinn. Why would he do that, I asked myself, and then the full realization broke: Gertrude Stein had given Alfred Hodder an essay. That meant she had written an essay, typed an essay, put it in a large envelope perhaps, carried it to New York on the train. It was an essay she typed, an essay on women, an essay no Stein enthusiast, past or present, had ever seen, catalogued, read, or heard of. Could this be true? Where was the envelope? Where was the essay?

I considered. Mamie Gwinn would never have saved it. For who was Gertrude Stein to her? An annoying upstart, a throwback. But naturally I had to look, and when no such essay appeared among Mamie Gwinn's papers, even disguised as something else, I was not particularly surprised. Nonetheless, I filled out another library slip—this last time to fetch a box of miscellany. It arrived, and I rifled through the nondescript folders within, one by one.

Gertrude Stein had given Alfred Hodder an essay. Hodder had given it to Mamie Gwinn. Mamie Gwinn more or less gave it to me.

I pulled out of one of the unmarked folders eight typed legal sheets unsigned and, at first glance, innocuous. They bore the beguiling title "Degeneration in American Women." I leafed through. Penned at the top of each sheet was a page number. There were also corrections, several on a page, written in a clean, legible script. All these were sharply familiar. I had seen Stein's cursive on hundreds of manuscripts, letters, and cards.

I tried to regain my bearings. Corrections in Stein's hand, while telling, did not in themselves prove this paper her brainchild. Nonchalantly, I asked the young woman at the front desk if I could have the pages photocopied. I felt flushed and unexplainably furtive. When the copy was made, I rushed out of the library, leaving my bracelet on the table.

"Degeneration in American Women" was likely written for publication, perhaps in the *Journal of the American Medical Association*, for it begins as a reply to the quasi-medical study by George J. Engelmann, "The Increasing Sterility of American Women," which was published in that same journal on October 5, 1901. Dr. Engelmann, it seems, had deplored the falling birthrate among white, educated, middle-class American women; so did the author of "Degeneration," who sent the New Woman packing: "It will only be when women succeed in relearning the fact that the only serious business of life in which they cannot be entirely outclassed by the male is that of child bearing that they will once more look with respect upon their normal and legitimate function." Here was the sentiment, almost verbatim, of "Fernhurst." With a twist. Biology was destiny all right, and women were the losers in the battle of the sexes—except in the matter of childbirth.

Like "Fernhurst," the targets of "Degeneration" were the Carey Thomases and Mamie Gwinns of the women's movement. "Degeneration" condemned their overeducated tendency to mistake women's "cleverness and intelligence for effective capacity for the work of the world"—an ivory tower dictum that shattered on contact with the "real business of life" where "the male code is the only possible one." Stein had told Hodder she didn't much like it, though nothing could be done. Such was nature.

But was "Degeneration" actually written by Gertrude Stein? In the furious weeks that followed, I ran to libraries, inspected sources, returned to tale. Dates coincided; references coincided. I checked the typeface of "Degeneration" against that of the 1899 Stein paper "The Value of College Education for Women" (also unsigned), which Dr. Claribel Cone, its recipient, had the courtesy to identify and date for posterity. Mamie Gwinn had not been so kind and yet, judging from the typeface alone—which matched—it looked as if she who loathed Stein's essay had, for reasons of her own, preserved it.

Evidence was mounting. And not just external evidence: there was, for instance, the matter of style, which suggested I found the very first, perhaps unintentional, example of Stein's signature preoccupation with rhythm, as well as her habit of omitting punctuation, particularly commas; her customary, if restless, string of independent clauses, her passion for participles and the repetitive structures she looped with a biblical *and*. Even the tendency to run phrases together seemed to anticipate her later, more deliberate linguistic adventures. The leitmotif of *The Making of Americans* literally appeared, word for word, in "Degeneration": the notion of "right living" with its celebration of the "normal functions of living, walking, talking, thinking, being, eating and drinking."

At Princeton again, I hunted for Mamie Gwinn's reaction, if any, to the essay Hodder had sent her. As I suspected, Gwinn had been appalled but, fortunately, not struck dumb. Her angry reply was yet more confirmation, for it countermanded the arguments of Stein's essay virtually word for word. "Degeneration" was indeed the paper Mamie Gwinn despised. By now the identity of the author was incontrovertible—it was Gertrude Stein.

A disillusioned, reactionary, and defiant Gertrude Stein had appeared before me one scorching New Jersey afternoon, stilted, full of bluff, and holier-than-thou. This Stein was canny, too, for the title of her essay, "Degeneration in American Women," summoned both the pseudo-scientific jargon of eugenics, a late-nineteenth-century passion I knew she rather enjoyed, and that of the sexologists, for whom biological degeneracy spelled homoeroticism. Was this also Stein's meaning?

It's impossible to know for sure. Yet "Degeneration" was written when when she faced a series of crucial transformations, having given up one career for another in light of her recent failure at medical school and, what's more, having redefined her own sexuality in light of a recent and, despite its anguish, liberating lesbian love affair. The declamations of "Degeneration," then, make ironic sense, coming from one who had just abandoned medicine by failing obstetrics. By defining femininity in conventional terms and instructing women to return home, Stein restored their power, or thought she did, granting women a separate, uncontested sphere. But since she also equated the feminine with enslavement, she chose otherwise for herself; she elected the writer's life, not motherhood and, as a woman who loved other women, exempted herself from the rule of maternity she casually prescribed for others. "Of course it is not meant that there are not a few women in every generation who are exceptions to this rule," she declared, "but these exceptions are too rare to make it necessary to subvert the order of things in their behalf and besides if their need for some other method of expression is a real need there is very little doubt but that the opportunity of expression will be open to them." She was the exceptional woman whose need for expression was raw and real.

In this, "Degeneration" also augurs the announcement that would later offend many: Stein's almost flat assertion of her genius. It also, however, exposes her stake in it. Perhaps Stein had to do more than repudiate the future she urged on other women and go far beyond them. Perhaps that too is one wellspring of her remarkable drive. And perhaps, even, she had to reject America as well, soon to leave it far behind, the expatriate supreme.

Was Stein a feminist? "Degeneration" renders that question obsolete. Its author was brash, and rife with the conflicts in a mere woman would later conceal or convert muscle: she would never be a motherhood; she who would be canonized as one of the most creatively liberated women of the century counseled the mundane and conservative—but not for herself. And this lesbian Jew who loved democracy, inspiring women and men to discover themselves, also spoke a nativist language, urging white middle-class American women to submit to a round of putative or biological givens.

The paradoxes of "Degeneration" are the paradoxes of Gertrude Stein, neither radical nor philistine, feminist nor foul; in "Degeneration" she is a twenty-eight-year-old woman grappling with her life and on its threshold. She is alive, complex, jam-packed with contradiction—and the biographer's true find.

American Scholar, Fall 1997.

Bibliography

Aiken, Conrad. "We Ask for Bread." *The New Republic* 78 (4 April 1934): 219.

Alsop, Joseph, Jr. "Gertrude Stein on Writing." *The New York Herald-Tribune Books* 10 January 1937: 2.

Anderson, Sherwood. "Four American Impressions." *The New Republic* 32 (11 October 1922): 171.

"And She Triumphed in the Tragic Turnip Field!" *Cleveland (Ohio) Leader* 21 June 1914.

Armitage, Gilbert. "A Word on Gertrude Stein." *Oxford Magazine* 17 June 1926: 584.

Ashleigh, Charles. "Steinese Literature." *Chicago Evening Post* 7 August 1914.

Auden, W. H. "All About Ida." *The Saturday Review of Literature* 23 (22 February 1941): 8.

Barnes, Djuna. "Matron's Primer." *Contemporary Jewish Record* 8 (June 1945): 342-43.

Bechtel, Louise Seaman. "Gertrude Stein for Children." *The Horn Book* 15 (September 1939): 286-91.

Becker, May Lamberton. "Books for Young People." *The New York Herald-Tribune Books* 24 September 1939: 6.

Bodenheim, Maxwell. "To Gertrude Stein." *Poetry* 57 (December 1940): 193.

"Book Is a Book." *The New Yorker* 20 (19 February 1944): 18-19.

Brégy, Katherine. "War." *Commonweal* 32 (23 August 1940): 373.

"Briefly Noted." *The New Yorker* 22 (9 November 1946): 124.

"Briefly Noted: *Paris France* by Gertrude Stein." *The New Yorker* 16 (13 July 1940): 68.

Bromfield, Louis. "Gertrude Stein, Experimenter with Words." *The New York Herald-Tribune Books* 3 September 1933: 1, 2.

Burke, Kenneth. "The Impartial Essence." *The New Republic* 83 (3 July 1935): 227.

_____. "Two Brands of Piety." *The Nation* 138 (28 February 1934): 256-58.

Burton, Richard. "Posing." *Minneapolis Bellman* 17 October 1914: 5.

Buss, Kate. "The Writing of Gertrude Stein and *Geography and Plays*." *Voices* 2 (Summer 1923): 29-32.

Butcher, Fanny. "The Literary Spotlight." *Chicago Tribune* 11 August 1946: 4:9.

Canby, Henry Seidel. "Cheating at Solitaire." *The Saturday Review of Literature* 11 (17 November 1934): 290.

Cane, Melville. "Appeal to Gertrude." *The New Yorker* 10 (3 November 1934): 69.

Cerf, Bennett. "Trade Winds." *The Saturday Review* 25 (5 September 1942): 20.

Chamberlain, Dorothy. "Her France, Her Paris." *The New Republic* 103 (22 July 1940): 123-24.

Corbett, Sgt. Scott. "Give Me Land." *Yank* 2 (11 November 1945): 17.

Cowley, Malcolm. "Gertrude Stein, Writer or Word Scientist?" *The New York Herald-Tribune Weekly Book Review* 24 November 1946: 1.

Crawford, John W. "Incitement to Riot." *New York Call* 19 August 1923.

C., R. M. "Books, Books, Books." *The New Yorker* 8 (20 February 1932): 69-70.

Damon, Maria. "Gertrude Stein's Jewishness, Jewish Social Scientists, and the 'Jewish Question.'" *Modern Fiction Studies* 42 (Fall 1996): 489-506.

Davies, Hugh Sykes. "Books of the Quarter." *The Criterion* 15 (July 1936): 752-55.

D., K. "When Helen Furr Got Gay With Harold Moos." *Vanity Fair* 21 (October 1923): 27.

"Dr. Lowes Finds *Tender Buttons* Poetic Asparagus." *St. Louis Post-Dispatch* 29 March 1916.

Dodge, Mabel. "Speculations, or Post-Impressionism in Prose." *Arts and Decoration* 3 (March 1913): 173-74.

Eagleson, Harvey. "Gertrude Stein: Method in Madness." *Sewanee Review* 44 (April-June 1936): 164-77.

Elias, Robert H. "Letters: A Response to Maurice Zolotow." *Story* 10 (February 1937): 108-109.

Faÿ, Bernard. "A Rose is a Rose." *The Saturday Review of Literature* 10 (2 September 1933): 1-3.

"Fiction, But Not Novels." *Kansas City Star* 18 December 1909.

Flanner, Janet. "History Tramps Down the Champs-Elysées." *The New York Herald-Tribune Books* 23 June 1940: 1.

_____. "Letter from Paris." *The New Yorker* 22 (10 August 1946): 36-37.

"Flat Prose." *The Atlantic Monthly* 114 (September 1914): 430-32.

Fletcher, John Gould. "A Stone of Stumbling." *American Review* 5 (June 1935): 379-84.

Flint, F. Cudworth. "Contemporary Criticism." *Southern Review* 2 (Spring 1936): 208-13.

"Futurist Essays." *Los Angeles Times* 9 August 1914.

"A Futurist Novel." *Philadelphia Public Ledger* 10 April 1910.

Gannett, Lewis. "Books and Things." *The New York Herald-Tribune* 7 November 1934.

"Gertrude Stein." *New York City Call* 7 June 1914.

"Gertrude Stein in Critical French Eyes." *Literary Digest* 88 (6 February 1926): 58, 60-62.

"Gertrude Stein Interprets Accurately the National Political Situation." *Boston Herald* 25 March 1924.

"Gertrude Stein, Plagiary." *New York Evening Sun* 13 June 1914.

Gold, Michael. "Gertrude Stein: A Literary Idiot." *Change the World!* London: Lawrence & Wishart, 1936. 23-26.

Goldberg, Isaac. "A Critic Has a Headache." *Haldeman-Julius Weekly* 1 October 1927.

Haldane, Charlotte. "Gentlemen Prefer." *English Review* 62 (May 1936): 528-30.

Hemingway, Ernest. "The True Story of My Break with Gertrude Stein." *The New Yorker* 2 (12 February 1927): 23.

"Hogarth Essays." *Times Literary Supplement* 25 November 1926: 848.

Hubbell, Lindley Williams. "A Letter to Gertrude Stein." *Pagany* 1 (Spring 1930): 37.

_____. "The Plain Edition of Gertrude Stein." *Contempo* 3 (25 October 1933): 1, 4.

Jones, Ruth Lambert. "A Visit from St. Nicholas." *New York City Evening Post* 22 December 1923.

K., A. S. "The Same Book from Another Standpoint." *Little Review* 4 (July 1914): 63.

K., G. E. "Miss Stein Applies Cubism to Defenseless Prose." *Baltimore Sun*
    25 August 1923.

Knickerbocker, William S. "Stunning Stein." *Sewanne Review* 4 (October-
    December 1933): 499.

Kreymborg, Alfred. "Gertrude Stein: Hoax and Hoaxtress." *The New York
    Telegraph* 7 March 1915: 6.

Krutch, Joseph Wood. "A Prepare for Saints." *The Nation* 138 (4 April
    1934): 396, 398.

Laughlin, James IV. "New Words for Old." *Story* 9 (December 1936): 105,
    107, 110.

Lerman, Leo. "A Wonderchild for 72 Years." *The Saturday Review* 29 (2
    November 1946): 17-18.

London, Blanche. "The Career of a Modernist." *New York Jewish Tribune*
    6 March 1931: 2, 6.

_____. "Gertrude Stein." *New Palestine* 16 (5 April 1929): 298-300.

Loy, Mina. "Communications: Gertrude Stein." *Transatlantic Review* 2.3
    (1924): 305-9.

_____. "Communications: Gertrude Stein (Continued)." *Transatlantic
    Review* 2.4 (1924): 427-30.

Mann, Klaus. "Two Generations." *Decision* 1 (May 1941): 71-74.

Marquis, Don. "Gertrude Is Stein, Stein Gertrude." *The New York Sun* 15
    October 1914: 10.

_____. "Gertrude Stein's Hints for the Table." *The New York Sun* 28 August
    1914: 6.

_____. "Gertrude Stein on the War." *The New York Sun* 2 October 1914:
    12.

_____. "The Golden Group." *The New York Sun* 26 March 1915: 10.

_____. "Taking Up Music in a Serious Way." *The New York Sun* 18
    January 1915: 10.

_____. "Thoughts of Hermione, a Modern Young Woman." *The New York
    Sun* 13 October 1914: 12.

_____. "Thoughts of Hermione." *The New York Sun* 13 March 1915: 6.

_____. "To G. S. and E. P." *The New York Sun* 3 October 1914: 6.

Marshall, Marguerite Mooers. "Futurist Man's Dress to Be a One-Piece
    Suit …" *Toledo (Ohio) Blade* 9 July 1914.

Mellquist, Jerome. "And Paris." *Commonweal* 33 (29 November 1940): 148.

Mencken, H. L. "A Cubist Treatise." *Baltimore Sun* 6 June 1914: 4.

_____. "Literary Survey." *Vanity Fair* 21 August 1923: 923.

Mongan, Agnes. "Stein on Picasso." *The Saturday Review of Literature* 19 (18 March 1939): 11.

Moore, Marianne. "Perspicuous Opacity." *The Nation* 143 (24 October 1936): 484, 486.

Nash, Ogden. "They Don't Speak English in Paris." *New York American* 22 March 1934.

Nathan, George Jean. "The Theatre: Stein on the Table." *Vanity Fair* 42 (May 1934): 49.

Norman, Sylva. "Words and Waste." *The Nation and Athenæum* 45 (13 April 1929): 52.

"Notable Piece of Realism." *Boston Globe* 18 December 1909.

O'Brien, Justin. "Miss Stein and France." *The Nation* 151 (27 July 1940): 76.

"Officer, She's Writing Again." *Detroit News* 6 June 1914.

"Our Own Polo Guide: The Game Explained à la Gertrude Stein." *The New York Sun* 13 June 1914.

Paul, Elliot H. "From a Litterateur's Notebook." *Chicago Tribune* (Paris Edition) 22 May 1927: 7.

Paulding, C. G. "Let Them Talk and Talk." *Commonweal* 44 (2 August 1946): 384-85.

"*Picasso*." *The Nation* 148 (29 April 1939): 508.

Porter, Katherine Anne. "Everybody is a Real One." *The New York Herald Tribune* 16 January 1927: 1-2.

Pulsifer, Harold T. "The Stein Songs and Poetry." *Outlook* 134 (6 June 1923): 139.

Rago, Henry. "Gertrude Stein." *Poetry* 69 (November 1946): 93-97.

Rascoe, Burton. "Self-Confidential." *The Saturday Review of Literature* 17 (4 December 1937): 11, 56.

Redman, Ben Ray. "The Importance of Being Earnest." *The Saturday Review of Literature* 28 (10 March 1945): 8, 30.

Reid, B. L. *Art By Subtraction: A Dissenting Opinion of Gertrude Stein.* Norman OK: U of Oklahoma P, 1958.

Rogers, Robert Emons. "New Outbreaks of Futurism." *Boston Transcript* 11 July 1914: 12.

Rönnebeck, Arnold. "Gertrude Was Always Giggling." *Books Abroad* 18 (October 1944): 3-7.

Schwartz, Delmore. "Gertrude Stein's Wars." *The Nation* 160 (24 March 1945): 339-40.

Seibel, Fred O. "Movie of a Man Trying to Read What Gertrude Stein Says About America." *Richmond Times Dispatch* 12 March 1935.

"The Shape of Things." *The Nation* 163 (10 August 1946): 142-43.

Sillen, Samuel. "Obituary of Europe and Gertrude Stein." *New Masses* 25 (7 December 1937).

Sitwell, Edith. "Miss Stein's Stories." *The Nation & The Athenæum* 33 (14 July 1923): 492.

Skinner, B. F. "Has Gertrude Stein a Secret?" *The Atlantic Monthly* 153 (January 1934): 50-57.

S., L. W., M. L. E., and L. S. E. "In Memoriam: Gertrude Stein, 1898." *Radcliffe Quarterly* 30 (August 1946): 21.

Smith, Harrison. "A Rose for Remembrance." *The Saturday Review* 29 (10 August 1946): 11.

S., R. "Crossword Puzzle." *The New York Sun* 30 October 1936.

Stimpson, Catharine R. "Gertrude Stein and the Lesbian Lie." *American Women's Autobiography*. Ed. Margo Culley. Madison: U of Wisconsin P, 1992. 152-66.

Sullivan, Frank. "The Autobiography of Alice B. Sullivan." *The New Yorker* 9 (1 July 1933): 13-14.

Swan, Nathalie. "Stein on Picasso." *The New Republic* 99 (5 July 1939): 259.

"*Three Lives*. By Gertrude Stein." *The Nation* 90 (20 January 1910): 65.

"*Three Lives*." *Washington (D. C.) Herald* 12 December 1909.

Troy, William. "A Note on Gertrude Stein." *The Nation* 137 (6 September 1933): 274-75.

"Two Futile Attempts to Rival the Style of Gertrude Stein." *Indianapolis (Indiana) News* 15 August 1923.

"*Useful Knowledge*." *New Statesman* 33 (13 April 1929): 22.

Van Vechten, Carl. "Gertrude Stein: An Epilogue." Syndicated Column. 7 November 1946. Rpt. in Bruce Kellner, "Baby Woojums in Iowa." *Books at Iowa* 26 (April 1977):3-18.

_____. "Gertrude Stein Memorial." 22 May 1947. Unpublished. Beinecke Rare Book and Manuscript Library, Yale University Library, New Haven.

_____. "How to Read Gertrude Stein." *Trend* 7 (August 1914): 553-57.

_____. "Medals for Miss Stein." *The New York Tribune* 13 May 1923: 9: 20.

"The Virtue of Intolerance." *The Saturday Review of Literature* 2 (27 February 1927): 585.

Wagner-Martin, Linda. "Notes from a Women's Biographer." *Narrative* 1.3 (October 1993): 265-68.

Warshow, Robert S. "Gerty and the G. I.s." *The Nation* 163 (5 October 1946): 383-84.

"We Nominate for the Fall of Fame: Gertrude Stein." *Vanity Fair* (August 1922): 72.

"What Are Masterpieces." *The Nation* 151 (23 November 1940): 512.

Willard, Donald B. "The Latest Thing in Prose Style." *Boston Globe* 31 October 1923.

Williams, William Carlos. "A 1 Pound Stein." *Rocking Horse* 2 (Spring 1935): 3-5.

_____. "The Work of Gertrude Stein." *Pagany* 1 (Winter 1930): 41-46.

Wilson, Edmund. "A Guide to Gertrude Stein." *Vanity Fair* 21 (September 1923): 60, 80.

_____. "Nonsense." *The New Republic* 58 (20 February 1928): 21-22.

_____ and Chauncey Hackett. "Slightly Pied Pipers." *The New Republic* 101 (20 December 1939): 266-67.

Wineapple, Brenda. "Gertrude Stein and the Lost Ark." *American Scholar* 66 (Fall 1997): 107-12.

Winter, Ella. "Gertrude Stein Comma." *Pacific Weekly* 2 (12 April 1935): 172-73.

Zolotow, Maurice. "Letter: A Response to James Laughlin." *Story* 10 (January 1937): 196-97.

Index

174, 175, 180, 185, 190, 236, 241
Cummings, E. E., 27, 115, 193, 200, 220, 221, 222

Dodge, Mabel,
  friendship with Stein, 156, 167
  on Stein, 151-154, 162
  publicizes Stein, 2, 7
  Stein writes about, 15, 24, 29, 66, 78, 148, 157, 173-174, 201, 270, 272-273, 274

Eliot, T. S., 38, 102, 115, 116, 193, 200
Evans, Donald, 2, 20, 154, 157
Everybody's Autobiography
  accessibility of, 285, 310, 311
  contrasted to *Alice B. Toklas*, 2
  experimentalism of, 302
  reviews of, 104-107, 315-17, 320
  sexuality in, 312-313, 315, 318, 319-321

Faulkner, William, 132
Faÿ, Bernard, 39, 55-63, 78, 315, 330
Fernhurst, 313, 344, 346-350
Flanner, Janet, 116, 280, 327
Flaubert, Gustave, 172
Fletcher, John Gould, 85
Four Saints in Three Acts
  compared to *Cantos* (Pound), 211-214
  contrasted to other Stein works, 114, 144, 227, 295
  reviews of, 70-78,
  style of, 82, 88, 218-220, 282
Futurism, 12, 13, 18, 19, 21, 22, 28, 163, 164, 231-233, 236, 241, 243, 244

Geographical History of America, The, philosophy in, 224, 298, 299, 300, 301, 302, 303, 304, 305, 307
  reviews of, 98-106
Geography and Plays
  and Sherwood Anderson, 192, 215
  and *Tristram Shandy* (Sterne), 195
  compared to other Stein works, 88, 174, 201
  experimentalism of, 176-178, 184, 190
  parody of, 248-249
  reviews of, 23, 24, 27, 28-31
  style in, 37, 88, 190
Gold, Mike, 208-211
Gris, Juan, 29, 37, 65-66, 68, 79, 200, 326
Gwinn, Mamie, 345-351

Hemingway, Ernest
  influenced by Stein, 38, 132, 150, 193, 200, 214, 282-283, 285
  parody of Stein, 254-255
  popularity compared to Stein's, 3, 326
  Stein writes about, 66, 67, 68, 78, 121, 311
  writing compared to Stein's, 314-315
Hodder, Alfred, 337-343
How to Write, 6, 52, 54
Hubbell, Lindley Williams, 52, 257

Ida, 126-130, 228, 307

James, Henry, 12, 24, 39, 68, 84, 157, 172, 218, 255, 282, 284, 294, 312, 320

About the Editor

KIRK CURNUTT is Associate Professor of English at Troy State University, Montgomery. He is the author of *Wise Economies: Storytelling and Brevity in American Short Stories* (1997) and *Ernest Hemingway and the Expatriate Modernist Movement* (2000).